THE SOUND OF GENESIS - Vol. 1

The Complete Guitar Transcriptions of

FOXTROT

by

Paulo De Carvalho

ISBN: 978-0-578-94011-3
ISBN-13: 978-0-578-94011-3

CONTENTS

Foreword

Ever since I first met Paulo, I was amazed that he had managed to analyze chord shapes and harmonies on my own work that I had long forgotten myself. Turning his attention to Genesis' 1972 album *Foxtrot*, he has applied his rigorous and focused style to what has become for fans a classic album of the early band. Paulo has taken on the hydra headed monster and remains undefeated by its challenges.

I highly recommend this book for anybody who wants to dissemble and play the Genesis music that has inspired musicians from all genres for many years.

I'm sure you'll enjoy this wonderfully comprehensive book as a key to numerous Genesis secrets!

Steve Hackett

June 18,2021

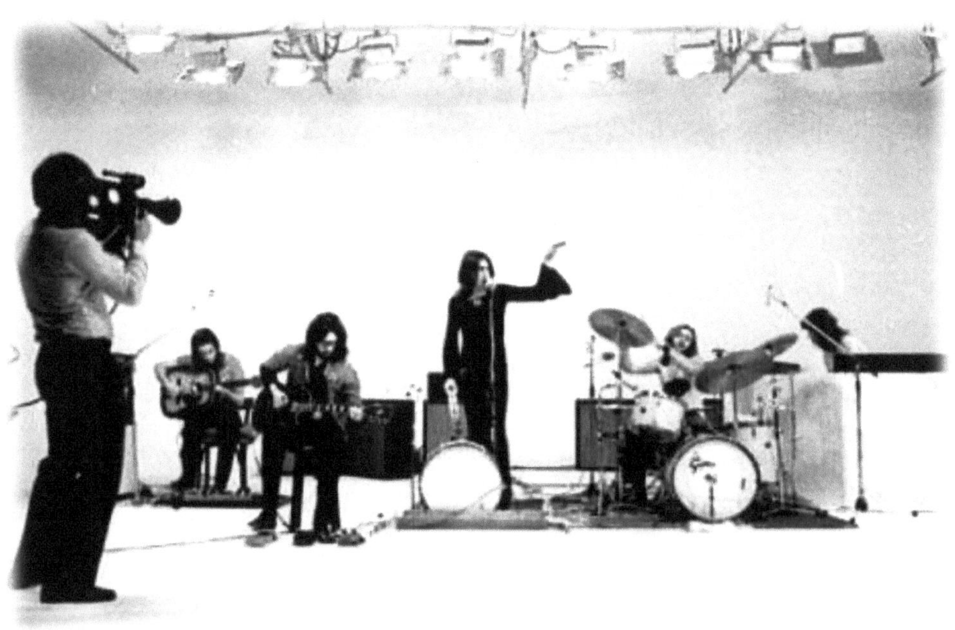

Photo 1: Genesis' promotional photo
Kindly provided by Alan Hewitt
'The Waiting Room Online' editor

PREFACE

The Complete Guitar Transcriptions of Foxtrot is the first volume within the series *The Sound of Genesis*, a complete guitar transcription series of Genesis' albums, which complements my other series, *The Sound of Steve Hackett*, so far comprised of an introductory songbook *A Selection of Guitar Transcriptions from His Solo Career*; Volume 1: *The Complete Guitar Transcriptions of Voyage of the* Acolyte, and Volume 2: *The Complete Guitar Transcriptions of Please Don't Touch!* Since its conception, as per the title of the series, my primary goal has been to exalt the sound that Genesis created, which inspired me from a very young age.

On the path of Steve Hackett Solo Career's transcriptions, Genesis' series presents, for the first time, transcriptions of the entire album *Foxtrot*, including the explanation of the gears and equipment used in the studio, along with the guitar adaptation of some parts for the flute and keyboards. During my transcriptions and adaptions, I continuously amazed myself with many delightful details that Steve input in his works. One may have a hard time hearing considerable harmonic parts in the guitar on the original recording of *Foxtrot* due to the layers of sounds. I wanted to retrieve these details in a very accurate way for my transcriptions. I needed not only a pen and paper for this task. I made some excellent use of *Protools*, *Sibelius*, and *AnytunePro+*, making possible numerous hours of transcriptions of many nuances on the album. Steve himself has reviewed the book, and he wrote a foreword for it.

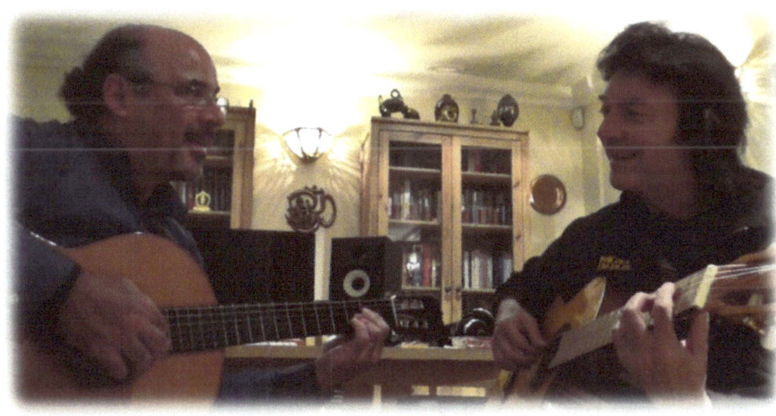

After transcribing the songs, I met with Steve, with whom I played all the songs from the album and requested him to answer my questions on each piece, for I wanted to get the exact shape of the chords as accurately as possible. We played together for hours and hours, and Steve tried his best to remember all the details.

Other vital collaborators in this process were Tony Banks, Jo Greenwood (Tony Smith's personal management), Paul Whitehead (*Foxtrot*'s album cover artist), Richard Macphail (Genesis road manager), Jo Hackett, Mario Giammetti (*Dusk Italian Genesis Magazine* founder and director), Alan Hewitt (*The Waiting Room Online* editor), John Burns (*Foxtrot*'s audio engineer), and Dr. Marcos Nogueira (professor of Graduate Studies at the School of Music of Federal University of Rio de Janeiro, who reviewed the music sheets), my dear children Gabriel and Giulia De Carvalho (text revision), my wife and violinist Maluh De Felice (content design supervision), and Sergio Lestingi (overall review).

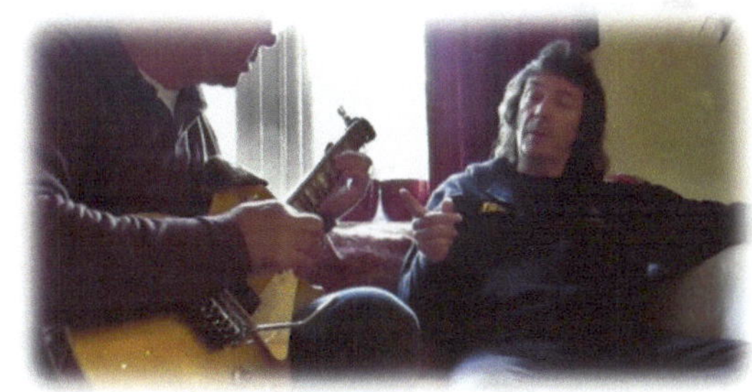

Photos 2 and 3: Steve Hackett (right) explains details of his techniques to Paulo De Carvalho (left) in his home in London, UK.
Photo by Paulo De Carvalho.

New to this volume is the art that Paul Whitehead exclusively created for the songbook's front and back covers with original elements he used in his *Foxtrot*'s art. To honor his work, I wrote a section that contains unprecedented information he shared explaining details of Whitehead's *Foxtrot* front and inside covers.

With this songbook in hand, I hope you will be able to appreciate all the details and music subtleness I transcribed, and you will enjoy playing *Foxtrot* as much as I do.

Paulo De Carvalho

REHEARSAL/STUDIO

"I remember the first time I got a cassette [of Supper's Ready's recording]. I used to have a cassette player in the truck, which was very unusual back then. Whenever we were going, whenever we got in the van to go to a gig, a rehearsal, or wherever else, we were playing Supper's Ready. It was like a religious ritual because the day couldn't really start properly without listening to it. It just touched us so much."
Richard Macphail

Genesis rehearsed *Foxtrot*'s album in two different places (East Sussex and Una Billings School of Dance) and then recorded it in London at Island Studios between August and September 1972.

During my interviews, Richard Macphail, tour manager for Genesis from 1969 to 1973, explained: "Phil's mother and her work partner ran a Barbara Speake Acting School, which Phil attended. In this way, he had a career as a young actor. He appears as an extra in *A Hard Day's Night*. They knew the Una Billings Dance Studio, and that is how they got that place. It wasn't very convenient because it was in the basement; getting the mellotron on the very narrow stairs was very difficult. I live kilometers away from there now. Whenever I pass by, I remember Phil telling me the first time we went there. In this street on the Shepherds Bush Road, in the opposite corner, there is a big pub, 'The Richmond.' That pub is still there. I used to go in the morning with the roadies to set up. The band would come in around 10 am. I would go to the office to deal with money, staff, gigs, then we used to go to the music shops to buy guitar strings, drumsticks, tambourines, microphones, and I would come back about 4 or 5 o'clock in the afternoon.

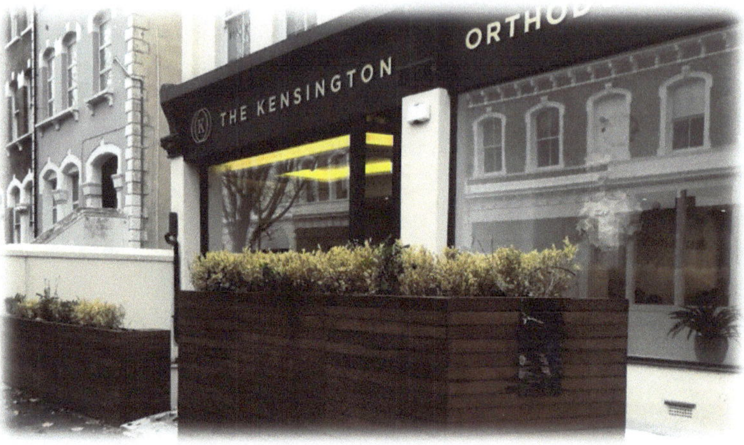

Photo 5: The building where Una Billings Dance Studio used to be and where Genesis composed and rehearsed parts of Foxtrot. Nowadays it is a dentist's office. Photo by Paulo De Carvalho.

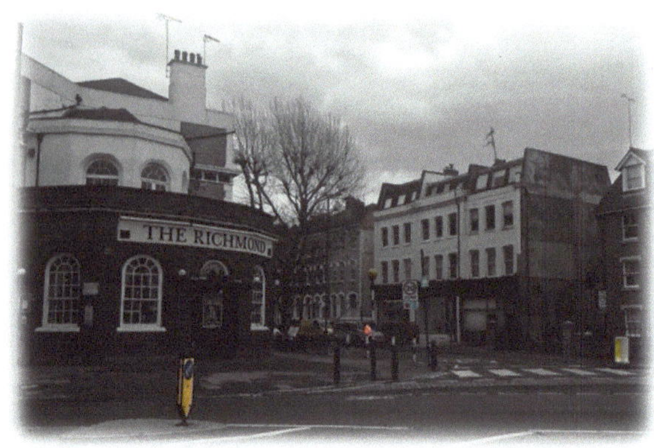

Photo 6: Pub 'The Richmond,' across which Genesis composed and rehearsed parts of Foxtrot. Photo by Paulo De Carvalho.

The other place where they wrote some of *Supper's Ready* was Tony Stratton-Smith's mix house. He had a house in East Sussex, south of London. All the Charisma's bands went down in the Summer to write their new records. Over the Summer, the typical thing was writing and recording a new album and then going on the road in September, October, and November to promote the album that came out. In those years, that was always the rhythm. They recorded *Foxtrot* in Basing Street. It was an old church. Many famous people recorded there."

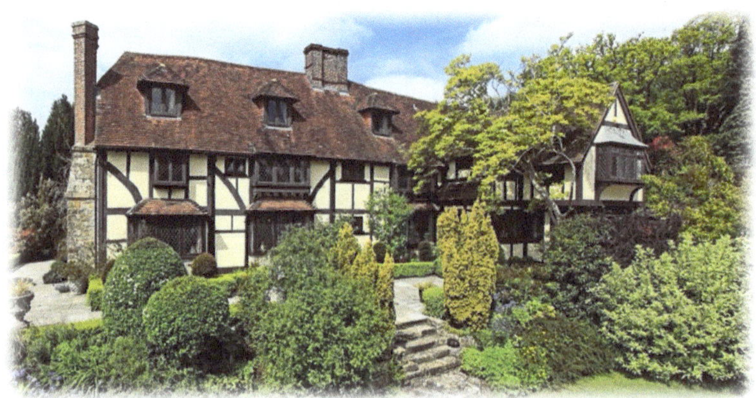
Photo 7: Tony Stratton-Smith's house in East Sussex, London, where Genesis composed and rehearsed parts of Foxtrot.

Richard continued: "*Trespass* came out. We replaced John Mayhew, Phil came very quickly. After Anthony Phillips left, we couldn't find a guitarist right away. We did some gigs as four pieces. We got Tony a Horner electric piano that he plugged into his amp on the side of the stage, put a fuzz box on it, and played the guitar solos on the organ, the harmonies with his left hand. We did several gigs like that. After a few weeks, Steve came, and the classic five pieces came together. They set about writing and recording *Nursery Cryme*. We had high hopes for it because things were building very slowly, not set on fire.

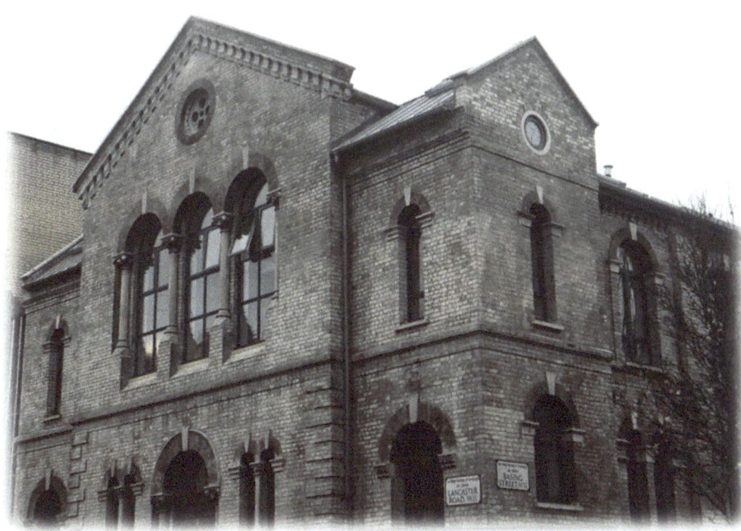

Photo 8: "Island Studios" in Basing Street, where Foxtrot was recorded and mixed. Photo by Paulo De Carvalho.

We were playing for twenty people in the basement outside somewhere, and we got invited to Italy. It was unbelievable. I had no idea how many people had bought Genesis albums at that time in Italy, of course. We arrived on April 72. Suddenly, we were playing in these huge places, with thousands of people who just loved it. The Italians, they clap, they somehow pick up the emotion, and they all start cheering and clapping in the middle of the songs. It was a very pleasant surprise, seeing them singing along the songs. Then the band realized they needed to keep going because if they liked it in Italy, why wouldn't everybody else do?

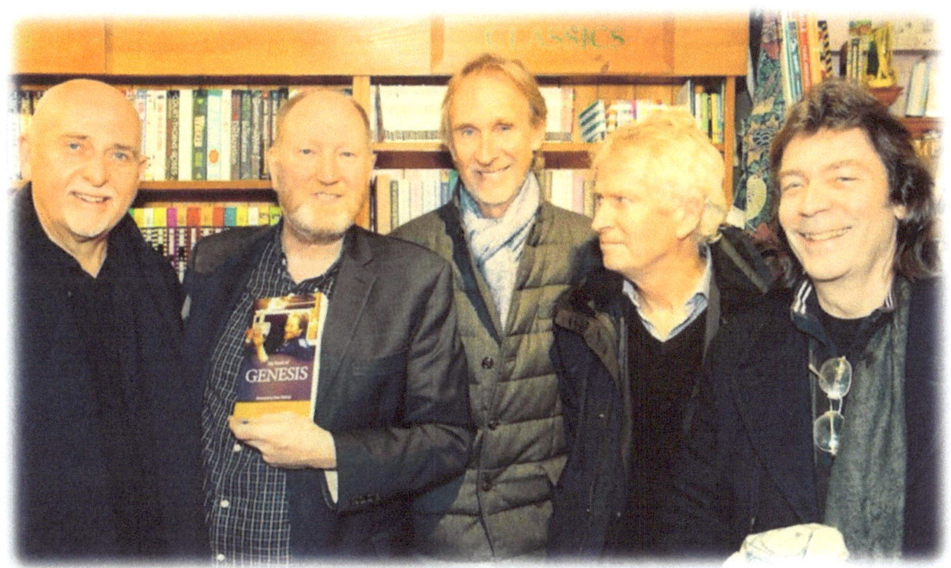

Photo 9: Richard Macphail holding 'My Book of Genesis' of his authourship. On his left, Peter Gabriel. On his right: Mike Rutherford, Tony Banks, and Steve Hackett. Photo kindly provided by Richard Macphail.

I was in the middle of the crowd, mixing the sound. We were underequipped for a place like that, but it did not matter because the concerts were in basketball places, very echoey. What I could do was very limited, but they loved it; we loved it. Everybody got to the gig at about 10 or 11 in the morning. We backed the truck to the stage, unloaded everything, and everybody was doing their own thing. I was concentrating on the PA and microphones. We had multi-cords, big cables going from stage to the mixer. You had to plug everything in the way you wanted in the mixer. We had two roadies with us, and they would help set up. Everybody set up their own stuff, which was great, did a soundcheck, and then went to eat this incredible Italian meal. The promotor ordered everything because we didn't know how to order, and then we got back to the hotel and collapsed, slept like the dead, and then got up and did the concert. It was crazy but wonderful. We haven't had recorded *Foxtrot* yet, but *Can-utility* was part of it.

A significant time came along with the Italy tours. The most important thing about this Italian tour is that it gave the band an enormous boost in confidence. Then we recorded Foxtrot. In his concerts, Genesis tried to perform the best live tracks from the three albums, and of course, *Supper's Ready*, a long piece, and after that, we usually finished with *The Return of Giant Hogweed*. It was a good cross-section of the entire band's work at that time. Live, the music was always brilliant.

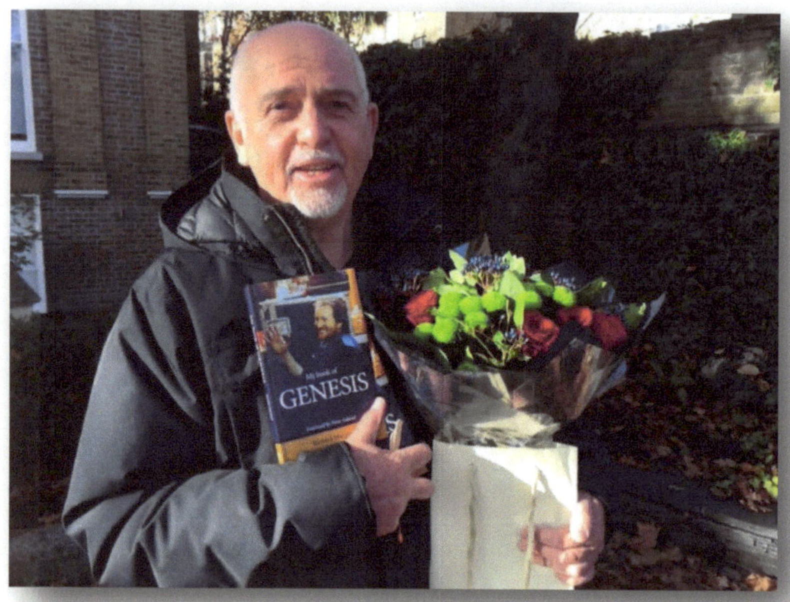

Photo 10: Peter Gabriel holding Richard Macphail's book.
Photo kindly provided by Richard Macphail

Richard Macphail commented on *Foxtrot*: "It was the first time with John Burns, the new producer /engineer. I thought he was much better than John Anthony. He really captured the sound better, but I think the band was better too. They were learning about recording and getting better at it. He was the first one to really capture how good they were on record. I was always disappointed with the sound of *Nursery Cryme* and *Trespass*, just because I heard them play every night and they could sound better than that. Funnily enough, one of the things to do with my decision to leave the band in 1973 was that I felt that with *Foxtrot* they had really made a record that sounded like them, and in a way, my job was done. I wanted the world to know how good they were, and with *Foxtrot,* we achieved that."

Indeed, John Burns told me: "Richard is absolutely right. I was important for Genesis in the early days when it came to the technical side of how to realize their creative vision. I was confident with using the new multitrack technology and understood what Genesis was trying to do where previous producers/engineers had not. I immediately took charge of the sessions and guided the group productively in the studio. In those days, it was frowned upon in the music industry to record in sections, but I knew that this would be the only way to handle *Suppers Ready*, and I saw no reason not to. This process of working out how to record their songs also helped Genesis tackle the technical challenge of performing them as well."

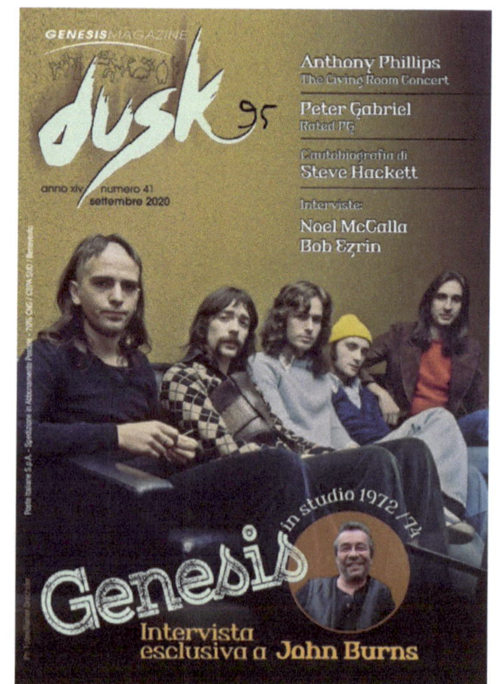

Photo 11: Italian Magazine Dusk cover containting John Burns' exclusive interview

In his interview for *Genesis Italian Magazine Dusk*, Burns remarks that "*Foxtrot* needed many edits, especially in Supper's Ready. The various sections of the song were recorded separately, sometimes on different days. There could be different microphone placements on the drums or different keyboards used. The edits were made with a white wax crayon to mark, with a 45-degree razor blade, a cut when it was necessary, for example, also to consider the

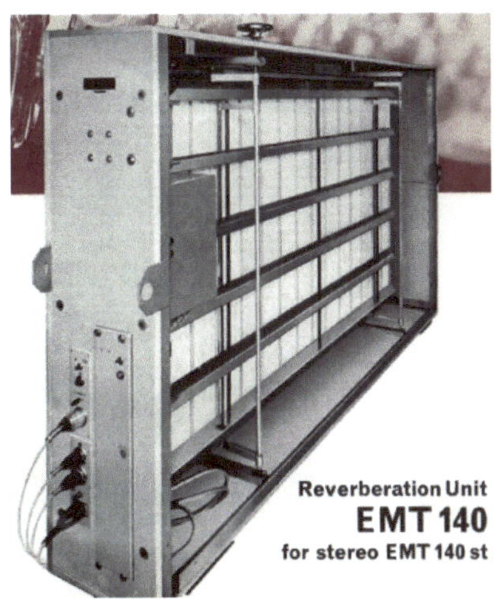

Photo 12: EMT 140 Plate Reverb used in Foxtrot.
Promotional Photo

decay tail of a crash plate. Thus, an edit was also to include the beginning of the sound of the crash cymbal. Edits could be recorded on the joints, which would otherwise have seemed very unnatural. I was confident in my ability to manage the process of cutting and joining sections of the tape, so I could take the situation into my own hands and lead the sessions from a practical point of view. In this way, I took control of the whole process and stopped referring to David Hitchcock as soon as I understood the situation. I started running the sessions myself. At first, Peter had his own microphone drum, but I said 'no.' It would interfere with mixing Phil's drums. Peter was then 'banned' from the control room, but he accepted it."

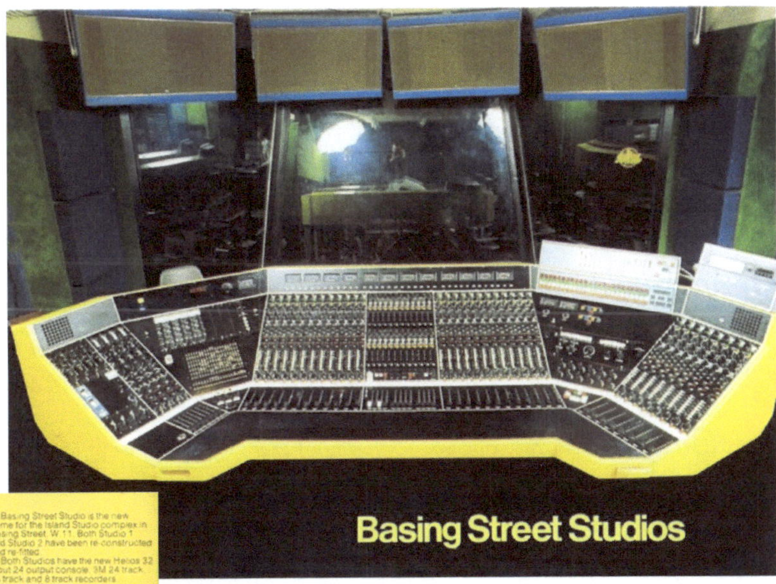

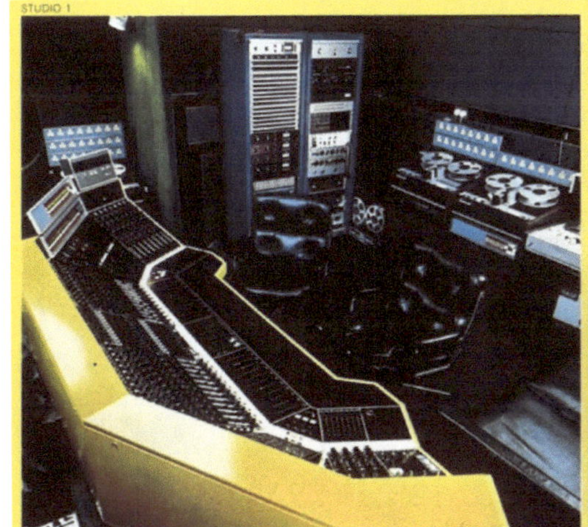

Basing Street Studio is the new name for the Island Studio complex in Basing Street, W 11. Both Studio 1 and Studio 2 have been re-constructed and re-fitted.

Both Studios have the new Helios 32 input 24 output console, 3M 24 track, 16 track and 8 track recorders
24M series Dolbys
UREI Graphic Equalisers
4 UREI Limiters
UREI Filters
2 Pultecs
6 Keepex Expanders
EMT Digital Delay
Tannoy speakers with alternative choice of Altecs and JBL.

Studio 1 is 60ft × 40ft × 25ft with a capacity of 80 musicians (this studio is an ideal size for Promo films).

Studio 2 is 20ft × 30ft × 10ft with a capacity of 20 musicians.

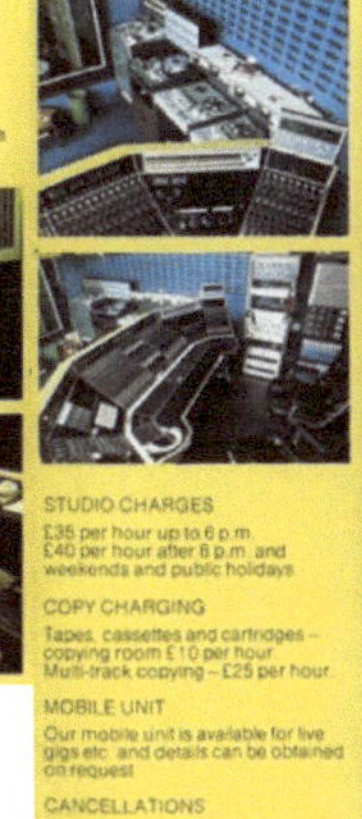

STUDIO CHARGES
£35 per hour up to 6 p.m.
£40 per hour after 6 p.m. and weekends and public holidays

COPY CHARGING
Tapes, cassettes and cartridges – copying room £10 per hour
Multi-track copying – £25 per hour.

MOBILE UNIT
Our mobile unit is available for live gigs etc. and details can be obtained on request

CANCELLATIONS
Between 4 days and 48 hours the charge will be 50%. Within 48 hours the charge will be 100%.

Bookings can be made with Penny Hansen at 01-229 1229

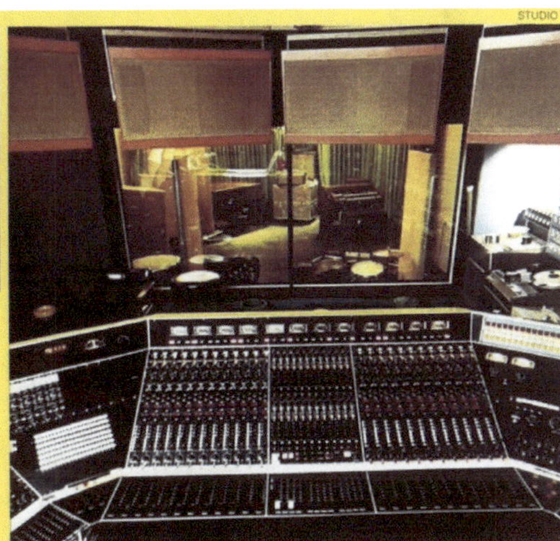

Photos 13-15: "Basing Street Studios" (Island Studios)
Promotional Photo

FOXTROT

1 – *Watcher of the Skies*
2 – *Time Table*
3 – *Get 'Em Out by Friday*
4 – *Can-Utility and the Coastliners*
5 – *Horizons*
6 – *Supper's Ready*
I. *Lover's Leap*
II. *The Guaranteed Eternal Sanctuary Man*
III. *Ikhnaton and Itsacon and Their Band of Merry Men*
IV. *How Dare I Be So Beautiful?*
V. *Willow Farm*
VI. *Apocalypse in 9/8 (Co-Starring the Delicious Talents of Gabble Ratchet)*
VII. *As Sure as Eggs is Eggs (Aching Men's Feet)*

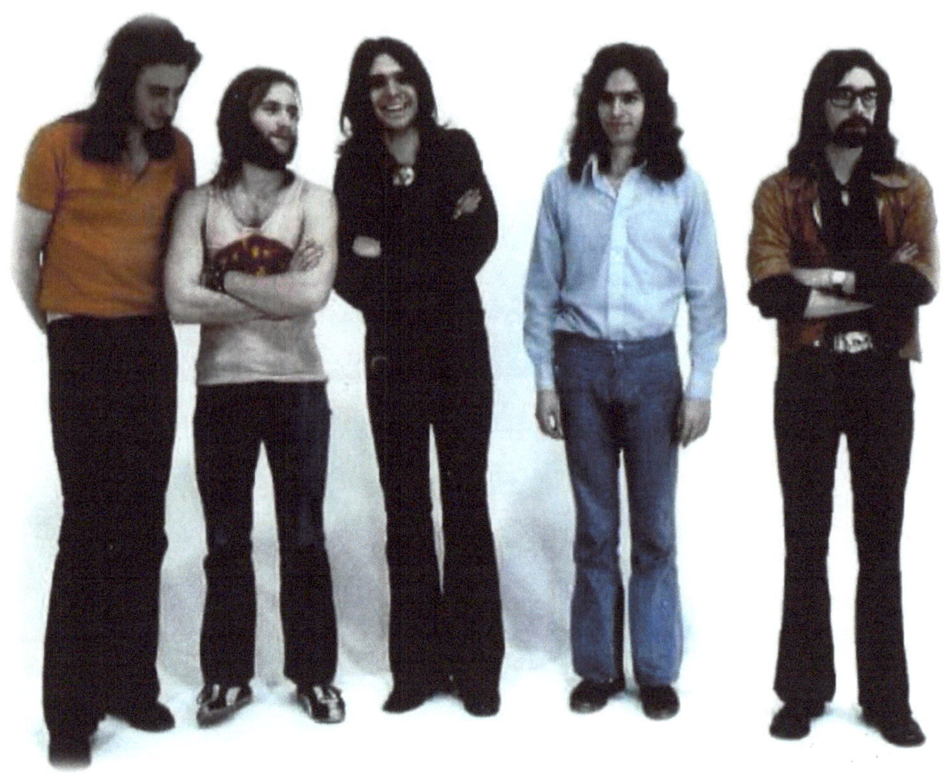

Photo 4: From 'The Waiting Room Online'
Promotional photo. Kindly provided by Alan Hewitt

Players/Instruments:

Steve Hackett: Gibson Les Paul Custom, Yamaha six-string steel acoustic, Hagstrom BJ-12-string

Tony Banks: Mellotron MK II, Hammond L122, Hohner Pianet N, Acoustic Piano, Hagstrom BJ-12-string

Peter Gabriel: Lead Vocals, Flute, Oboe

Phil Collins: Drum, Assorted Percussion, Backing Vocal

Mike Rutherford: Rickenbacker 4001 Bass, Vox Bass pedal, Hagstrom BJ-12-string, Cello

All titles composed, arranged, and performed by Genesis

Produced by David Hitchcock and Genesis

Engineering by John Burns

Equipment & stage sound: Richard MacPhail

Recorded at: Island Studios, London, England (August-September 1972)

Genesis' Shows at the Time of Foxtrot's Release Advertisements, Program, and Ticket

Foxtrot was released on **October 21st, 1972**.

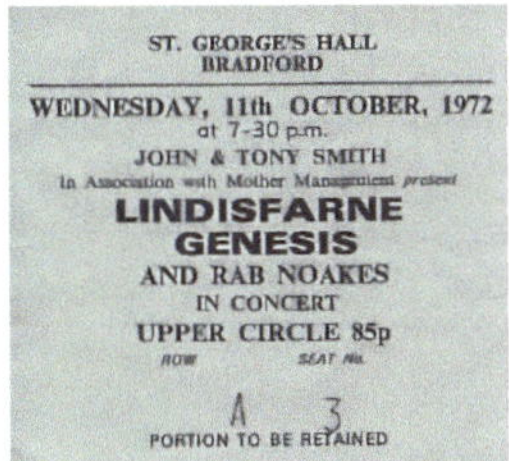

Photo 16: Show Advertisement
St Georges Hall, Bradford
October 11th, 1972
Kindly provided by
Alan Hewitt, The Waiting Room Online editor

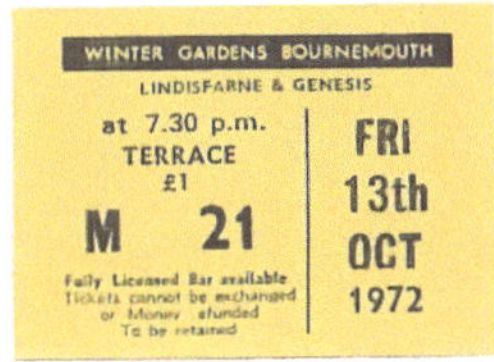

Photo 17: Show ticket
Winter Gardens Bournemouth
October 13th, 1972
Kindly provided by
Alan Hewitt, The Waiting Room Online editor

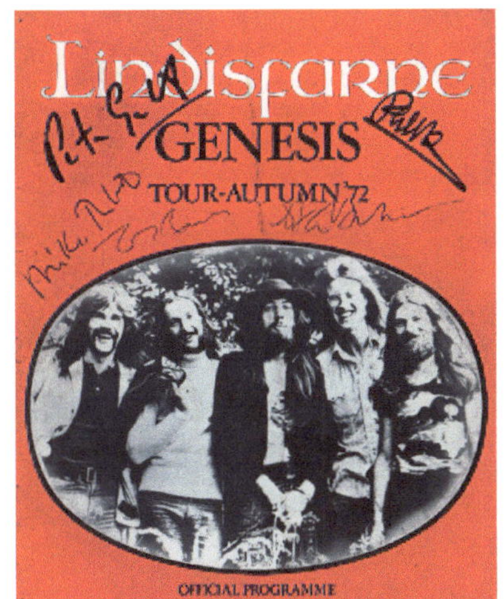

Photo 18: Show Program
Genesis Tour
Fall 1972
Kindly provided by
Alan Hewitt, The Waiting Room Online editor

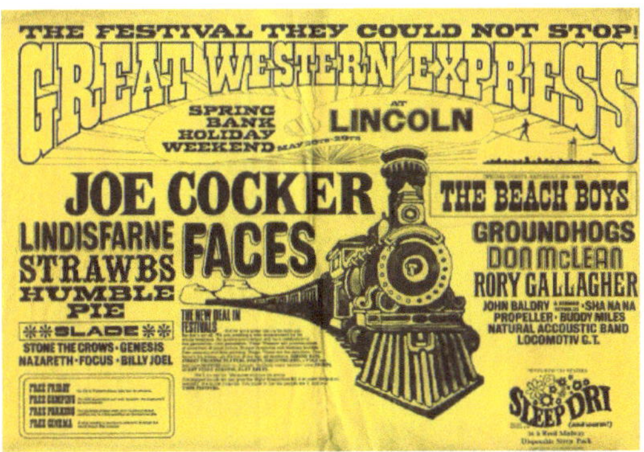

Photo 19: Great Western Express Festival
May 26-29th, 1973
Kindly provided by
Alan Hewitt, The Waiting Room Online editor

PAUL WHITEHEAD

In my interview with Paul Whitehead, he described how he came up with the art for the covers of *Trespass* (1970), *Nursery Cryme* (1971), and *Foxtrot* (1972):

"I was painting those days based in watercolor, and pen, and ink drawings. I had an exhibition in London and the producer John Anthony saw the paintings. He came and asked me if I wanted to work on the cover of Genesis' second album [*Trespass*]. I had no idea who Genesis was, but I got along very well with Peter Gabriel.

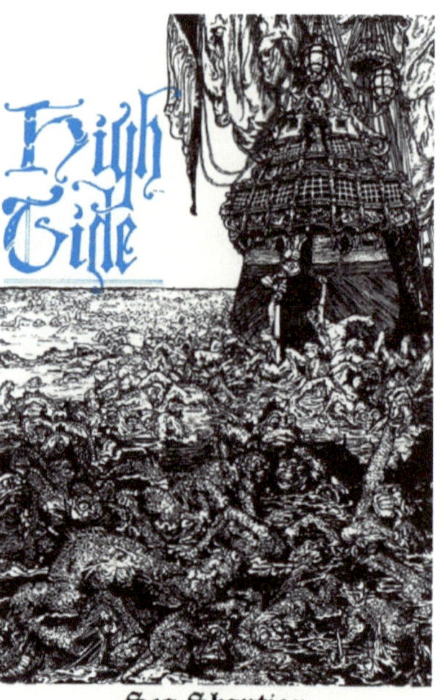

Photo 20: Whitehead's cover of the debut album "Sea Shanties" by the English band 'High Tide" (1969)

Peter gave me some of the songs and provided all the lyrics. The songs were a kind of pastoral romantic twelve-string guitar. I was working for a month on a canvas on a detailed painting: a king and a queen in love looking out of the kingdom. The Cupid came up behind and ambushed them. I had gotten maybe halfway through when Peter Gabriel called me and said that he thought the idea we had was not going to work because he had just written another song called *The Knife*, which was kind of violent, and maybe the image would not fit with the theme. I had already done 2/3 of the work, so I said, 'Ok, let me think about it. Let me hear the music.' I was not a lazy artist, but I didn't want to waste work. I wondered how I could still use it on the cover. The idea of the knife came as, in those days, an Italian artist had used a razor blade and slashed canvas in straight lines. He was in the contemporary museum of London. I asked Peter if he wanted me to do the same. He asked me: 'Do you want to do that, to slash your painting?' I said, 'yes, of course.' We thought of taking a picture of the cut. We wanted a professional who could photograph the cut from an upright view. I rented a knife, the sort of the ones Scottish guys wore in their socks from a movie stuff shop, and that could serve as a model, that would go with the painting. They called it *sgian dubh*. I put the painting over a piece of plywood, took the razor, and cut the artwork. Everybody was surprised. It worked correctly, implied violence… in the beauty. The guys in Genesis were thrilled and had a lot of great feedback from people at record stores. They didn't sell many records, but the public had noticed the cover, and they wanted me to do the cover of their next album too.

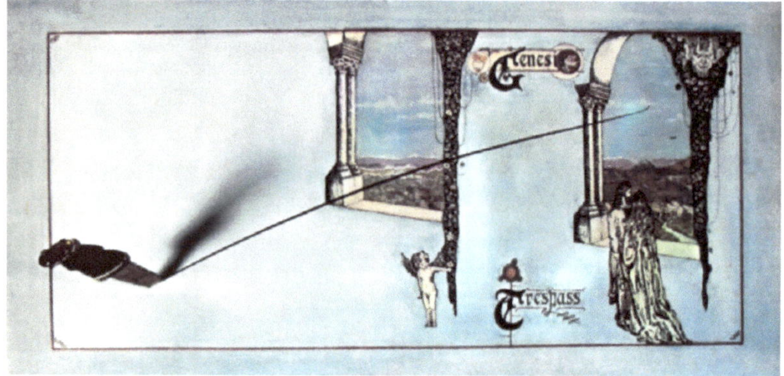

Photo 21: Whitehead's cover of 'Trespass'

We talked about their third album [*Nursery* Cryme]. *The Musical Box* was kind of violent as well. Somehow, we got into a conversation about *croquet*, which is a very English game. It is the kind of game one plays properly, usually wanting to screw up one's partner. The idea is to get your ball in front of the other person. It sort of implies violence: very English. I listened to the song's lyrics, and I had an idea: 'why couldn't she play cricket with his brother's head?'

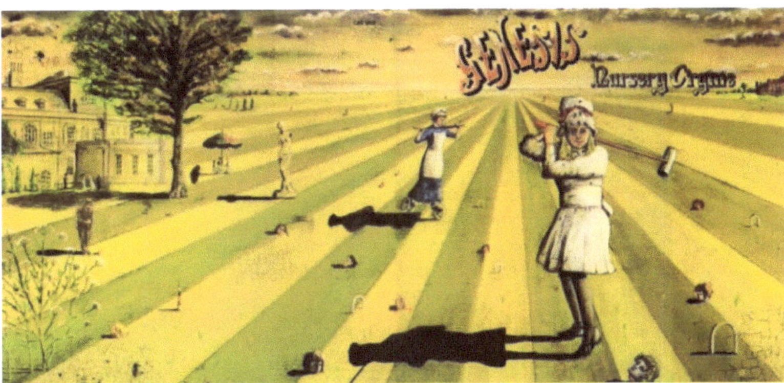

Photo 22: Whitehead's cover of 'Nursey Cryme'

The title *Nursery Cryme* was my idea. I used the '*y*' because it was an old Victorian English spelling, and still, it would work well in the record store. It was the 70's, and all the horror films had not come out yet. Movies with horror content were not with the blood and stuff you see nowadays, so the song was kind of shocking. *Nursery Cryme* sold very well, and everybody liked its cover. In the first printing, the color was too yellow, but everybody loved it. After years, with more reproduction, it was getting worse and worse.

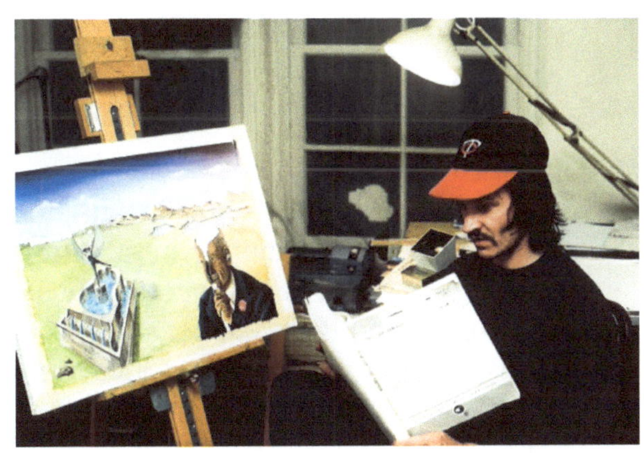
Photo 23: Whitehead's art for Armando Gallo's book cover 'I Know What I Like'. Kindly provided by Paul Whitehead

With *Foxtrot*, I was primarily working with Peter. We lived close, so we got to each other places. He brought me the songs and lyrics; *Supper's Ready* appeared. I did a little sketch focusing on the grand vision of the apocalypse's four horses: a compelling image. I created *Foxtrot*'s art combining it with elements of *Nursery Cryme* so that there was some continuity in the 'world' of Genesis. I used the croquet tournament, a symbol of power, to link them: croquet symbolizes the English aristocracy and their hobbies or sports, and so does fox hunting. We showed it to the others. They gave some inputs, but not much. They were happy to let me do my things. The same with the record company; they didn't interfere. They asked me if I had any thoughts on the title of the album. They had a lot of ideas with kind of long names. I thought on the 'F' in the morse code when they fly a plane: 'Charlie, Foxtrot...' Then, because of the fox, I suggested *Foxtrot*. When they printed the cover, they also never got the color right. The original *Foxtrot* artwork was stolen, along with *Nursery Cryme*, from Charisma Records when the staff found out Virgin had bought Charisma.

Those three covers, *Trespass*, *Nursery Cryme*, and *Foxtrot*, represent three years of my work. I was twenty-five years old and hired to do a cover. It was just a job to me, and I always did my best. I still don't understand how, after so many years, so many people admire these works. Sometimes it is a curse because I am a much better painter now and have much better ideas, but people don't want to look at my new stuff. Not that Genesis is a bad band to be associated with: they opened many doors for me.

I moved to Los Angeles in early 74. At the time, it was not easy to work. International phone calls were costly. It was a very different world. My last work with Genesis was lettering for *Genesis Live*."

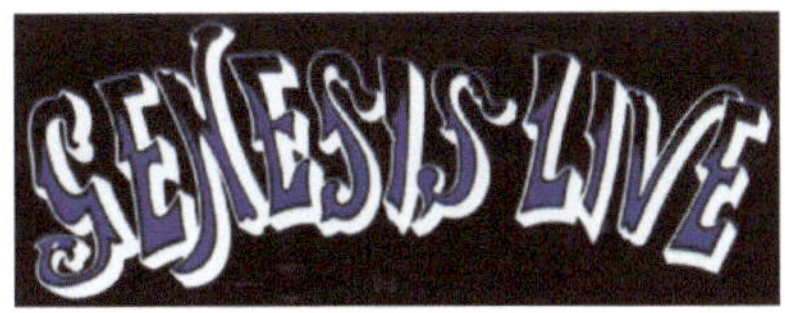

Paul Whitehead comments on details on his *Foxtrot*'s Covers:

THE FRONT AND BACK COVERS

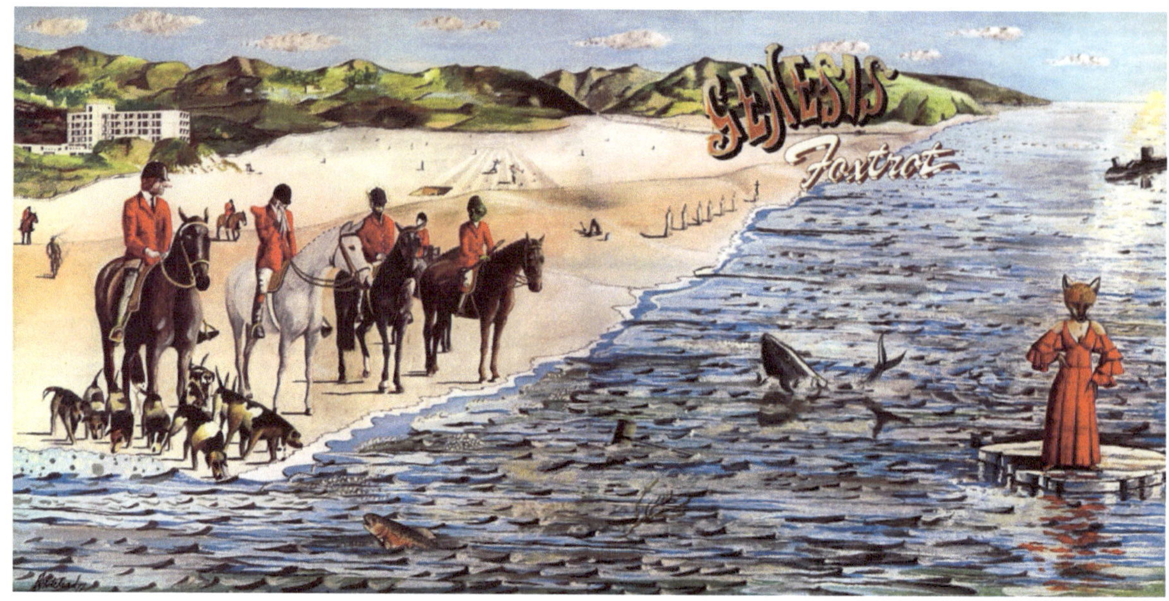

Photo 24: Foxtrot's Front Cover - painting by Paul Whitehead

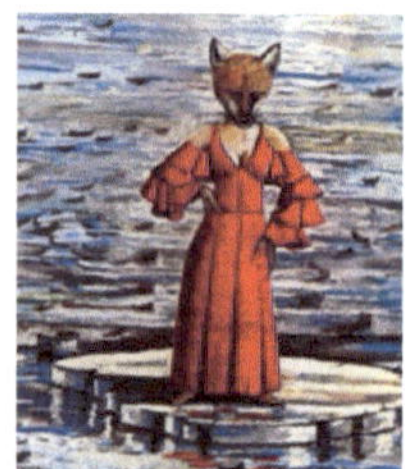

Fox and Ice: "Peter or Tony asked me if there was some other English institution or game that could have a knocker. I thought it could be foxhunting because it is disgusting that rich people chase a poor little fox. We could even incorporate the horses. One thing about the fox is that it is cunning, and it tries to get away from hunters. At that time, several of my friends who had been to America were coming back to England talking about girls as foxes, 'I met this nice fox.' I thought, 'let us make the fox in drag, so she dresses as a woman and hides from the hunters.' That would be a clever way to getaway. Peter and I talked about how water is unique because it has three different forms: if it's freezing, it's ice; if it is medium warm, it is water; if it is hot, it is a steam cloud. Staying in a piece of ice in the water is brave."

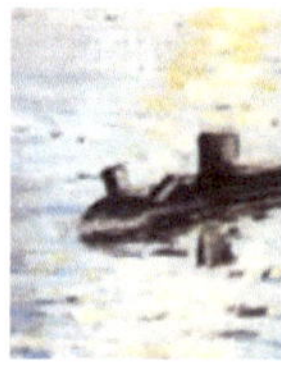

Submarine: "In those days, Americans used a base in Scotland called *Holy Loch* for their nuclear submarines. They would patrol the coastal regions of Russia in a game of brinksmanship. English people were pissed off with the US because they reasoned that the Russians would bomb England before America if anything happened. The idea of throwing nukes in that beautiful part of rural Scotland was repugnant to the English and Scottish."

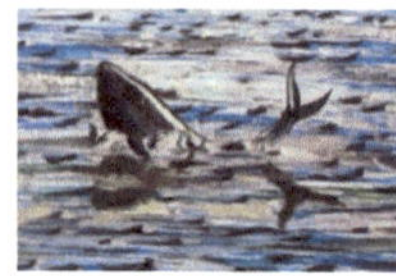

Dolphins and Fish: "That was all to do with pollution in the sea. In the 70's we were already talking about pollution in the sea. Peter likes dolphins because they are intelligent. My thought was to have dolphins and the fishes getting some fresh air because the sea was so polluted."

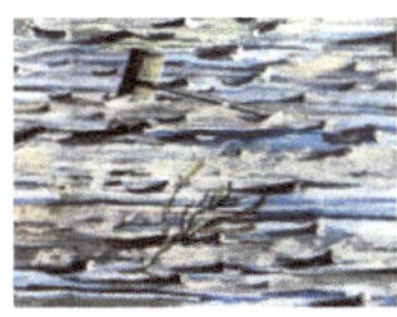

Hogweed and Croquet Mallet: "Reference from *Nursery Cryme*'s songs *The Return of the Giant Hogweed* and *Musical Box*."

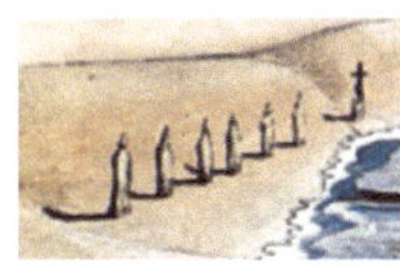

Six shrouded men: "It refers to *Supper's Ready* part about six saintly shrouded men. They move slowly, and the seventh walks in front with a cross held high."

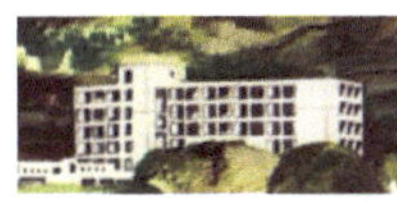

Building: "The white building was a *Holiday Inn* because I could see a lot of hotels in the future for Genesis while touring. That was like a prediction."

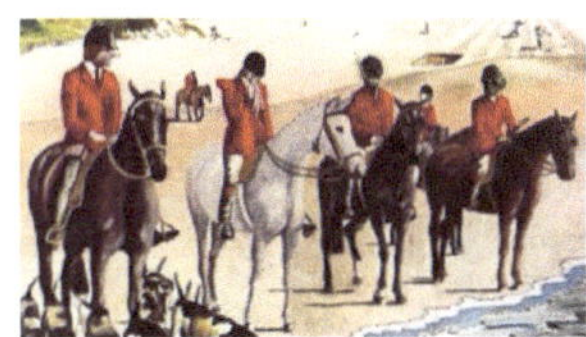

Four Horsemen of the Apocalypse: "The four horsemen are hunters: just like British high society members, they are frustrated. The character on the white horse is weeping because the disguised fox had escaped on the water on the top of an ice floe. The pale horse death, the pestilence, the starvation represents the plagues in the apocalypse; the guy on the left was kind of Nixon, a liar with a big nose. To show how turned on the fourth horse was, I placed him hidden by the green-headed horseman as he gets closer to the fox. Again, pretty girls in America were known as 'foxes' at that time."

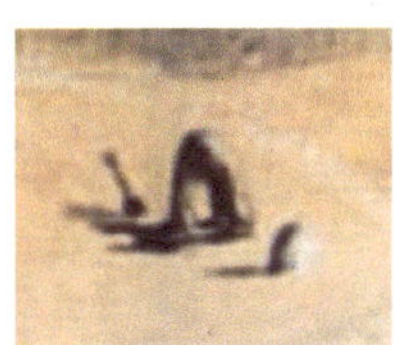

Man Burying the Head in the Sand: "The man with his head in the sand represents the elements of society that indulge in selective amnesia, like an ostrich when chased. Lots of anger was going on in the world. Not wanting to be confronted, the man hid his head in the sand."

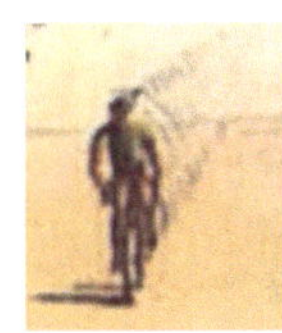

Guy Riding a Bicycle by the Sand: "Have you ever tried to ride a bike in the sand? It's impossible. I like the aspect of painting that allows you to depict the impossible. It turned out Peter Gabriel used to go to meetings by bicycle."

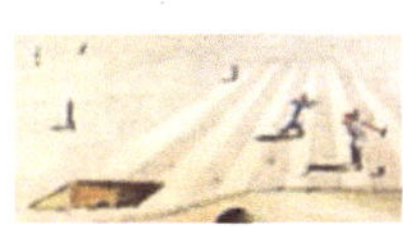

The Hole in the Ground: "That relates to *Nursery Cryme*: where the house was, now there is a hole."

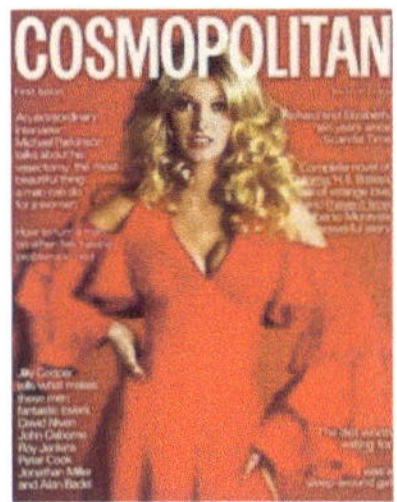

The Cover of Cosmopolitan Magazine: Paul Whitehead's inspiration for the Fox in Drag: "Remember I told you pretty women used to be called "foxes" in America, right? My girlfriend at the time used to have this Cosmopolitan Magazine. The red dress was on the front cover. That was a perfect dress for a disguise: a drag fox in a red dress."

THE INSIDE COVER

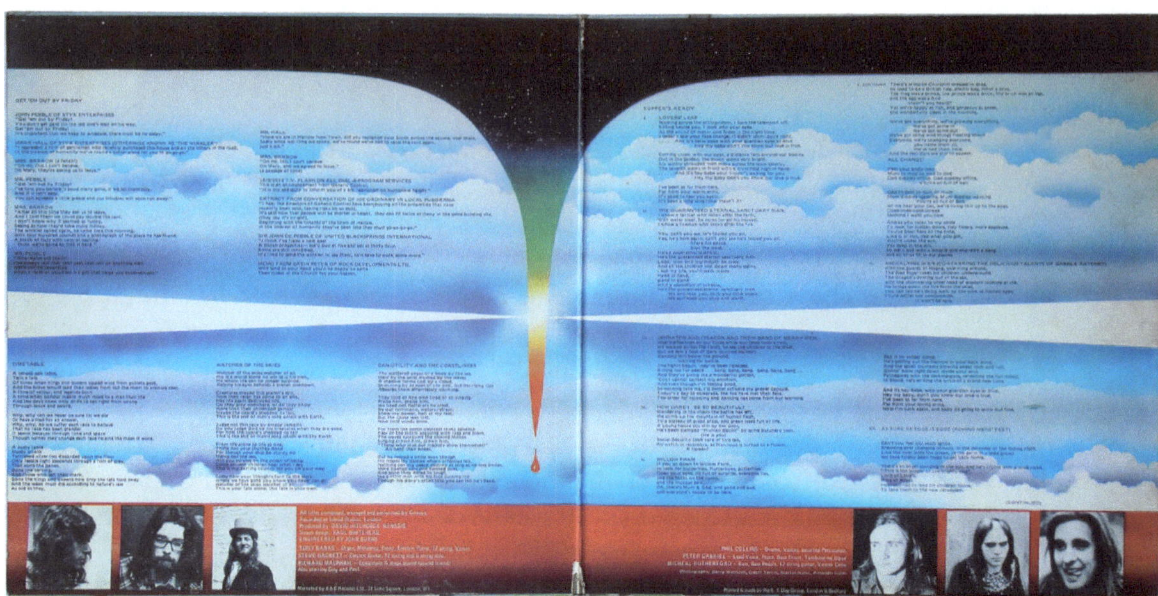

Photo 25: Foxtrot's Inside Cover - painting by Paul Whitehead

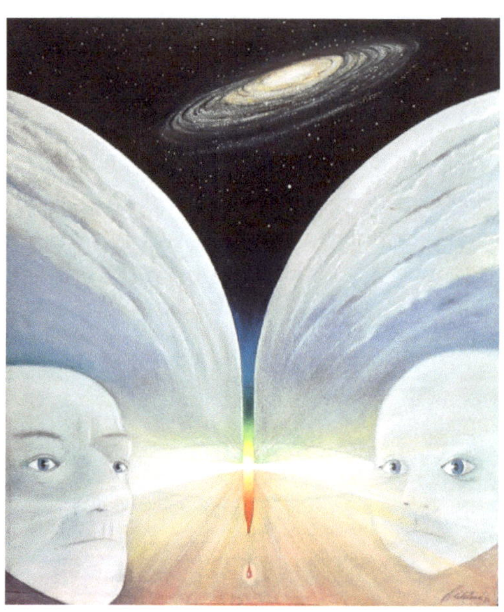

Photo 26: 'Inner Space is White, Outer Space is Black, and Life is the Rainbow in Between' painting by Paul Whitehead with ideas that he used in the inside cover of 'Foxtrot'

"Peter Gabriel once came to my studio and noticed one of my paintings. The original picture had a man, a little baby, and the idea was life. The cosmos was coming down, changing colors, and becoming blood. I named it *Inner Space is White, Outer Space is Black, and Life is the Rainbow in Between*. Peter asked me: 'Can we use that idea somehow?'

As in Joni Mitchell's song *Woodstock*, I always thought that we are composed of stardust, that we are all made of components of someone from the past, that we carry a piece of people from history in ourselves. That was the genesis of that painting: the idea of dust and atomic matter of the cosmos condensing down through the rainbow and becoming blood, flesh and bones, the inspiration for the inside cover image.

UFO: The song *Watchers in the Skies* inspired me to include this UFO [detail on the bottom of the right page, above the red stripe, in the clouds]. I believe there is evidence that aliens have played with our evolution in the past. Maybe they have manipulated our DNA. I saw a documentary that theorized that they had messed with caveman's DNA and made them stronger and more intelligent so that they could work for them mining gold."

Based on elements he used on *Foxtrot*, Paul Whitehead specially created artworks for this songbook's front and back covers.

www.paulwhitehead.com

During the *Foxtrot Era*, Steve used a Wah-wah pedal before the Fuzz to add a different tone quality, boosting specific frequencies. He used a two-way switch to create high harmonics.

He used a Volume Swell pedal to make the guitar sound like a violin. The guitar player must attack with the volume off and then turn it up to produce a *crescendo*. One should not hear the contact of the pick with the string.

Steve used the Volume Swell after the Fuzzes, even though he had used it sometimes before the Fuzzes, such as in his previous album *Nursery Cryme* on *The Fountain of Salmacis* and *Seven Stones*.

Sometimes Steve used the Fuzz pedal with a saturated Fuzz-Tone. He selected the neck pickup, which had its tone control all the way back, attenuating high frequencies, and reducing the noise created by the Fuzz.

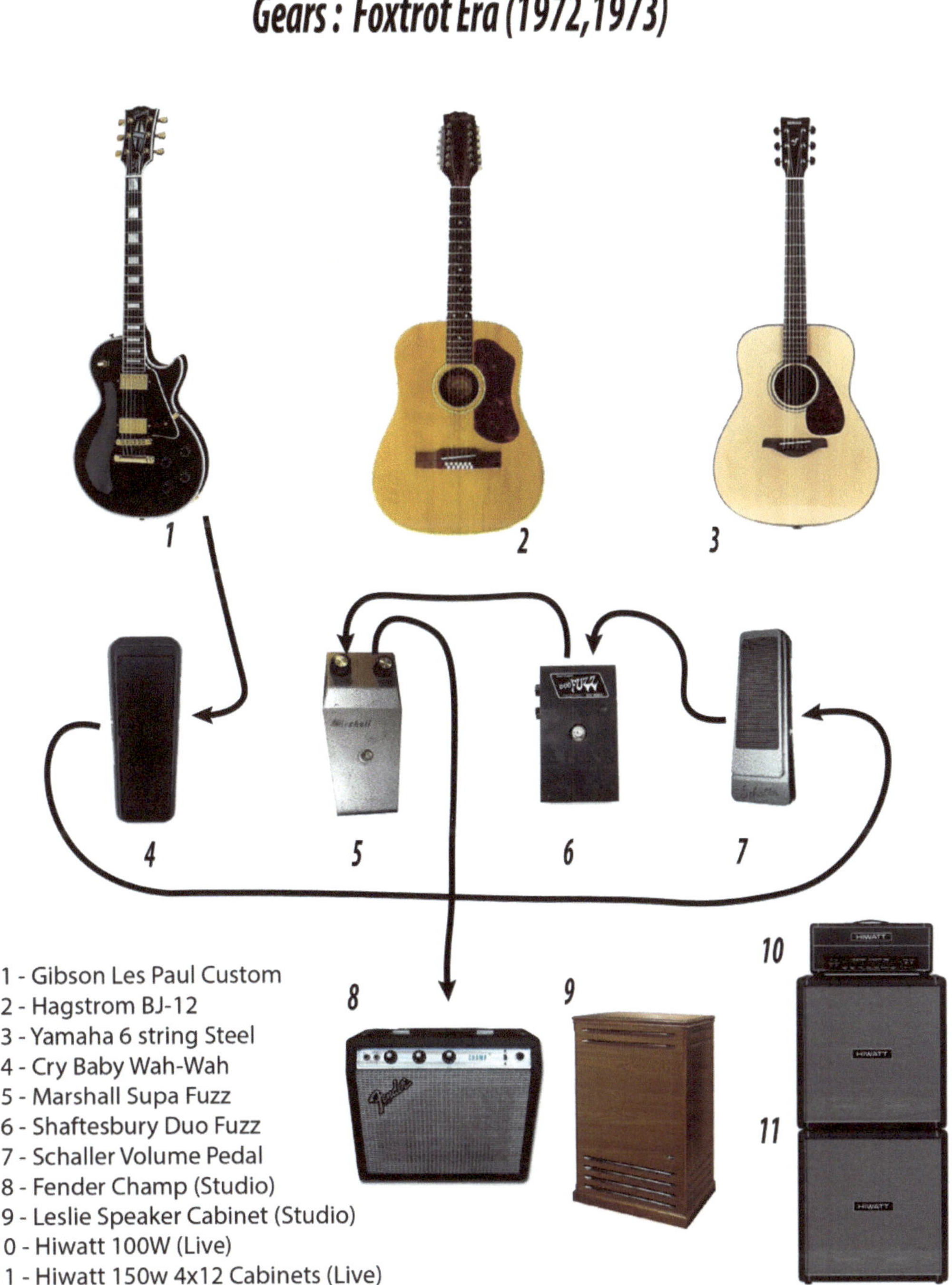

Chart showing one of the ways Steve used to connect the pedals during the Foxtrot Era.
Based on 'The Sound of Steve Hackett, A Selection of Guitar Transcriptions from His Solo Career'
Conceptualized and assembled by Paulo De Carvalho

WATCHER OF THE SKIES

"We were rehearsing the song in 'Reggio Emilia Palasport' in Italy (April 12th,1972). The promoters were watching, and they found it was good because it sounded powerful in a big space. I remember hearing this when I was downstairs. I could hear the mellotron shaking the building. Sounded like a spaceship."

Steve Hackett

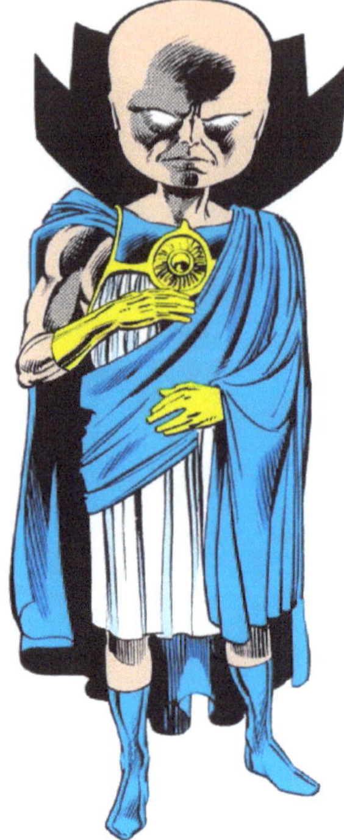

Photo 27: Uatu The Watcher™ @Marvel-Characters: Cartoon that inspired Mike and Tony to write the lyrics of 'Watchers of the Skies'

Steve was a big mellotron fan, and he asked the group to buy one, so they bought one from King Crimson. In King Crimson's rehearsal place, they had three mellotrons. They wanted to sell one of them, and they bought the Mark II. They needed four men to lift it: one on each corner. Steve told me: "It looked like a funeral coffin (the weight was 160 kg). It was a double-manual keyboard with 18 sounds on the right hand, and one could combine two sounds by toggling the switch to put it between A and B. On the right-hand side, one plays notes, chords, and on the left-hand side, prerecorded riffs, just like the intro of the Beatles' song *Bungalow Bill* is preset in the mellotron. The mellotron brass is an instantly recognized sound, with a massive attack on every note, but it would considerably change when mixed with strings. Tony was using mellotron brass and strings [samples in between slots A and B] together, having the English accordion doing the bass in the left hand."

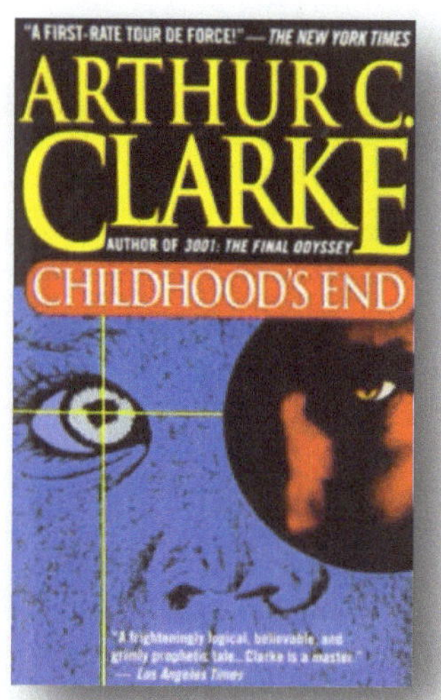

Photo 28: "Childhood's End', book by Arthur C. Clarke - Inspiration for the lyrics of 'Watchers of the Skies'

Tony Banks explained to me: "After I got my mellotron, I did these two cool chords that just sounded good. I played these two chords a lot. They had such a wonderful sound and quality. And so, I just run the rest of it. Go away from that and then come back to it with an idea. You play the chords a few times initially and then go elsewhere and come back to it. And when you come back to the second time, it's kind of a comforting sort of feeling because the nature of the chord changes at the end. Writing comes in, and the song takes over, and I thought: I'm going to use these two chords as a sort of basis of all the songwriting."

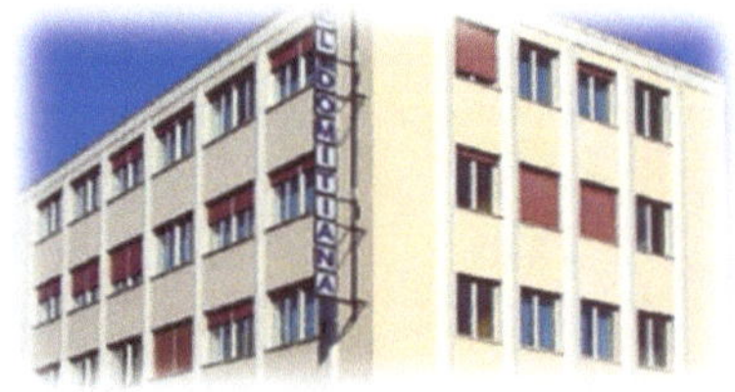

Photo 29: Hotel Domitiana in Naples, Italy. From the view of the top of the building, Tony and Mike got inspired to begin to write the lyrics of 'Watchers of the Skies.' It is a Best Western hotel nowadays.

Tony and Mike wrote the lyrics based on Arthur C. Clarke's *Childhood's End.* The inspiration came when they were on the top of a building looking out. Tony told me: "We just looked at as long as nobody was there at all. So, we wrote in lots of ideas, the people kind of disappeared from the planet. And then also the other thing was the novel character called *The Watcher*: he couldn't take part of it, but he would watch from far." Tony knew there was going to be a combination of the use of those two ideas. He didn't like the way the music and the lyrics worked together, finding out that some lines were a bit clumsy."

"The guitar in the song is clean most of it, using natural amp distortion, but when going to the solo, I just used the Duo Fuzz. I introduced the Duo Fuzz again when we played the muted part and the [guitar] scream. At that time, when I played live, I didn't use reverb in concerts," Steve commented.

There is a unique feature in this album. As Steve stressed: "The volume pedal that I used would deliver more distortion the louder I played, as I put the volume pedal down. In the end, there were just single notes using the volume pedal to make a natural distortion of the amp slightly.

We played very loud at the top of the *crescendo*: the idea was going from very quiet to loud. I think it's one of the best *crescendo*s in all of rock and roll. The version on the album is a little bit too fast, but at the time, Genesis performed live in a more comfortable tempo, though we were still racing in the ending wherever we were going to polymeters. I think we always used to rush towards the finale, nonetheless, having an extraordinary tension of chords, magnificently dissonant. Tony used to say the best bit of the song is the beginning and the end. I think the song lyrics are excellent. Live we changed it a little bit the accent, but I prefer the accent we used in the album. Phil had the idea of the rhythm."

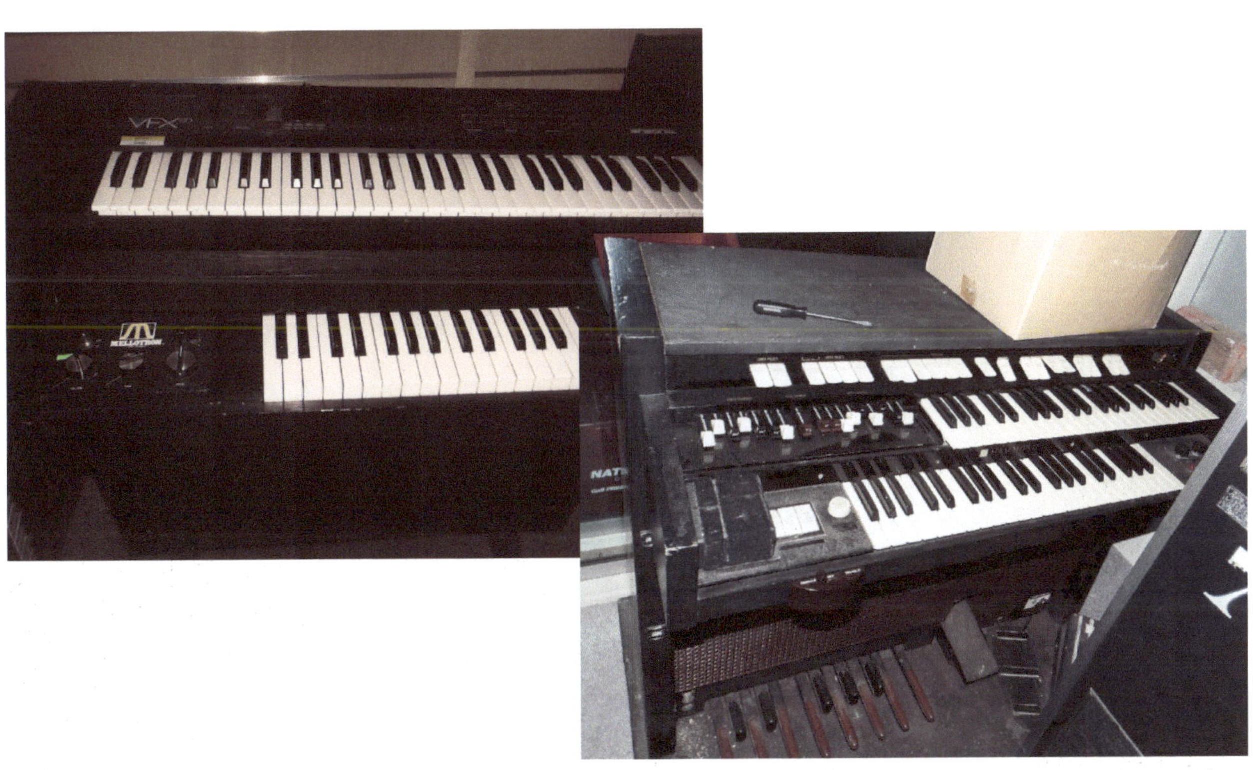

Photos 30 & 31: Tony Bank's Mellotron (left) and Hammond (right)
From Genesis web-fanzine 'The Waiting Room Online'
Kindly provided by Alan Hewitt

Players/Instruments:

Peter Gabriel: Vocal
Tony Banks: Hammond L122, Mellotron MK II, Backing Vocals
Steve Hackett: Black Gibson Les Paul Custom
Mike Rutherford: Rickenbacker 4001 Bass, Vox Bass Pedal, Backing Vocals
Phil Collins: Drums, Backing Vocals

Watcher of the Skies: Guitar Specifics

Chord Shapes

At the time of Genesis, Steve played the chords differently from nowadays. As he mentioned: "Back in those days, I used to do it because, at the time, this produced the best sound in natural amp distortion. I played the F#s in an octave, including B with finger 1, just getting the overtone. Nowadays, I use just power chord with two notes."

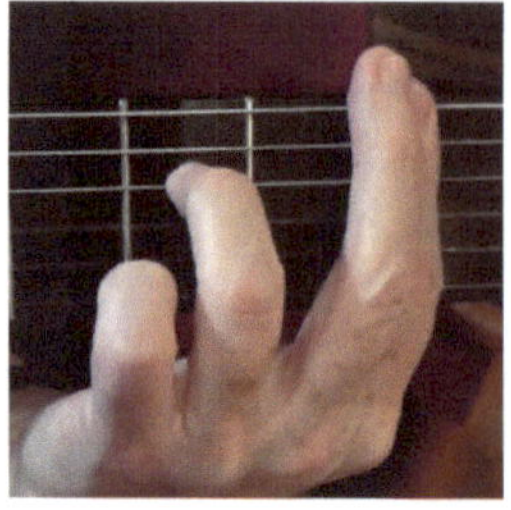

Photo 32: Steve showing how he used to play
Photo by Paulo De Carvalho

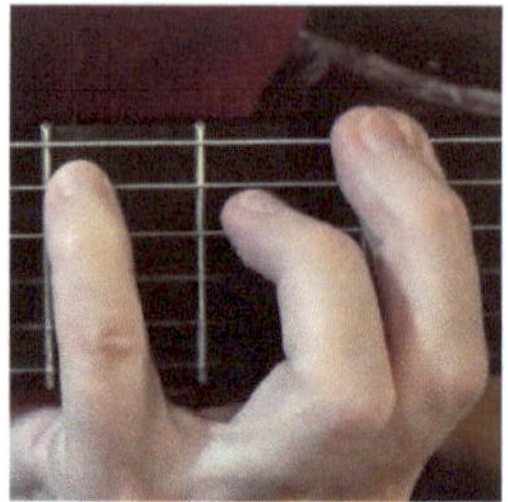

Photo 33: Steve showing how he plays nowadays
Photo by Paulo De Carvalho

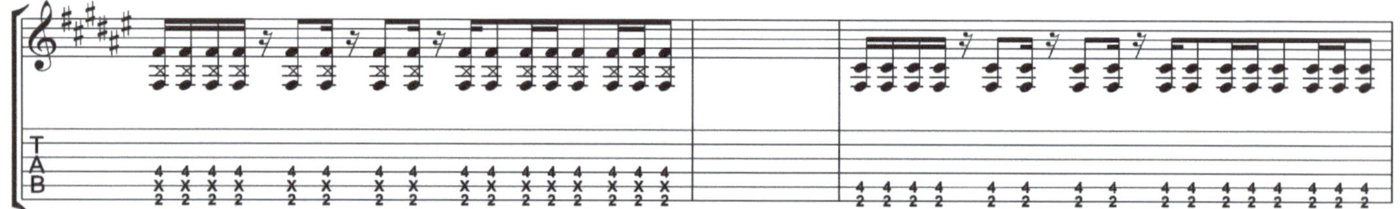

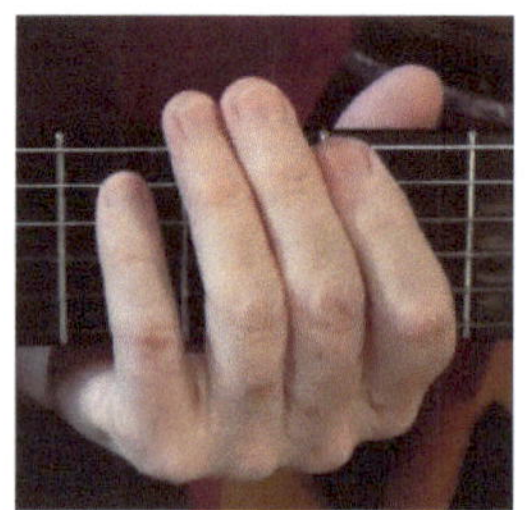

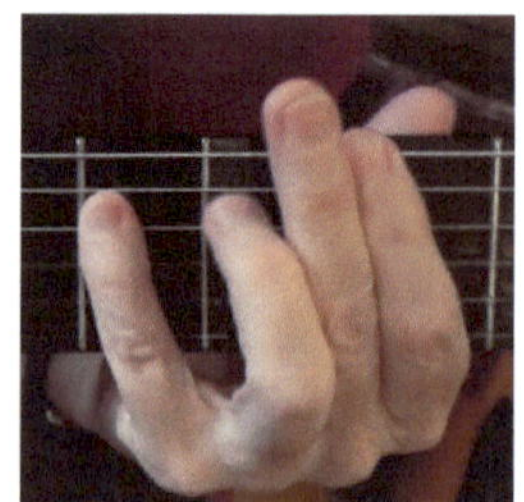

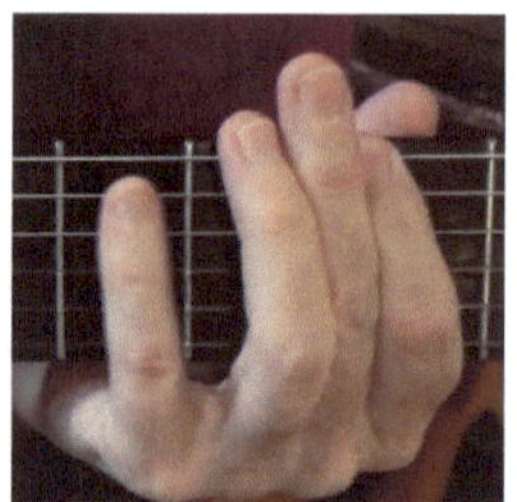

Photos 34-36: Steve showing the riff below - Photos by Paulo De Carvalho

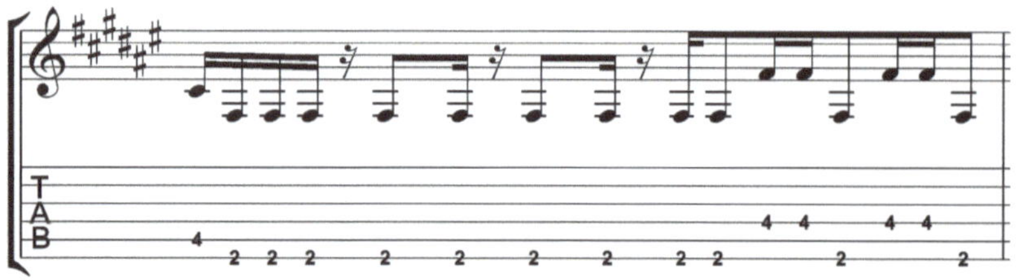

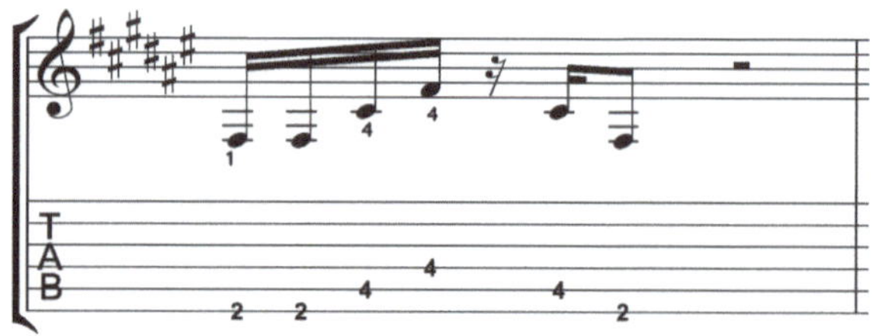

Screaming Guitar

The screaming guitar part is only the Duo Fuzz with reverb that makes that noise. "It was kind of a non-chord: the chord is not so important. Nothing that I played after those days sounded like that again. It was lost with that equipment. I struck at the same time as Phil hit the cymbals. The main thing was not to sound like a chord, but as a noise [photo 31]," Steve told me.

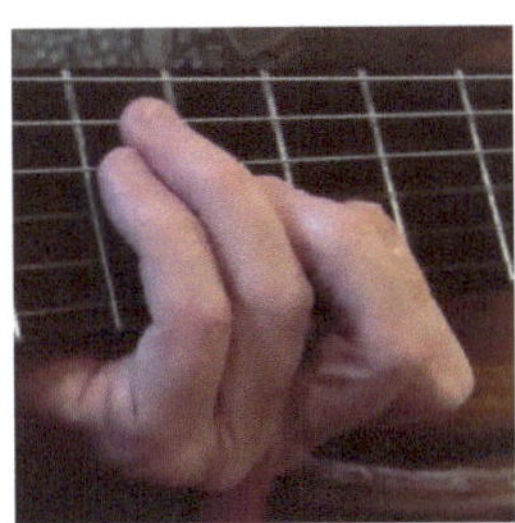

Photo 37: Steve showing the Screaming Guitar over the B chord
Photos by Paulo De Carvalho

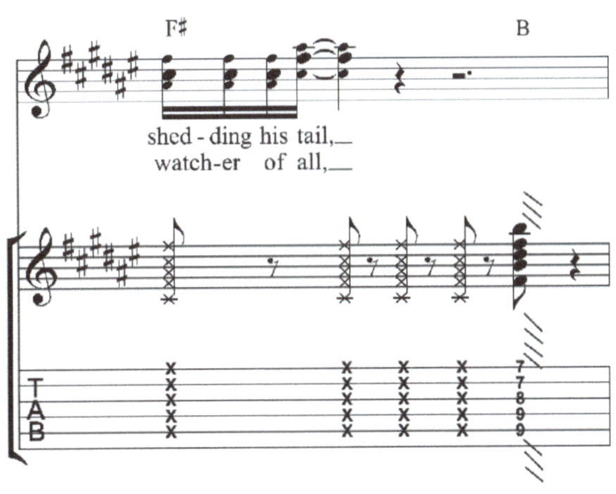

Solo Using Duo Fuzz

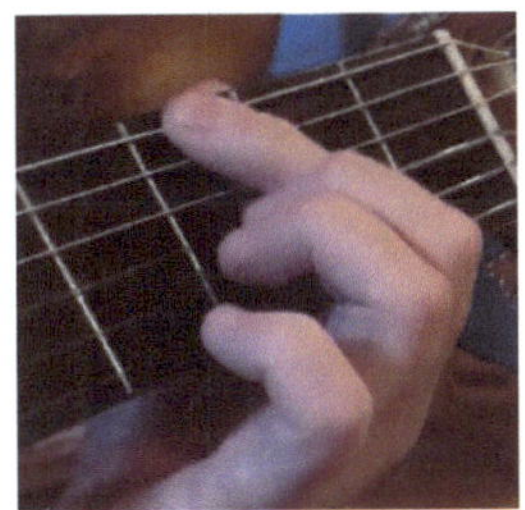

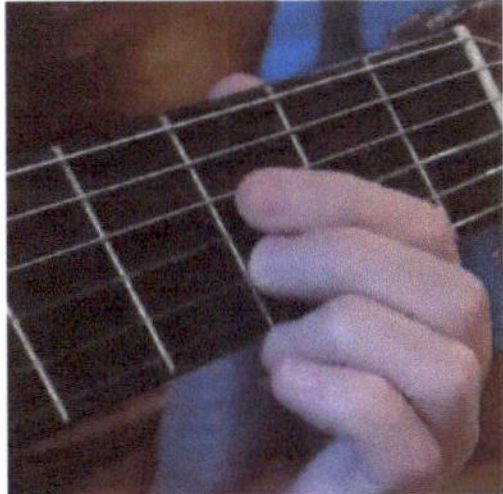

Photos 38-39: Steve showing the Gm6 and C/G chords - Photos by Paulo De Carvalho

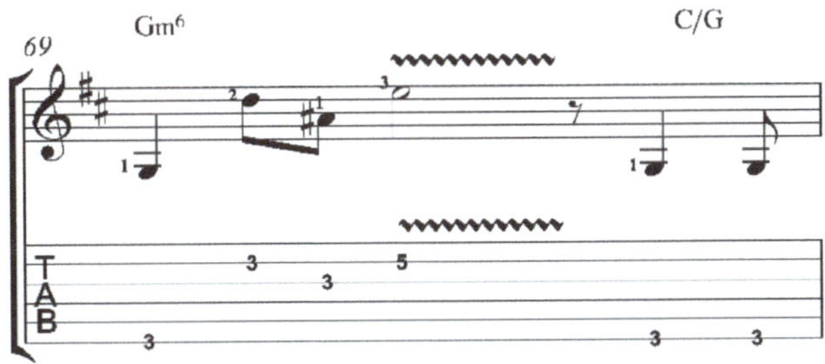

Polymeters

Tony played in 6/4 while Steve and Mike played in 4/4:

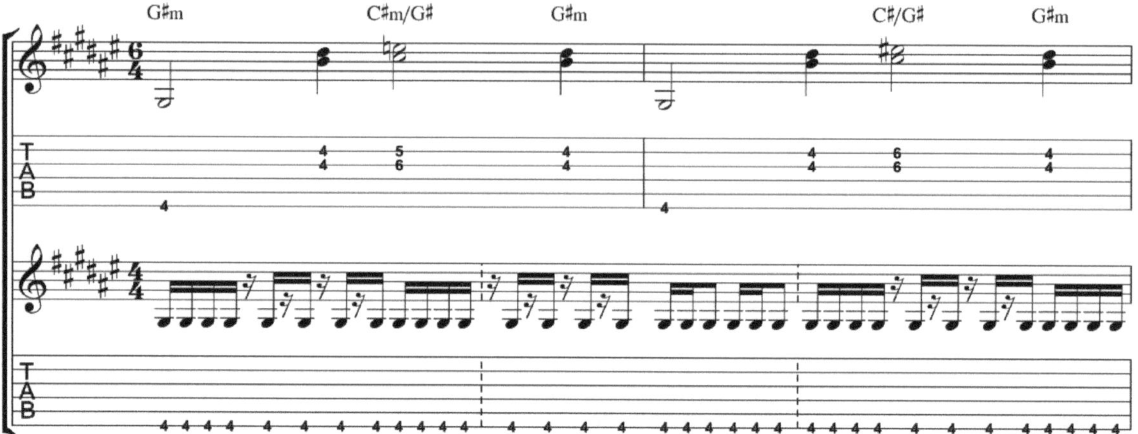

from Genesis - *Foxtrot*

Watcher of the Skies

by T. Banks, P.Collins, P. Gabriel, S. Hackett, M. Rutherford

Transcribed by Paulo De Carvalho

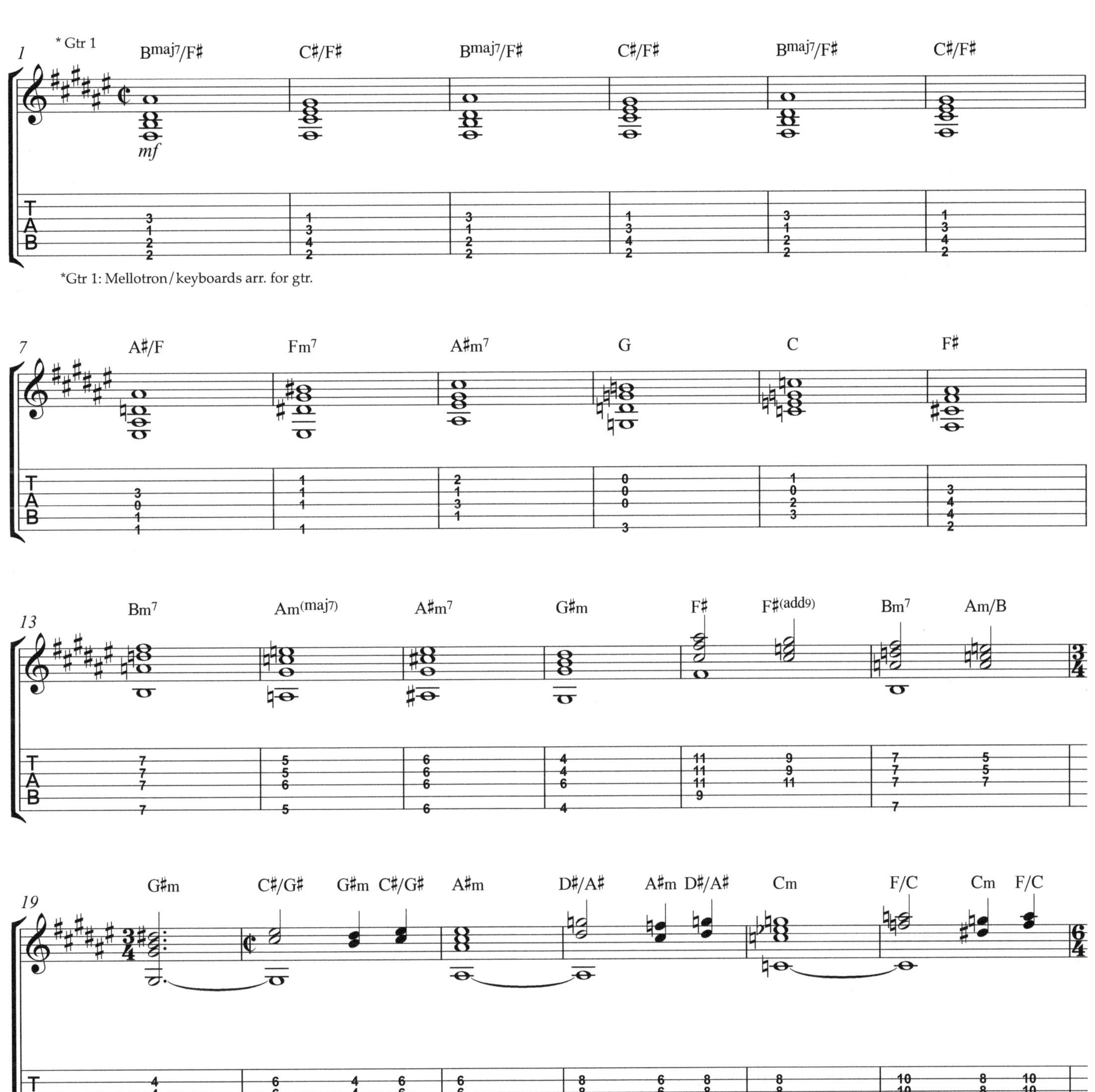

*Gtr 1: Mellotron/keyboards arr. for gtr.

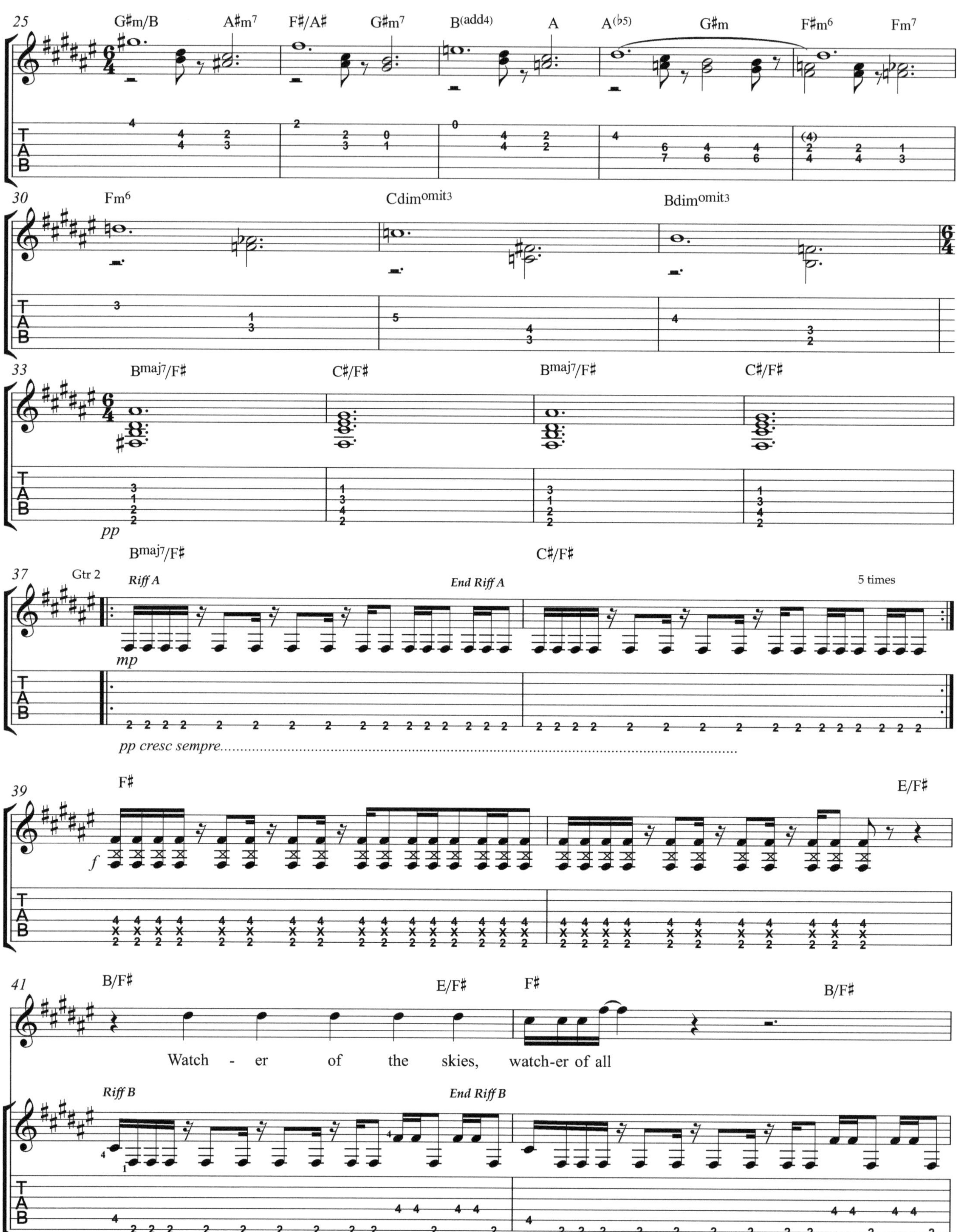
25
G♯m/B
A♯m7
F♯/A♯
G♯m7
B(add4)
A
A(♭5)
G♯m
F♯m6
Fm7
30
Fm6
Cdimomit3
Bdimomit3
33
Bmaj7/F♯
C♯/F♯
Bmaj7/F♯
C♯/F♯
pp
Bmaj7/F♯
C♯/F♯
37
Gtr 2
Riff A
End Riff A
5 times
mp
pp cresc sempre.........
39
F♯
E/F♯
f
41
B/F♯
E/F♯
F♯
B/F♯
Watch - er of the skies, watch-er of all
Riff B
End Riff B

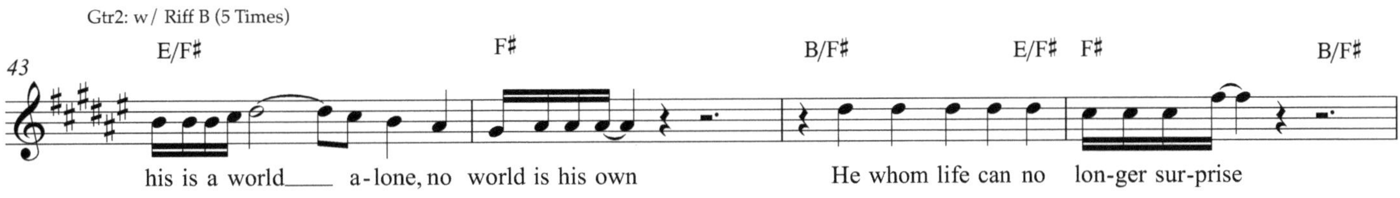
Gtr2: w/ Riff B (5 Times)
43
E/F♯ F♯ B/F♯ E/F♯ F♯ B/F♯
his is a world___ a-lone, no world is his own
He whom life can no lon-ger sur-prise

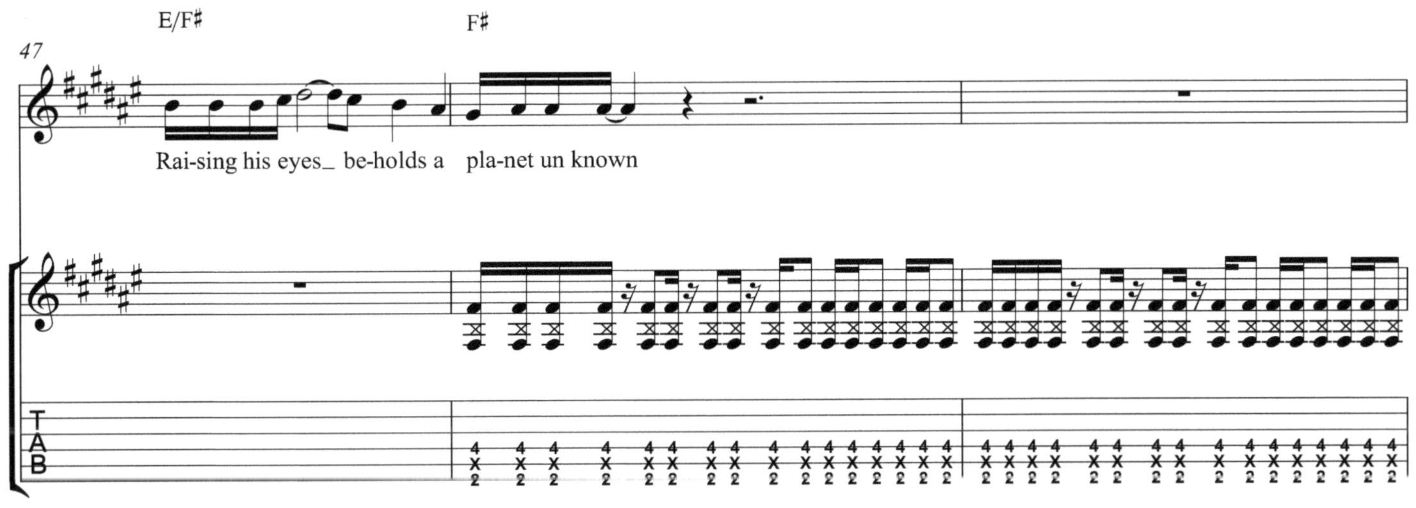
47
E/F♯ F♯
Rai-sing his eyes_ be-holds a pla-net un known
T
A
B

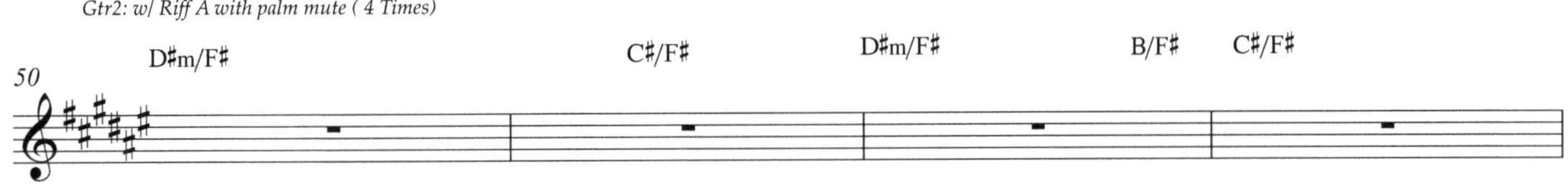
Gtr2: w/ Riff A with palm mute (4 Times)
50
D♯m/F♯ C♯/F♯ D♯m/F♯ B/F♯ C♯/F♯

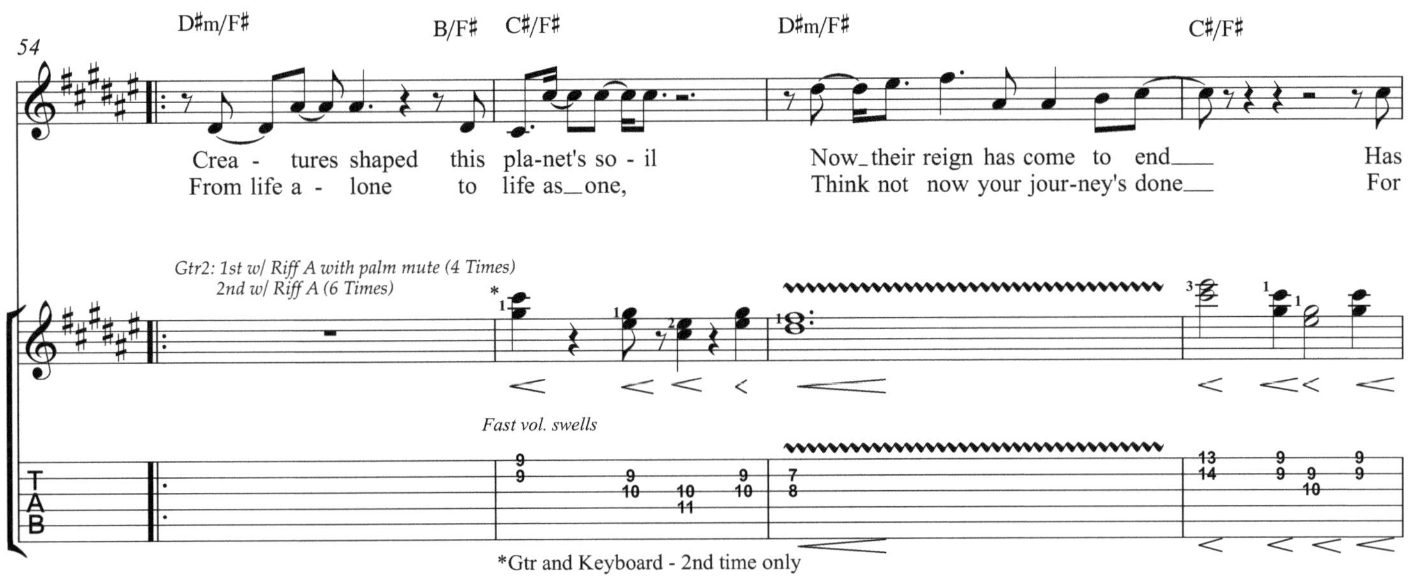
54
D♯m/F♯ B/F♯ C♯/F♯ D♯m/F♯ C♯/F♯
Crea - tures shaped this pla-net's so - il
Now_their reign has come to end___ Has
From life a - lone to life as_one,
Think not now your jour-ney's done___ For
Gtr2: 1st w/ Riff A with palm mute (4 Times)
2nd w/ Riff A (6 Times)
Fast vol. swells
T
A
B
*Gtr and Keyboard - 2nd time only

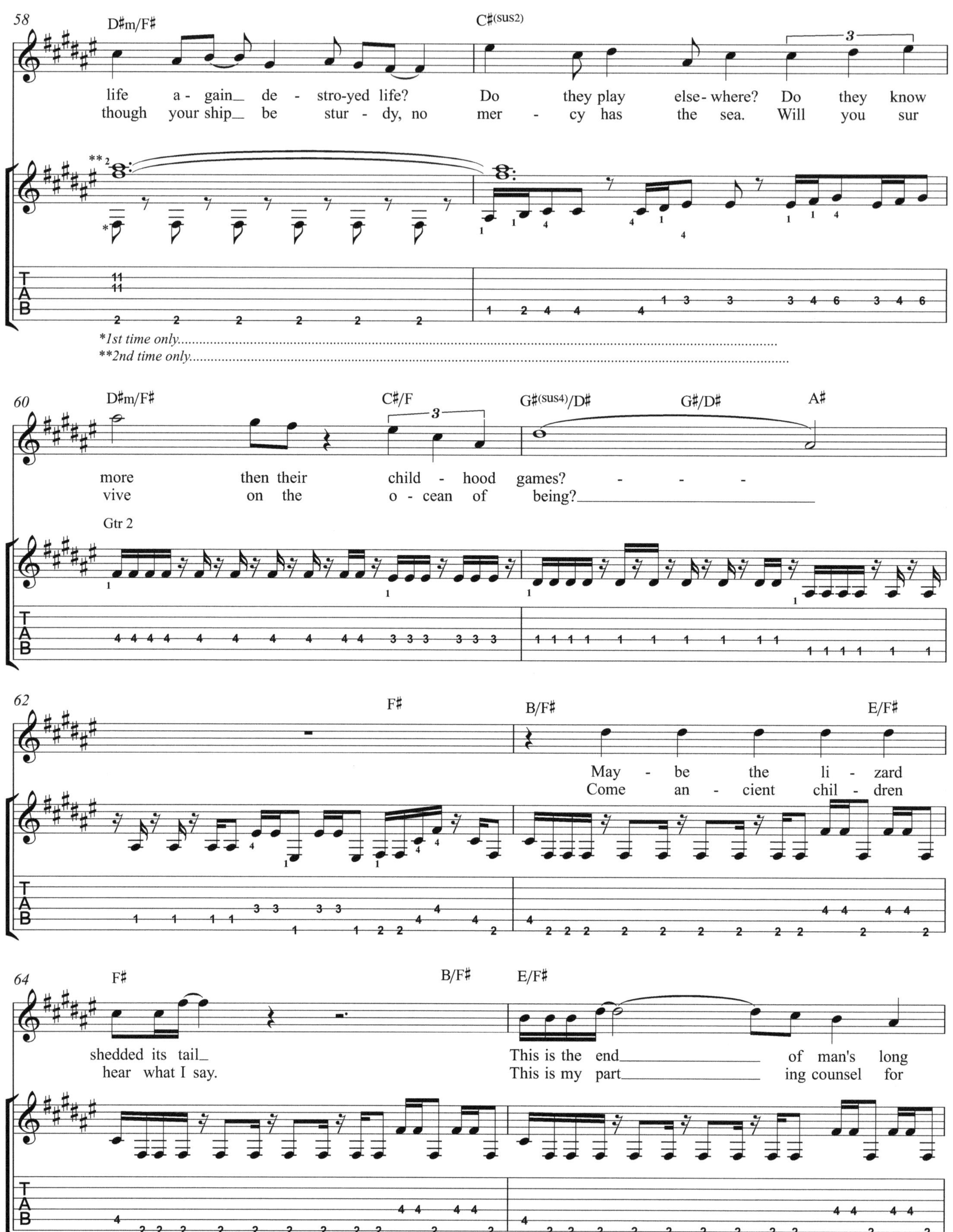
58
D♯m/F♯
C♯(sus2)
life a - gain_ de - stro-yed life? Do they play else- where? Do they know
though your ship_ be stur - dy, no mer - cy has the sea. Will you sur
*1st time only.
**2nd time only.
60
D♯m/F♯
C♯/F
G♯(sus4)/D♯
G♯/D♯
A♯
more then their child - hood games? - - -
vive on the o - cean of being?
Gtr 2
62
F♯
B/F♯
E/F♯
May - be the li - zard
Come an - cient chil - dren
64
F♯
B/F♯
E/F♯
shedded its tail_ This is the end_ of man's long
hear what I say. This is my part_ ing counsel for

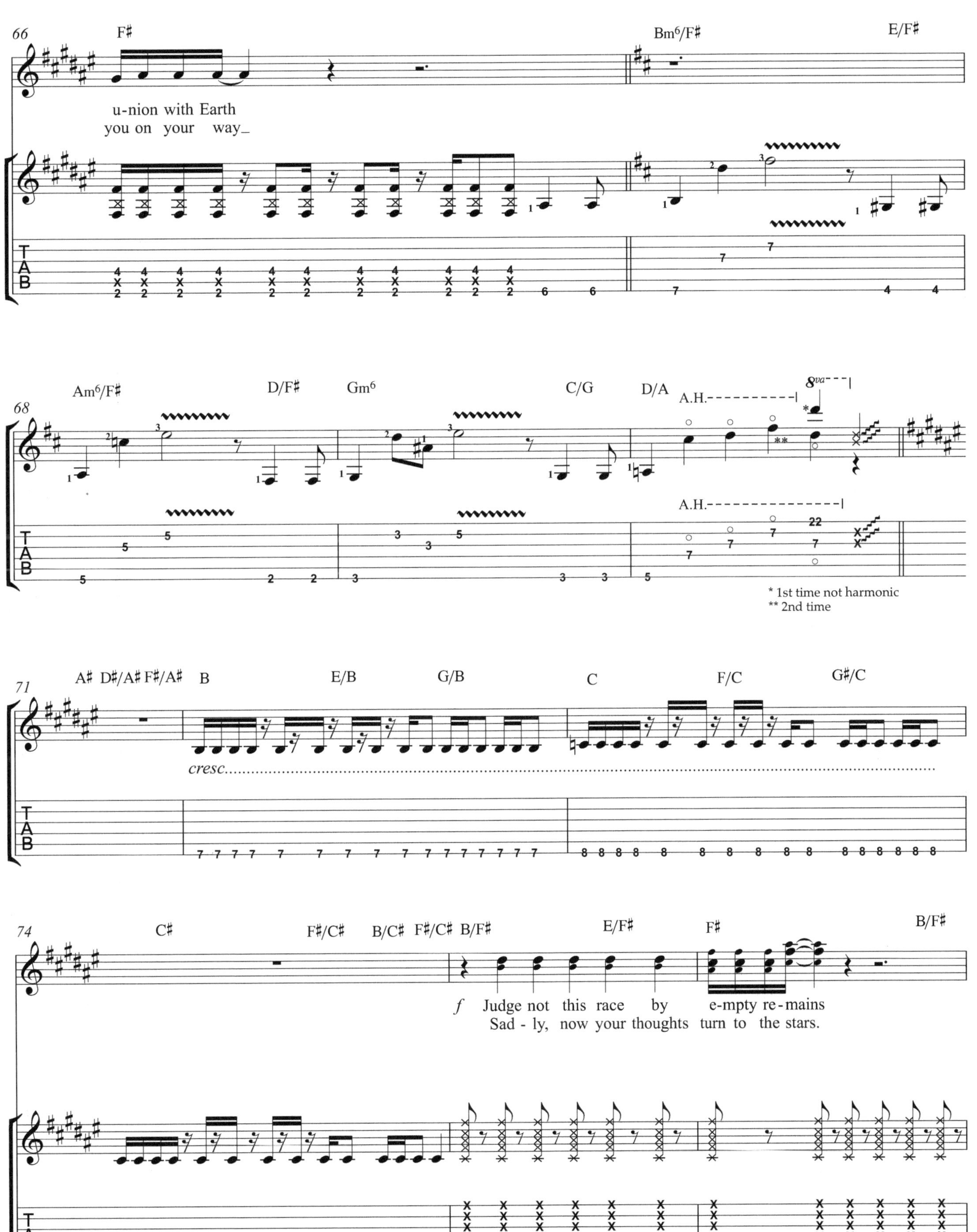
66
F♯
Bm6/F♯
E/F♯
u-nion with Earth
you on your way_
68
Am6/F♯
D/F♯
Gm6
C/G
D/A
A.H.
8va
* 1st time not harmonic
** 2nd time
71
A♯ D♯/A♯ F♯/A♯
B
E/B
G/B
C
F/C
G♯/C
cresc.
74
C♯
F♯/C♯
B/C♯
F♯/C♯
B/F♯
E/F♯
F♯
B/F♯
f
Judge not this race by e-mpty re-mains
Sad - ly, now your thoughts turn to the stars.

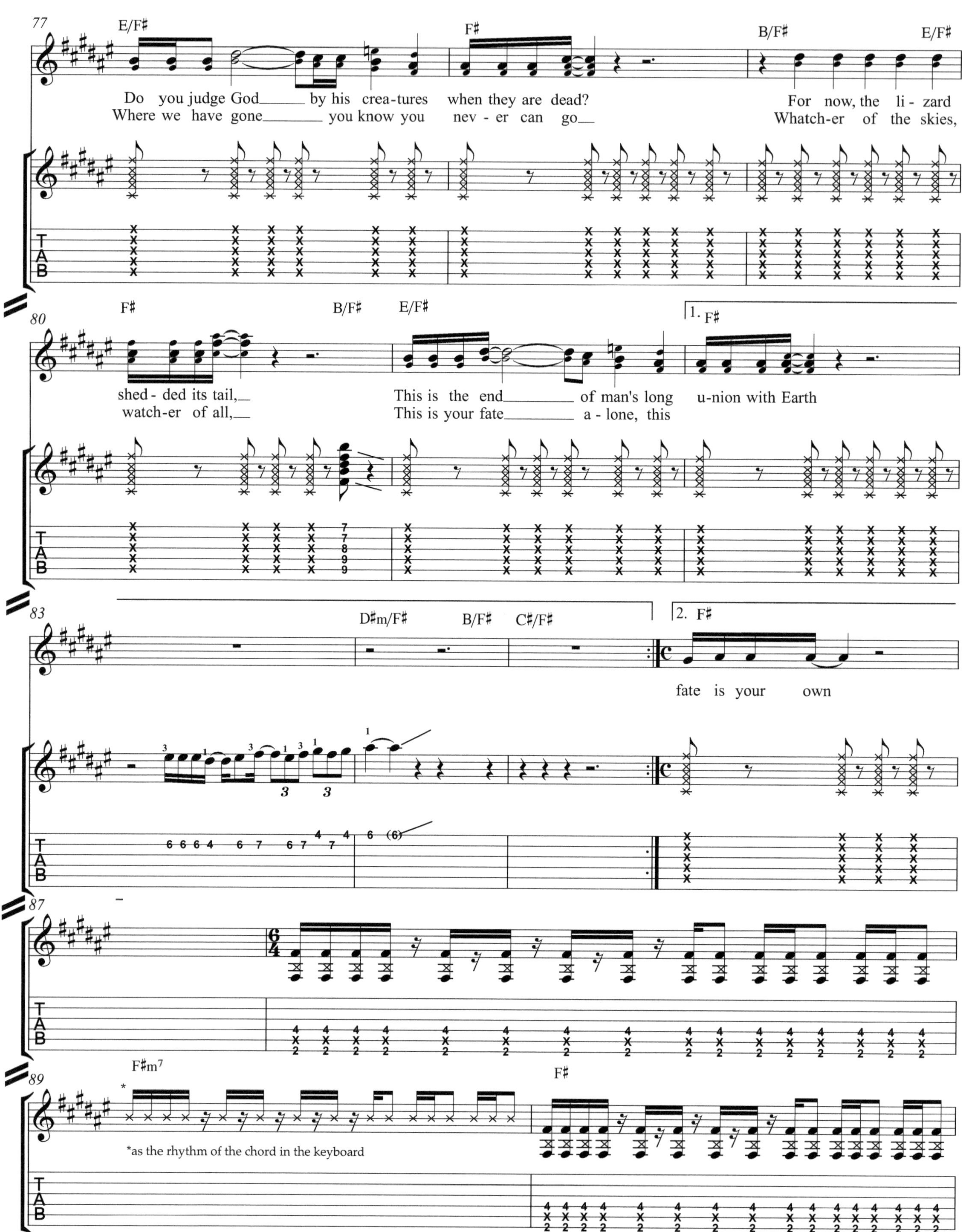
77
E/F♯
F♯
B/F♯
E/F♯
Do you judge God by his crea-tures when they are dead? For now, the li - zard
Where we have gone you know you nev - er can go Whatch-er of the skies,
80
F♯
B/F♯
E/F♯
1. F♯
shed - ded its tail, This is the end of man's long u-nion with Earth
watch-er of all, This is your fate a - lone, this
83
D♯m/F♯
B/F♯
C♯/F♯
2. F♯
fate is your own
87
89
F♯m7
F♯
*as the rhythm of the chord in the keyboard

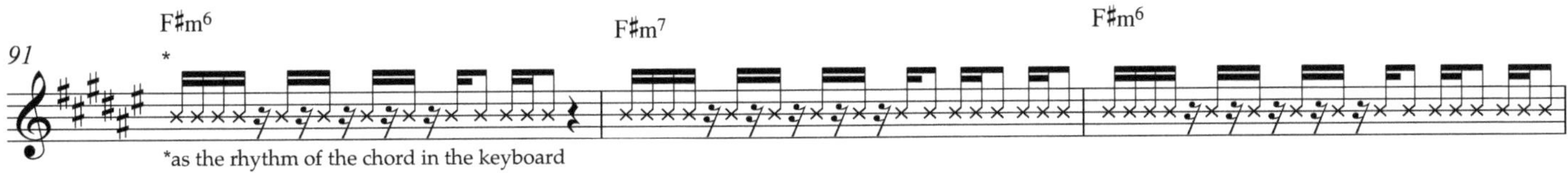
91
F♯m6
F♯m7
F♯m6
*as the rhythm of the chord in the keyboard

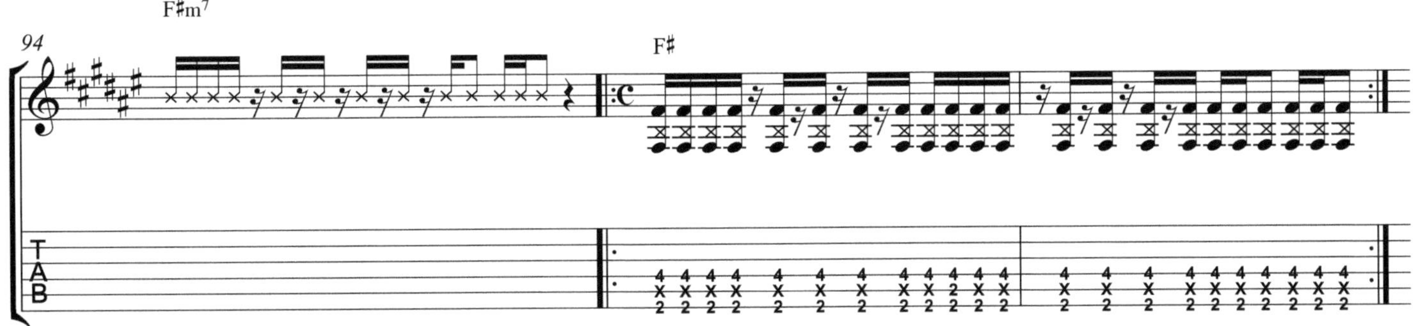
94
F♯m7
F♯

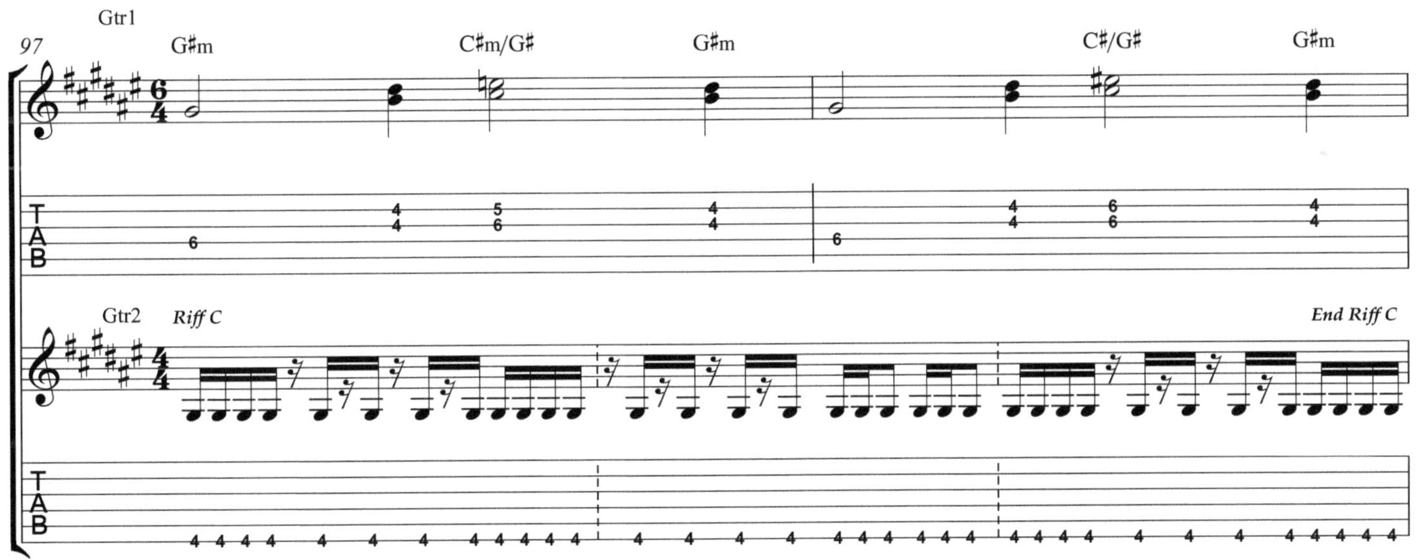
Gtr1
97
G♯m
C♯m/G♯
G♯m
C♯/G♯
G♯m
Gtr2
Riff C
End Riff C

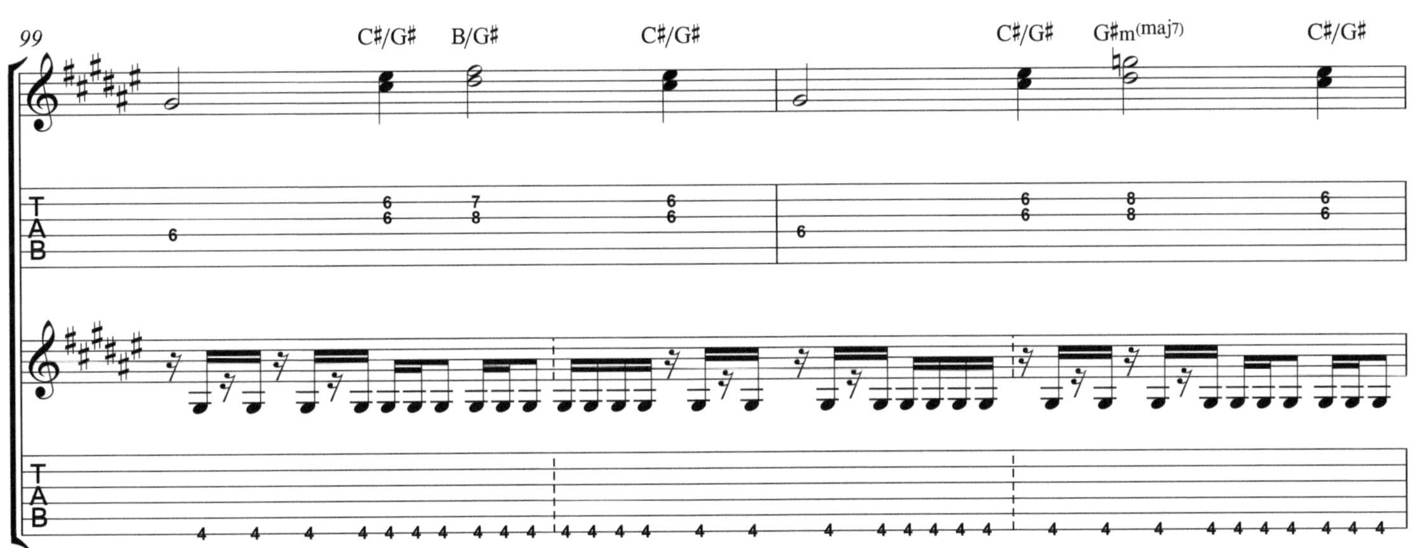
99
C♯/G♯
B/G♯
C♯/G♯
C♯/G♯
G♯m(maj7)
C♯/G♯

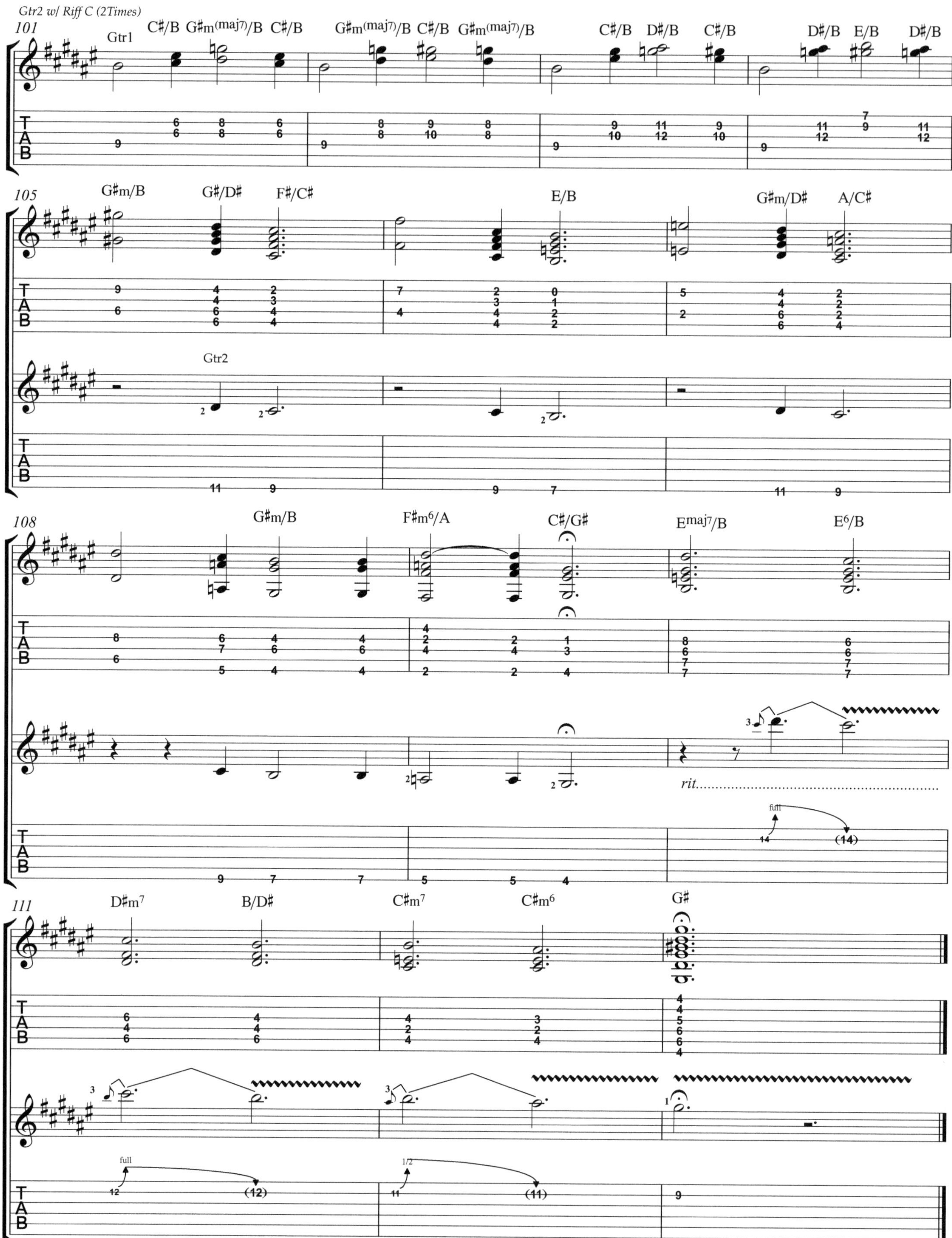
Gtr2 w/ Riff C (2Times)
101
Gtr1
C♯/B G♯m(maj7)/B C♯/B
G♯m(maj7)/B C♯/B G♯m(maj7)/B
C♯/B D♯/B C♯/B
D♯/B E/B D♯/B
105
G♯m/B G♯/D♯ F♯/C♯
E/B
G♯m/D♯ A/C♯
Gtr2
108
G♯m/B
F♯m6/A C♯/G♯
Emaj7/B E6/B
rit.
full
111
D♯m7 B/D♯
C♯m7 C♯m6
G♯
full
1/2

WATCHER OF THE SKIES
BY GENESIS

INTRO

II: Bmaj7/F# I C#/F# :II (play 3 times)

I A#/F I Fm7 I A#m7 I G I C I F# I

I I Bm7 I Am(maj7) I A#m7 I G#m I

I F# F#(add9) I Bm7 Am/B I G#m I C#/G# G#m C#/G# I

I A#m I D#/A# A#m D#/A# I Cm I F/C Cm F/C I

I G#m/B A#m7 I F#/A# G#m7 I B(add4) A I

I A(b5) G#m I F#m6 Fm7 I Fm6 I Cdim(omit3) I Bdim(omit3) I

II: Bmaj7/F# I C#/F# :II (play 7 times)

I F# I E/F#I

B/F# E/F# F# B/F#
WATCHER OF THE SKIES, WATCHER OF ALL

E/F# F#
HIS IS A WORLD ALONE, NO WORLD IS HIS OWN

B/F# E/F# F# B/F#
HE WHOM LIFE CAN NO LONGER SURPRISE

E/F# F#
RAISING HIS EYES BEHOLDS A PLANET UNKNOWN

I D#m/F# I C#/F# I D#m/F# B/F# I C#/F# I

D#m/F# B/F# C#/F#
CREATURES SHAPED THIS PLANET'S SOIL

D#m/F# C#/F#
NOW THEIR REIGN HAS COME TO END

D#m/F# C#(sus2)
HAS LIFE AGAIN DESTROYED LIFE? DO THEY PLAY ELSEWHERE?

D#m/F# C#/F G#(sus4) /D# G#/D# A# F#
DO THEY KNOW MORE THAN THEIR CHILDHOOD GAMES?

B/F# E/F# F# B/F#
MAYBE THE LIZARD SHEDDED ITS TAIL

E/F# F#
THIS IS THE END OF MAN'S LONG UNION WITH EARTH

I Bm6/F# E/F# I Am6/F# D/F# I Gm6 C/G I D/A I

I A# D#/A# F#/A# I B E/B G/B I C F/C G#/C I C# F#/C# B/C# F#/C# I

```
B/F#                      E/F#      F#               B/F#
    JUDGE NOT THIS RACE BY EMPTY REMAINS

E/F#                                           F#
DO YOU JUDGE GOD BY HIS CREATURES WHEN THEY ARE DEAD?

B/F#                        E/F#     F#              B/F#
    FOR NOW, THE LIZARD SHEDDED ITS TAIL

E/F#                                    F#
THIS IS THE END OF MAN'S LONG UNION WITH EARTH


| F#        |          | D#m/F#    B/F#  | C#/F#        |


D#m/F#                      B/F#  C#/F#
   FROM LIFE ALONE  TO   LIFE  AS ONE

D#m/F#
     THINK NOT NOW YOUR JOURNEY'S DONE

C#/F#       D#m/F#                                 C#(sus2)
      FOR THOUGH YOUR SHIP BE STURDY, NO MERCY HAS THE SEA

               D#m/F#         C#/F         G#(sus4)/D#    G#/D#   A#     F#
WILL YOU SURVIVE ON THE OCEAN OF BEING?

B/F#                            E/F#   F#                   B/F#
   COME ANCIENT CHILDREN HEAR WHAT I SAY

E/F#                                       F#
THIS IS MY PARTING COUNSEL FOR YOU ON YOUR WAY


| Bm6/F#   E/F# | Am6/F#   D/F# | Gm6    C/G | D/A        |
| A#   D#/A#   F#/A# | B   E/B   G/B | C   F/C   G#/C | C#   F#/C#  B/C# |


B/F#                E/F#               F#                     B/F#
   SADLY, NOW YOUR THOUGHTS TURN TO THE STARS

E/F#                                          F#
WHERE WE HAVE GONE YOU KNOW YOU NEVER CAN GO

B/F#                          E/F#   F#                 B/F#
    WATCHER OF THE SKIES, WATCHER OF ALL

E/F#                                   F#
THIS IS YOUR FATE ALONE, THIS FATE IS YOUR OWN


| F#        |         | F#m7      | F#        | F#m6       | F#m7       | F#m6        | F#m7         ||: F#        |         :||
| G#m   C#m/G#  G#m |    C#/G#  G#m |     C#/G#  B/G#   C#/G# |     C#/G#  G#m(maj7)  C#/G# |
|      C#/B   G#m(maj7)/B   C#/B |     G#m(maj7)/B    C#/B    G#(maj7)/B |     C#/B  D#/B C#/B |     D#/B  E/B   D#/B|
| G#m/B     G#/D#    F#/C# |         E/B |      G#m/D#   A/C# |      G#m/B     | F#m6/A      C#/G#     |
| Emaj7/B      E6/B | D#m7      B/D# | C#m7      C#m6 | G#          ||
```

TIME TABLE

"My idea for this song was to play with Tony to make it sound like one instrument." Steve Hackett

"That's awesome how we did things. Steve and I used to play quite like the idea that it wouldn't necessarily tell who was who." Tony Banks

Tony Banks composed the music and the lyrics of *Time Table*. He did some parts of the words with Mike, not initially thinking the band would record it. He thought it was not necessarily a Genesis piece, but he played it on the piano for the band, and they liked it; thus, they decided to use it. As Tony remarked, "*Time Table* is quite a nice sort of contrast to the rest of the record because of its structure as a song, verse-chorus, and the rest of it. The other pieces are longer and rambling."

Steve used Tony's two handmade Leslie cabinets. He tried to play the guitar as a Beatles' piano in a simplistic but handy way to help the song's pace. In some parts, Steve uses the Marshall Super Fuzz.

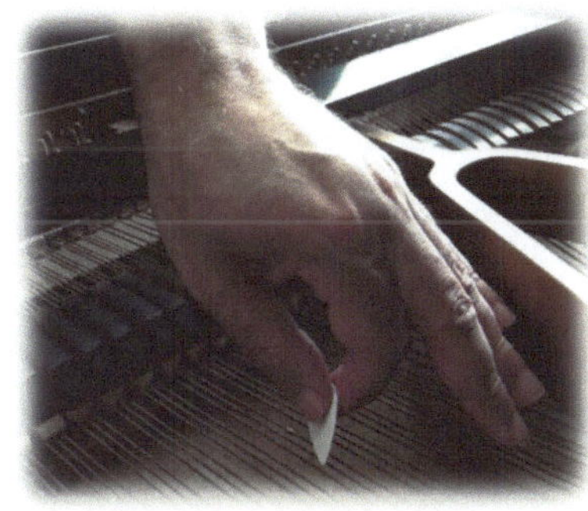

Photo 40: A pianist showing how Tony played the piano solo with a pick.
Photo by Sergio Lestingi

For the solo, Tony plucked into the piano. He used the plectrum on the strings of the piano. As he noticed: "It was just a different way of playing. It was like a harpsichord or something. It was quite a fun, nice sound. Without the damper, one can get strange harmonics coming in, which could sound a bit nasty, so I remember doing it in quite a few takes."

In his interview with the Italian magazine *Dusk* (September 2020, issue number 41), John Burns, Foxtrot's sound engineer, clarifies: "Tony Banks played the solo piano overdubs with a pick on the high pitch strings. I used duct tape to dampen the other two strings [the piano strings are arranged in groups of three for each note on the keyboard] so that I could play one string at a time. Recording overdubs took time, and bending over the grand piano was uncomfortable for the player."

In our interview, Tony commented: "The guitar on *Time Table* is nice, through the Leslies and stuff. Steve liked things just to sound differently. He was an honest player. He didn't necessarily want it to sound like a guitar all the time, which worked very well. I liked to do the same thing. We could both be experimenting at the same time and going to get some good results like that. Sometimes it was just an unexpected harmony. We often played listening to each other because we did a lot in harmony unison and tried to find a differentiated sound."

Players/Instruments:

Peter Gabriel: Vocal, Flute
Tony Banks: Piano, Hohner Pianet N
Steve Hackett: Black Gibson Les Paul Custom
Mike Rutherford: Rickenbacker 4001 Bass
Phil Collins: Drums, Percussion, Backing Vocals

Time Table: Guitar Specifics

"Part of how we approached things is too much as if it were another instrument. Sometimes for the benefit of the music; sometimes to its detriment." Steve Hackett

In the section starting on measure 23, Steve used a Super Fuzz, not using the entire volume on the bridge pickup guitar, using just a bit of distortion. He wanted it to be a Beatles' guitar sound. He played the guitar with the Leslie doubling some of the piano parts.

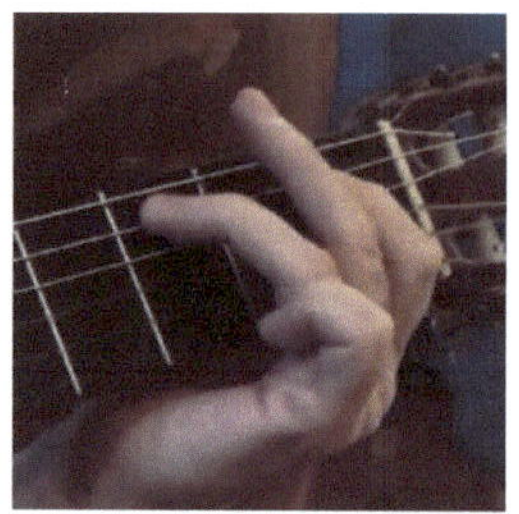
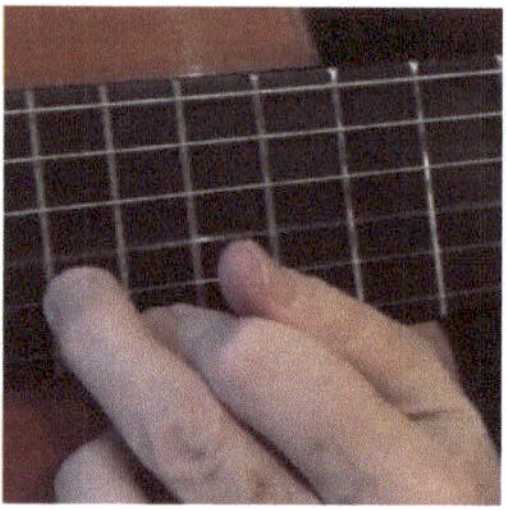

Photos 41-42: Steve showing how to play the section that starts on measure 23 [below]
Photos by Paulo De Carvalho

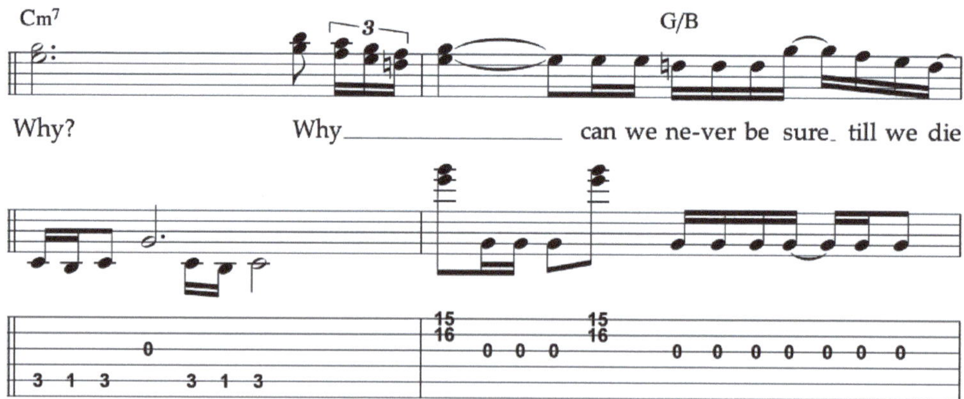

from Genesis - *Foxtrot*

Time Table

by T. Banks, P.Collins, P. Gabriel, S. Hackett, M. Rutherford

Transcribed by Paulo De Carvalho

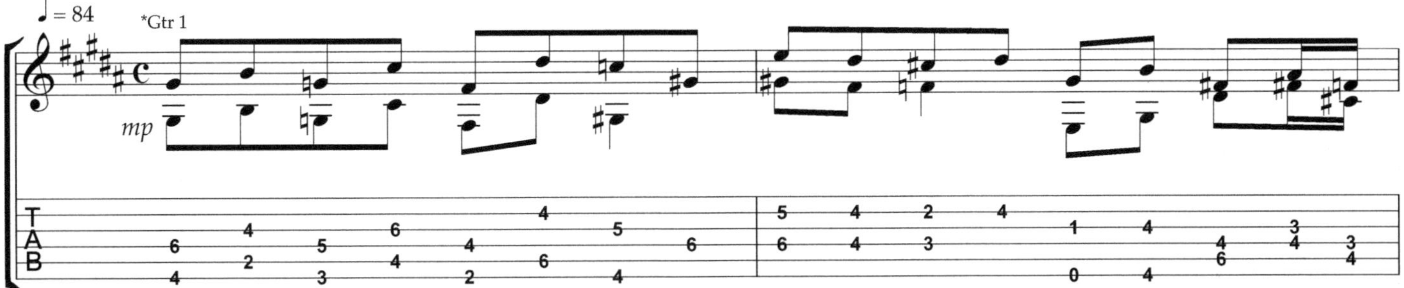

*Gtr 1: Piano/Keyboard arr. for gtr.

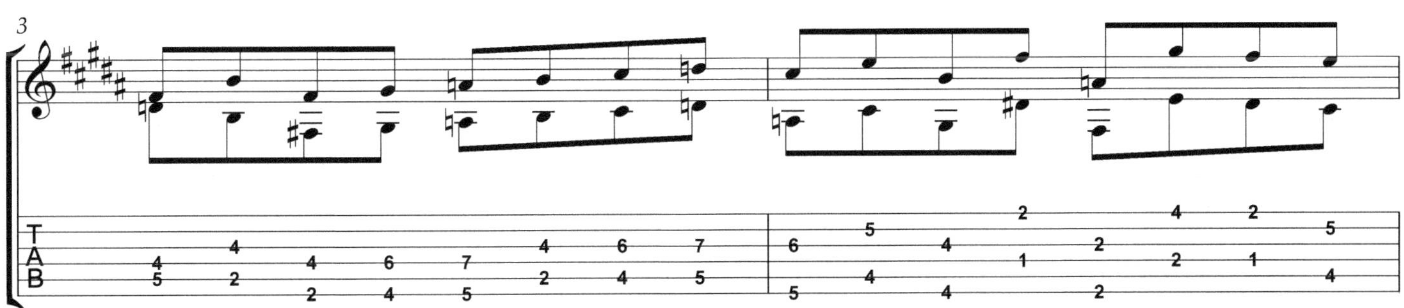

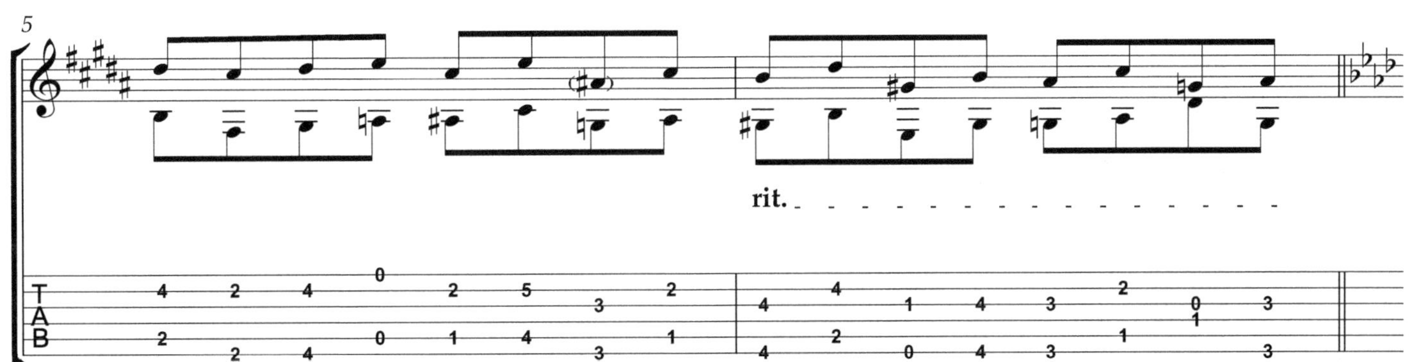

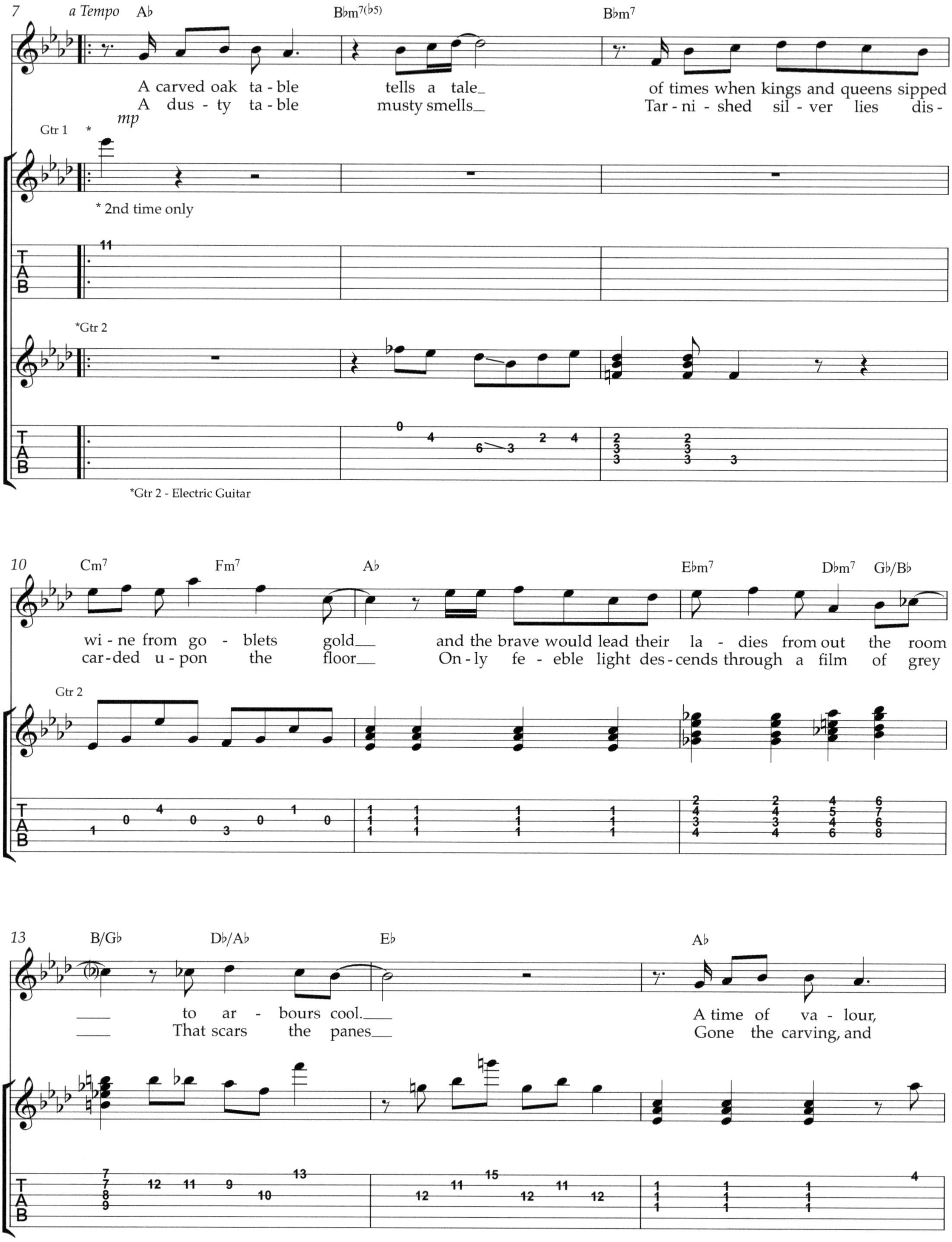

7 *a Tempo* Ab Bbm7(b5) Bbm7

A carved oak ta - ble tells a tale_ of times when kings and queens sipped
A dus - ty ta - ble musty smells_ Tar - ni - shed sil - ver lies dis -

Gtr 1 * *mp*

* 2nd time only

*Gtr 2

*Gtr 2 - Electric Guitar

10 Cm7 Fm7 Ab Ebm7 Dbm7 Gb/Bb

wi - ne from go - blets gold__ and the brave would lead their la - dies from out the room
car - ded u - pon the floor__ On - ly fe - eble light des - cends through a film of grey

Gtr 2

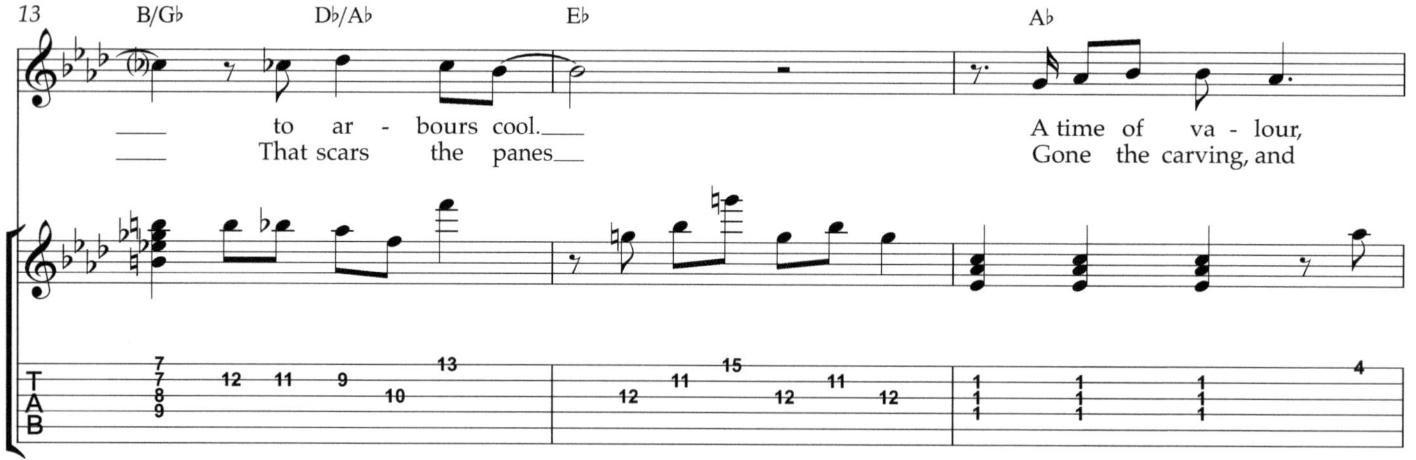

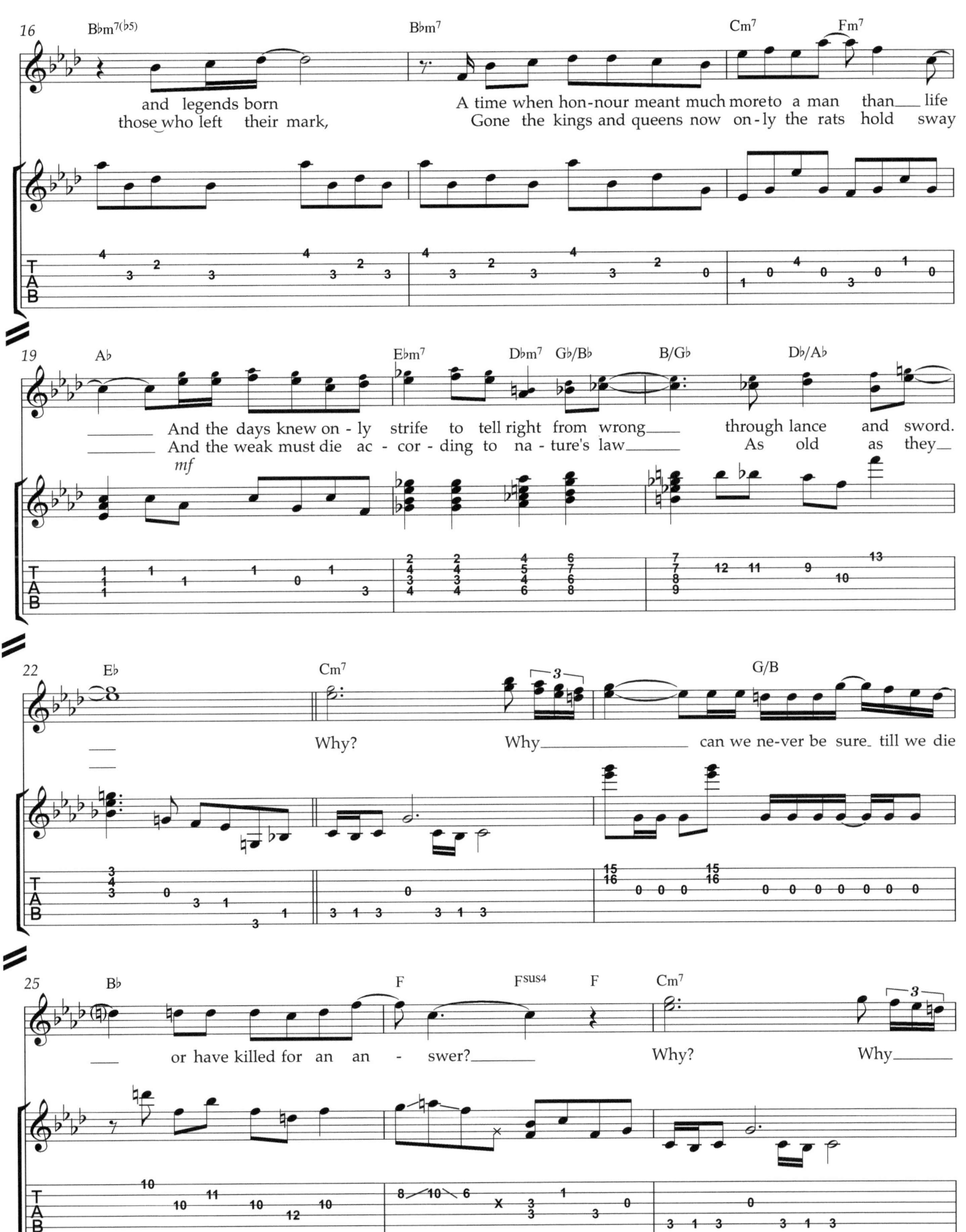
16
Bbm7(b5)
Bbm7
Cm7
Fm7
and legends born
those who left their mark,
A time when hon-nour meant much more to a man than life
Gone the kings and queens now on-ly the rats hold sway
19
Ab
Ebm7
Dbm7
Gb/Bb
B/Gb
Db/Ab
And the days knew on-ly strife to tell right from wrong
And the weak must die ac-cor-ding to na-ture's law
through lance and sword.
As old as they
mf
22
Eb
Cm7
G/B
Why?
Why
can we ne-ver be sure till we die
25
Bb
F
Fsus4
F
Cm7
or have killed for an an-swer?
Why?
Why

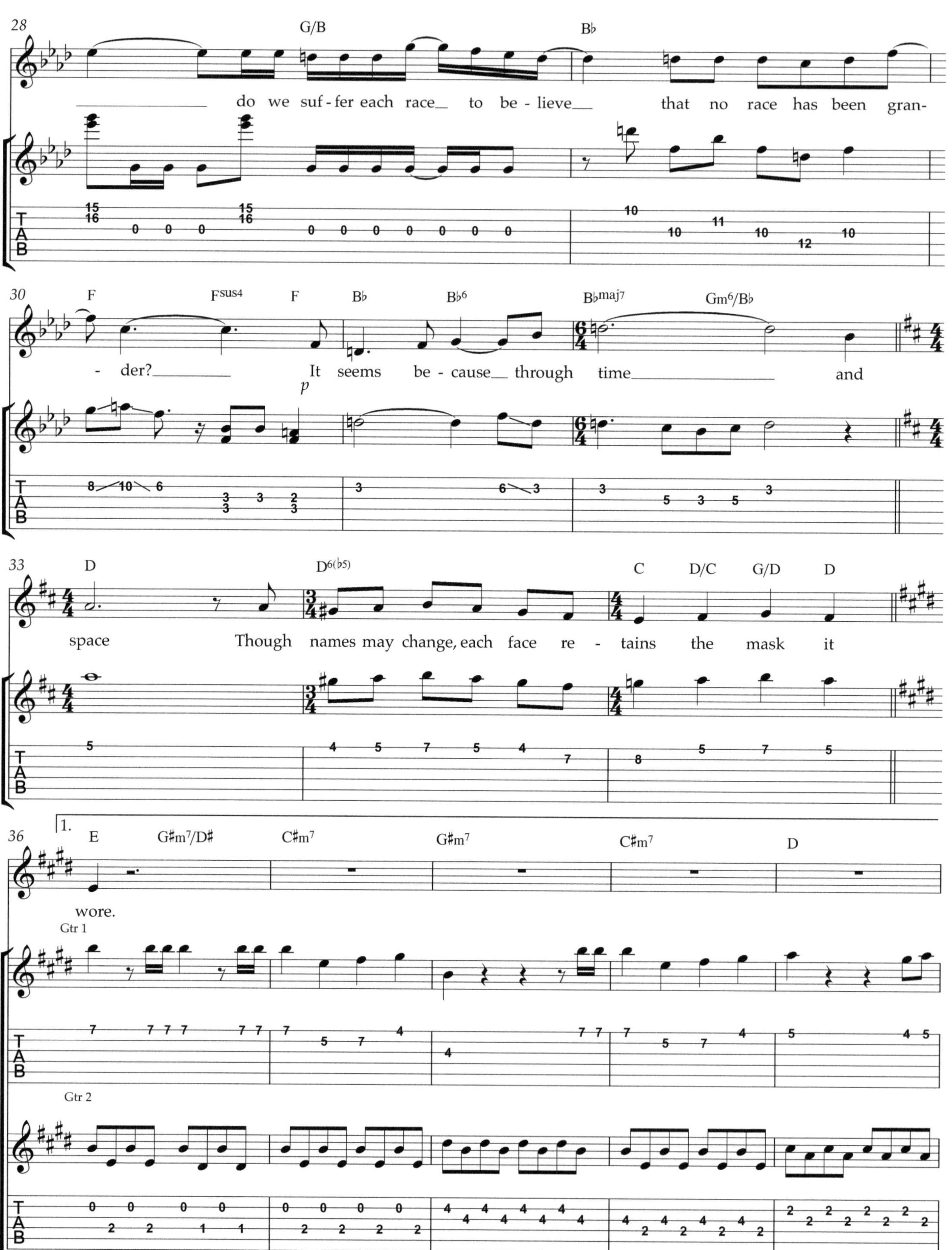
28
G/B
B♭
do we suf - fer each race to be - lieve that no race has been gran-
30
F
Fsus4
F
B♭
B♭6
B♭maj7
Gm6/B♭
- der? It seems be - cause through time and
p
33
D
D6(♭5)
C
D/C
G/D
D
space Though names may change, each face re - tains the mask it
36
1.
E
G♯m7/D♯
C♯m7
G♯m7
C♯m7
D
wore.
Gtr 1
Gtr 2

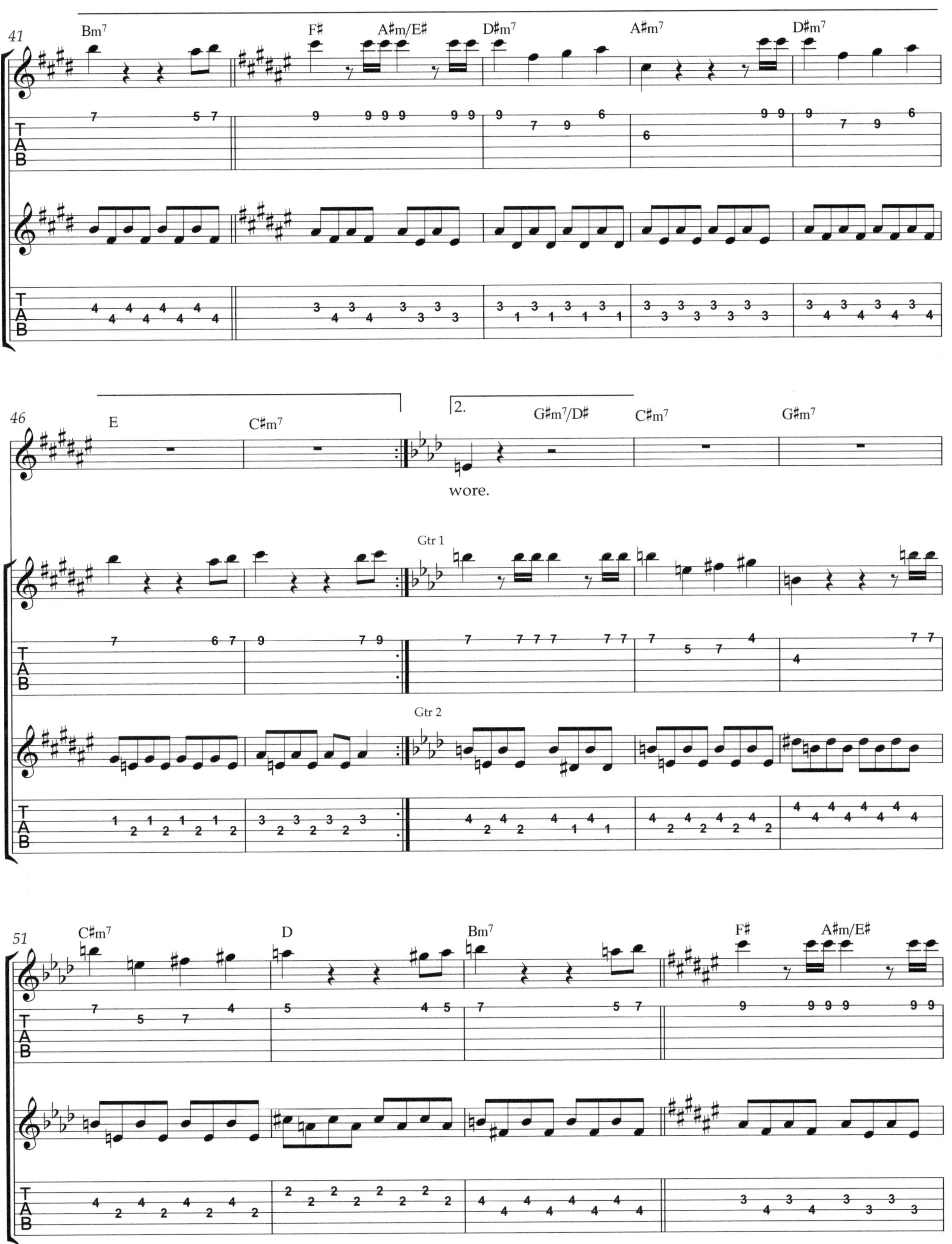
41
Bm7
F♯
A♯m/E♯
D♯m7
A♯m7
D♯m7
46
E
C♯m7
2.
G♯m7/D♯
C♯m7
G♯m7
wore.
Gtr 1
Gtr 2
51
C♯m7
D
Bm7
F♯
A♯m/E♯

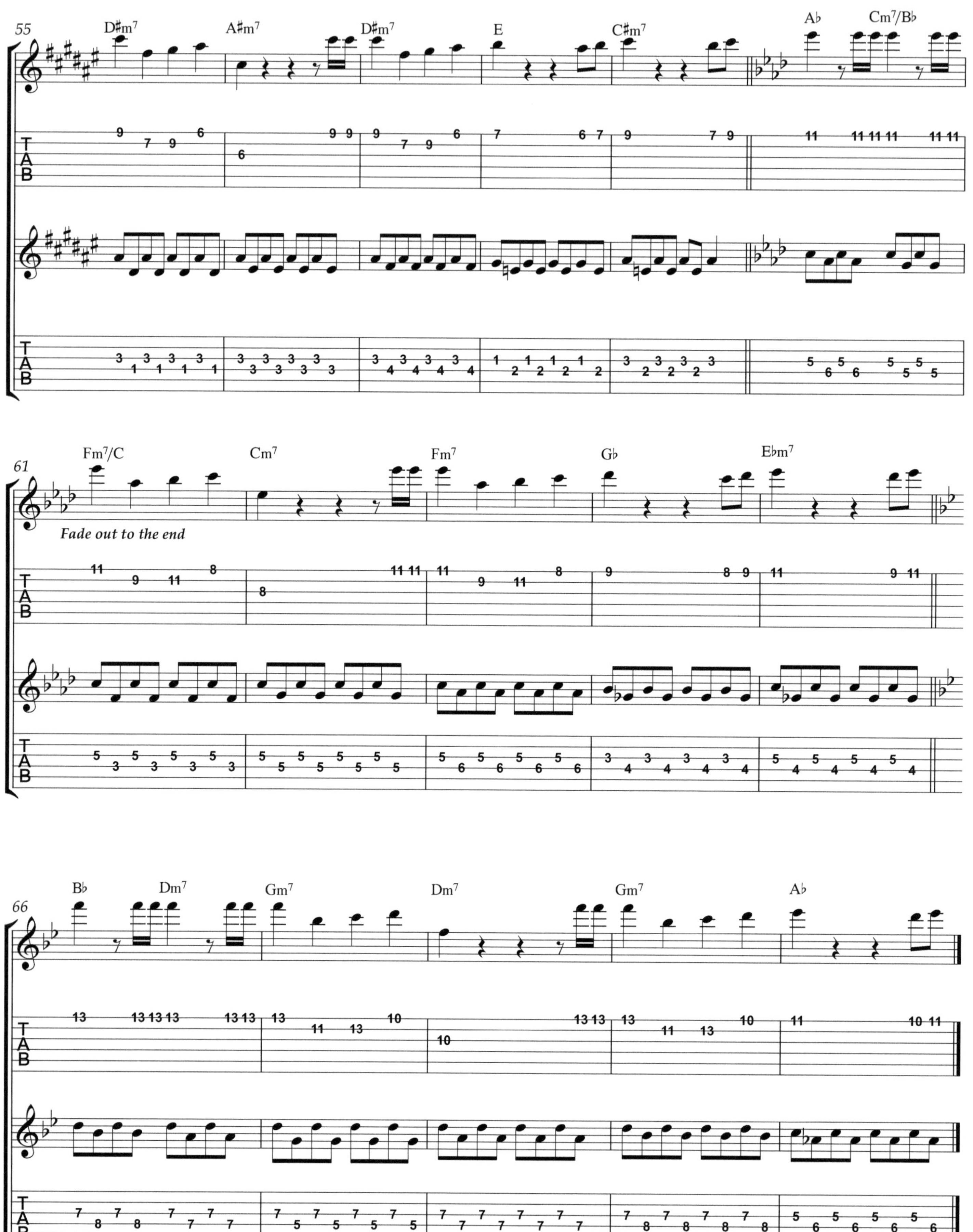
55
D♯m7
A♯m7
D♯m7
E
C♯m7
A♭
Cm7/B♭
61
Fm7/C
Cm7
Fm7
G♭
E♭m7
Fade out to the end
66
B♭
Dm7
Gm7
Dm7
Gm7
A♭

TIME TABLE

BY GENESIS

[INTRO]

Ab Bbm7(b5)
A CARVED OAK TABLE TELLS A TALE

Bbm7 Cm7 Fm7
OF TIMES WHEN KINGS AND QUEENS SIPPED WINE FROM GO - BLETS GOLD

Ab Ebm7 Dbm7 Gb/Bb
AND THE BRAVE WOULD LEAD THEIR LADIES FROM OUT OF THE ROOM

B/Gb Db/Ab Eb
TO ARBOURS COOL

Ab Bbm7(b5)
A TIME OF VALOUR, AND LEGENDS BORN

Bbm7 Cm7 Fm7 Ab
A TIME WHEN HONOUR MEANT MUCH MORE TO A MAN THAN LIFE

Ebm7 Dbm7 Gb/Bb B/Gb
AND THE DAYS KNEW ONLY STRIFE TO TELL RIGHT FROM WRONG

Db/Ab Eb
THROUGH LANCE AND SWORD

Cm7 G/B
WHY? WHY CAN WE NEVER BE SURE TILL WE DIE

Bb F Fsus4 F
OR HAVE KILLED FOR AN ANS - WER?

Cm7 G/B
WHY? WHY DO WE SUFFER EACH RACE TO BELIEVE

Bb F Fsus4
THAT NO RACE HAS BEEN GRAN - DER?

F Bb Bb6 Bbmaj7 Gm6/Bb D
IT SEEMS BECAUSE THROUGH TIME AND SPACE

D6(b5) C D/C G/D D E
THOUGH NAMES MAY CHANGE, EACH FACE RETAINS THE MASK IT WORE

| E G#m7/D# | C#m7 | G#m7 | C#m7 | D | Bm7 | F# A#m/E# |

| D#m7 | A#m7 | D#m7 | E | C#m7 |

Ab Bbm7(b5)
A DUSTY TABLE, MUSTY SMELLS

Bbm7 Cm7 Fm7
TARNISHED SILVER LIES DISCARDED UPON THE FLOOR

```
Ab                          Ebm7                    Dbm7  Gb/Bb
ONLY FEEBLE LIGHT DESCENDS THROUGH A FILM      OF    GREY

B/Gb          Db/Ab             Eb
      THAT SCARS THE PANES

   Ab                               Bbm7(b5)
   GONE THE CARVING, AND            THOSE WHO LEFT THEIR MARK

Bbm7                                           Cm7            Fm7
    GONE THE KINGS AND QUEENS NOW ONLY THE RATS     HOLD SWAY

Ab                                    Ebm7            Dbm7  Gb/Bb
   AND THE WEAK MUST DIE ACCORDING TO  NA -  TURE'S    LAW

B/Gb          Db/Ab            Eb
         AS  OLD AS THEY


Cm7                       G/B
WHY? WHY CAN WE NEVER BE SURE TILL WE DIE

Bb                                F         Fsus4   F
   OR HAVE KILLED FOR AN ANS - WER?

Cm7                            G/B
WHY? WHY          DO WE SUFFER EACH RACE TO BELIEVE

Bb                                 F         Fsus4
   THAT NO RACE HAS BEEN GRAN - DER?

F    Bb         Bb6                    Bbmaj7  Gm6/Bb    D
  IT SEEMS BECAUSE THROUGH TIME                AND SPACE

           D6(b5)                                 C      D/C  G/D   D           G#m7/D#
THOUGH NAMES MAY CHANGE EACH FACE RETAINS  THE   MASK IT WORE
```

| C#m7 | | | D | Bm7 | F#   A#m/E# |

| D#m7 | A#m7 | D#m7 | E | C#m7 | Ab   Cm7/Bb | Fm7/C | Cm7 | Fm7 |

| Gb | Ebm7 | Bb   Dm7 | Gm7 | Dm7 | Gm7 | Ab ||

GET 'EM OUT BY FRIDAY

"Originally, we wrote the piece, and I was sort of just playing, changing lines and things and doing stuff. A lot of the time, we wrote these things in the rehearsal room.
I tried different signatures. When I played, they started doing a sort of a counter rhythm to it. It made it sound more engaging. Then we just saw quite a few bits and pieces: a little bit of mine on the guitar, which was one of the verses that Steve wrote.
And then we did all the middle section.
I think that a little about it was sort of improvisation."
Tony Banks

Many times, Genesis had an idea of a sound they wanted to make it. Sometimes it was just the two flutes: one played by Peter and the other one was, in reality, Tony on the Mellotron. "So ordinary, but that was quite a nice thing to be able to do," Tony told me.

Steve commented that everyone composed the song, but Peter did the lyrics. Steve used a Marshall Super Fuzz. The introduction is Steve on the guitar with Peter on the oboe.

Players/Instruments:
Peter Gabriel: Vocal, Flute, Oboe
Tony Banks: Hammond L122, Hohner Pianet N, Mellotron MK II, Hagstrom BJ-12
Steve Hackett: Black Gibson Les Paul Custom, Hagstrom BJ-12
Mike Rutherford: Rickenbacker 4001 Bass, Vox Bass Pedal
Phil Collins: Drums

Get'em Out by Friday: Guitar Specifics

In the section that starts on measure 20, Steve and Mike played the same line:

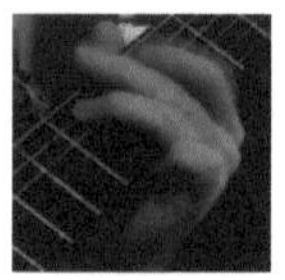
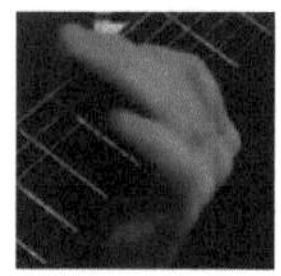
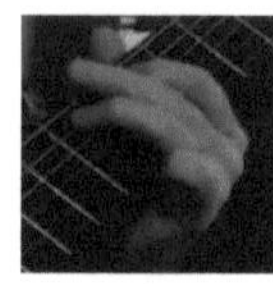
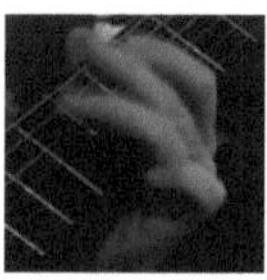
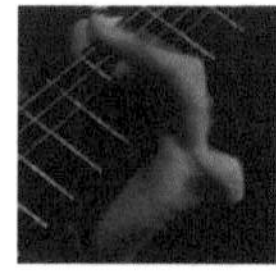
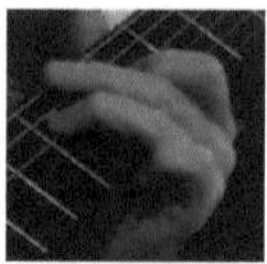

Photos 43-48: Steve showing the riff that starts on measure 20[below]. Photos by Paulo De Carvalho

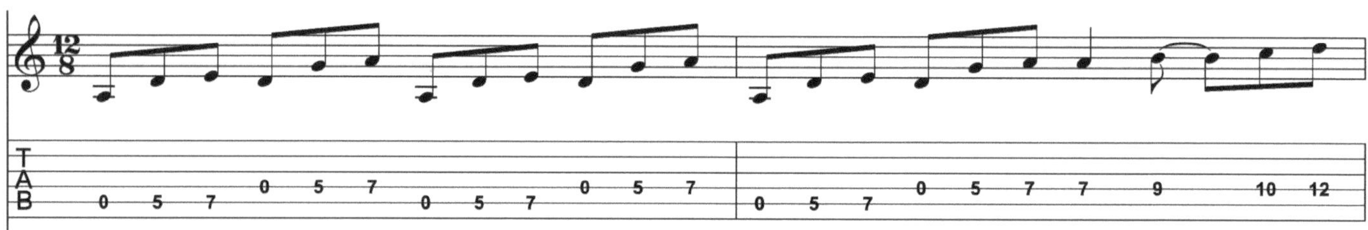

Before joining Genesis, Steve constantly played with his brother John Hackett on the flute. The line below was some of John's ideas:

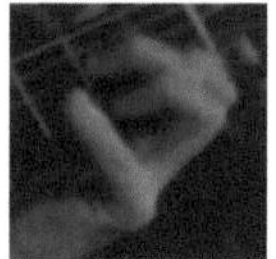
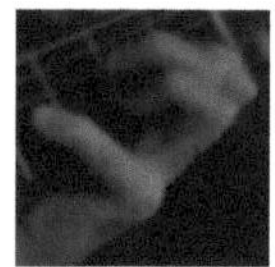

Photos 49-50: Steve showing the line that starts on measure 60 [below]. Photos by Paulo De Carvalho

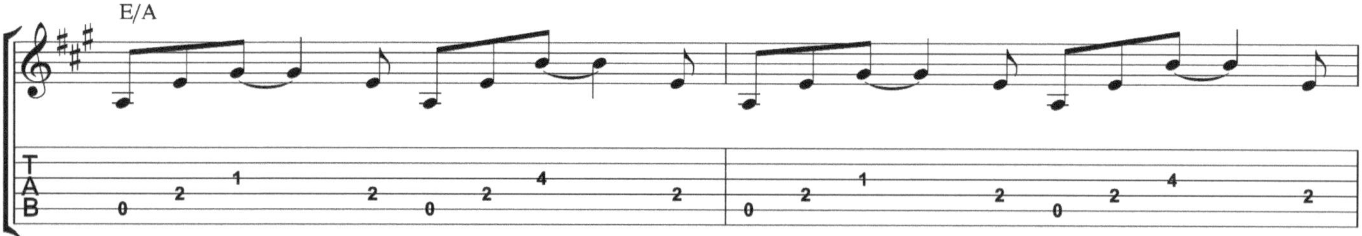

from Genesis - *Foxtrot*

Get'em out by Friday

Transcribed by Paulo De Carvalho

by T. Banks, P.Collins, P. Gabriel, S. Hackett, M. Rutherford

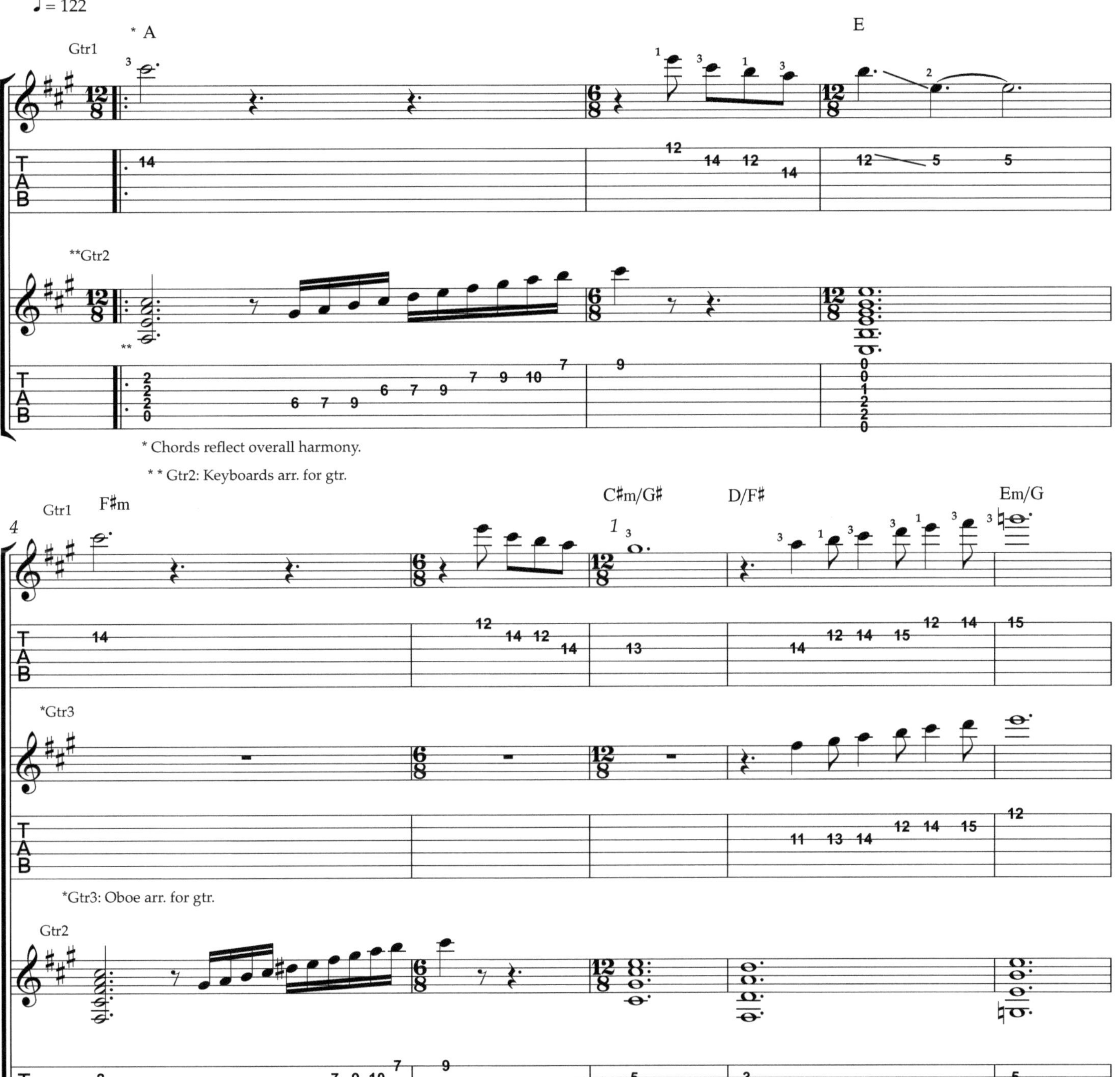

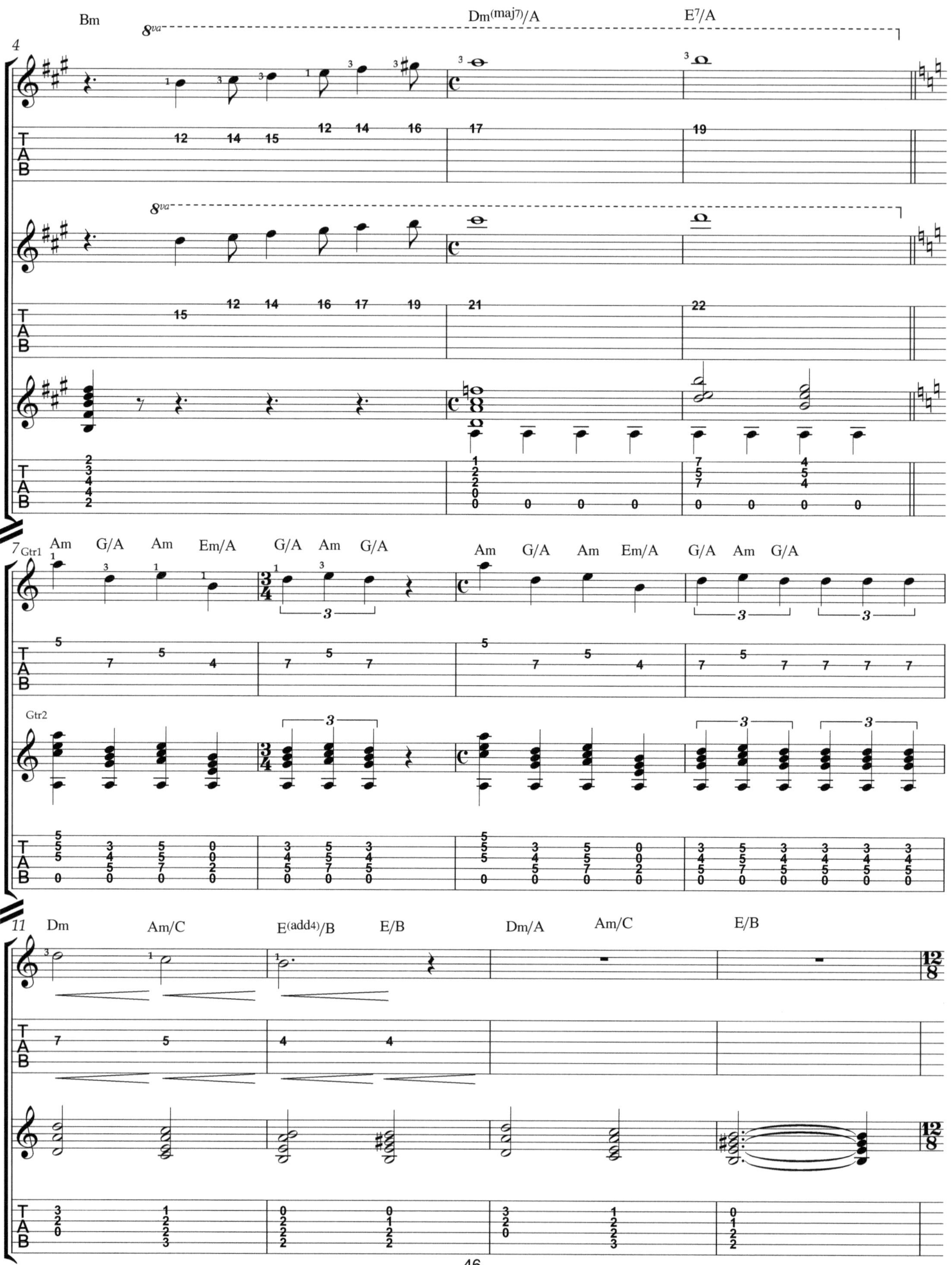
Bm
Dm(maj7)/A
E7/A
8va
Am
G/A
Em/A
Gtr1
Gtr2
Dm
Am/C
E(add4)/B
E/B
Dm/A

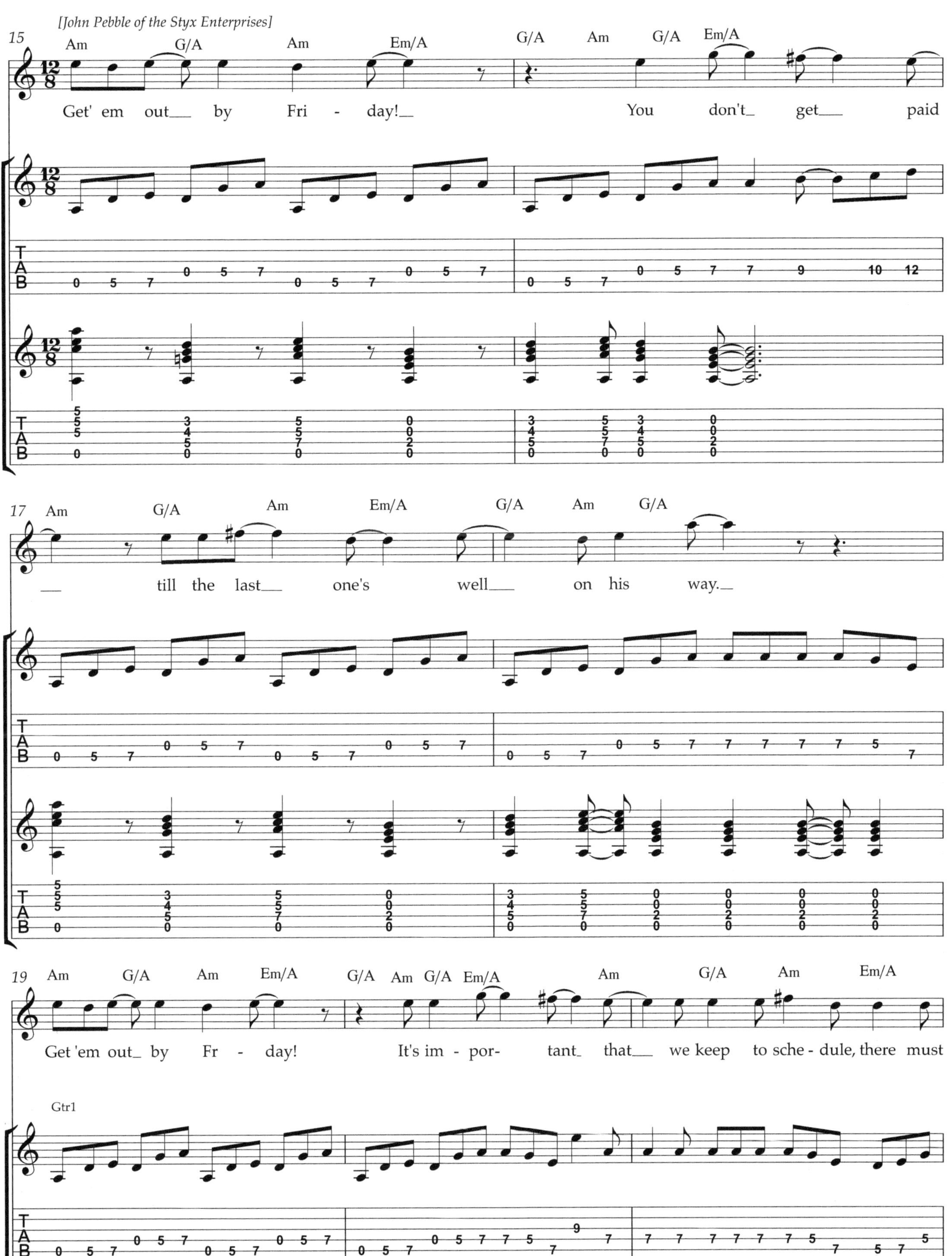
[John Pebble of the Styx Enterprises]
15
Am G/A Am Em/A G/A Am G/A Em/A
Get' em out__ by Fri - day!__ You don't_ get__ paid
17
Am G/A Am Em/A G/A Am G/A
__ till the last__ one's well__ on his way.__
19
Am G/A Am Em/A G/A Am G/A Em/A Am G/A Am Em/A
Get 'em out_ by Fr - day! It's im - por- tant_ that__ we keep to sche - dule, there must
Gtr1

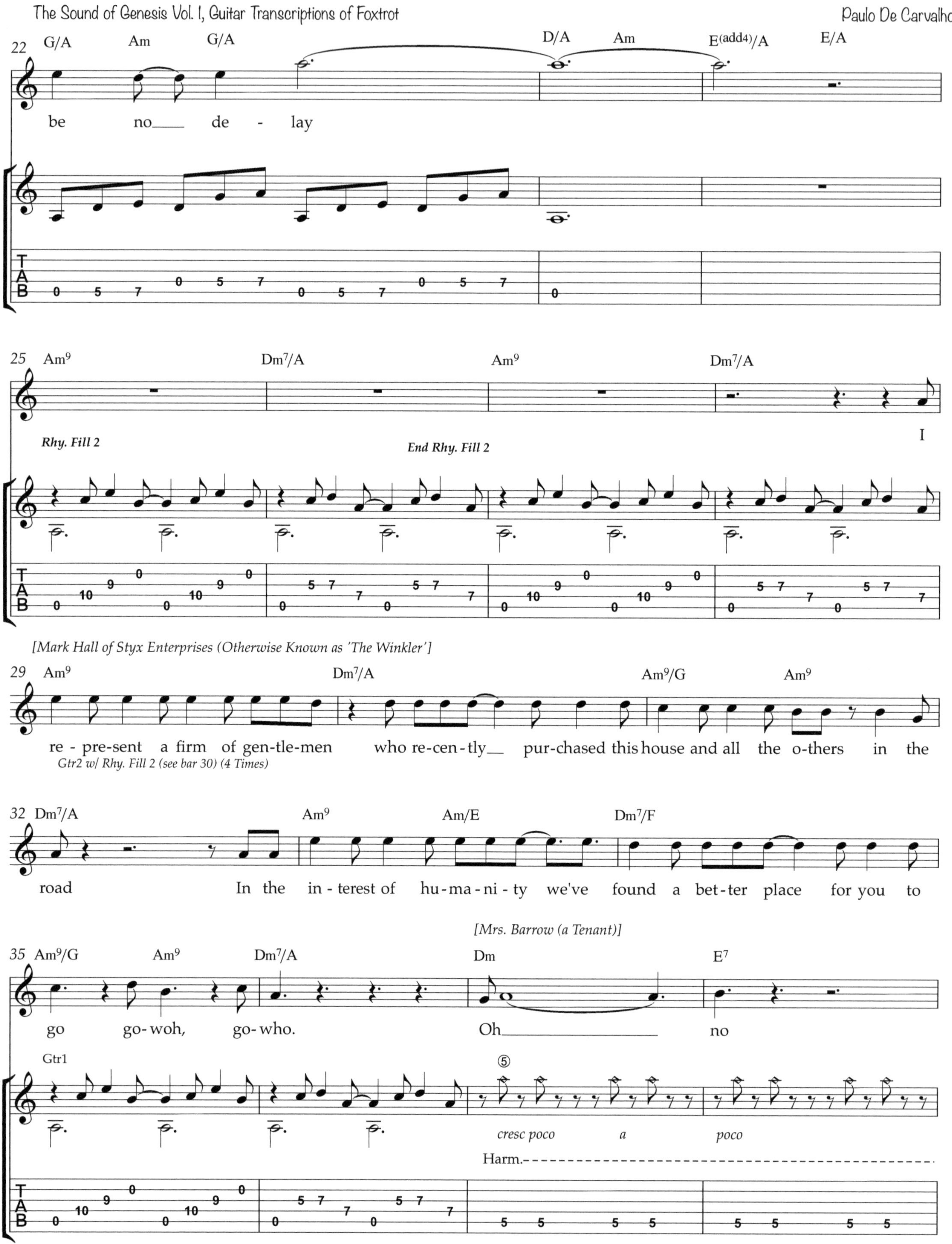
22 G/A Am G/A D/A Am E(add4)/A E/A
be no___ de - lay
T A B
0 5 7 0 5 7 0 5 7 0 5 7 0
25 Am9 Dm7/A Am9 Dm7/A
Rhy. Fill 2
End Rhy. Fill 2
I
[Mark Hall of Styx Enterprises (Otherwise Known as 'The Winkler']
29 Am9 Dm7/A Am9/G Am9
re - pre-sent a firm of gen-tle-men who re-cen-tly__ pur-chased this house and all the o-thers in the
Gtr2 w/ Rhy. Fill 2 (see bar 30) (4 Times)
32 Dm7/A Am9 Am/E Dm7/F
road In the in - terest of hu-ma-ni-ty we've found a bet-ter place for you to
[Mrs. Barrow (a Tenant)]
35 Am9/G Am9 Dm7/A Dm E7
go go-woh, go-who. Oh________ no
Gtr1
cresc poco a poco
Harm.

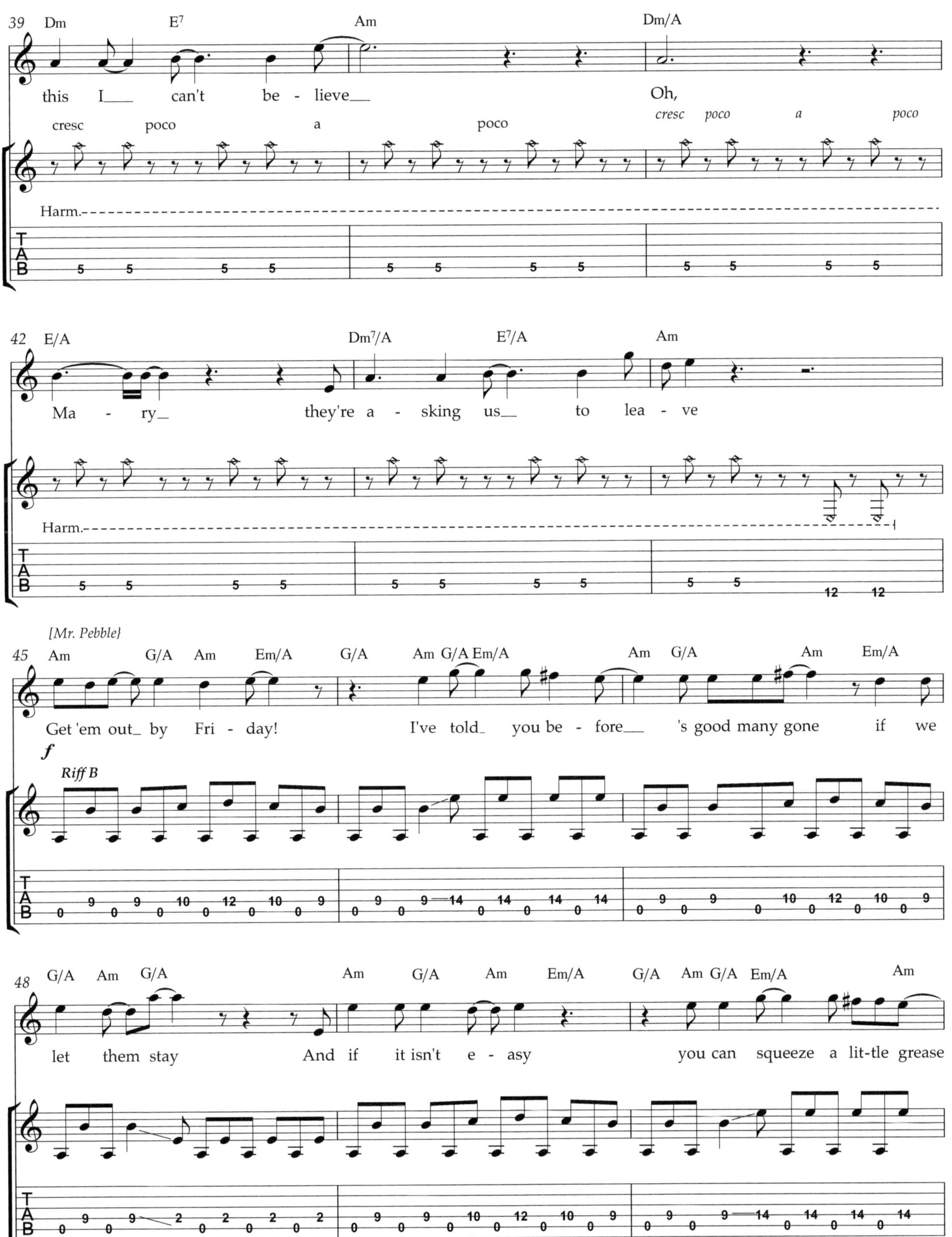
39 Dm E7 Am Dm/A
this I can't be - lieve Oh,
cresc poco a poco
cresc poco a poco
Harm.
42 E/A Dm7/A E7/A Am
Ma - ry they're a - sking us to lea - ve
Harm.
[Mr. Pebble]
45 Am G/A Am Em/A G/A Am G/A Em/A Am G/A Am Em/A
Get 'em out by Fri - day! I've told you be - fore 's good many gone if we
f
Riff B
48 G/A Am G/A Am G/A Am Em/A G/A Am G/A Em/A Am
let them stay And if it isn't e - asy you can squeeze a lit-tle grease

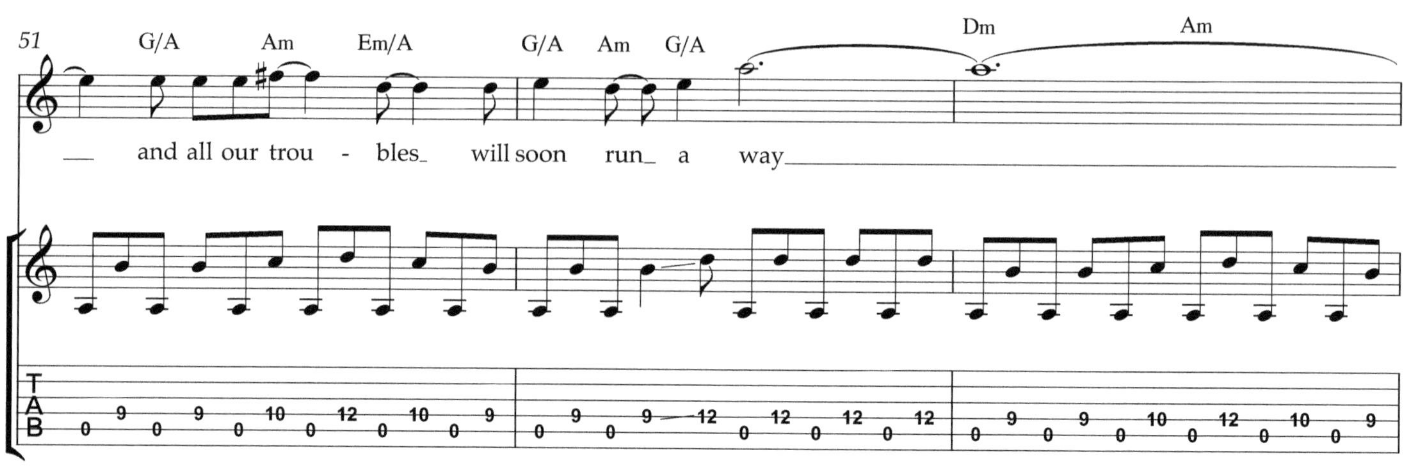
51
G/A
Am
Em/A
G/A
Am
G/A
Dm
Am
and all our trou - bles will soon run a way
T
A
B

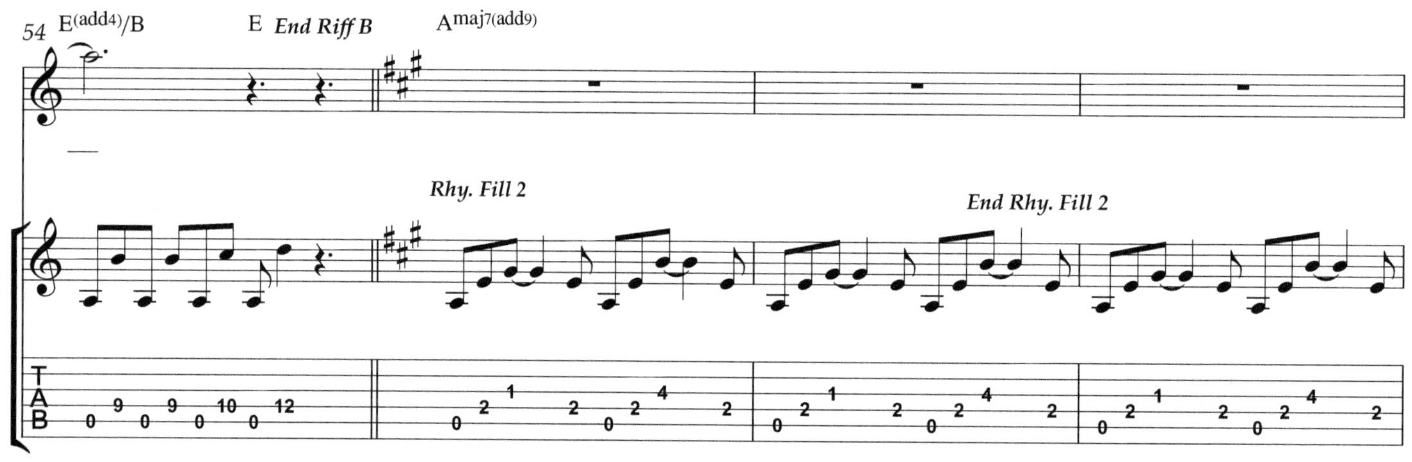
54
E(add4)/B
E End Riff B
Amaj7(add9)
Rhy. Fill 2
End Rhy. Fill 2
T
A
B

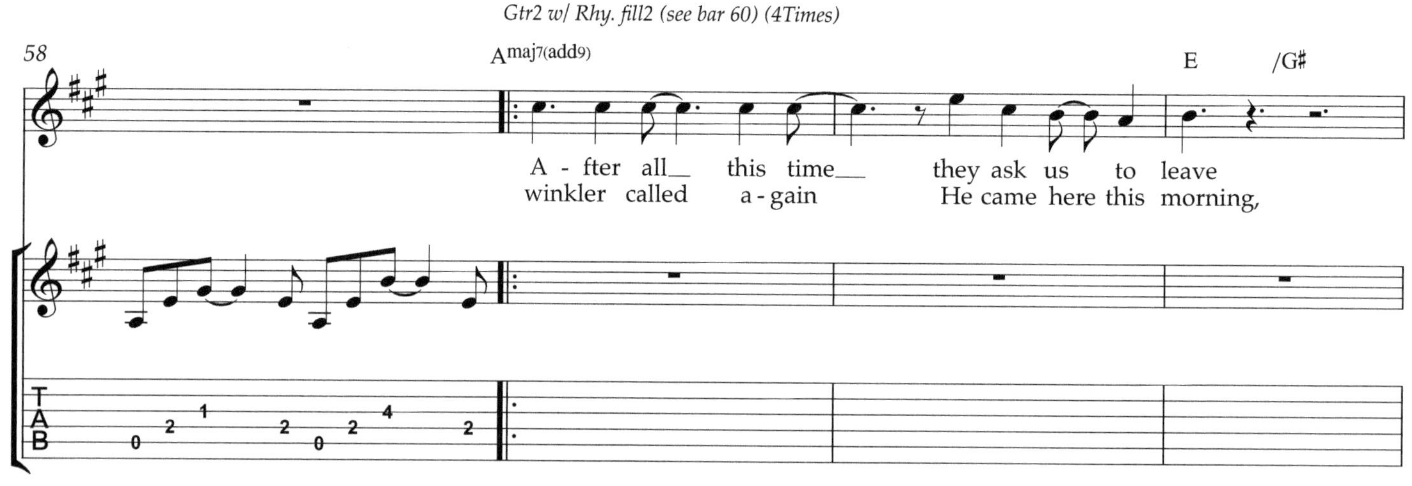
[Mrs. Barrow]
Gtr2 w/ Rhy. fill2 (see bar 60) (4Times)
58
Amaj7(add9)
E
/G#
A - fter all this time they ask us to leave
winkler called a - gain He came here this morning,
T
A
B

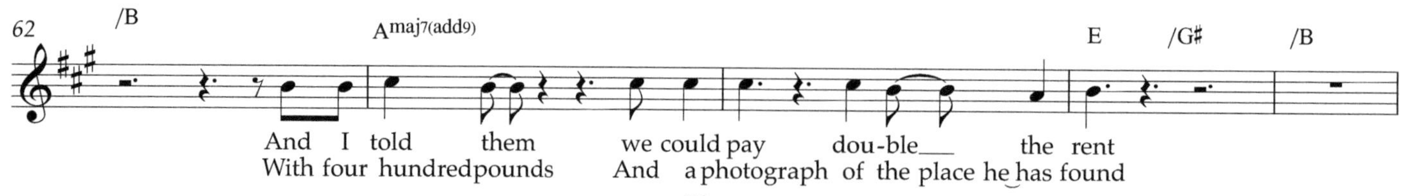
62
/B
Amaj7(add9)
E
/G#
/B
And I told them we could pay dou-ble the rent
With four hundred pounds And a photograph of the place he has found

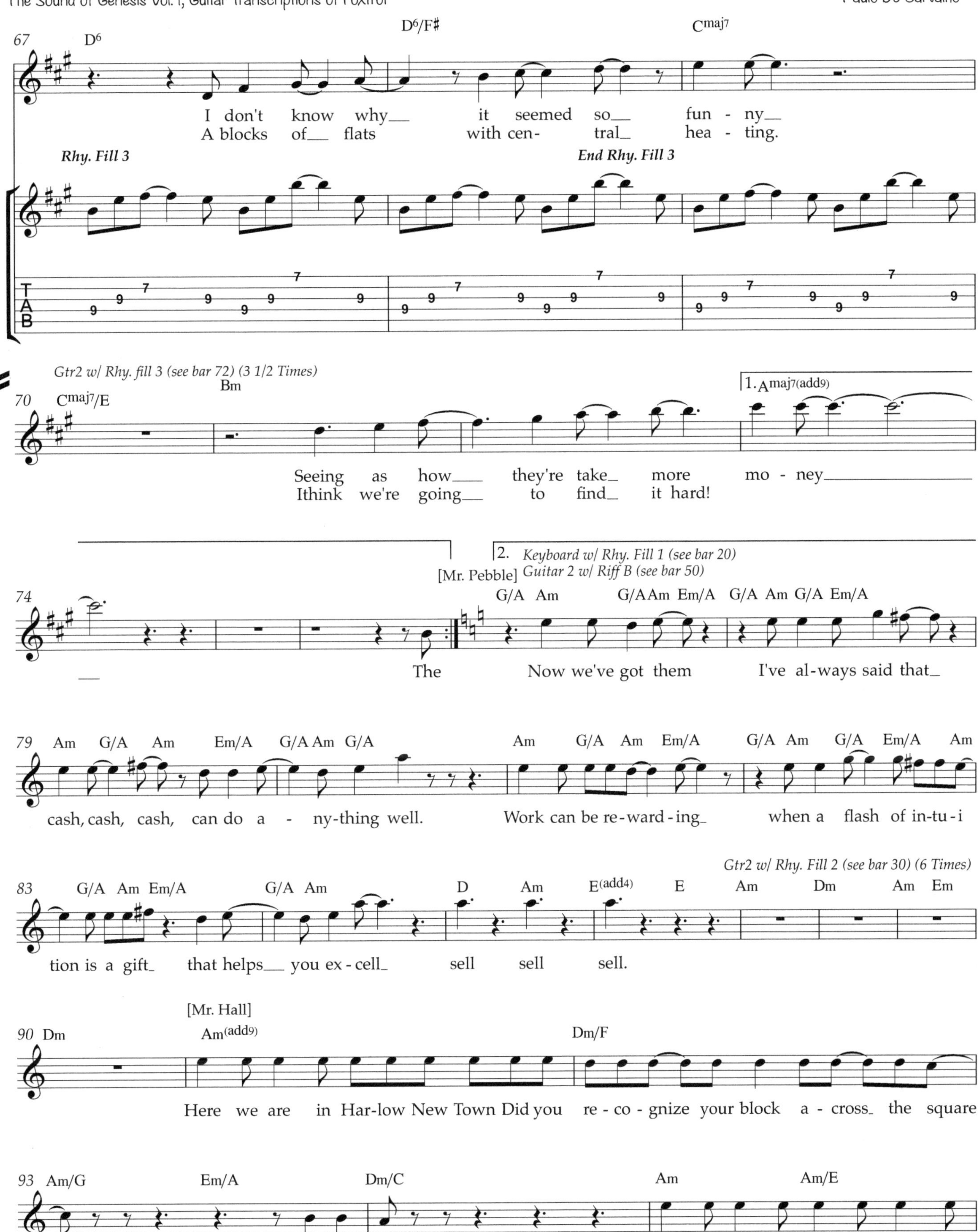
D6
D6/F#
Cmaj7
I don't know why it seemed so fun - ny
A blocks of flats with cen- tral hea - ting.
Rhy. Fill 3
End Rhy. Fill 3
Gtr2 w/ Rhy. fill 3 (see bar 72) (3 1/2 Times)
Cmaj7/E
Bm
1. Amaj7(add9)
Seeing as how they're take more mo - ney
Ithink we're going to find it hard!
2. Keyboard w/ Rhy. Fill 1 (see bar 20)
[Mr. Pebble] Guitar 2 w/ Riff B (see bar 50)
G/A Am G/A Am Em/A G/A Am G/A Em/A
The Now we've got them I've al-ways said that
Am G/A Am Em/A G/A Am G/A Am G/A Am Em/A G/A Am G/A Em/A Am
cash, cash, cash, can do a - ny-thing well. Work can be re-ward-ing when a flash of in-tu-i
Gtr2 w/ Rhy. Fill 2 (see bar 30) (6 Times)
G/A Am Em/A G/A Am D Am E(add4) E Am Dm Am Em
tion is a gift that helps you ex-cell sell sell sell.
[Mr. Hall]
Dm Am(add9) Dm/F
Here we are in Har-low New Town Did you re - co - gnize your block a - cross the square
Am/G Em/A Dm/C Am Am/E
o - ver there. Sad - ly since last time we spoke we've

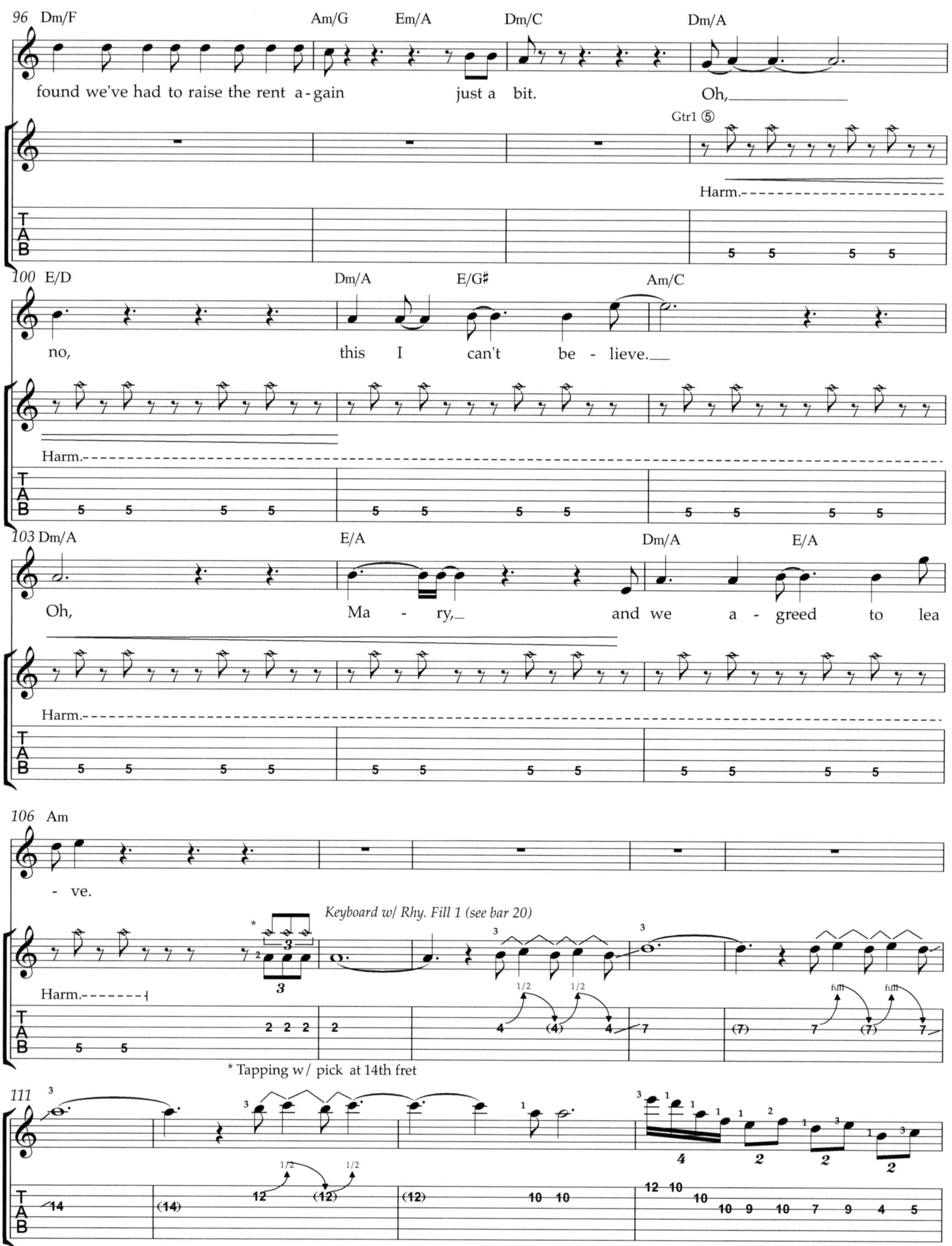
96 Dm/F
Am/G
Em/A
Dm/C
Dm/A
found we've had to raise the rent a-gain just a bit. Oh,
Gtr1 ⑤
Harm.
100 E/D
Dm/A
E/G♯
Am/C
no, this I can't be - lieve.
Harm.
103 Dm/A
E/A
Dm/A
E/A
Oh, Ma - ry, and we a - greed to lea
Harm.
106 Am
- ve.
Keyboard w/ Rhy. Fill 1 (see bar 20)
Harm.
* Tapping w/ pick at 14th fret
111

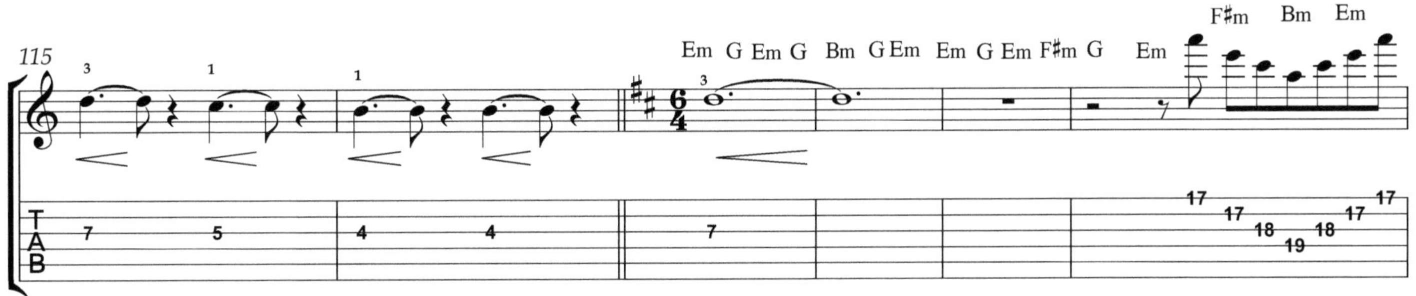
115
Em G Em G Bm G Em Em G Em F♯m G Em
F♯m Bm Em

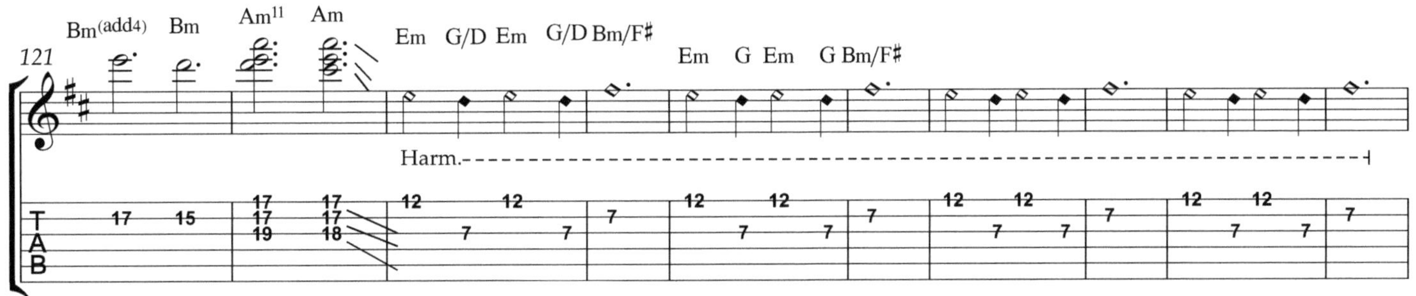
121
Bm(add4) Bm Am11 Am
Em G/D Em G/D Bm/F♯
Em G Em G Bm/F♯
Harm.

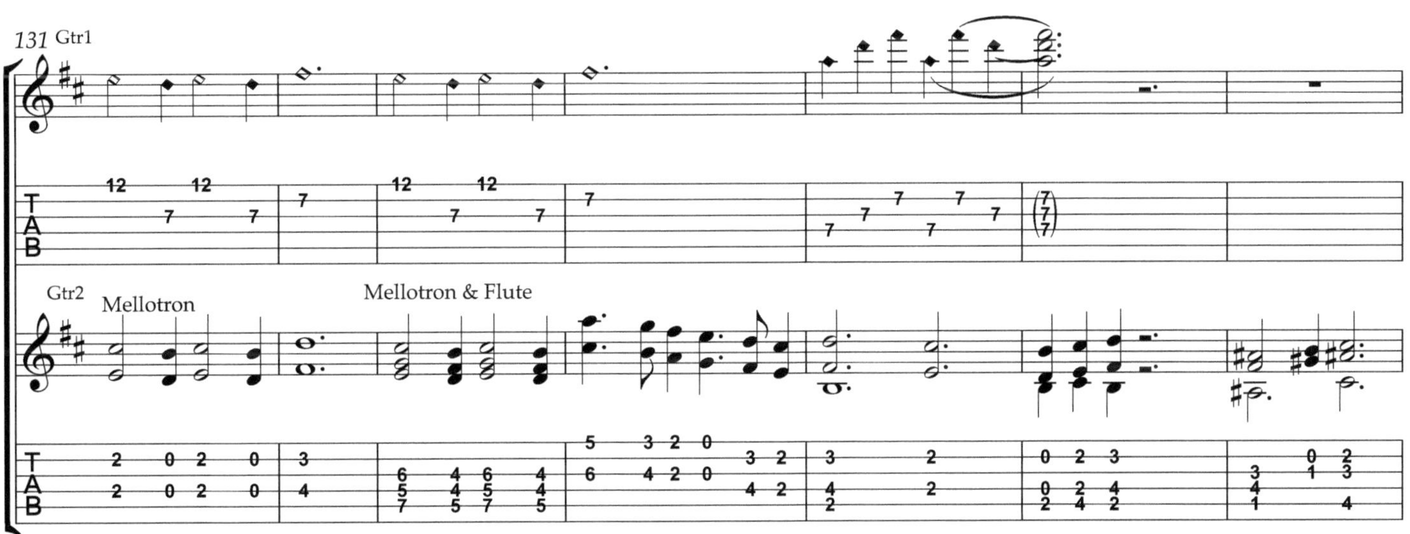
131 Gtr1
Gtr2
Mellotron
Mellotron & Flute

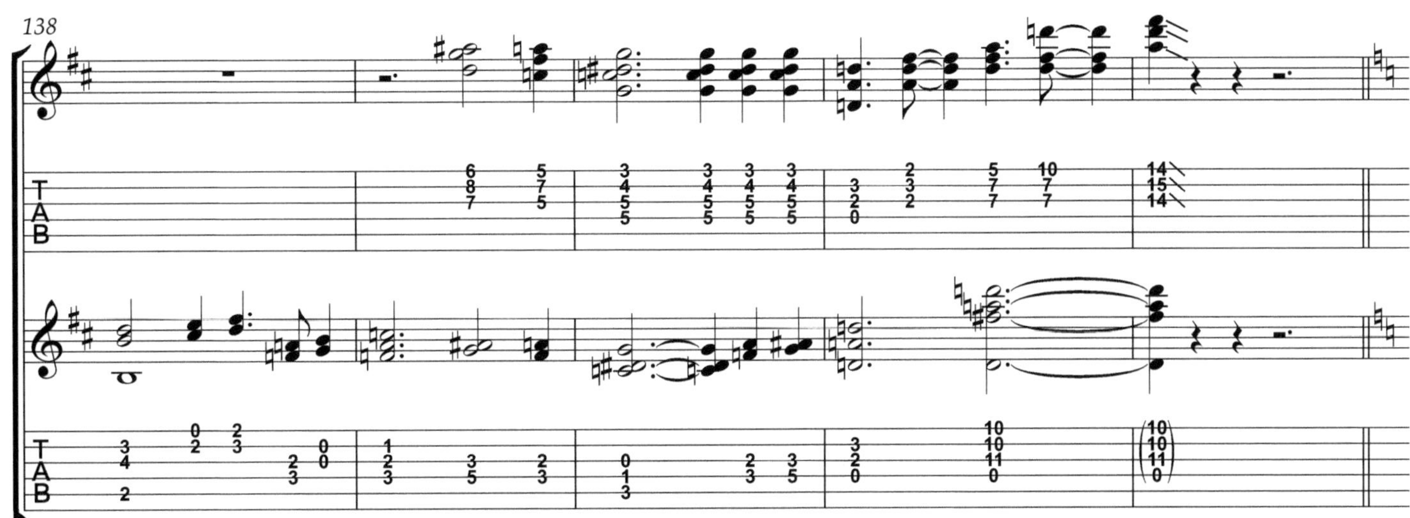
138

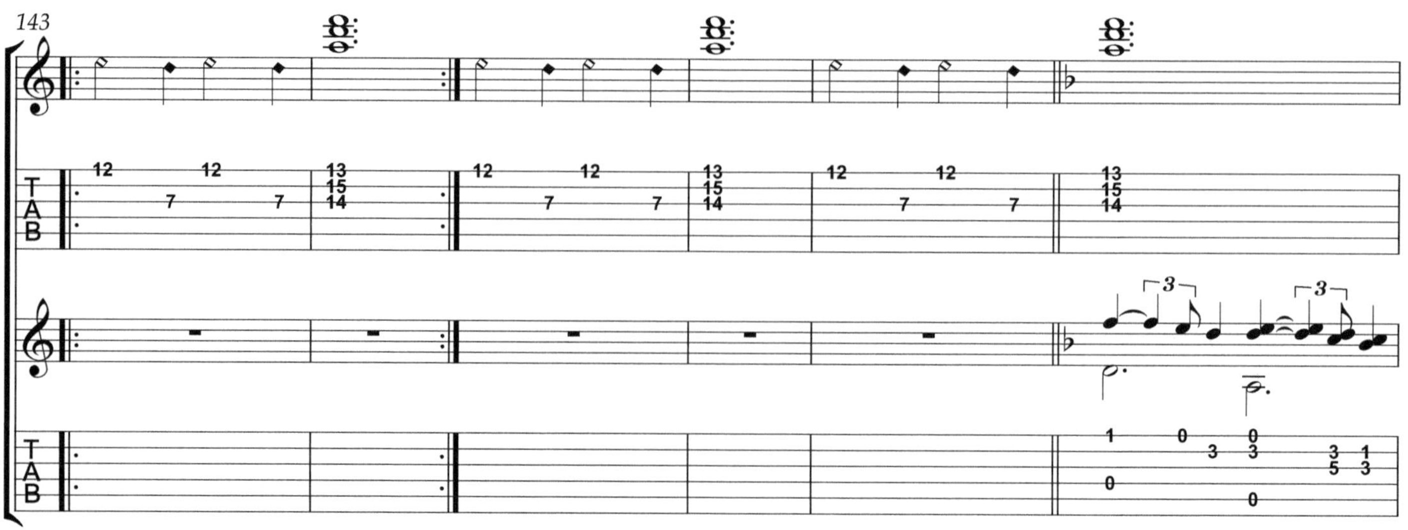

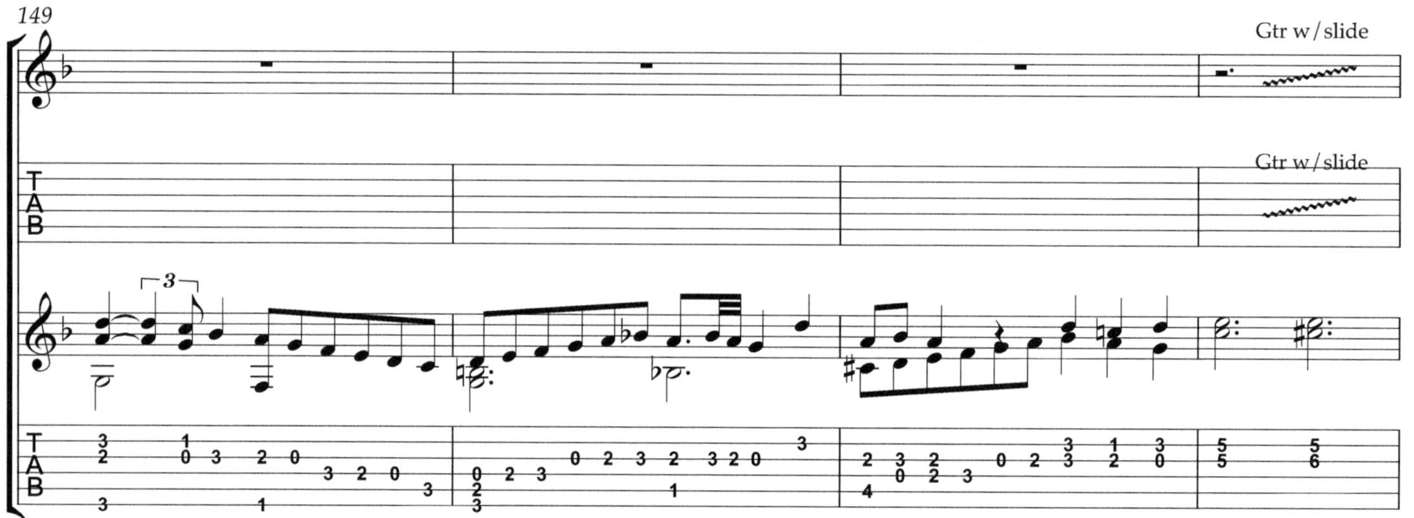

[18/9/2012 T.V. Flash on all Dial-A-Program services]

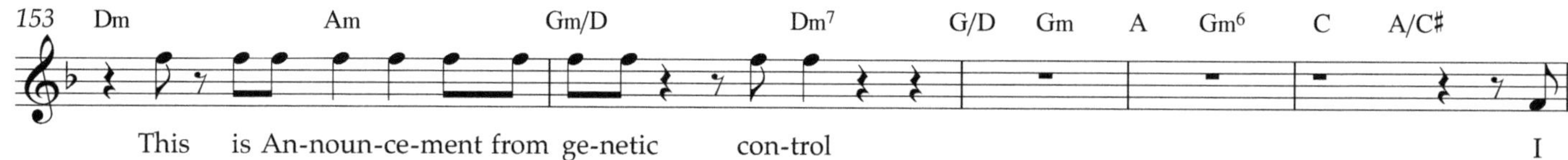

Spoken: It is my sad duty to inform you of a four restriction on humanoid height

[Extract from conversation of Joe Ordinary in local Puborama]

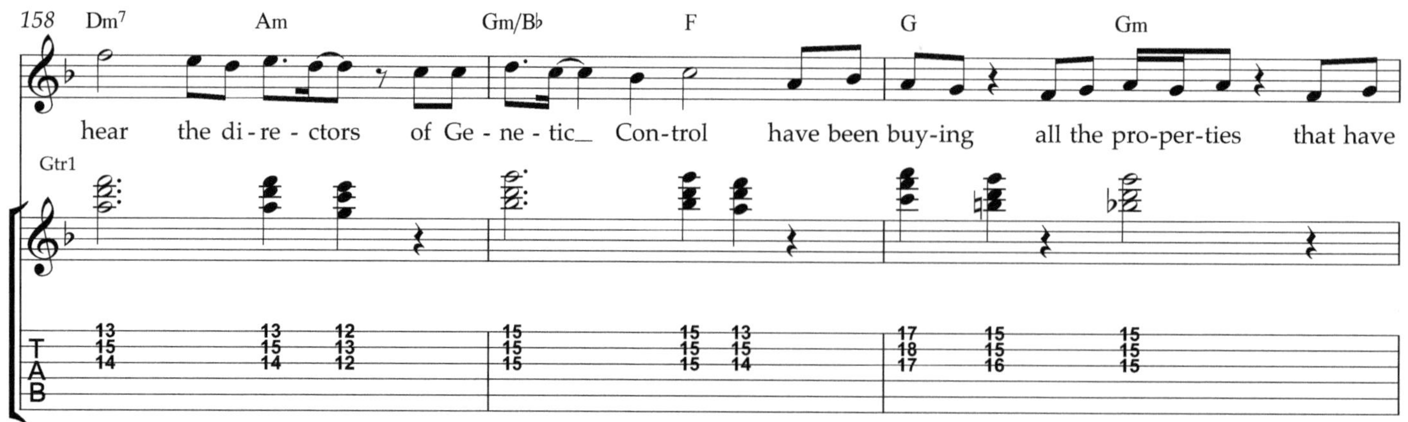

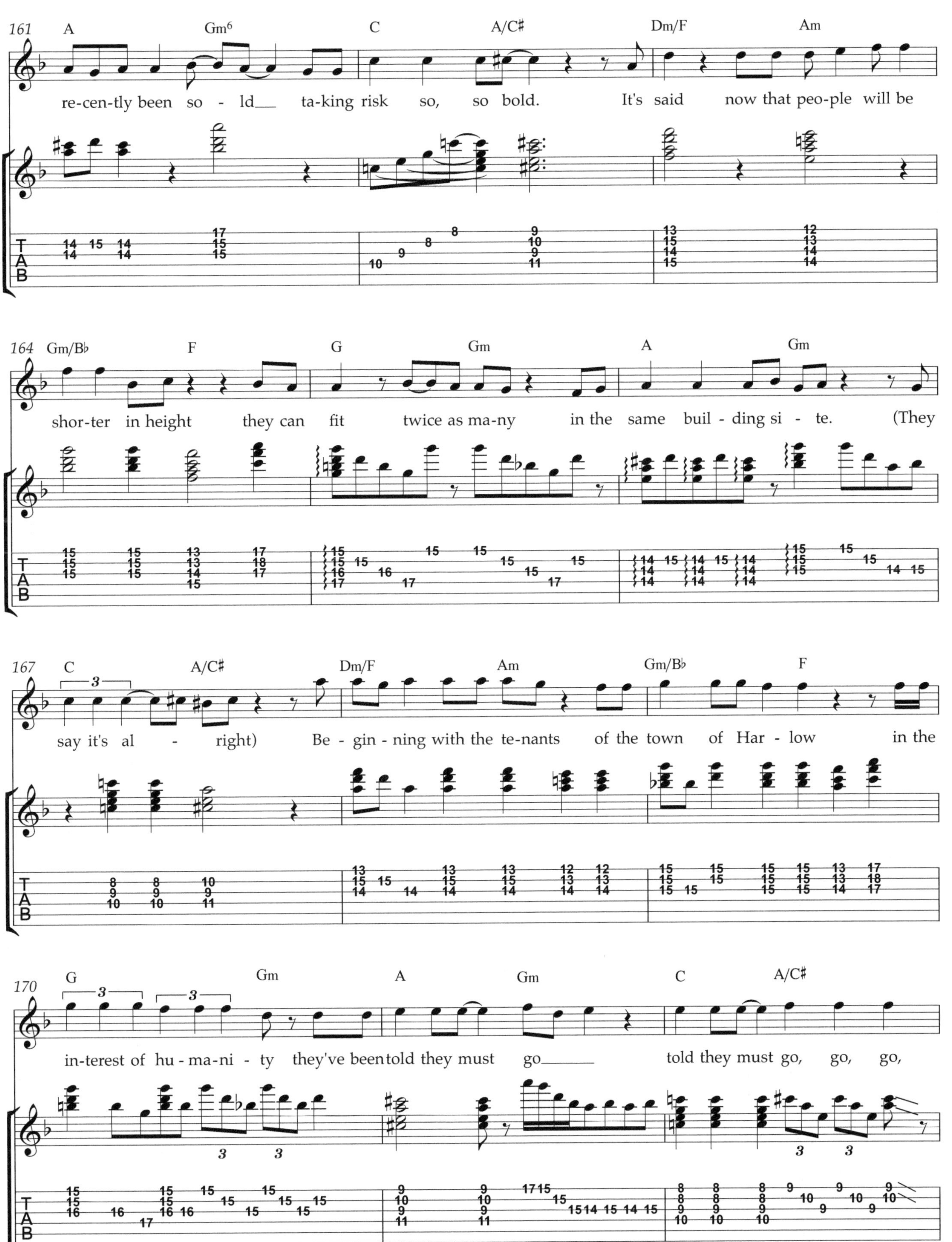
161
A Gm6 C A/C# Dm/F Am
re-cen-tly been so - ld___ ta-king risk so, so bold. It's said now that peo-ple will be
164
Gm/B♭ F G Gm A Gm
shor-ter in height they can fit twice as ma-ny in the same buil - ding si - te. (They
167
C A/C# Dm/F Am Gm/B♭ F
say it's al - right) Be - gin - ning with the te-nants of the town of Har - low in the
170
G Gm A Gm C A/C#
in-terest of hu - ma-ni - ty they've been told they must go___ told they must go, go, go,

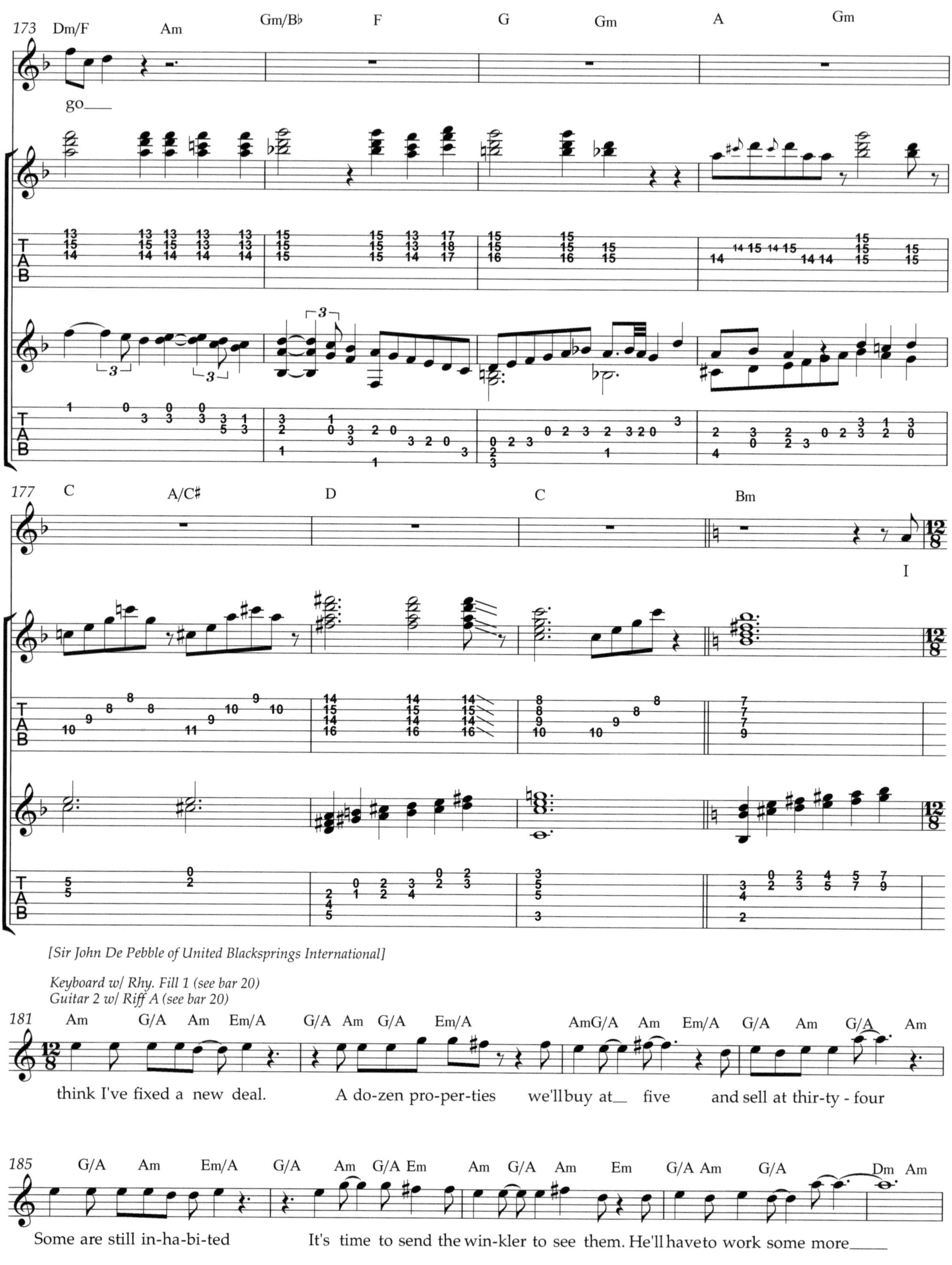

173 Dm/F Am Gm/B♭ F G Gm A Gm

go___

177 C A/C♯ D C Bm

I

[Sir John De Pebble of United Blacksprings International]

Keyboard w/ Rhy. Fill 1 (see bar 20)
Guitar 2 w/ Riff A (see bar 20)

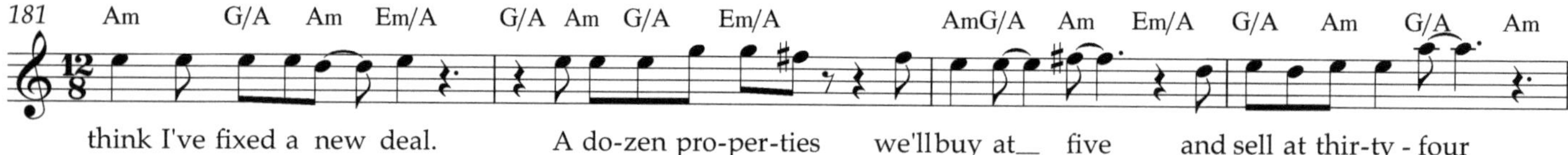

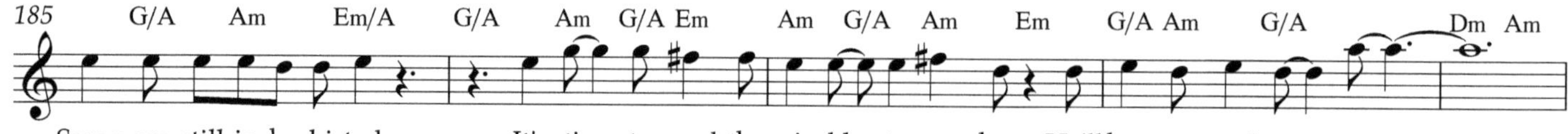

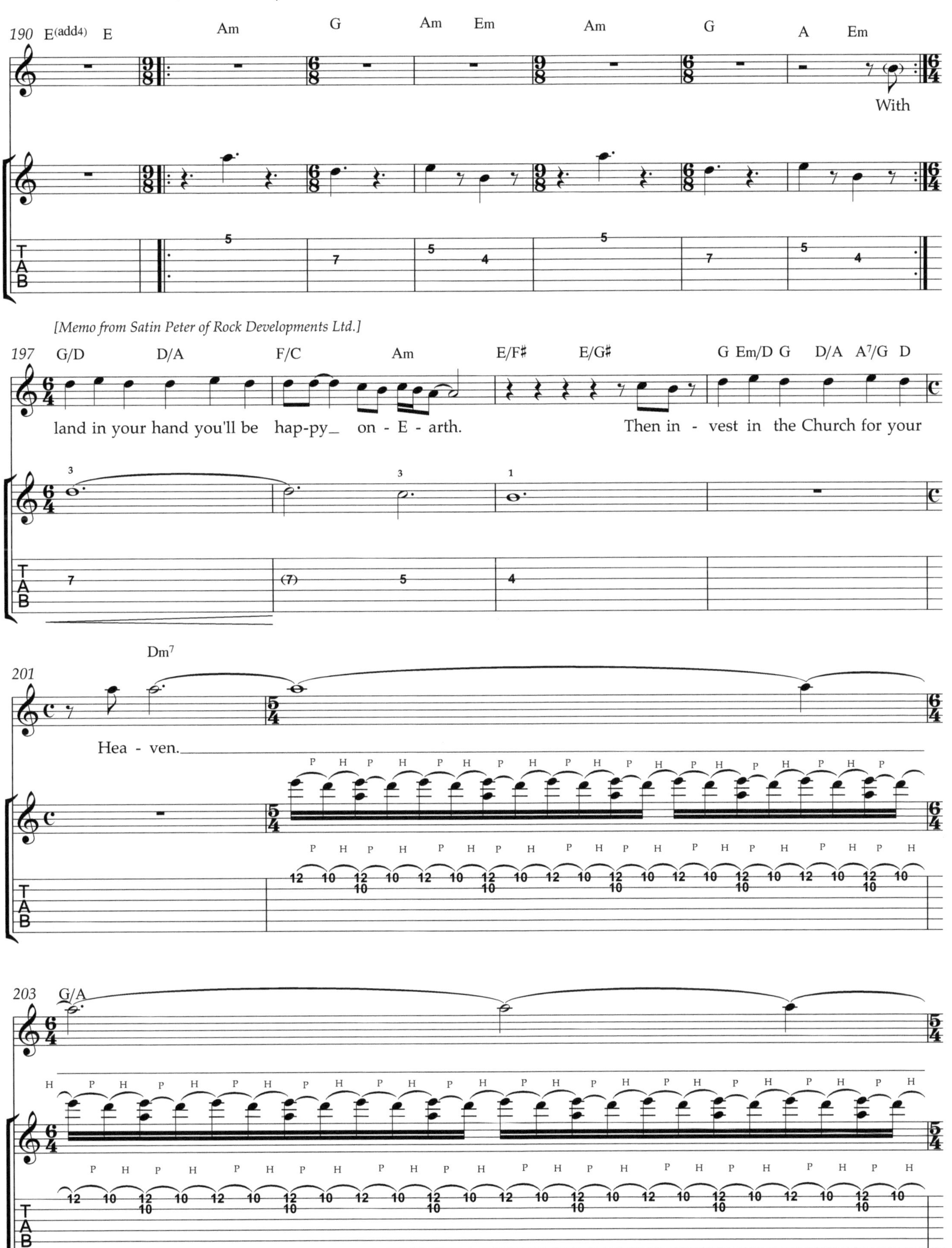
190
E(add4) E
Am
G
Am Em
Am
G
A Em
With
[Memo from Satin Peter of Rock Developments Ltd.]
197
G/D D/A F/C Am E/F♯ E/G♯ G Em/D G D/A A7/G D
land in your hand you'll be hap-py on - E - arth. Then in - vest in the Church for your
201
Dm7
Hea - ven.
203
G/A

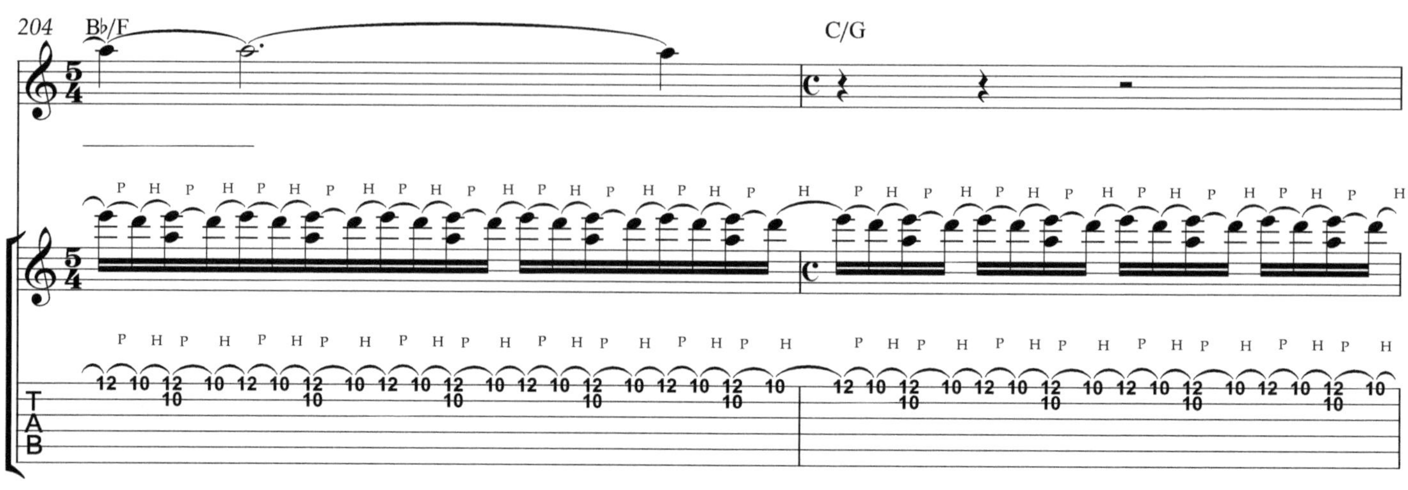
204
B♭/F
C/G

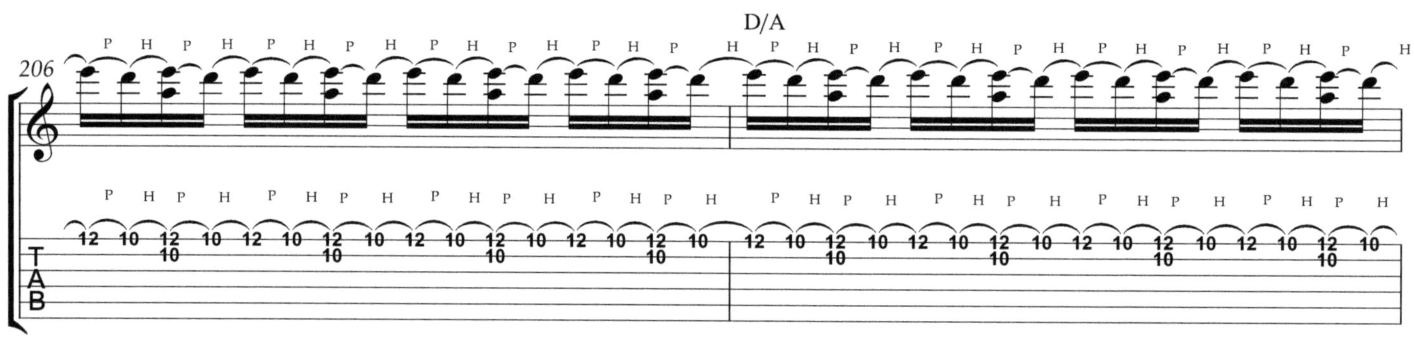
206
D/A

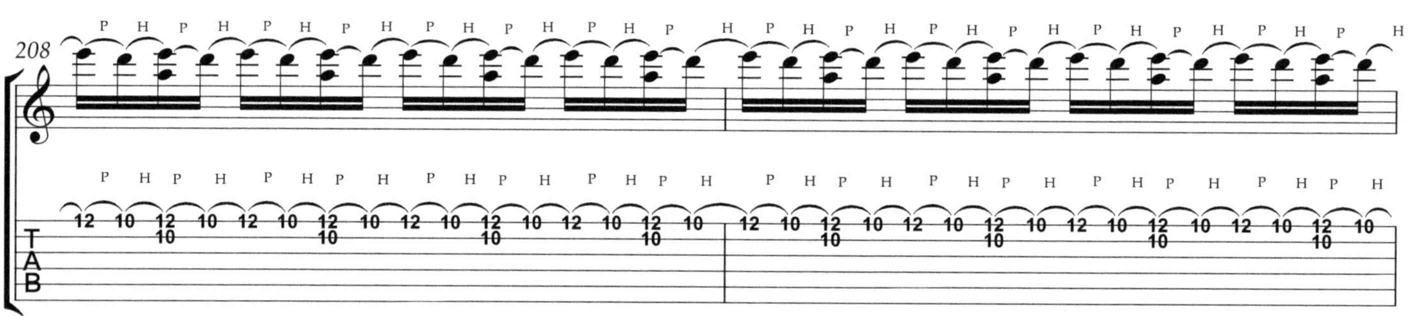
208

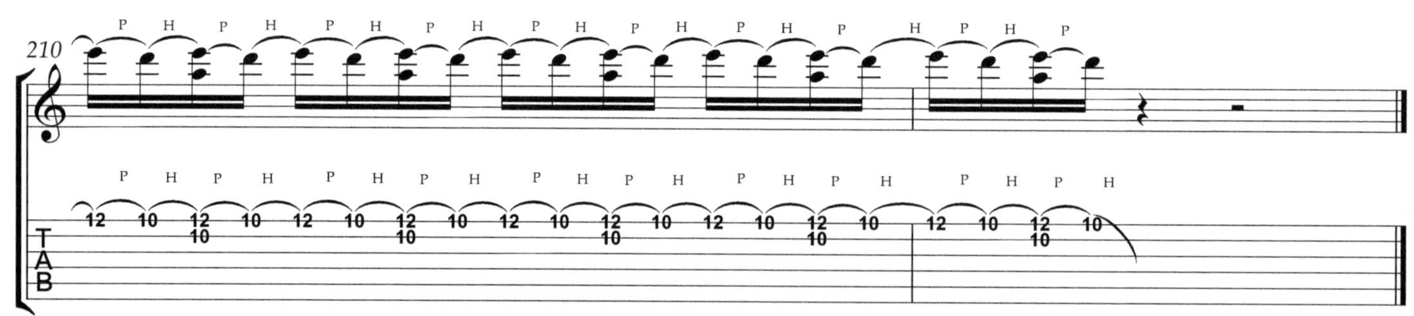
210

GET 'EM OUT BY FRIDAY

BY GENESIS

Intro:
| A | | E | F#m | | C#m/G# | D/F# | Em/G |
| Bm | Dm(maj7)/A | E7/A | Am G/A Am Em/A | G/A Am G/A | Am G/A Am Em/A | G/A Am G/A |
| Dm Am/C | E(add4)/B E/B | Dm/A Am/C | E/B |

[*John Pebble of Styx Enterprises*]
Am G/A Am Em/A
GET 'EM OUT BY FRIDAY!

G/A Am Em/A Am G/A Am Em/A G/A Am G/A
YOU DON'T GET PAID TILL THE LAST ONE'S WELL ON HIS WAY

Am G/A Am Em/A
GET 'EM OUT BY FRI -DAY!

G/A Am G/A Em/A Am G/A Am Em7/A G/A Am G/A
IT'S IM - PORTANT THAT WE KEEP TO SCHEDULE, THERE MUST BE NO DELAY

I D/A Am I E(add4)/A E/A I Am9 I Dm7/A I Am9 I Dm7/A I

[*Mark Hall of Styx Enterprises (otherwise known as "The Winkler")*]
Am9 Dm7/A Am9/G
I REPRESENT A FIRM OF GENTLEMEN WHO RECENTLY PURCHASED THIS HOUSE

Am9 Dm7/A
AND ALL THE OTHERS IN THE ROAD

Am9 Am/E
IN THE INTEREST OF HUMANITY

Dm7/F Am9/G Am9 Dm7/A
WE'VE FOUND A BETTER PLACE FOR YOU TO GO- GO - GO

[*Mrs. Barrow (a tenant)*]
Dm E7 Dm E7 Am
OH NO, THIS I CAN'T BELIEVE

Dm/A E/A Dm7/A E7/A Am
OH MARY, THEY'RE ASKING US TO LEA - VE

[*Mr. Pebble*]
Am G/A Am Em/A
GET 'EM OUT BY FRIDAY!

G/A Am G/A Em/A Am G/A Am Em/A G/A Am G/A
I'VE TOLD YOU BEFORE, 'S GOOD MANY GONE IF WE LET THEM STAY

Am G/A Am Em/A G/A Am G/A Em/A Am
AND IF IT ISN'T E - ASY YOU CAN SQUEEZE A LITTLE GREASE

G/A Am Em/A G/A Am G/A
AND ALL OUR TROUBLES WILL SOON RUN A-WAY

```
| Dm    Am    | E(add4)/B    E   | Amaj7(add9)  |  2   |  3   |  4   |


[Mrs. Barrow]
 Amaj7(add9)                                  E       /G#   /B
AFTER ALL THIS TIME, THEY ASK US TO LEAVE

        Amaj7(add9)                                   E        /G#  /B
AND I TOLD THEM WE COULD PAY DOUBLE THE RENT

D6                        D6/F#               CMaj7    Cmaj7/E
   I DON'T KNOW WHY      IT SEEMED SO FUNNY

Bm                                            Amaj7(add9)
    SEEING AS HOW THEY'D TAKE MORE MONEY

     Amaj(add9)                                         E          /G#  /B
THE WINKLER CALLED AGAIN. HE CAME HERE THIS MORNING

            Amaj(add9)                                                        E        /G#   /B
WITH FOUR HUNDRED POUNDS, AND A PHOTOGRAPH OF THE PLACE HE HAS FOUND

D6                        D6/F#                   Cmaj7        Cmaj7/E
   A BLOCK OF FLATS       WITH CENTRAL HEATING

Bm
     I THINK WE'RE GOING TO FIND IT HARD


[Mr. Pebble]
G/A  Am            G/A   Am     Em/A
     NOW WE'VE GOT THEM!

G/A  Am  G/A  Em/A              Am         G/A       Am       Em/A.  G/A   Am    G/A
     I'VE ALWAYS SAID THAT CASH CASH    CASH     CAN DO   A -     NY - THING WELL

Am          G/A     Am       Em/A
WORK CAN BE REWARD-ING

G/A  Am        G/A    Em/A              Am       G/A   Am   Em/A             G/AD      Am         D     Am    E(add4)  E
     WHEN A FLASH     OF INTU- I- TION IS  A GIFT      THAT HELPS      YOU   EXCEL SELL SELL SELL


| Am     | Dm      | Am    Em   | Dm     |


[Mr. Hall]
Am(add9)
HERE WE ARE IN HARLOW NEW TOWN

          Dm/F                                                    Am/G   Em/A          Dm/C
DID YOU RECOGNIZE YOUR BLOCK ACROSS THE SQUARE,                  OVER THERE?

Am                 Am/E                 Dm/F                                       Am/G   Em/A            Dm/C
SADLY SINCE LAST TIME WE SPOKE, WE'VE FOUND WE'VE HAD TO RAISE THE RENT AGAIN            JUST A BIT


[Mrs. Barrow]
Dm/A  E/D  Dm/A    E/G#               Am/C     Dm/A   E/A               Dm/A   E/A             Am
OH    NO, THIS  I CAN'T BELIEVE               OH     MARY, AND WE A-GREED TO LEA  - VE
```

Solo Guitar

[*A passage of time*]
[*18 September 2012 T.V. Flash on all Dial-A-Program Services*]

Dm Am Gm/D Dm7
THIS IS AN ANNOUNCEMENT FROM GENETIC CONTROL

G/D Gm A
[Spoken] "IT IS MY SAD DUTY TO INFORM YOU

A Gm6 C A/C#
OF A FOUR-FOOT RESTRICTION ON HUMANOID HEIGHT."

[*Extract from conversation of Joe Ordinary in Local Puborama*]
Dm7 Am Gm/Bb F G
"I HEAR THE DIRECTORS OF GE-NE - TIC CONTROL HAVE BEEN BUYING ALL THE

Gm A Gm6 C A/C#
PROPERTIES THAT HAVE RECENTLY BEEN SO - LD, TAKING RISK OH SO, SO BOLD

Dm/F Am Gm/Bb F
IT'S SAID NOW THAT PEOPLE WILL BE SHORTER IN HEIGHT

G Gm A Gm
THEY CAN FIT TWICE AS MANY IN THE SAME BUILDING SI - TE

C A/C#
(THEY SAY IT'S AL - RIGHT)

Dm/F Am Gm/Bb F
BEGINNING WITH THE TENANTS OF THE TOWN OF HARLOW

G Gm A Gm
IN THE INTEREST OF HUMANI - TY, THEY'VE BEEN TOLD THEY MUST GO

C A/C# Dm/F Am
TOLD THEY MUST GO-GO-GO-GO."

|Gm/B F | G Gm | A Gm | C A/C# | D | C | Bm |

[*Sir John De Pebble of United Blacksprings International*]
Am G/A Am Em/A
I THINK I'VE FIXED A NEW DEAL

G/A Am G/A Em /A Am G/A Am Em/A G/A Am G/A Am
A DOZEN PROPERTIES - WE'LL BUY AT FIVE AND SELL AT THIRTY FOUR

G/A Am Em/A
SOME ARE STILL IN -HABITED

G/A Am G/A Em Am G/A Am
IT'S TIME TO SEND THE WINKLER TO SEE THEM

Em G/A Am G/A Dm Am E Am G Am Em Am G A
HE'LL HAVE TO WORK SOME MORE.

[*Memo from Satin Peter of Rock Development Ltd.*]
Em G/D D/A F/C Am E/F# E/G#
WITH LAND IN YOUR HAND, YOU'LL BE HAPPY ON EARTH

G Em/D G D/A A7/G D Dm7
THEN INVEST IN THE CHURCH FOR YOUR HEAVEN

| G/A | Bb/F | C/G | | D/A | 2 | 3 | 4 | 5 ||

CAN-UTILITY AND THE COASTLINERS

"Steve had written pretty much the whole first half of the song, which was a nice piece of music. We liked it, and then we kind of had the improvised session. That was very much something written in the rehearsal." Tony Banks

Steve wrote the song and the lyrics. "Can-Utility" in the title comes from the name *Canute*. Steve explained that King Canute, also known as "Cnut, the great," was the king of the North Sea Empire (England, Denmark, and Norway) and died in 1035. People used to believe Cnut was so powerful that if he had told the waves to retreat, they would do so. But Steve commented that the king knew the difference between fantasy and reality, and he used to affirm that the king was not divine: he was human. The line "we *heed* not flatterers" in the song, written in Old English style, means "we do not listen to false, insincere people." Steve mentioned that C.S. Lewis probably [as in *Narnia* in *Please Don't Touch!*] had a little bit of influence on him with his character *Reepicheep* (from the book *The Chronicles of Narnia*): a little mouse, always talking in the most pompous way.

Steve used a twelve-string acoustic guitar and a Les Paul straight into a Fender amp. In the end, he used a Marshal Super fuzz. Years later, Steve used Coloursound, which mainly had the same sound in his opinion.

Hackett frequently used lead chords, which provided the lead lines in the melody, like syncopated orchestration. He explained that Mike liked to play chords not related to anything, but which worked well. Because they were just acoustic guitar players, they didn't get the big picture's value, but the pleasing thing was that it seemed to have worked.

Genesis played *Can-Utility and The Coastliners* in some concerts before recording it. One may have heard it in some bootlegs in Verone at *Lem Club's* show on April 9th, 1972, or in Pavia, Italy, on April 14th, 1972. Peter Gabriel used to announce it for fun as "Bye, Bye, Johnny."

Players/Instruments:
Peter Gabriel: Vocal, Flute, Oboe
Tony Banks: Hammond L122, Mellotron MK II
Steve Hackett: Black Gibson Les Paul Custom, Hagstrom BJ-12-string
Mike Rutherford: Hagstrom BJ-12-string, Rickenbacker 4001 Bass, Vox Bass Pedal
Phil Collins: Drums, Backing Vocals

Can-Utility and the Coastliners: Guitar Specifics

Intro

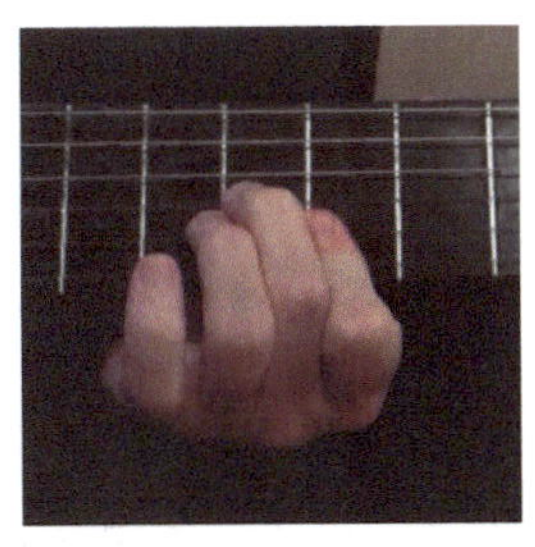
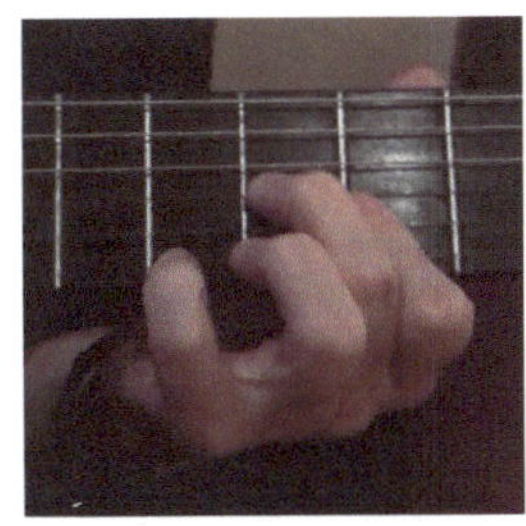
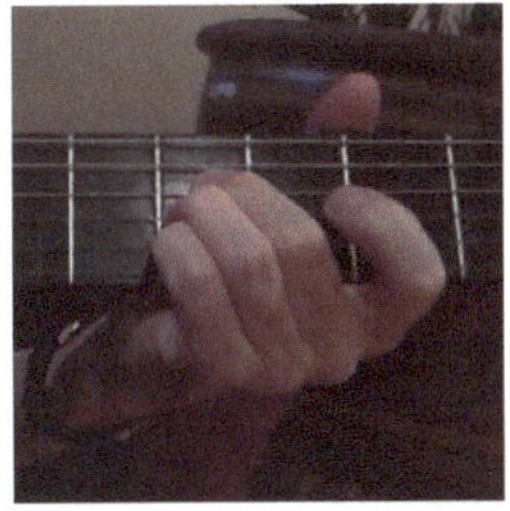

Photos 51-53: Steve showing the arpeggios that start on measure 1 [below] - Photos by Paulo De Carvalho

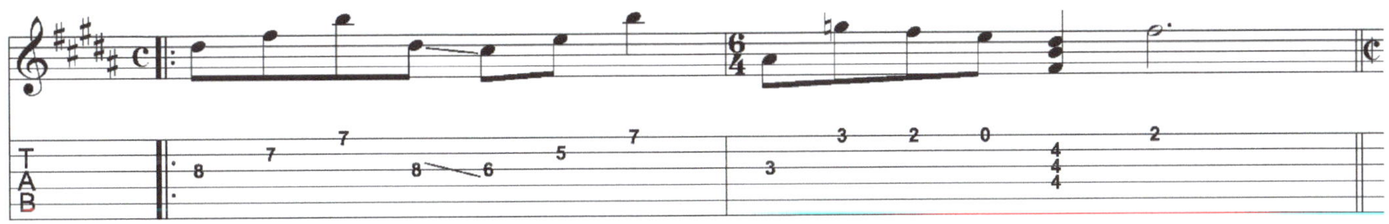

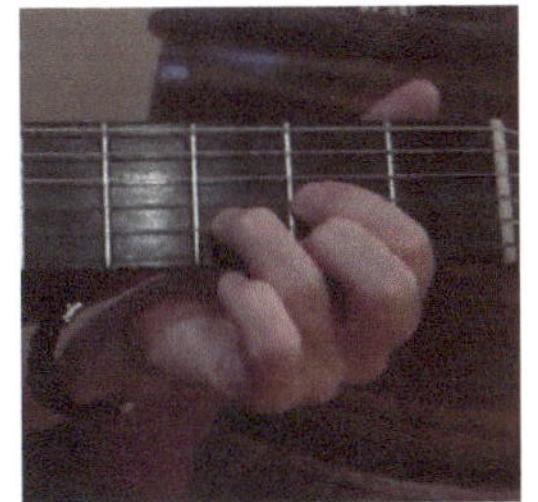
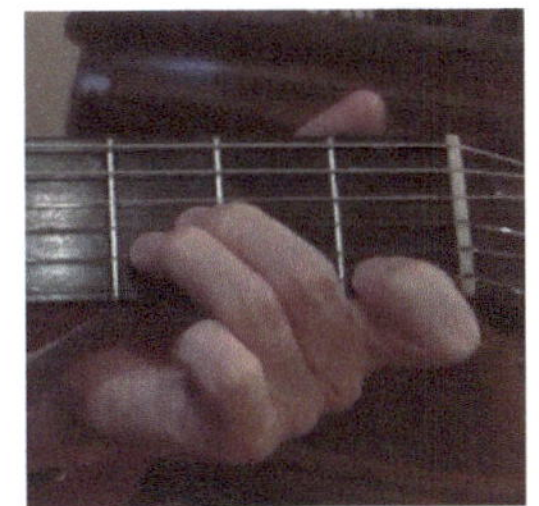
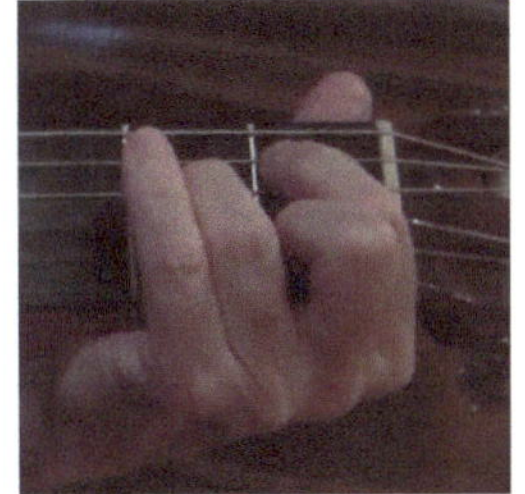
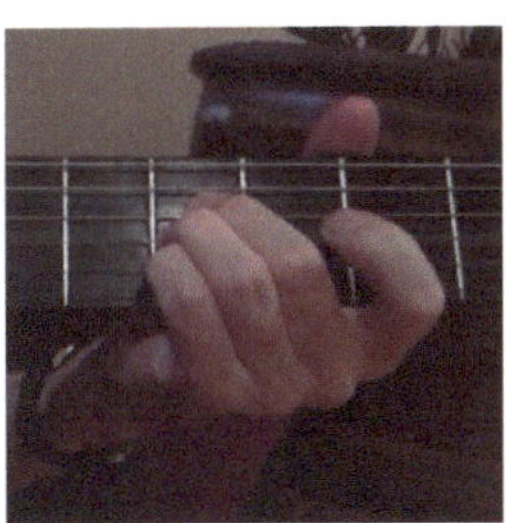

Photos 54-57: Steve continuing the arpeggios on measures 3-6 [below] - Photos by Paulo De Carvalho

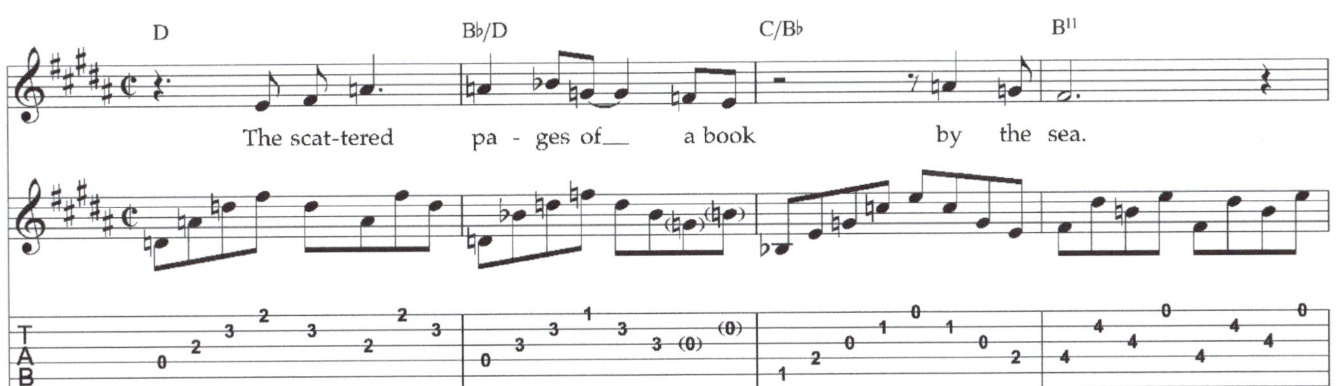

Middle Section

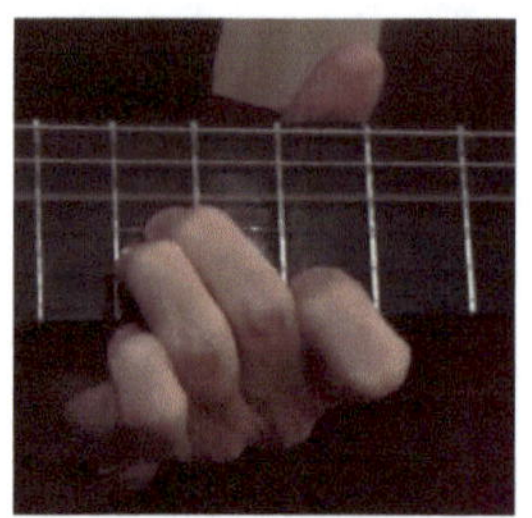

Photo 58: Steve playing measure 66 [right below]
Photo by Paulo De Carvalho

Steve playing measure 67 [right below] the way he recorded it
Photo not available

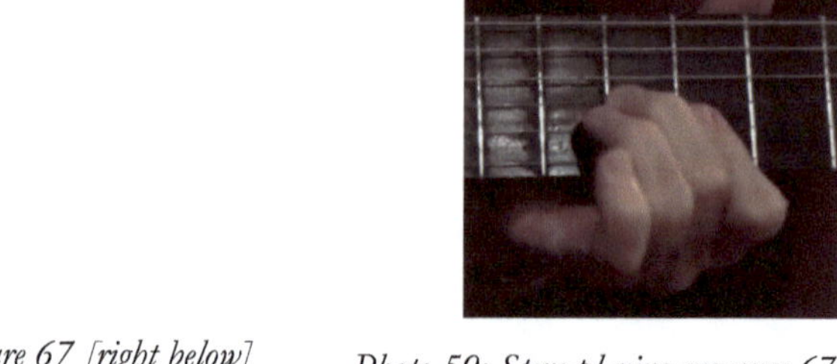

Photo 59: Steve playing measure 67[right below] the way he plays nowadays
Photo by Paulo De Carvalho

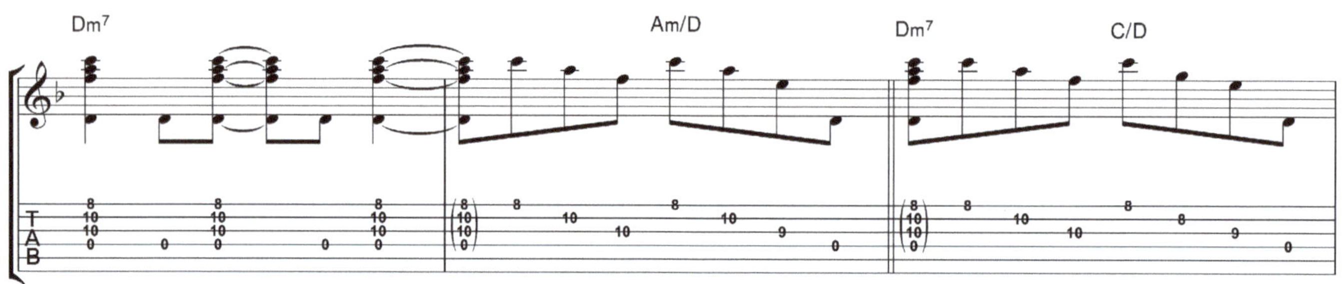

Final Section

Measures 214-217 top line shows the way Steve recorded.

Measures 214-217 bottom line shows the way Steve plays nowadays. Please notice the octave higher in the very last three notes.

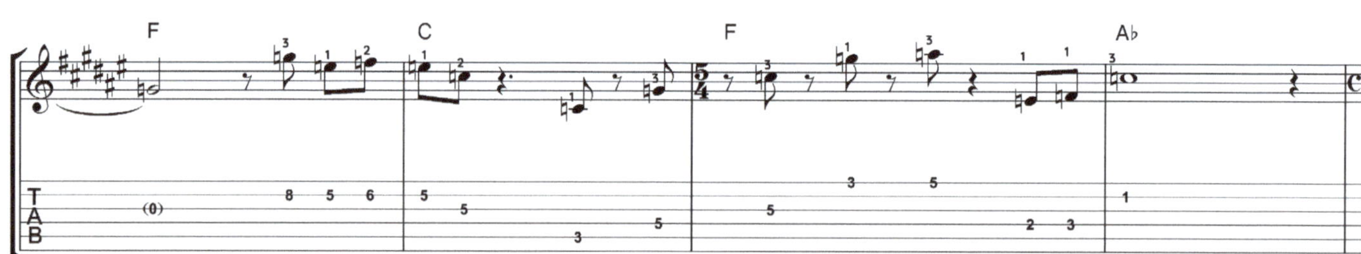

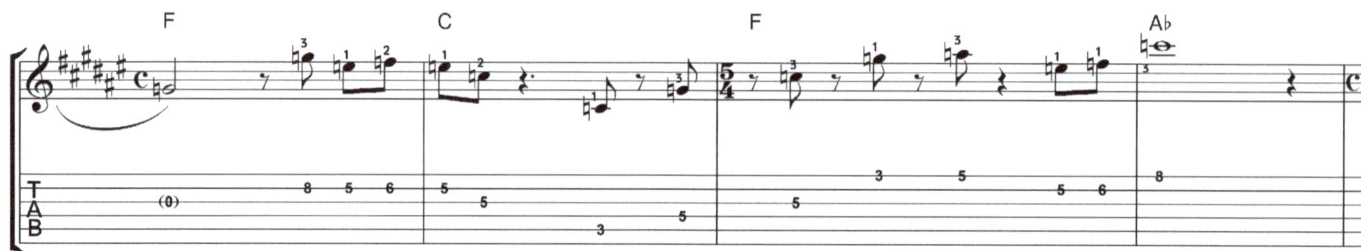

from Genesis - *Foxtrot*

Can-Utility and the Coastliners

by T. Banks, P.Collins, P. Gabriel, S. Hackett, M. Rutherford

Transcribed by Paulo De Carvalho

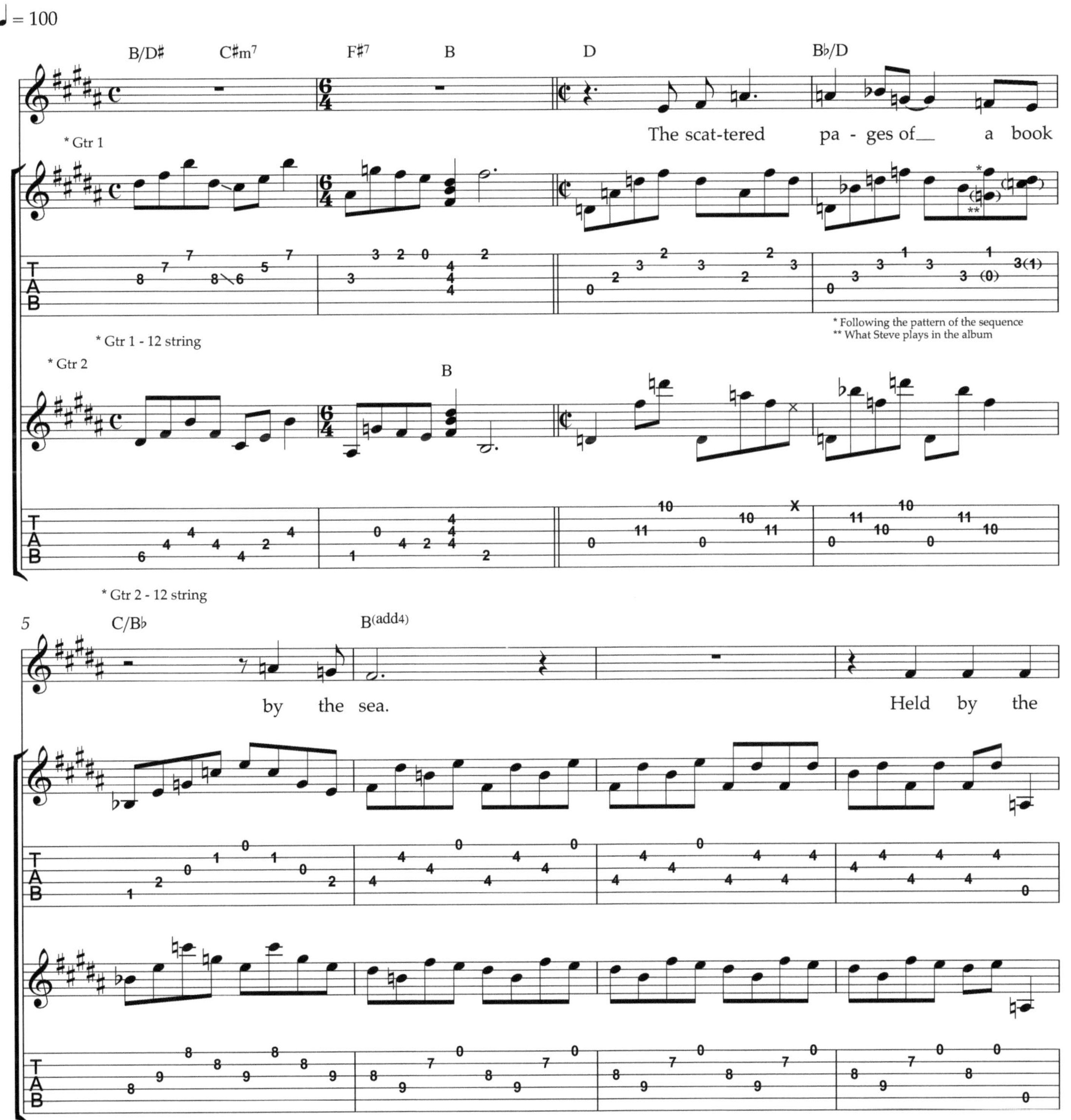

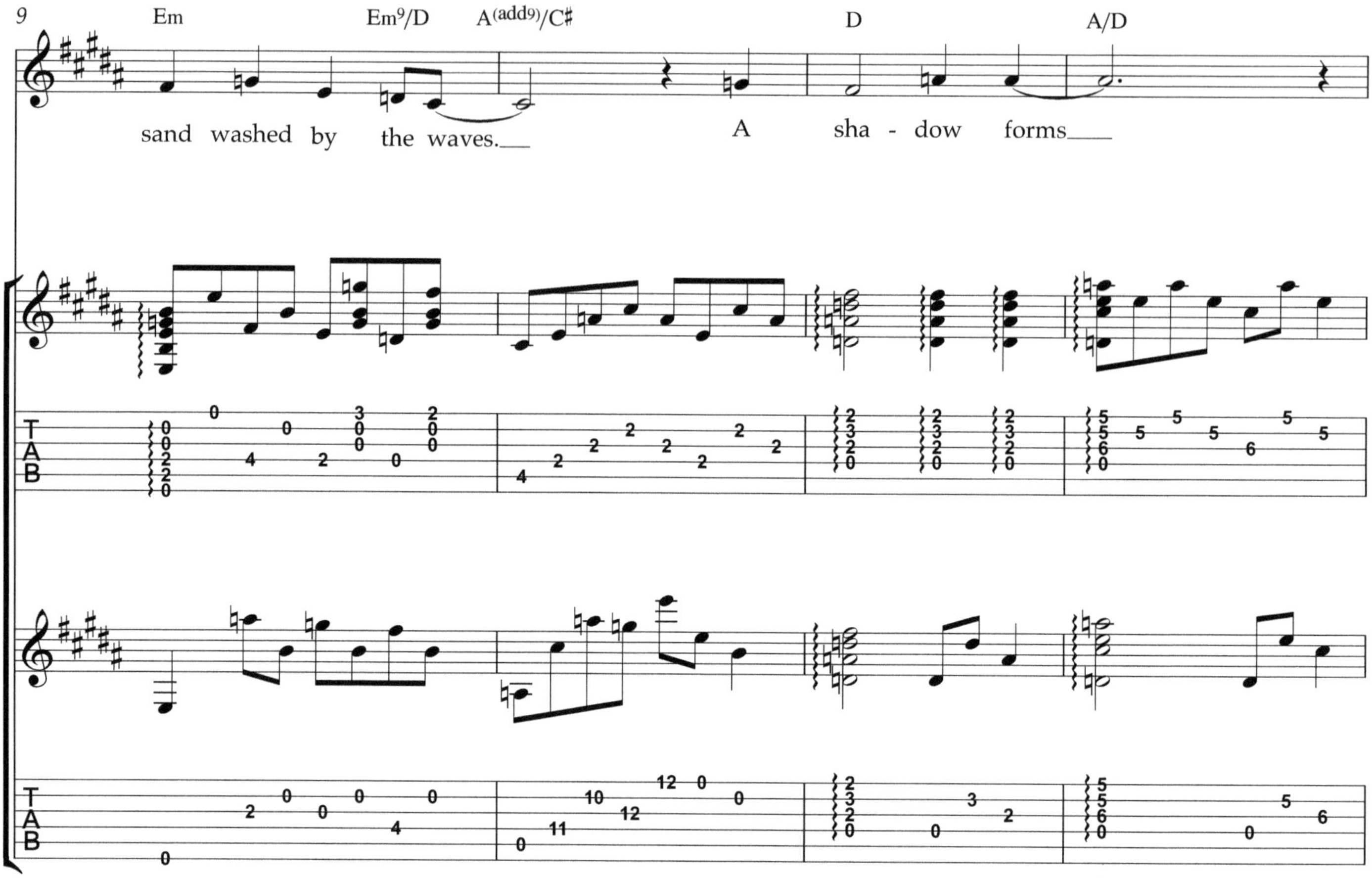

9 Em Em^9/D A$^{(add9)}$/C♯ D A/D

sand washed by the waves.___ A sha - dow forms___

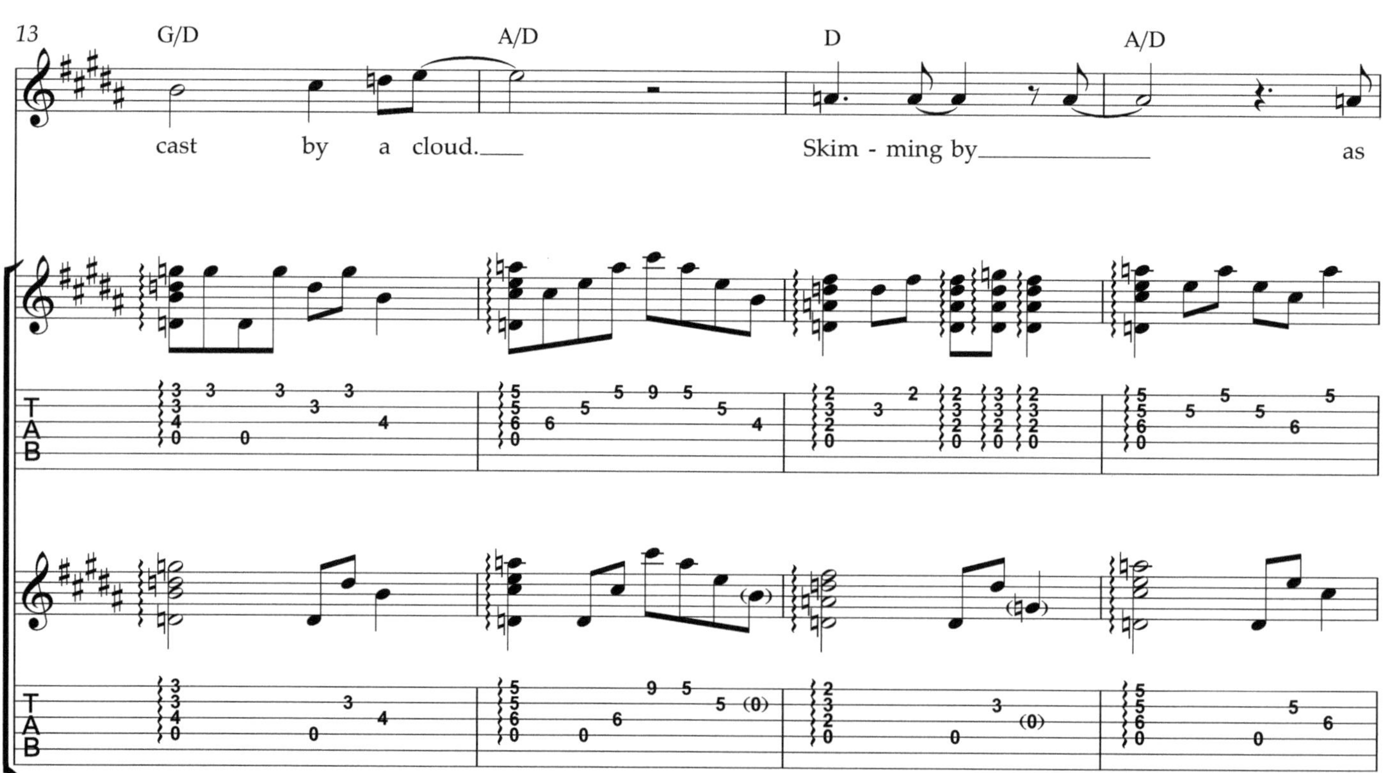

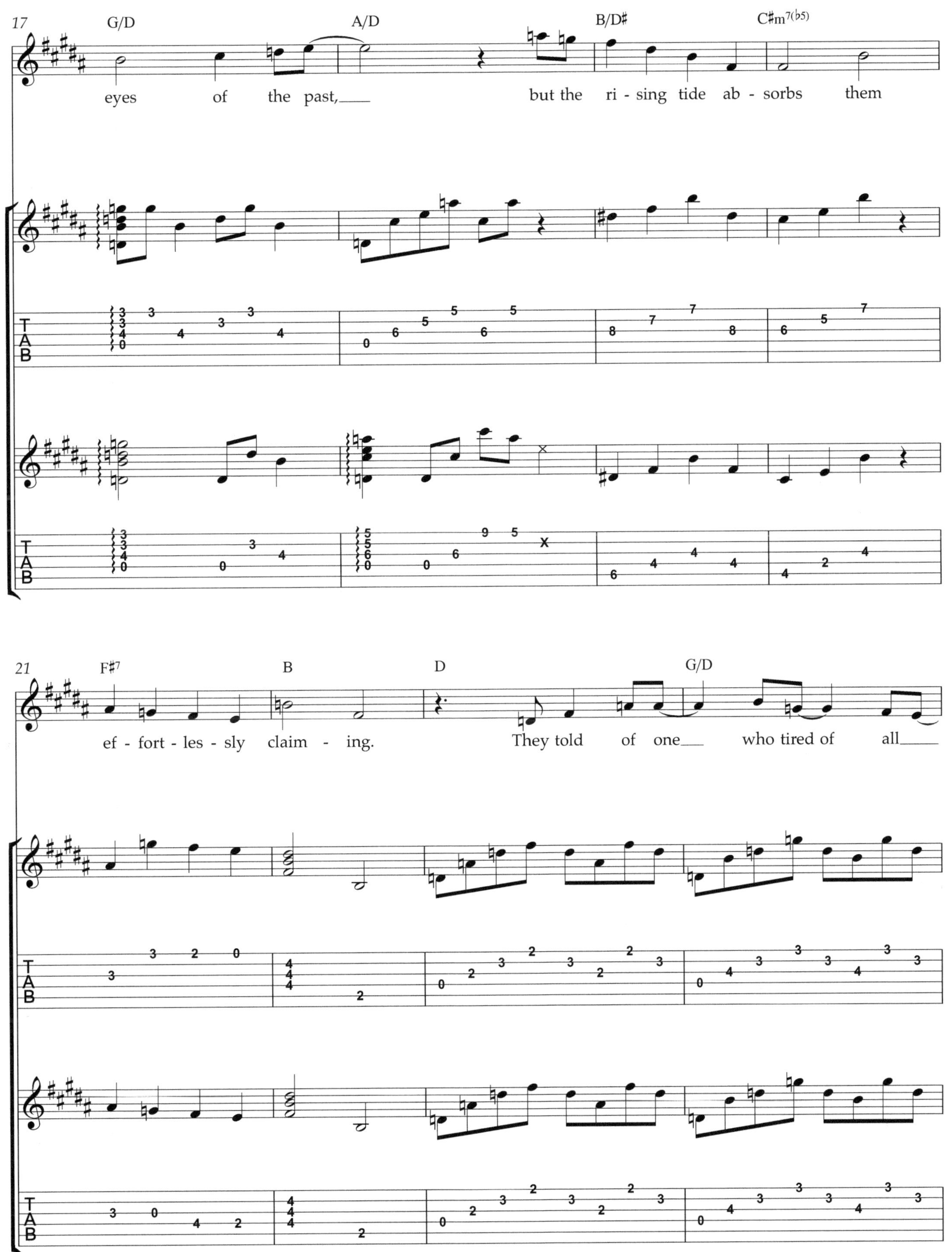
17
G/D
A/D
B/D♯
C♯m7(♭5)
eyes of the past, but the ri - sing tide ab - sorbs them
21
F♯7
B
D
G/D
ef - fort - les - sly claim - ing. They told of one who tired of all

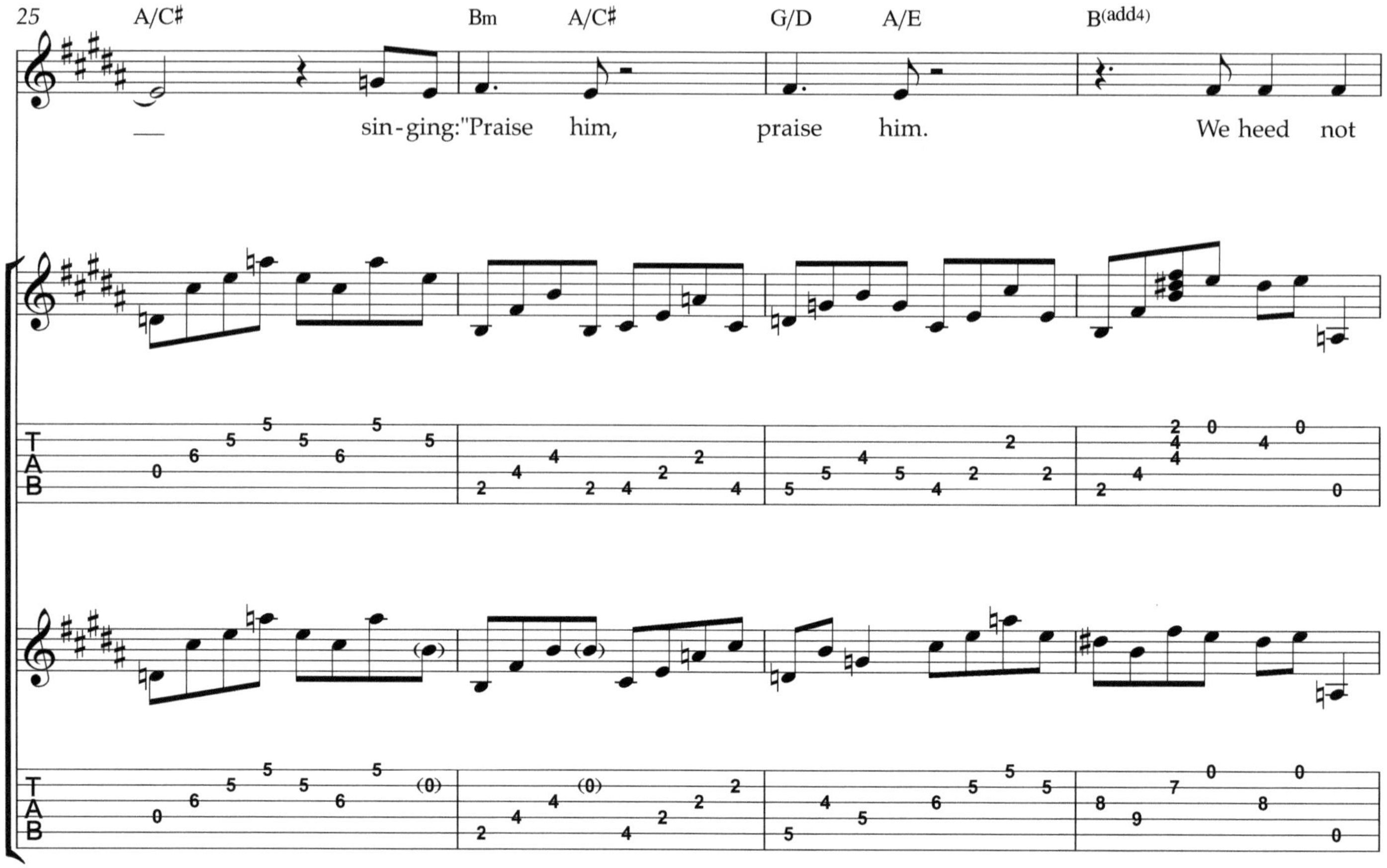

25 A/C♯ Bm A/C♯ G/D A/E B(add4)

— sin-ging:"Praise him, praise him. We heed not

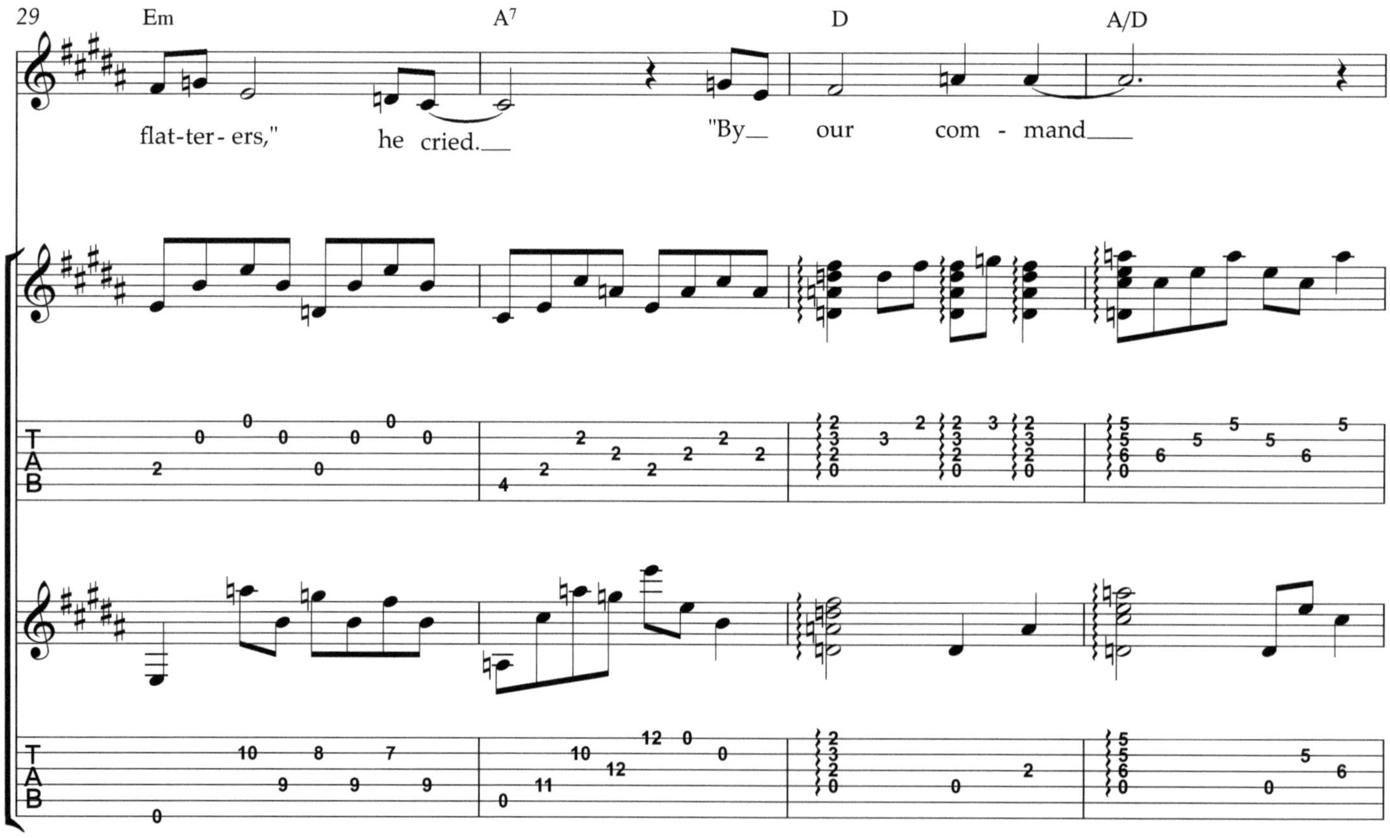

29 Em A^7 D A/D

flat-ter-ers," he cried.__ "By__ our com - mand___

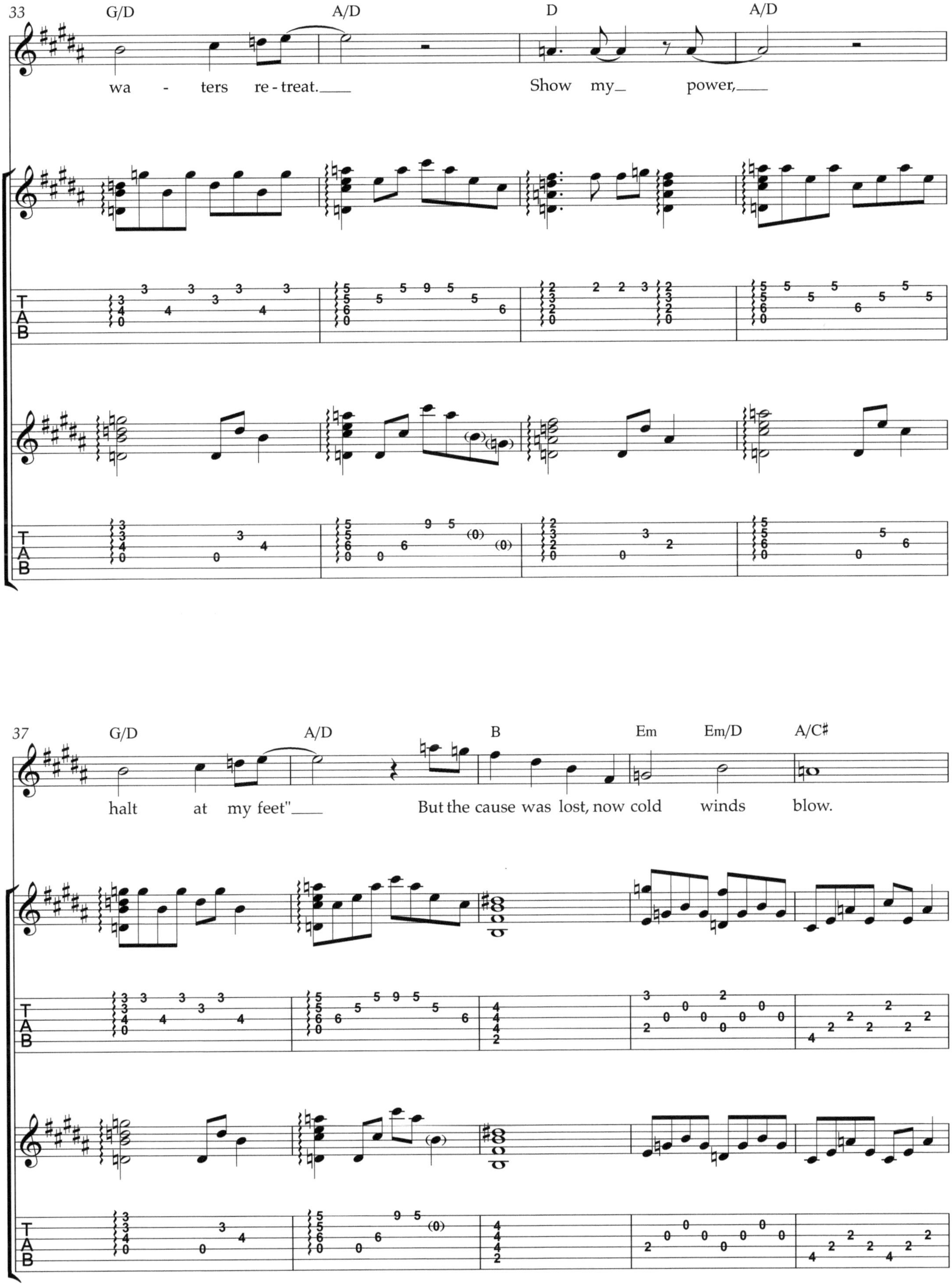

33

G/D A/D D A/D

wa - ters re - treat.____ Show my_ power,____

37

G/D A/D B Em Em/D A/C♯

halt at my feet"____ But the cause was lost, now cold winds blow.

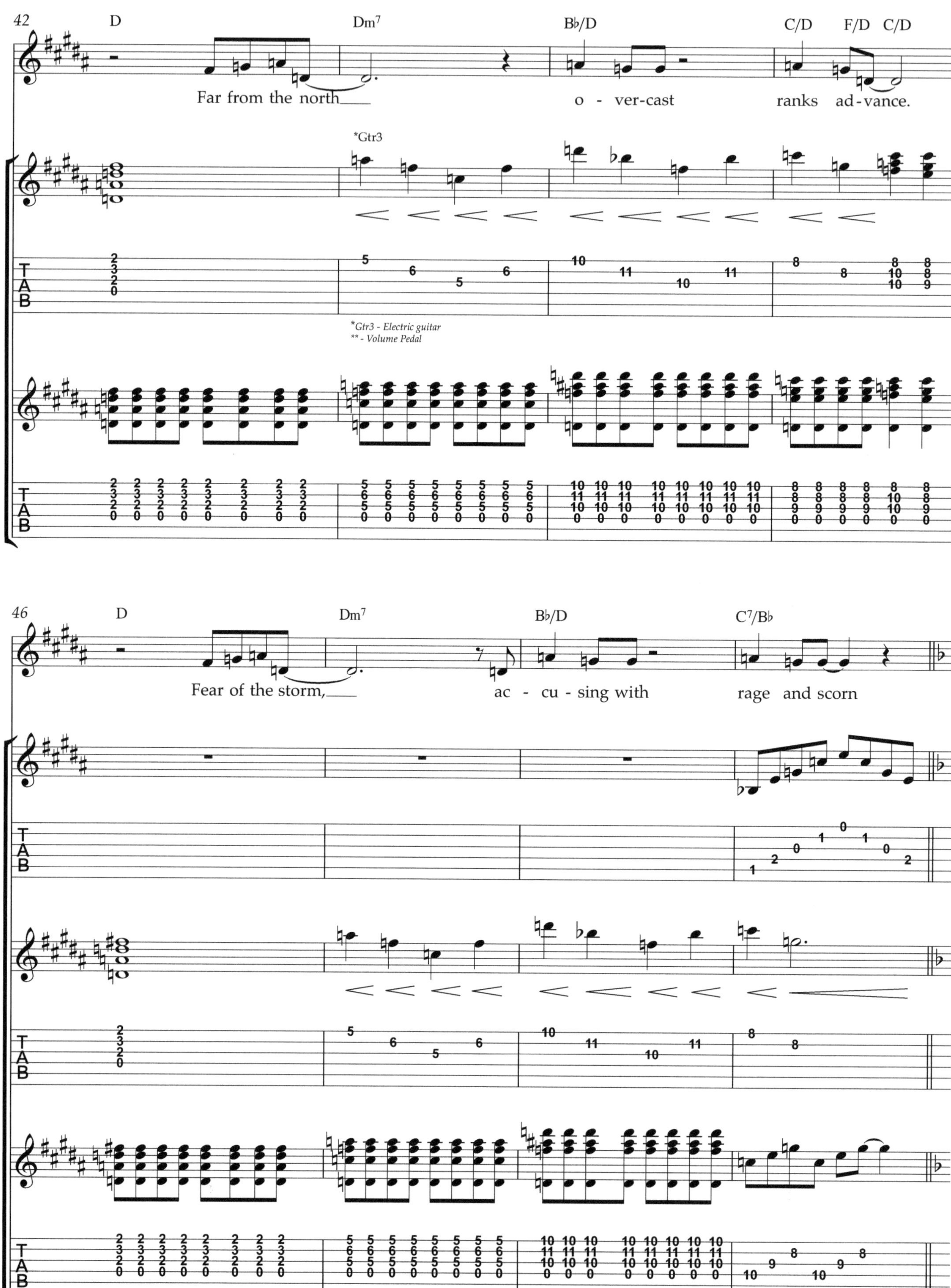
42
D
Dm7
B♭/D
C/D
F/D
C/D
Far from the north
o - ver-cast
ranks ad-vance.
*Gtr3
*Gtr3 - Electric guitar
** - Volume Pedal
46
D
Dm7
B♭/D
C7/B♭
Fear of the storm,
ac - cu - sing with
rage and scorn

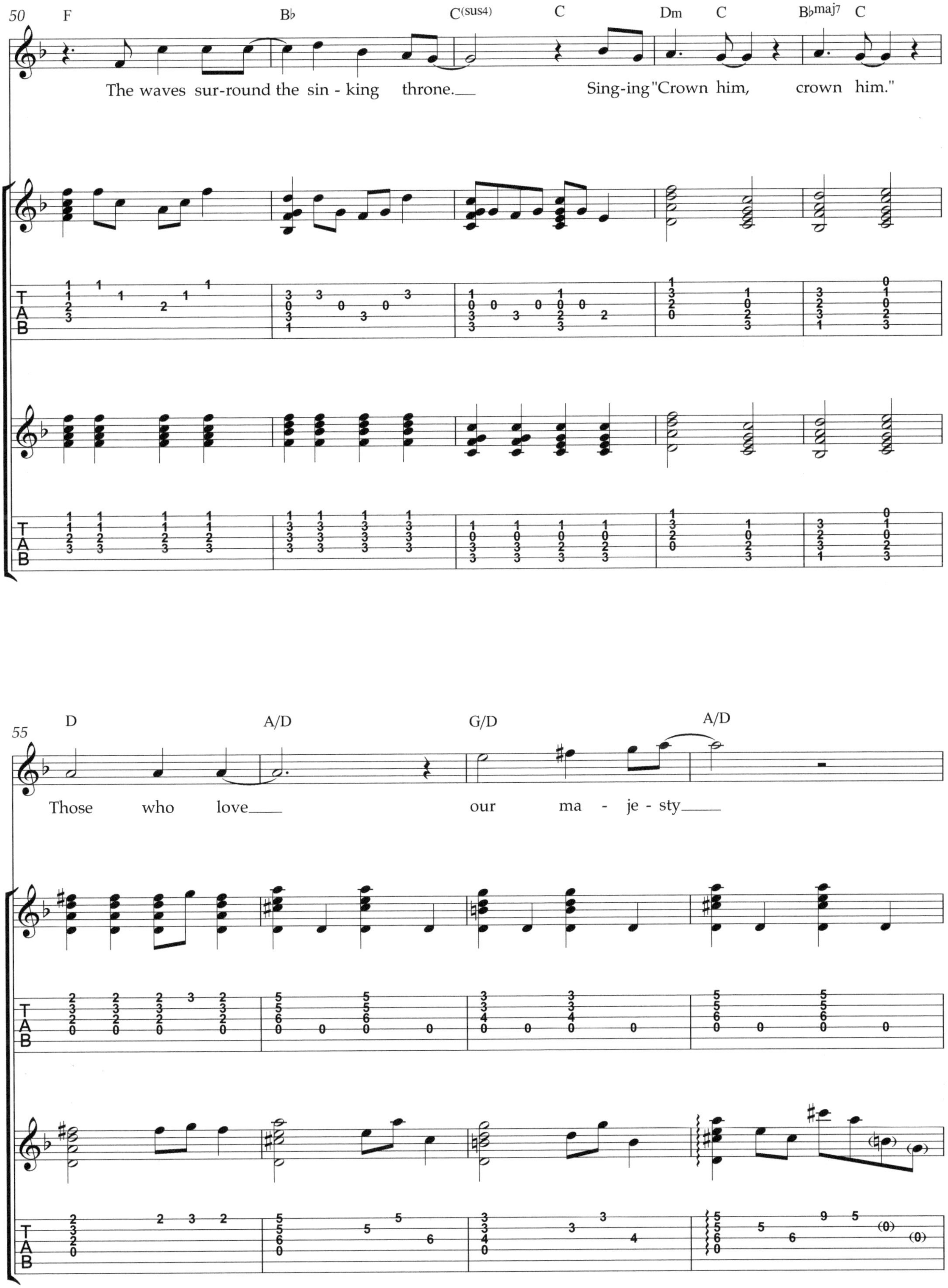

50

F B♭ C(sus4) C Dm C B♭maj7 C

The waves sur-round the sin - king throne.__ Sing-ing "Crown him, crown him."

55

D A/D G/D A/D

Those who love__ our ma - je - sty__

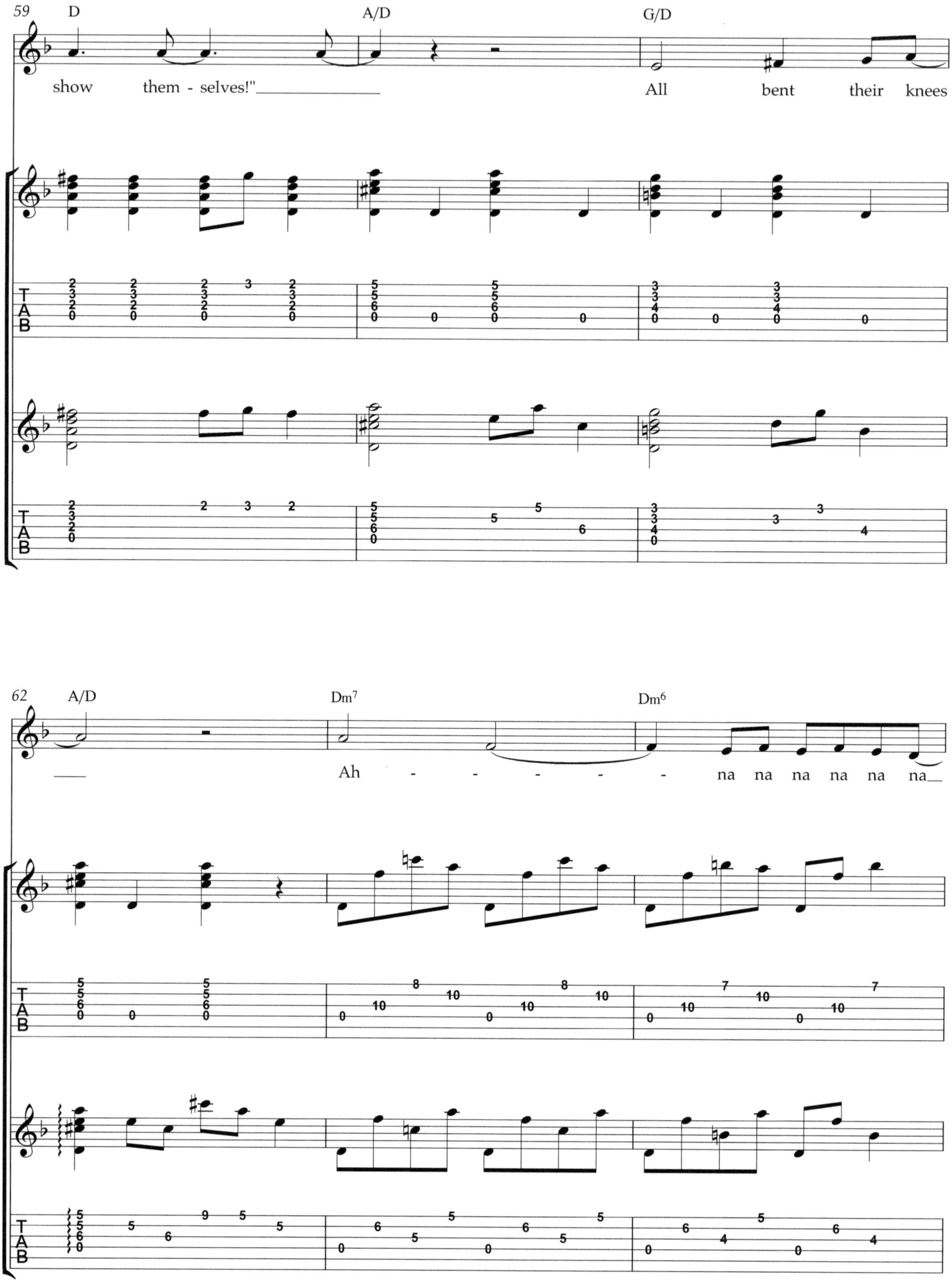

59 D A/D G/D

show them - selves!" All bent their knees

62 A/D Dm7 Dm6

Ah - - - - - na na na na na na

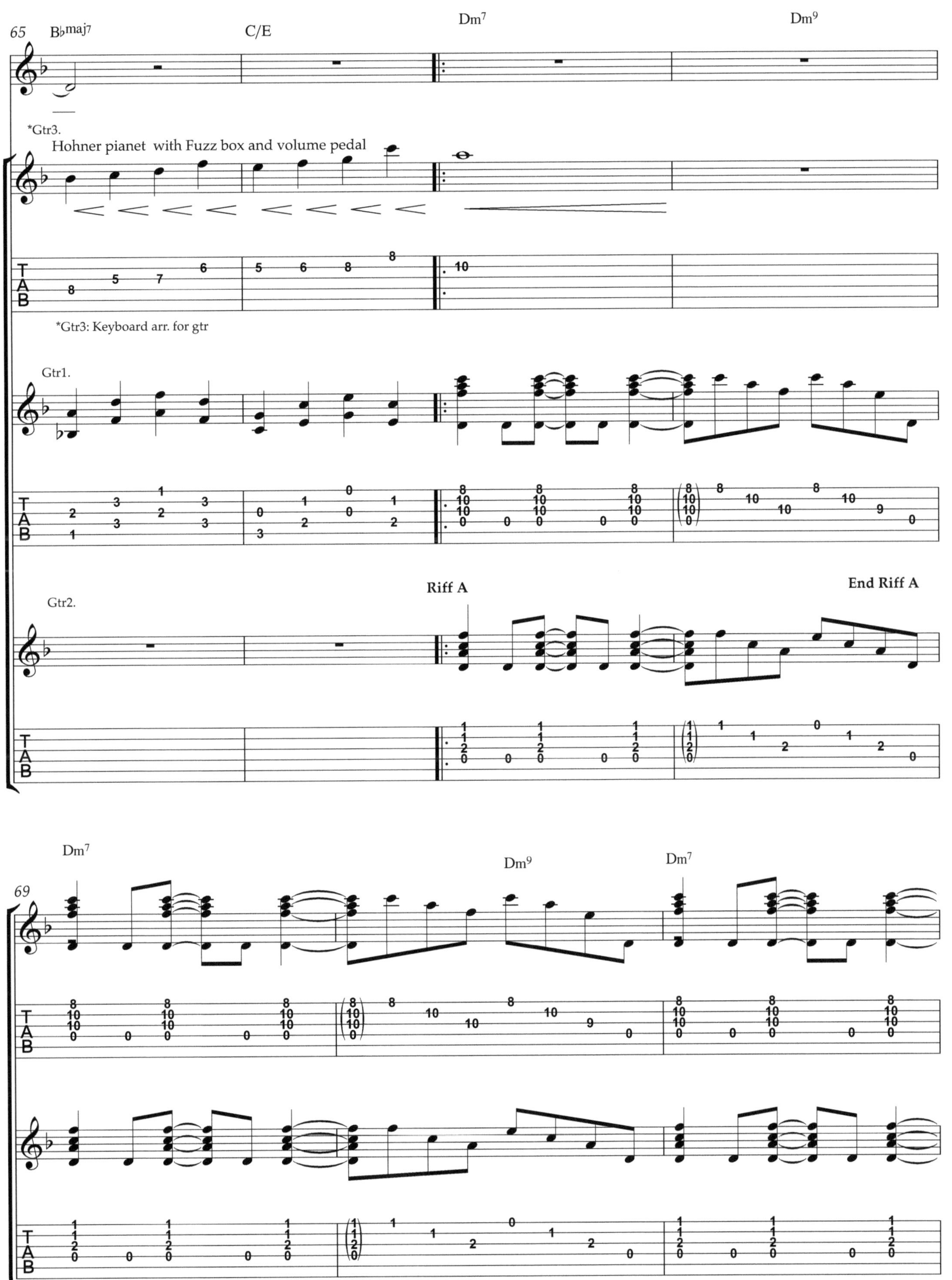
65
B♭maj7
C/E
Dm7
Dm9
*Gtr3.
Hohner pianet with Fuzz box and volume pedal
*Gtr3: Keyboard arr. for gtr
Gtr1.
Riff A
End Riff A
Gtr2.
69
Dm7
Dm9
Dm7

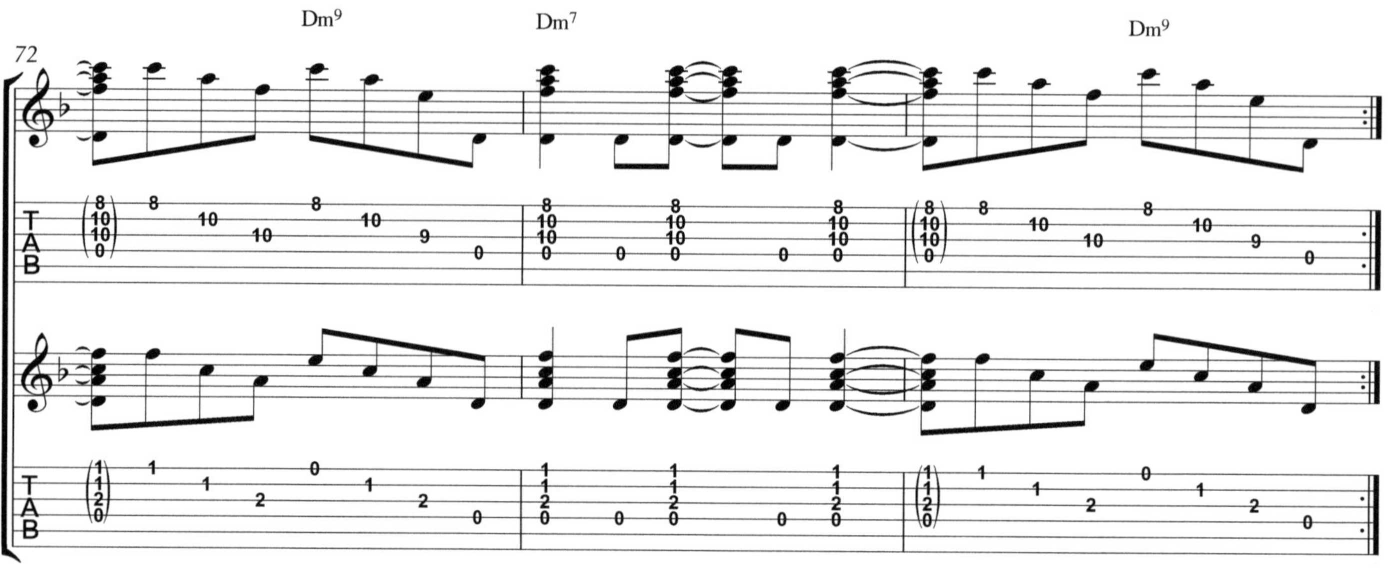

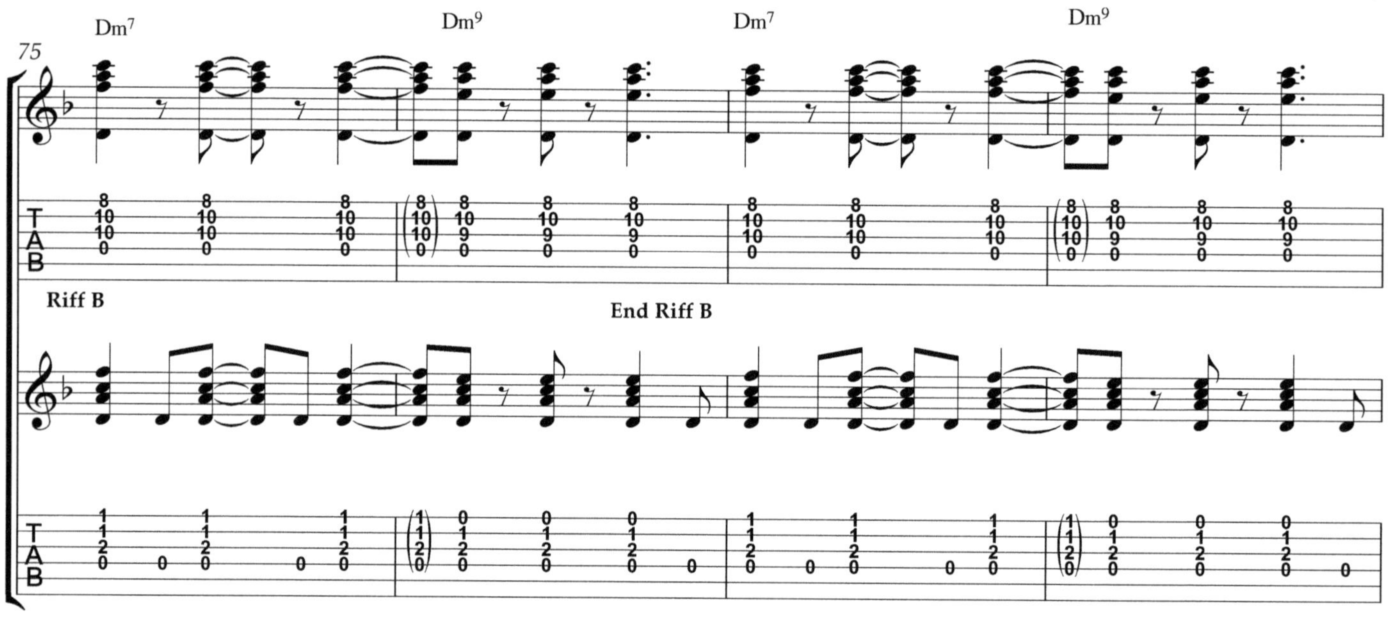

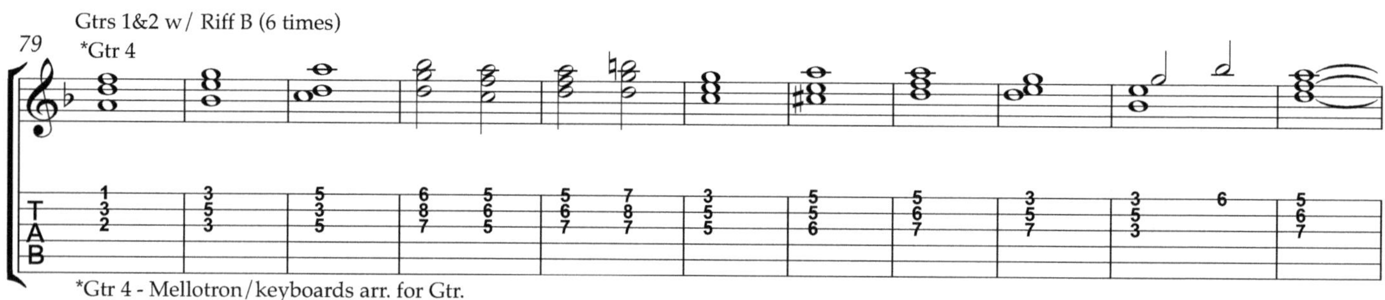

*Gtr 4 - Mellotron/keyboards arr. for Gtr.

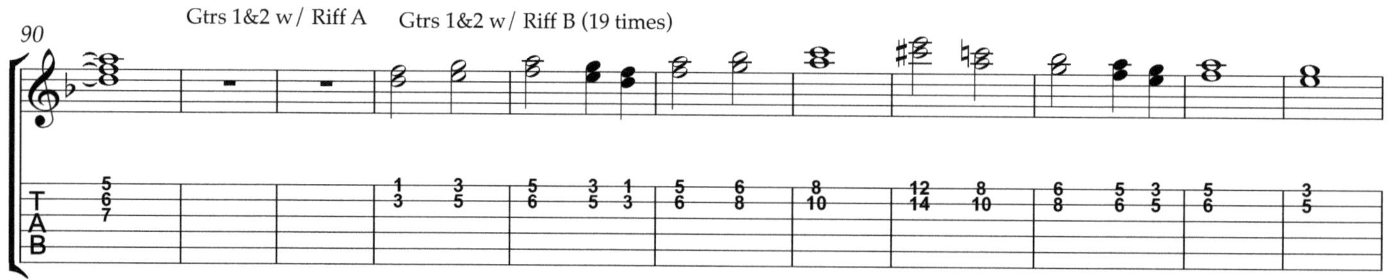

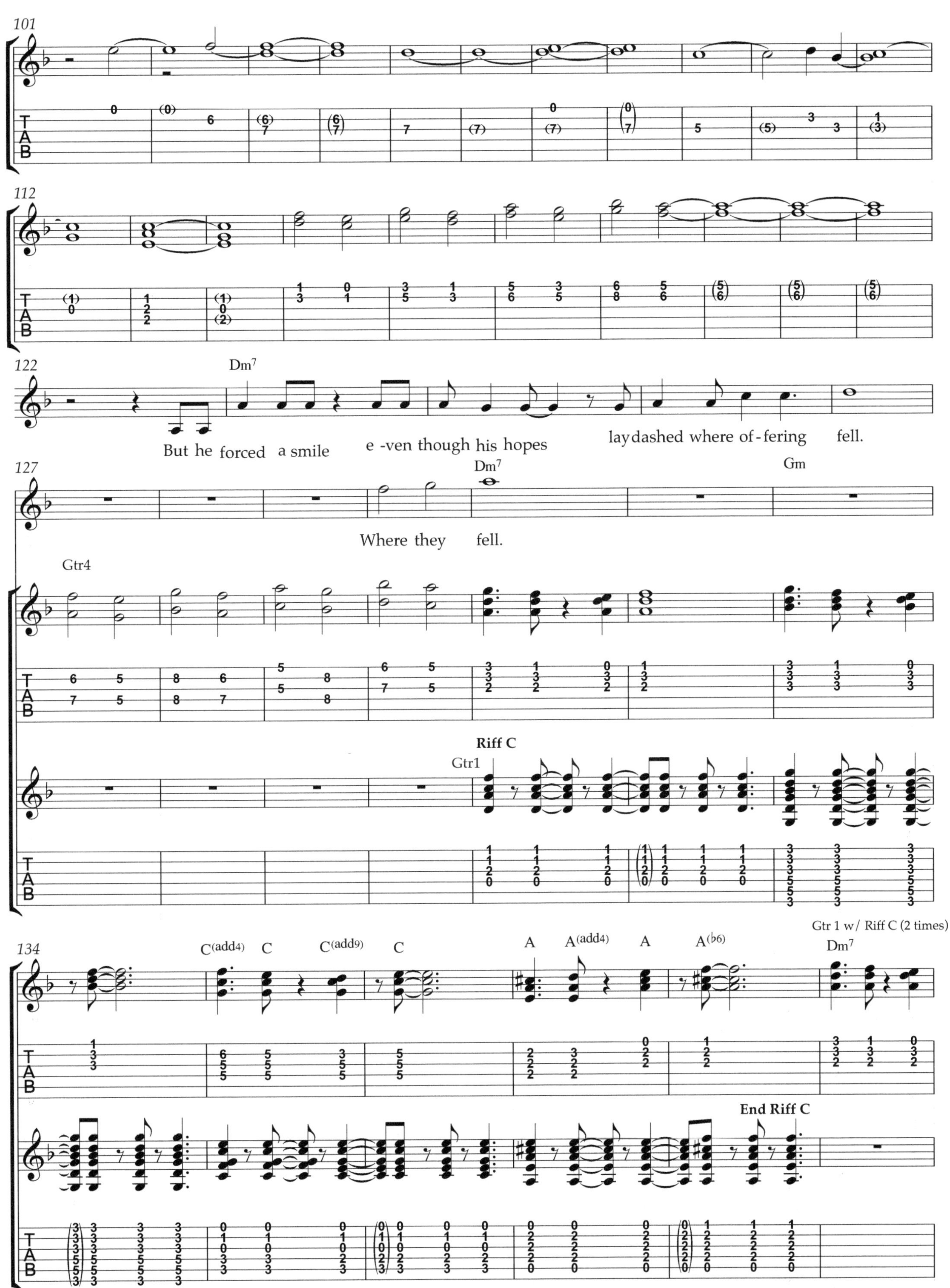
101
112
122
Dm7
But he forced a smile e -ven though his hopes lay dashed where of-fering fell.
127
Dm7
Gm
Where they fell.
Gtr4
Riff C
Gtr1
134
C(add4) C C(add9) C
A A(add4) A A(b6)
Gtr 1 w/ Riff C (2 times)
Dm7
End Riff C

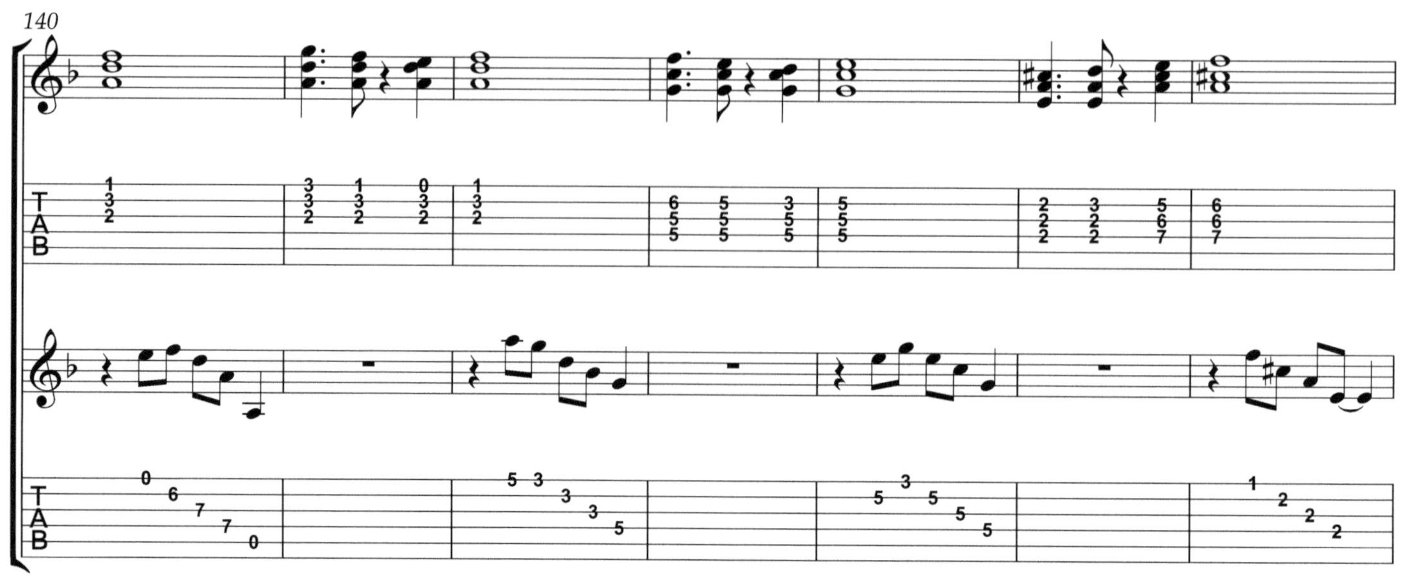
140

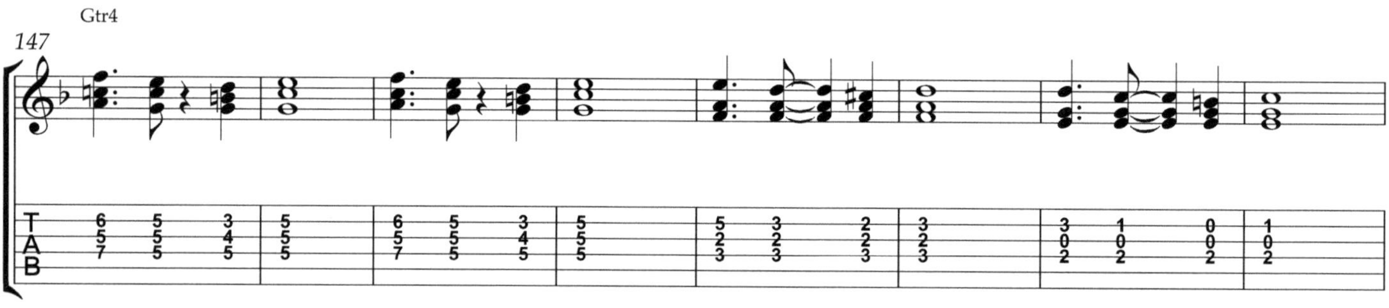
Gtr4
147

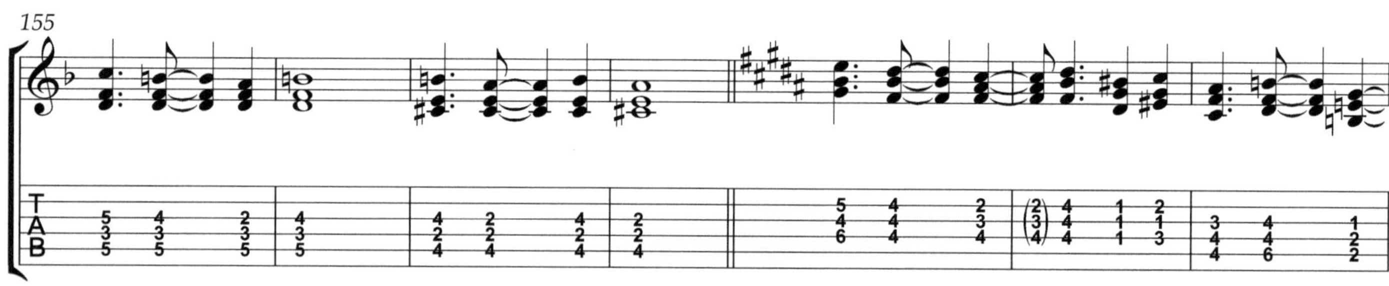
155

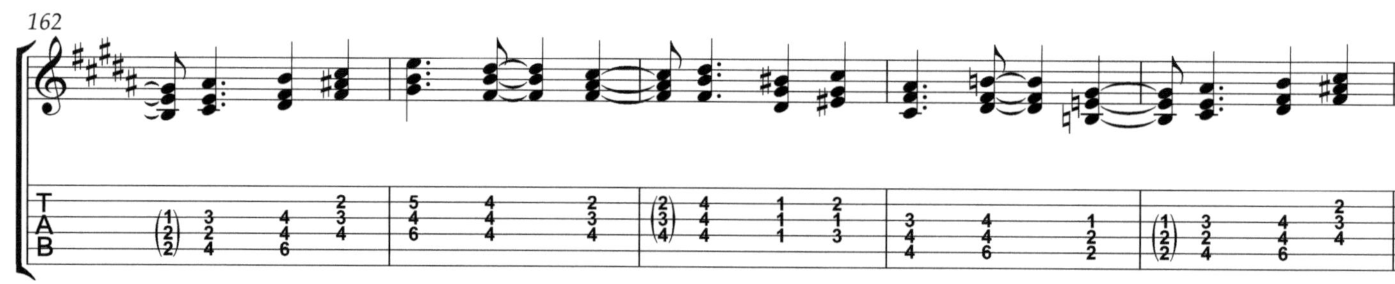
162

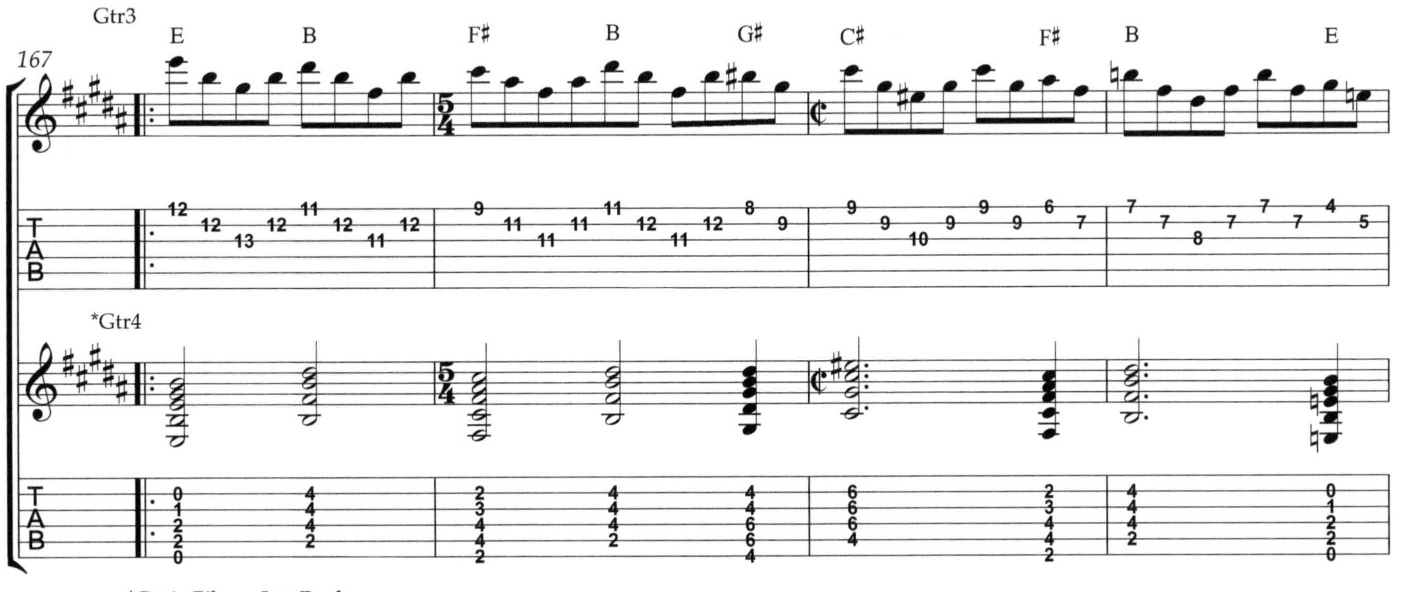

*Gtr4: Gibson Les Paul

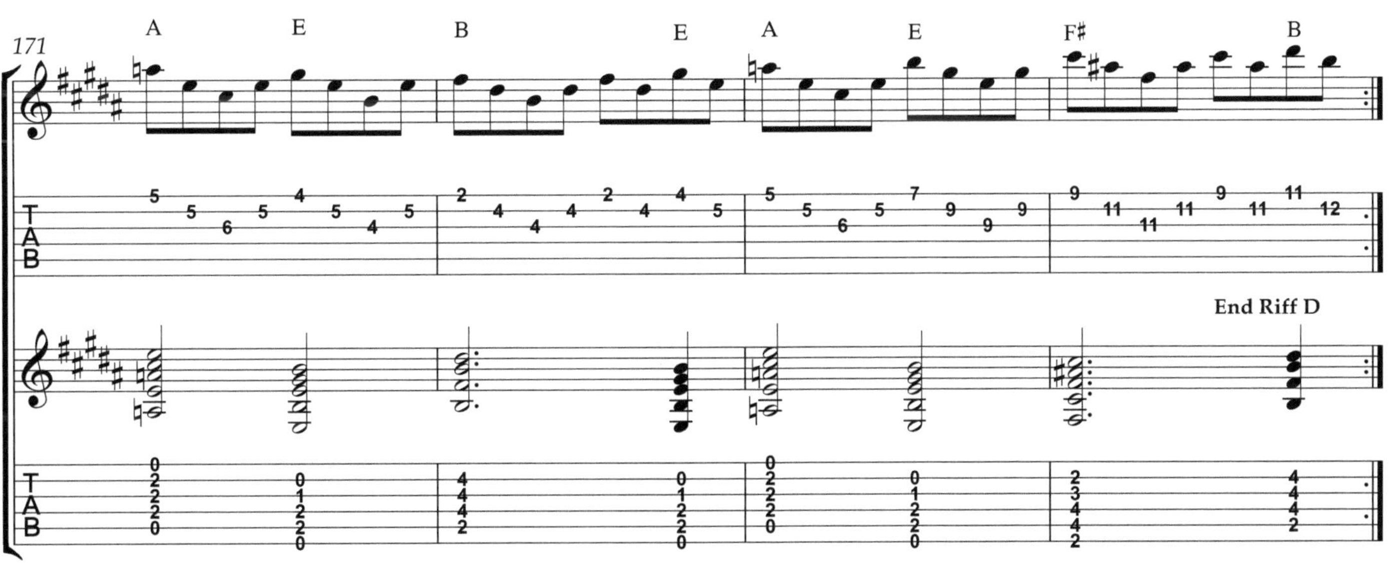

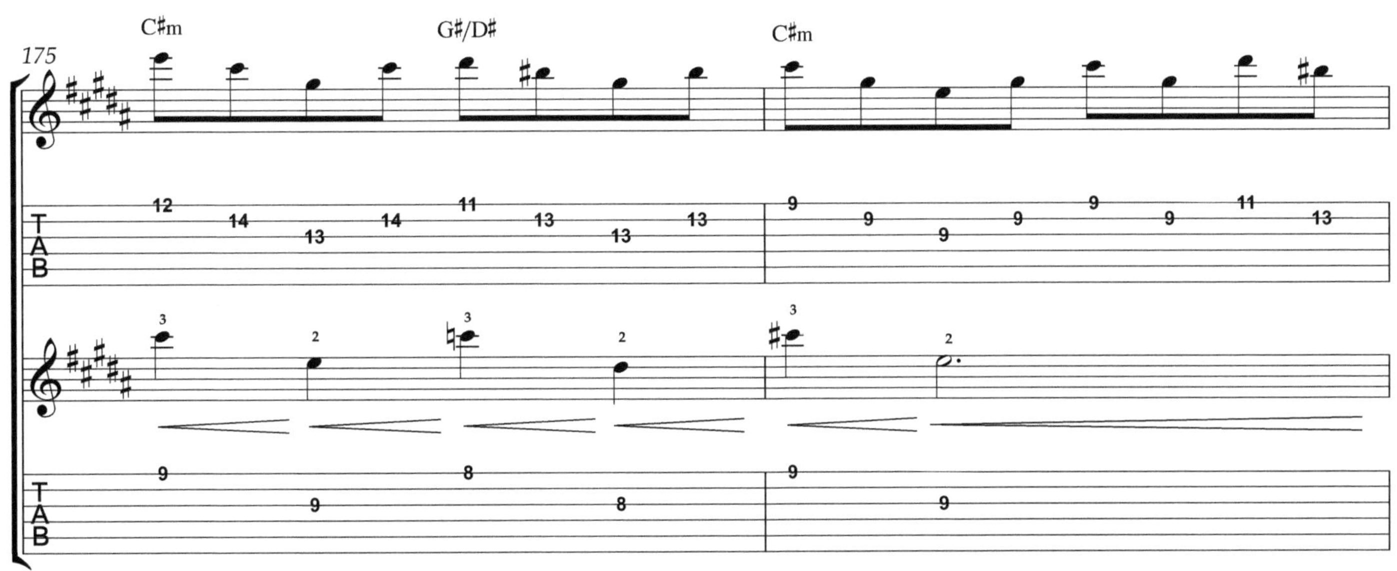

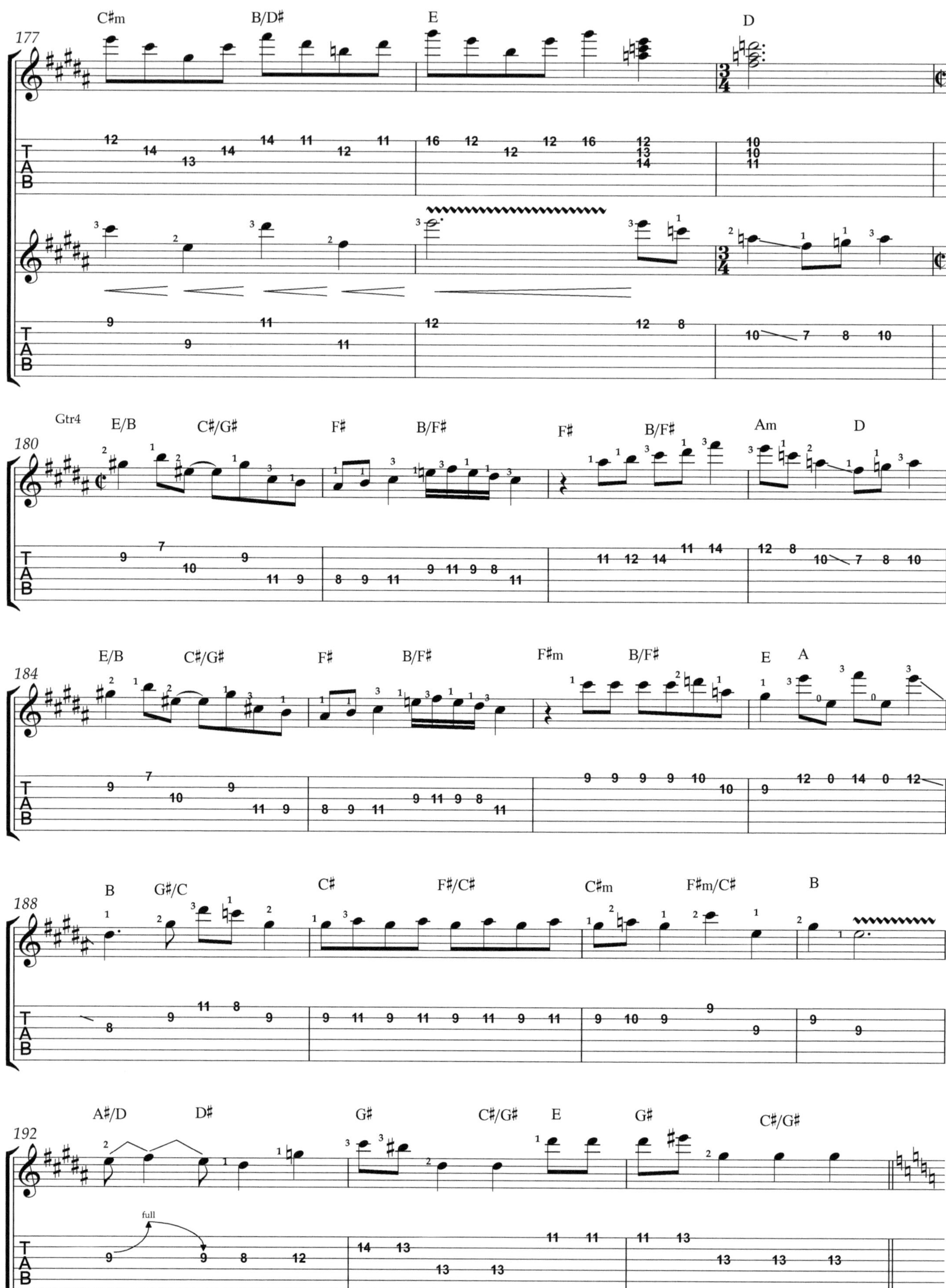
177
C#m B/D# E D
180
Gtr4
E/B C#/G# F# B/F# F# B/F# Am D
184
E/B C#/G# F# B/F# F#m B/F# E A
188
B G#/C C# F#/C# C#m F#m/C# B
192
A#/D D# G# C#/G# E G# C#/G#
full

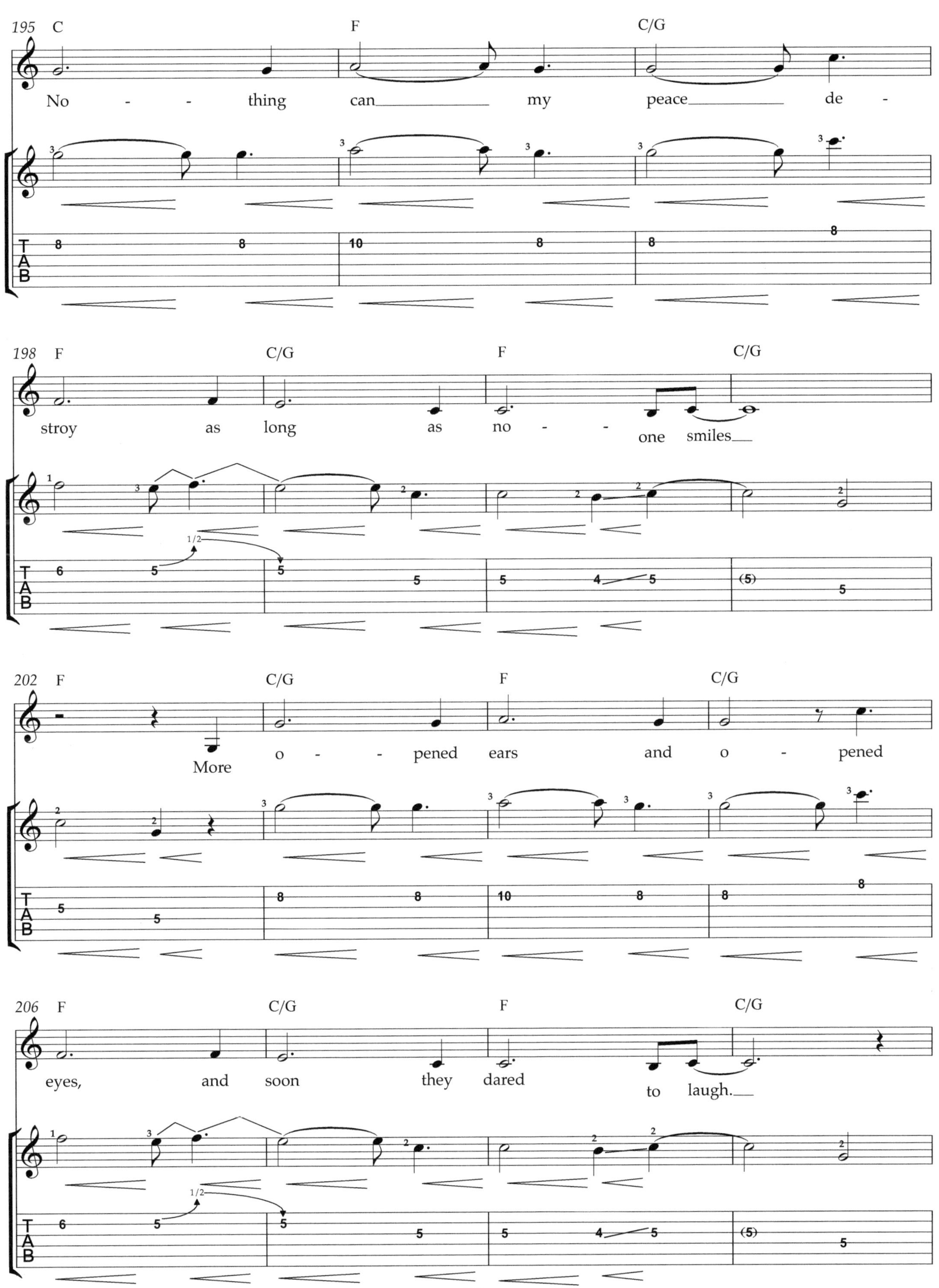
195
C
F
C/G
No - - thing can my peace de -
198
F
C/G
F
C/G
stroy as long as no - - one smiles
202
F
C/G
F
C/G
More o - - pened ears and o - pened
206
F
C/G
F
C/G
eyes, and soon they dared to laugh.

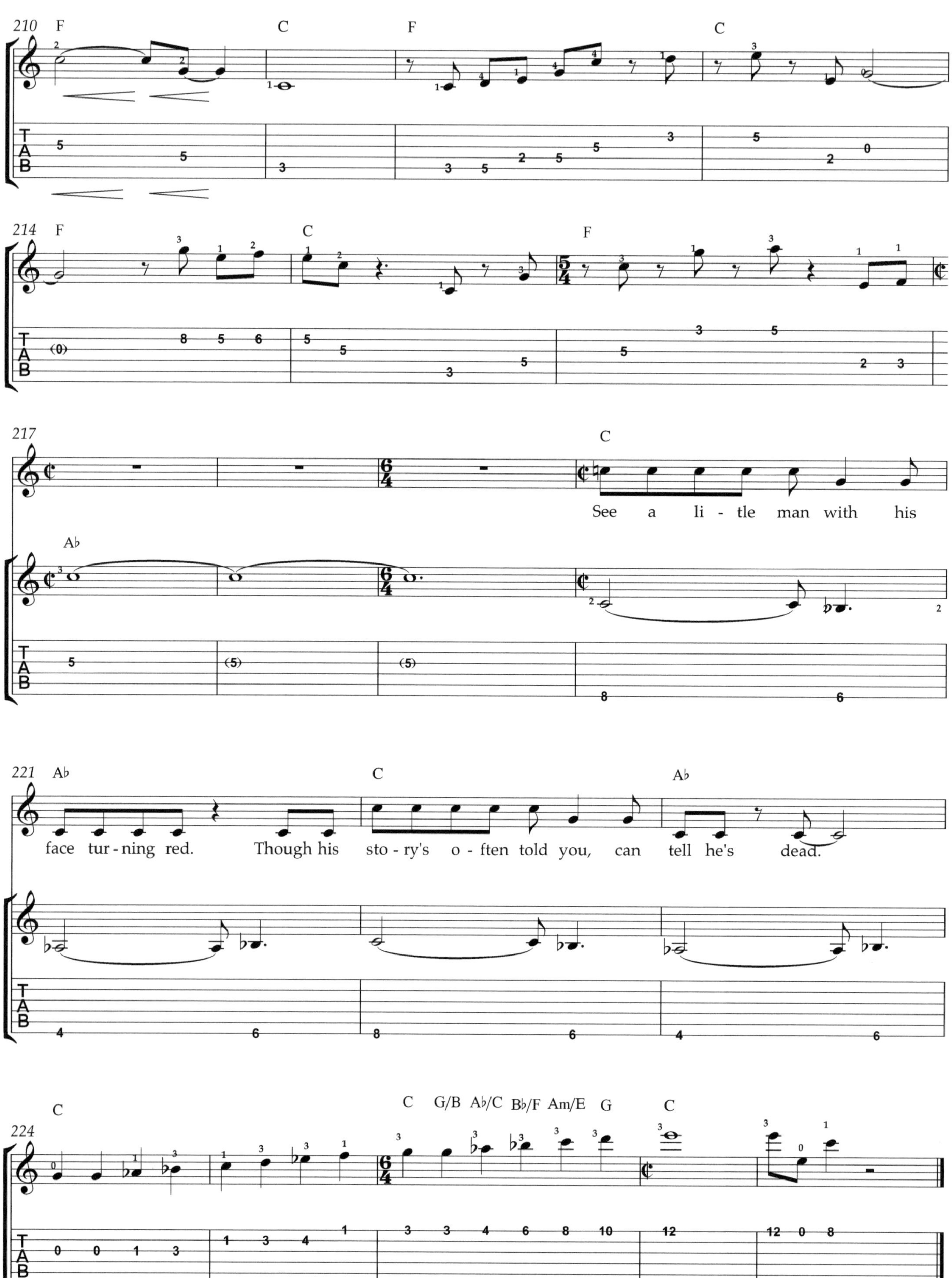
210 F
C
F
C
214 F
C
F
217
C
See a li - tle man with his
Ab
221 Ab
C
Ab
face tur - ning red. Though his sto - ry's o - ften told you, can tell he's dead.
224
C
C G/B Ab/C Bb/F Am/E G
C

CAN UTILITY AND THE COASTLINERS
BY GENESIS

```
| B/D#        C#m7        | F#7        B             |
D                         Bb/D               C/Bb          Badd4
   THE SCATTERED PAGES OF A BOOK        BY THE SEA
B11                  Em                             Em9/D    A (add9)/C#
    HELD BY THE SAND, WASHED  BY  THE WAVES
  D                      A/D  G/D                 A/D
A SHADOW FORMS         CAST BY A CLOUD
D                A/D    G/D                  A/D             B/D#
SKIMMING BY      AS EYES OF THE PAST,      BUT THE RISING TIDE
    C#m7(b5)        F#7              B
ABSORBS THEM EFFORTLESSLY CLAIMING


D                               G/D                           A/C#
      THEY TOLD OF ONE    WHO TIRED OF ALL        SINGING:
 Bm        A/C#  G/D     A/E
"PRAISE HIM, PRAISE HIM
Badd4             Em                                       A7
       WE HEED NOT FLATTERERS," HE CRIED
   D                     A/D  G/D                  A/D
"BY OUR COMMAND,        WATERS RETREAT
D                   A/D G/D                    A/D
SHOW MY POWER,      HALT AT MY FEET"
            B                           Em    Em/D    A/C#
BUT THE CAUSE WAS LOST, NOW COLD WINDS BLOW


D                                    Dm7  Bb/D        C/D      F/D      C/D
      FAR FROM THE NORTH            OVERCAST RANKS ADVANCE
D                                 Dm7       Bb/D            C7/Bb
      FEAR OF THE STORM,             ACCUSING WITH RAGE AND SCORN
F                                 Bb                        C(sus4)   C
   THE WAVES SURROUND THE SINKING THRONE                          SINGING:
 Dm        C       Bbmaj7   C
"CROWN HIM, CROWN HIM
D/F#                  A/E    G                 A/E  D/F#                     A/E         |
THOSE WHO LOVE          OUR MAJESTY,       SHOW THEMSELVES!"
G/D                        A/E
ALL BENT THEIR KNEES


Dm7      Dm6                                  Bbmaj7      C/E
AH                NA NA NA NA NA NA
```

II: Dm7 I Dm9 :II (play 8 times)

II: Dm7 I Dm9 :II (play 2 times)

43 measures (solo)

Dm7
BUT HE FORCED A SMILE EVEN THOUGH HIS HOPES LAY DASHED
Gm **Dm7**
WHERE OFFERINGS FELL WHERE THEY FELL

I Gm I IC (add4) C Cadd9 I C I A A(add4) A I A(add4, 5#) I Dsus4 Dm Dsus2 (guitars solo) I

27 measures (solo)

II: E B I F# B G # I C# F# I B E I

I A E I B E I A E I F# :II

I C#m G#/D# I C#m I C#m B/D# I E I I

I E/B C#/G# I F# B/F# I F# B/F# I Am D I E/B C#/G# I

I F# B/F# I F#m B/F# I E I B G#/C I C# F#/C# I C#m F#m/C# I

I B E I A#/D D# I G# C#/G# I G# C#/G# I

C F C/G F C/G F C/G
NOTHING CAN MY PEACE DESTROY AS LONG AS NO ONE SMILES
F C/G F C/G F C/G F C/G
MORE OPENED EARS AND OPENED EYES AND SOON THEY DARED TO LAUGH

II: F I C :II F I C I F I Ab I I I

C Ab
SEE A LITTLE MAN WITH HIS FACE TURNING RED
C Ab
THOUGH HIS STORY'S OFTEN TOLD, YOU CAN TELL HE'D DEAD

I C I IC G/B Ab/C Bb/F Am/E G I I II

HORIZONS

"*Horizons* appeared as an intro of *Supper's Ready* under a different title." *Steve Hackett*

"I never played Horizons live at that time because if I played it before Supper's Ready, I´d have to change quickly from the six-steel string guitar to the twelve-string guitar." Steve Hackett

Steve's inspiration to compose *Horizons* was Bach's cello suite #1 in G Major transcribed for the guitar in D Major and performed by the English classical guitarist Julian Bream. Steve remembered: "It took me a long time to compose it: about one year. When I played it to the band, I was not very confident, but Phil commented, "it sounded like there should be applause at the end." To record *Horizons*, Steve used a Yamaha six-steel string guitar using two Leslie cabinets, although he always plays it with nylon string guitar nowadays.

It took Steve four takes to record the song because "I couldn't mess it up," as he told me. Steve recorded it with just Bob Potter, sound engineer at the beginning of the recordings of *Foxtrot*. They did not plan that the take they had chosen would be final, but everybody liked how it sounded. Nor did they desire for it to come before *Supper's Ready*, but "Where else could we have put it on the album?" Steve thought, and he continued: "At those times, there were no pedals as chorus, so I liked to play my guitar through Leslie because it allowed me to get that type of effect."

Tony Banks told me *Horizons* was a "nice little piece that worked well as a break before we went to the long one, *Supper's Ready*, which was quite a challenge. Choosing to place *Horizons* right before it would help with the flow."

Steve remarked that that was the only time he played alone in a track during the Genesis era.

Player/Instrument:

Steve Hackett - Yamaha six-steel string guitar.

Horizons: Guitar Specifics

"Maybe it is not the correct way to play Horizons, but it is my way."
Steve Hackett

Nailpick

In photos 37 & 38, Steve shows how he plays the left-hand harmonics in the section below.

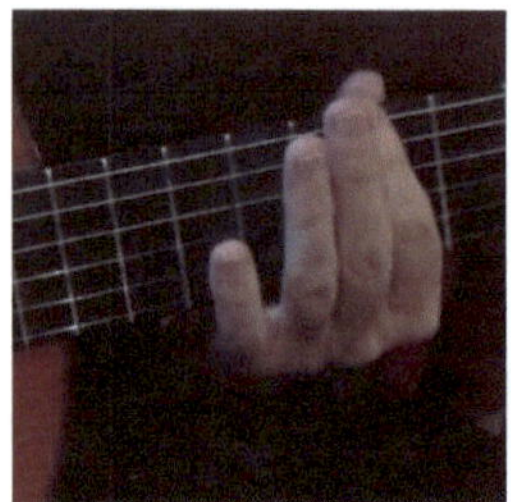

Photo 60: Steve playing the harmonics in measure 1, third and fourth beats [right below]
Photo by Paulo De Carvalho

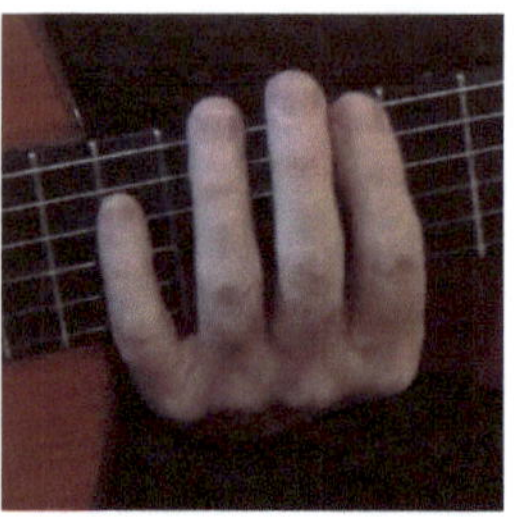

Photo 61: Steve playing the harmonics on measure 2, third and fourth beats [right below]
Photo by Paulo De Carvalho

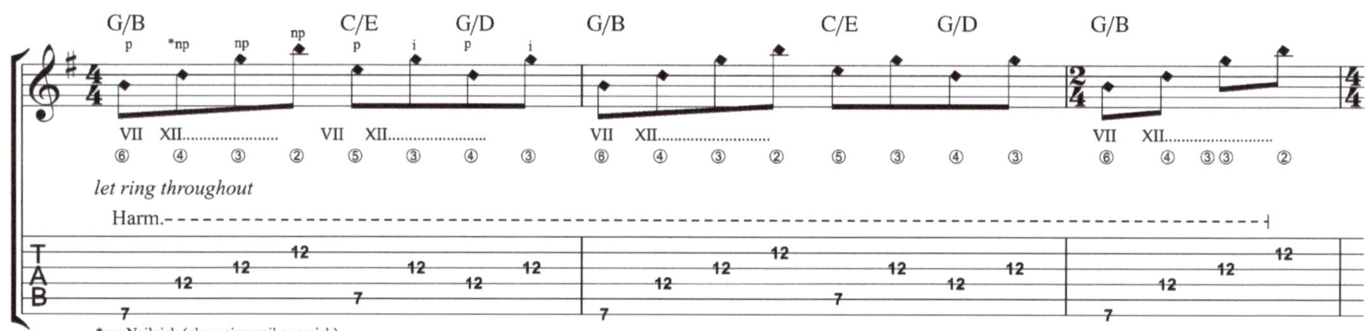

He uses the thumb and index fingers, and sometimes he puts the thumb (*p*) and index finger (*i*) together as a pick (plectrum), a '*nailpick*' (np), as I named and notated in the score [above]: a frequent right-hand technique of Steve's style.

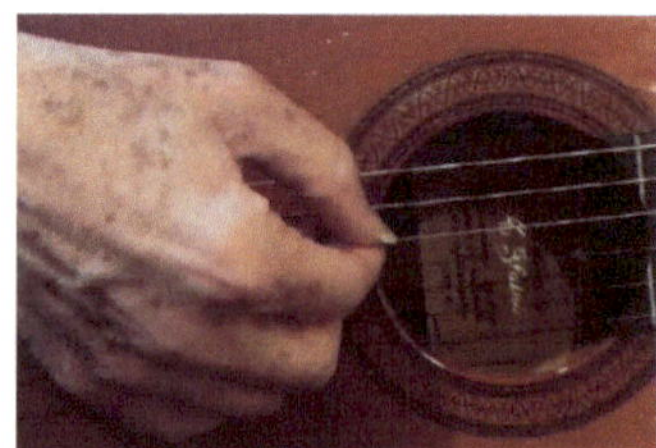

Photo 62: Steve showing a 'nailpick' [the thumb (p) and the index finger (i) together]
Photo by Paulo De Carvalho

Chord Shapes

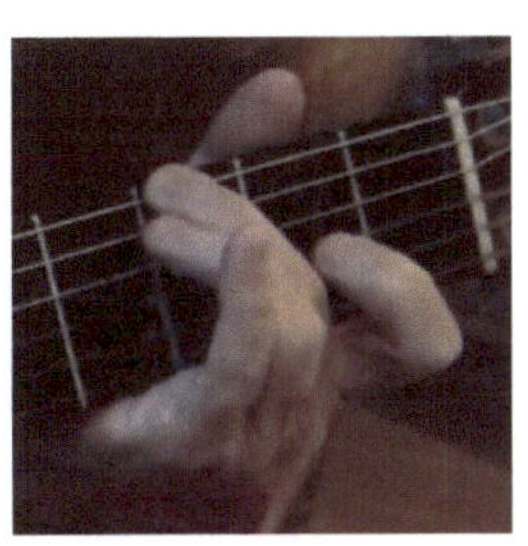

Photo 63: Steve playing
G(add9): measures 4-5 [right]
by Paulo De Carvalho

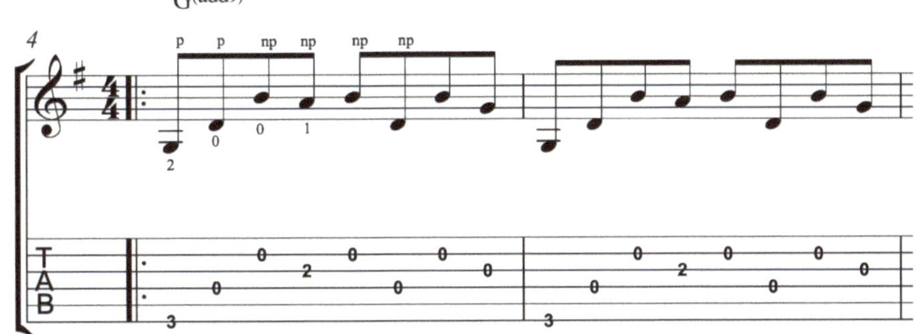

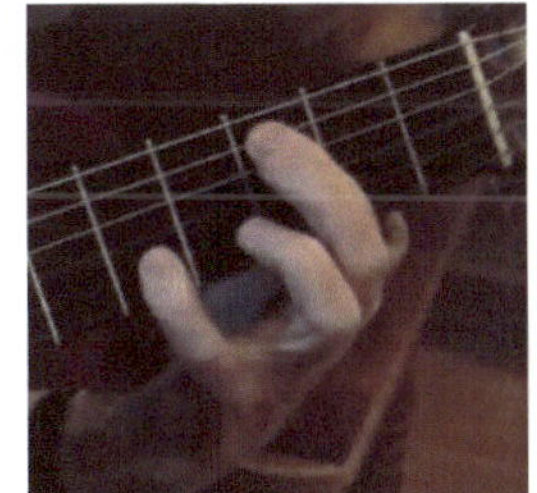

Photo 64: Steve playing
C6: measure10 [below]]
by Paulo De Carvalho

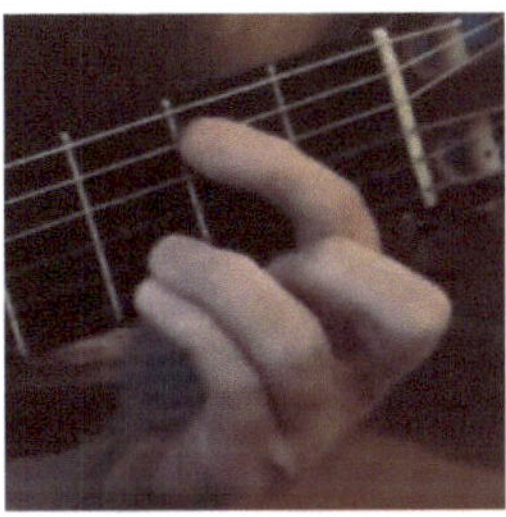

Photo 65: Steve playing
G/B: measure 10[below]
by Paulo De Carvalho

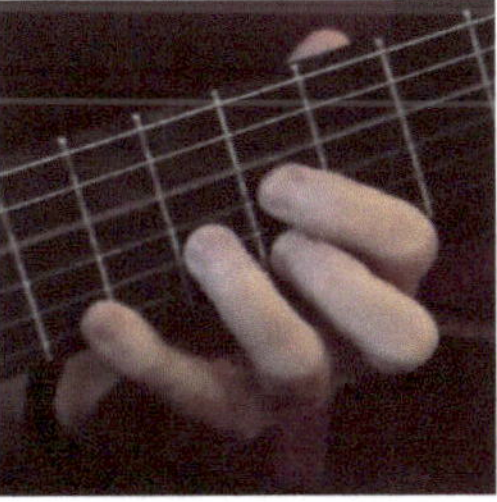

Photo 66: Steve playing
G/D: measure 11[below]
by Paulo De Carvalho

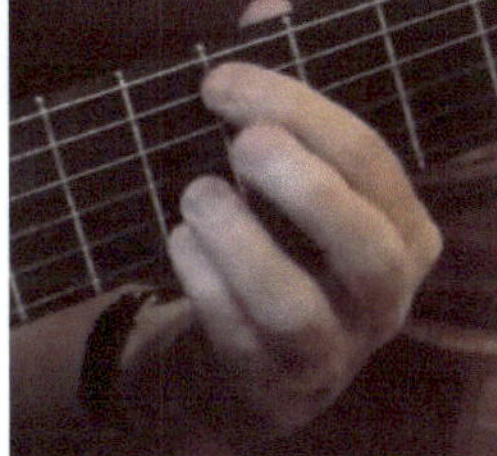

Photo 67: Steve playing
B/D#: measure 11[below]
by Paulo De Carvalho

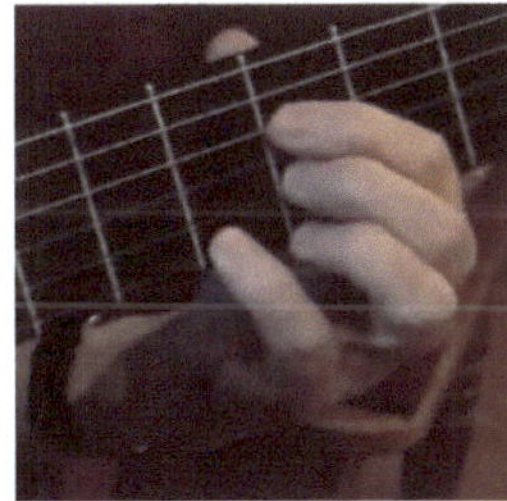

Photo 68: Steve playing
B7/F#: measure 11[below]
by Paulo De Carvalho

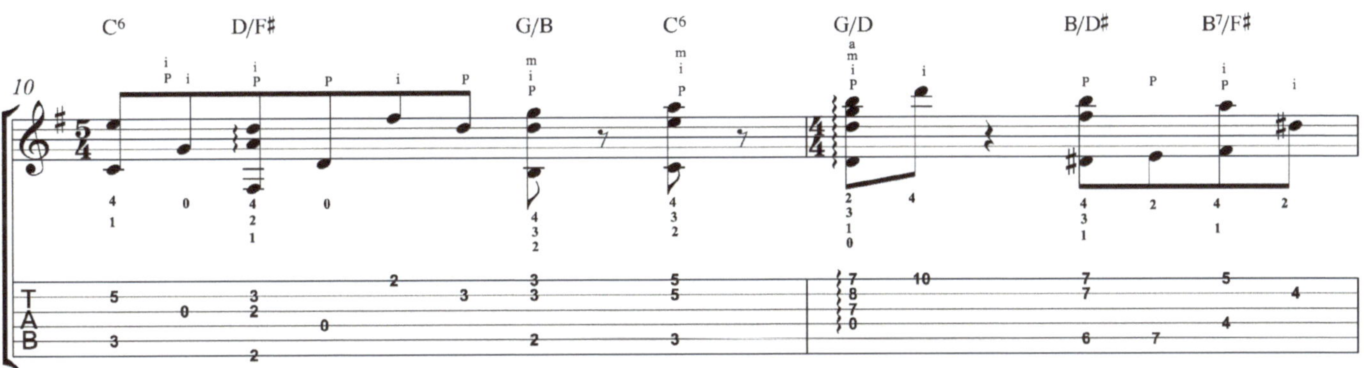

from Genesis - *Foxtrot*

Horizons

Transcribed by Paulo De Carvalho

by T. Banks, P.Collins, P. Gabriel, S. Hackett, M. Rutherford

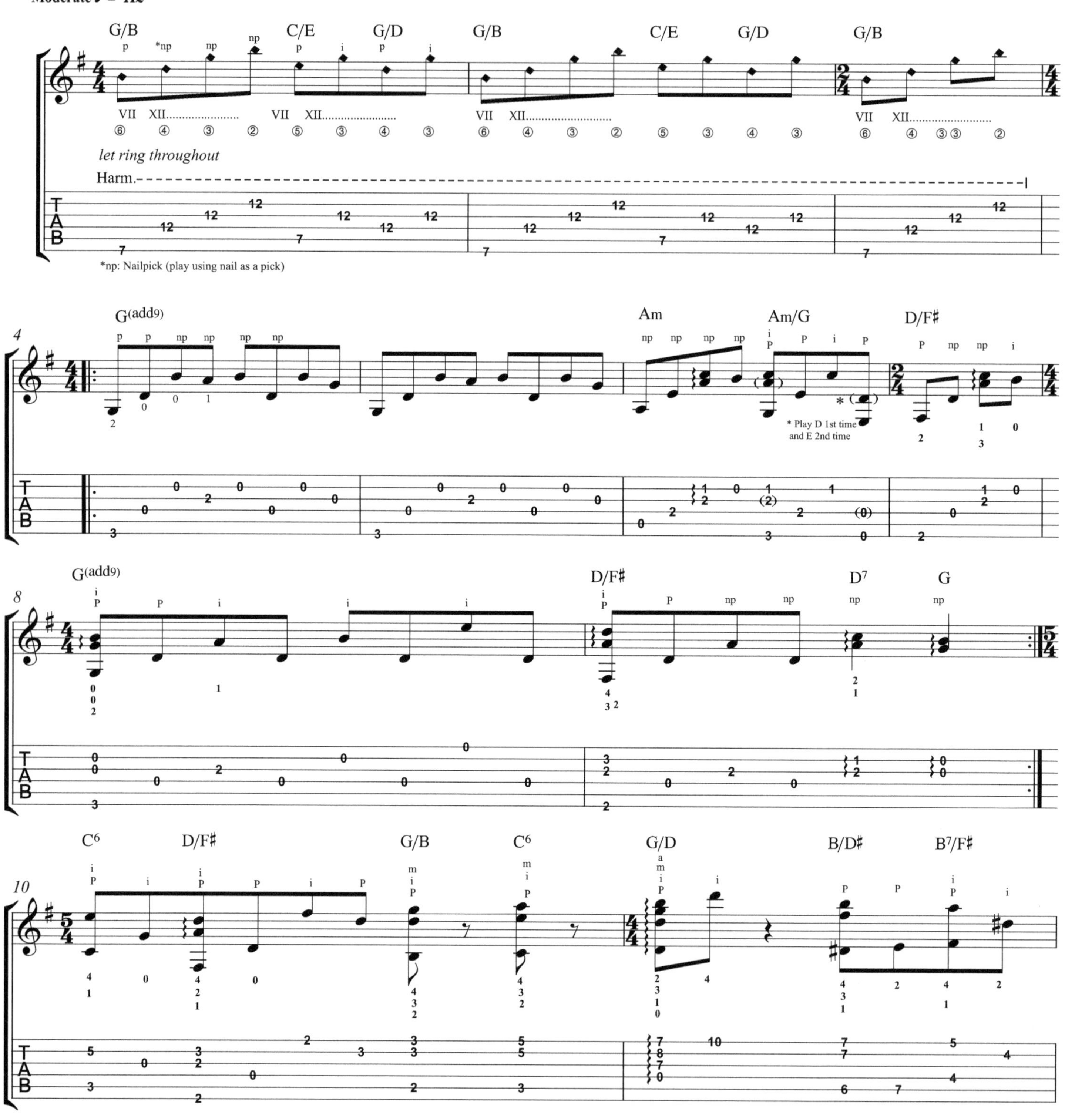

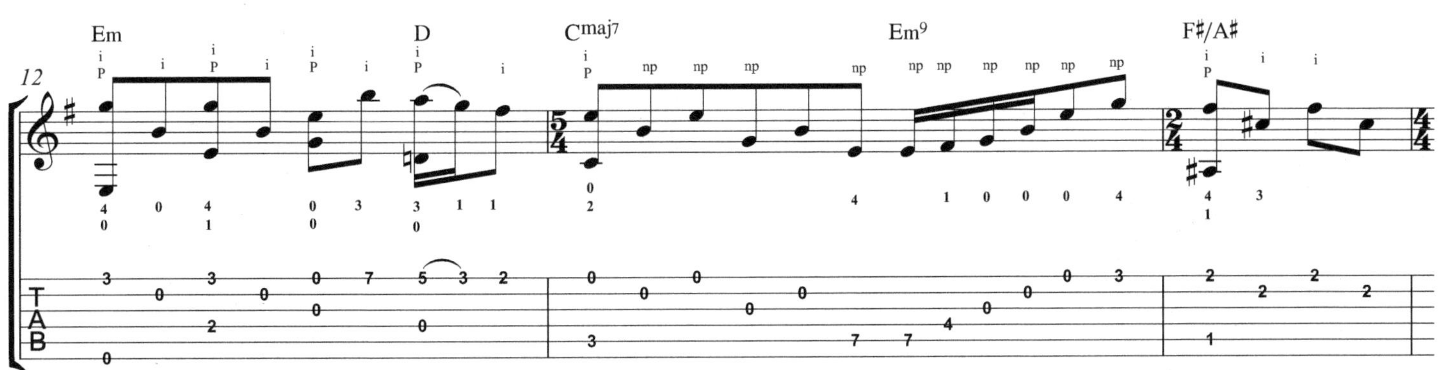
12
Em
D
Cmaj7
Em9
F#/A#
TAB

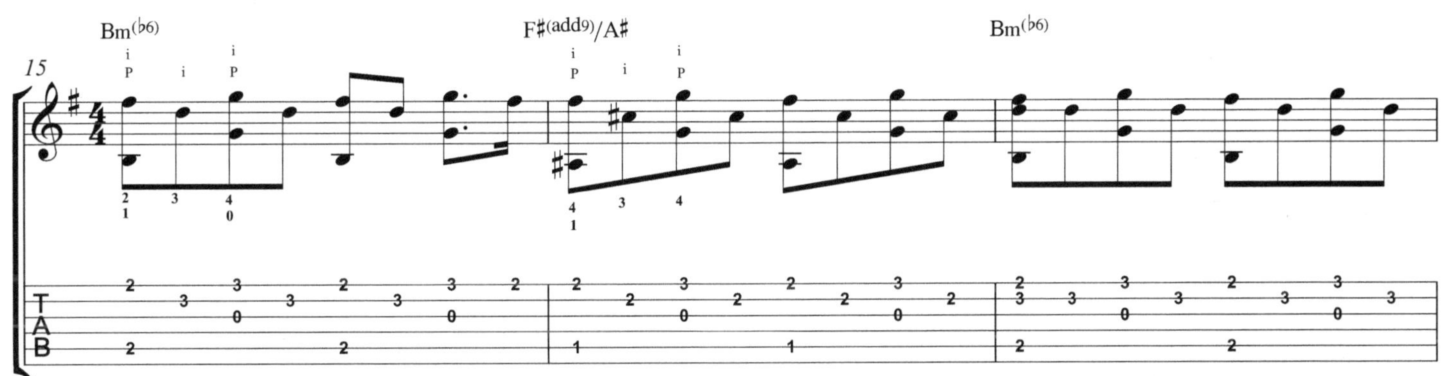
15
Bm(♭6)
F#(add9)/A#
Bm(♭6)
TAB

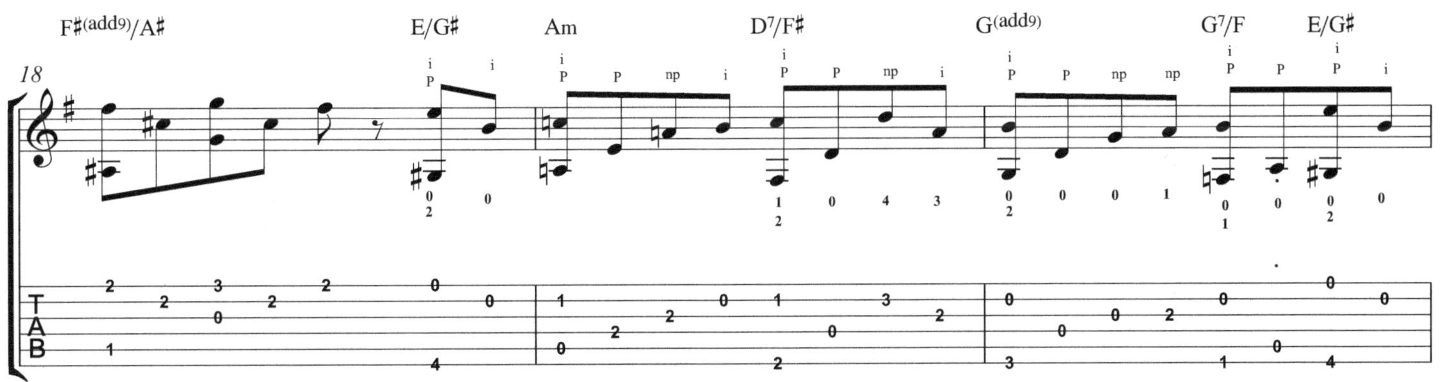
18
F#(add9)/A#
E/G#
Am
D7/F#
G(add9)
G7/F
E/G#
TAB

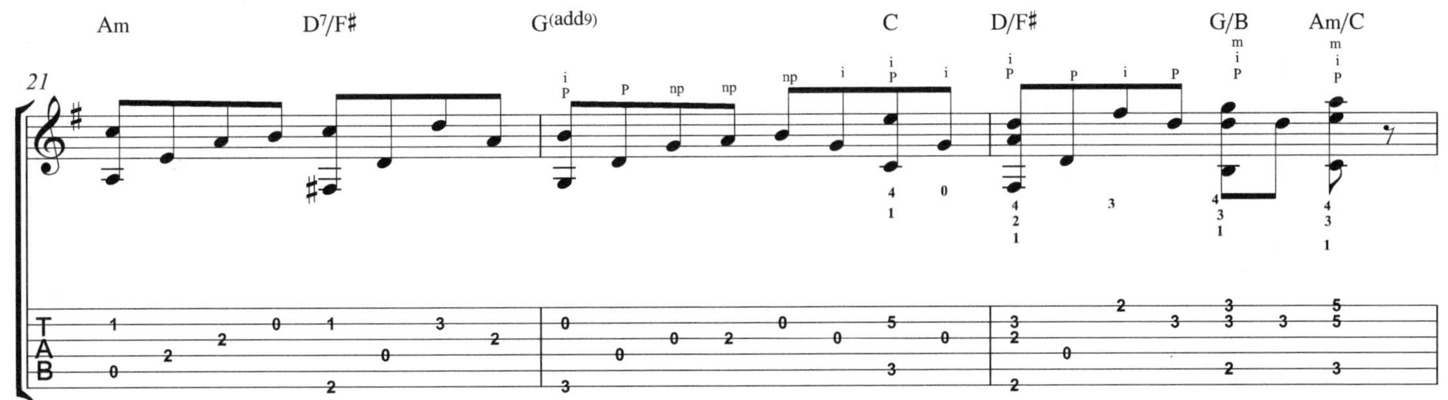
21
Am
D7/F#
G(add9)
C
D/F#
G/B
Am/C
TAB

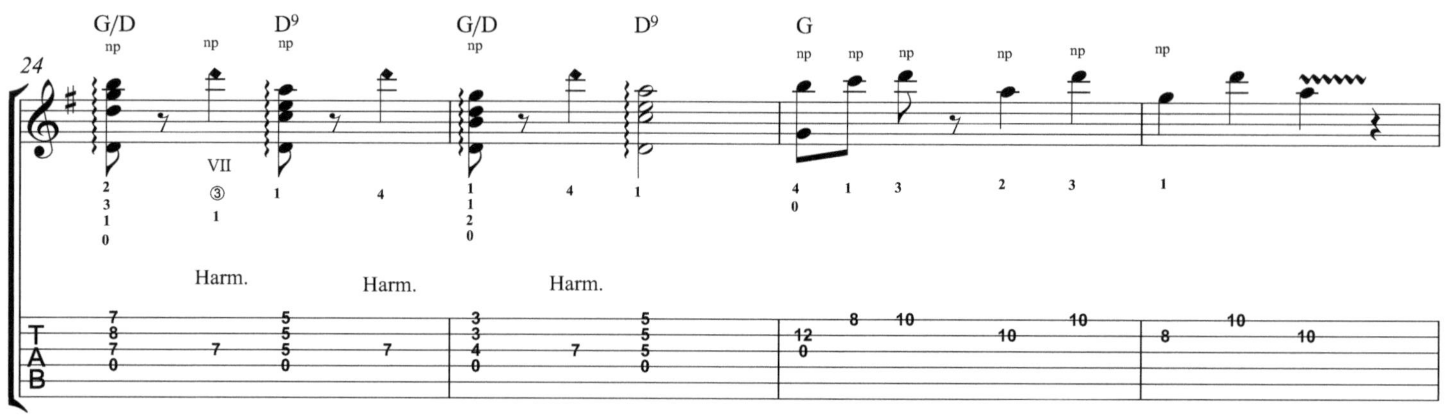
24
G/D
D9
G/D
D9
G
VII
Harm.
Harm.
Harm.
TAB

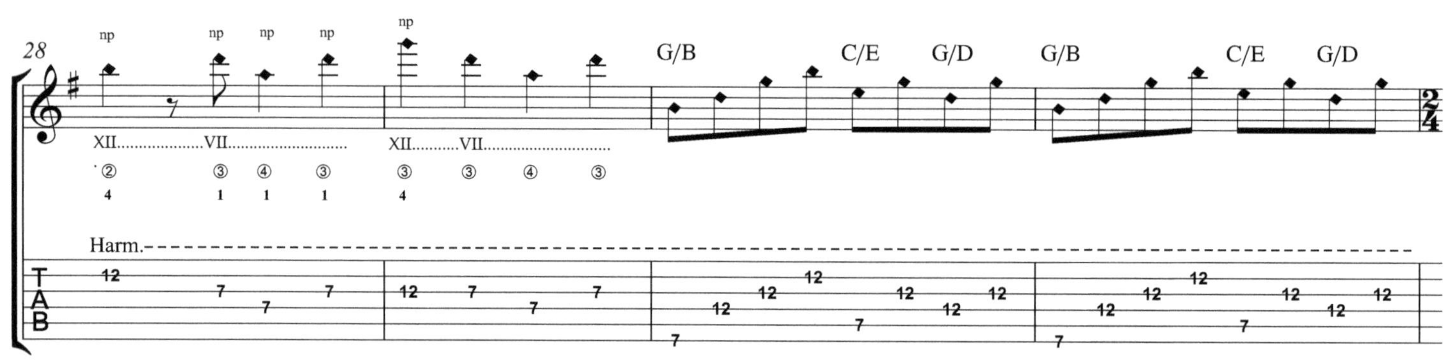
28
XII....................VII............................
XII...........VII.............................
G/B
C/E
G/D
G/B
C/E
G/D
Harm.
TAB

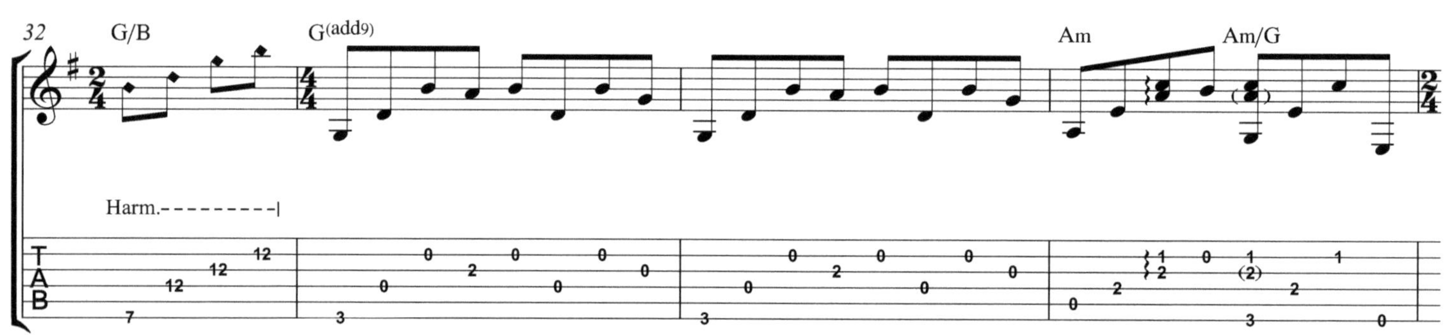
32
G/B
G(add9)
Am
Am/G
Harm.
TAB

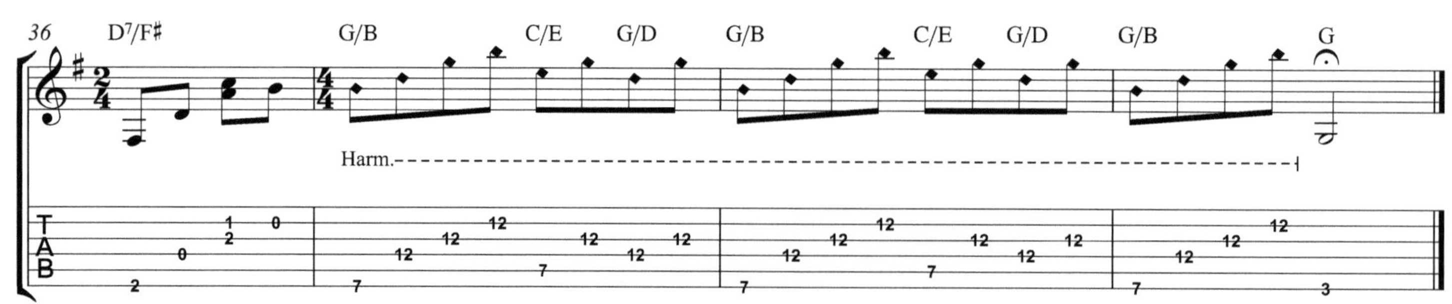
36
D7/F#
G/B
C/E
G/D
G/B
C/E
G/D
G/B
G
Harm.
TAB

SUPPER'S READY

This section contains parts of my interviews with Steve Hackett and Tony Banks.

"Genesis has always been about the writing." Tony Banks

I. LOVER'S LEAP

Steve: "I started the song with Mike and Tony on Hangstrons BJ-12-string - all playing the chords with the same shapes [see photos and score at the end of the section], and Peter and Phil on vocals. At the same time, Mike was playing Vox Bass Pedal, and sometimes, the cello. After a while, Tony played the Hohner Pianet N, and Peter, the flute. Phil was always on the percussion."

Tony: "It was my guitar part, and then we wrote the melody. It was one of those times when you got something that is probably special about it. It was an excellent place to start. I didn't know it was going to be such a long song. It was kind of a normal follow-up to *The Musical Box*, and we went through one or two ideas.

I played a twelve-string guitar through Leslie, which had a lot of depth. I always used a slow Leslie because of its grace, and it just made every song richer. I also played the Hohner Pianet through a fuzz. We got a slightly different effect out of it, rarely used because in those days we had the piano sound with a soft attack."

II. THE GUARANTEED ETERNAL SANCTUARY MAN

Steve: In this part of the song, I began to play with my Gibson Les Paul, and I used the Duo Fuzz.

Tony: "This one I wrote on the guitar a couple of years before recording it. When the kids sang: 'we will rock you, rock you little snake, we will keep you snug and warm,' I was on a Hammond organ, playing the same chord [Am6] from the beginning. It was just the secret joy of sounds, a nice quality. We got some kids on the street to sing that part. It was quite funny. I think we've worked very well in the context of the song, kind of the pure versus the evil."

III - IKHNATON AND ITSACON AND THEIR BAND OF MERRY MEN

Steve: "The solo in the middle is a written melody. I practiced it with Mike until I found something that I liked. I used the Duo Fuzz, but nowadays, I am using SamAmp."

IV. HOW DARE I BE SO BEAUTIFUL?

Tony: "In the recording, I played the acoustic piano, and John Burns [sound engineer], with the fader, would take away the instrument attack. So, at the beginning of each note, there was no sound. As I hold the note, he would raise the volume and then bring it down. That is how he got the effect that you hear in the recording."

V. WILLOW FARM

Steve: "On *Willow Farm,* I used the Duo Fuzz for single lines, but I recorded part of it just going to the amp using natural distortion."

Tony: "Peter Gabriel had previously composed the song. We took it and inserted it in the middle of *Supper's Ready*. I used the Mellotron Brass. I think I double-tracked the piano [the actual piano], the organ playing the top line with a bit of distortion. A good sound came out, quite quirky and exciting. The vocal performance on that was nice. It is a strong piece of music even just per se, outside *Supper's Ready*."

VI. APOCALYPSE IN 9/8

Steve: "In the vamp of *Apocalypse In 9/8*, I used a fender champ clean sound, but nowadays in the shows, to punch more, I use Pete Cornish Iron treble booster pedal.

In the end, I just used super fuzz with repeat echo: three guitars - two playing the harmony and one with another line, good phrases."

Tony: "This section was a solid piece of music with great vocal performance. It was just a great combination of sounds, a high point of our career at that point. It is just good and evil because obviously, the final part is pretty much good triumphing over bad. I think it has great lyrics, and it was fantastic on stage."

VII. A SURE AS EGGS IS EGGS

Steve: At the end of the song, I used Tonebender pedal, sometimes using it with volume pedal to remove the attack."

Tony: "Peter sounded fantastic. The idea of going from section to section without necessarily repeating them all the time was probably one of my biggest influences in the group.

Steve felt that *Supper's Ready* was the strongest moment of the older Genesis experience, and so did Tony. They are both very proud of that piece.

Players/Instruments:

Peter Gabriel - Lead & Backing Vocals, Flute, Oboe
Tony Banks - Hammond L122, Mellotron MK II, Hohner Pianet N, Hagstrom BJ-12 string, Acoustic Piano, Backing Vocals
Steve Hackett - Black Gibson Les Paul Custom, Hagstrom BJ-12-string
Mike Rutherford - Hagstrom BJ-12 string, Rickenbacker 4001 Bass, Vox Bass Pedal, Cello, Backing Vocals
Phil Collins - Drums, Backing Vocals, Percussion, Tubular Bells

Supper's Ready: Guitar Specifics

Chord Shapes

In photos 46-48, Steve shows the chords at the beginning of *Super's Ready*: Mike, Tony, and he played them together, precisely in the same way.

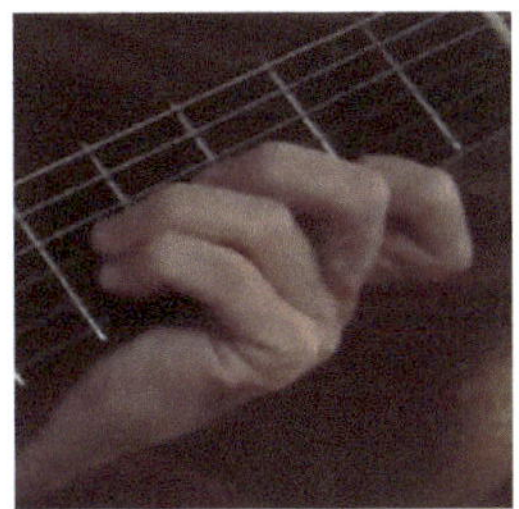

Photo 69: Steve playing
Am6: measure 1 [below]
by Paulo De Carvalho

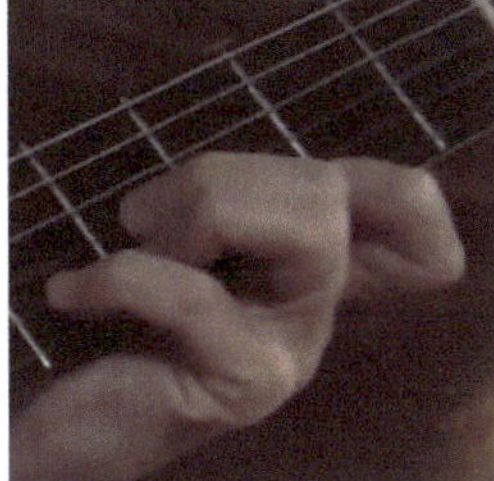

Photo 70: Steve playing
B(sus4): measure 3 [below]
by Paulo De Carvalho

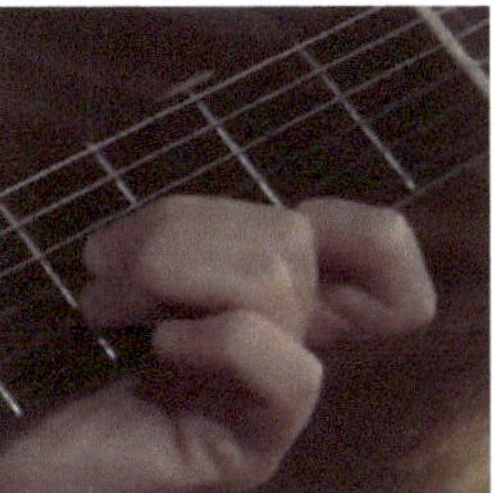

Photo 71: Steve playing
B: measure 4 [below]
by Paulo De Carvalho

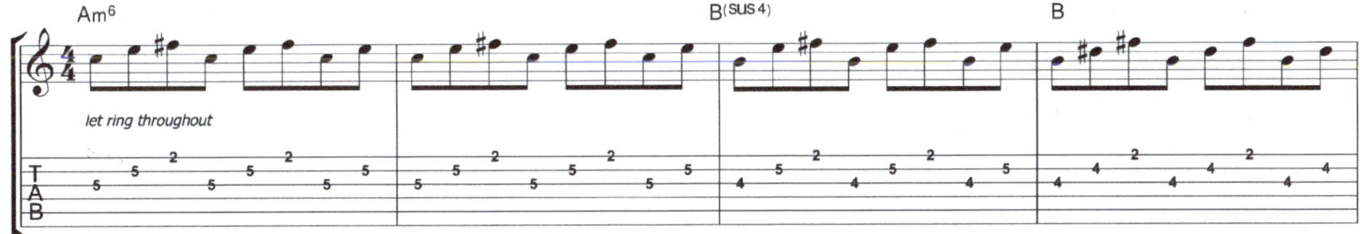

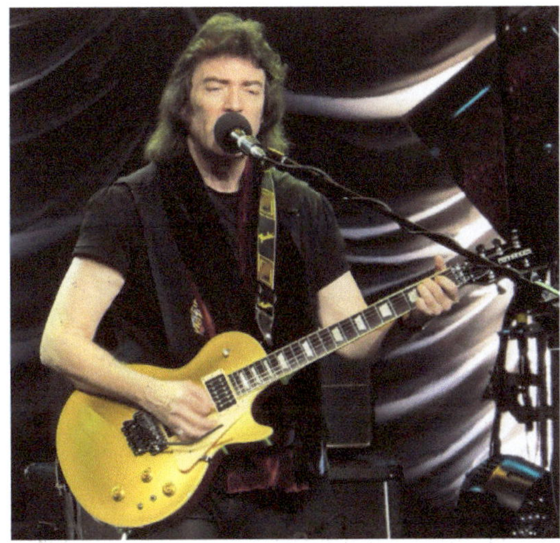

Photo 72: Steve Hackett
Photo by Paulo De Carvalho

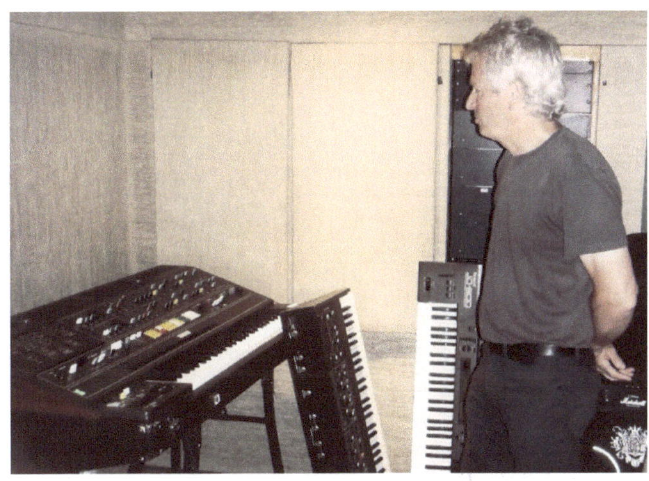

Photo 73: Tony Banks and his keyboards
Kindly provided by
Alan Hewitt, The Waiting Room Online editor

from Genesis - *Foxtrot*

Supper's Ready

by T. Banks, P.Collins, P. Gabriel, S. Hackett, M. Rutherford

Transcribed by Paulo De Carvalho

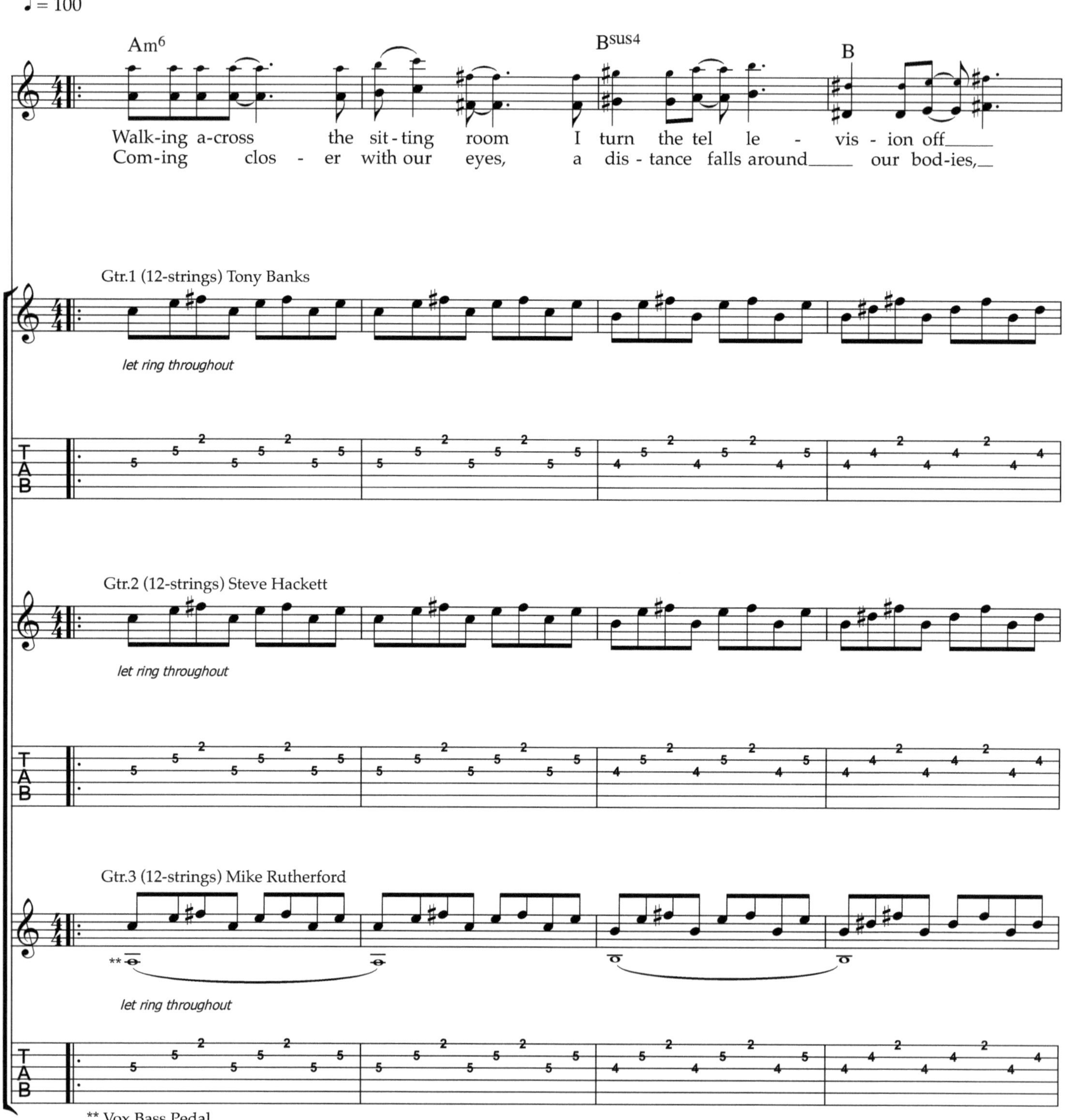

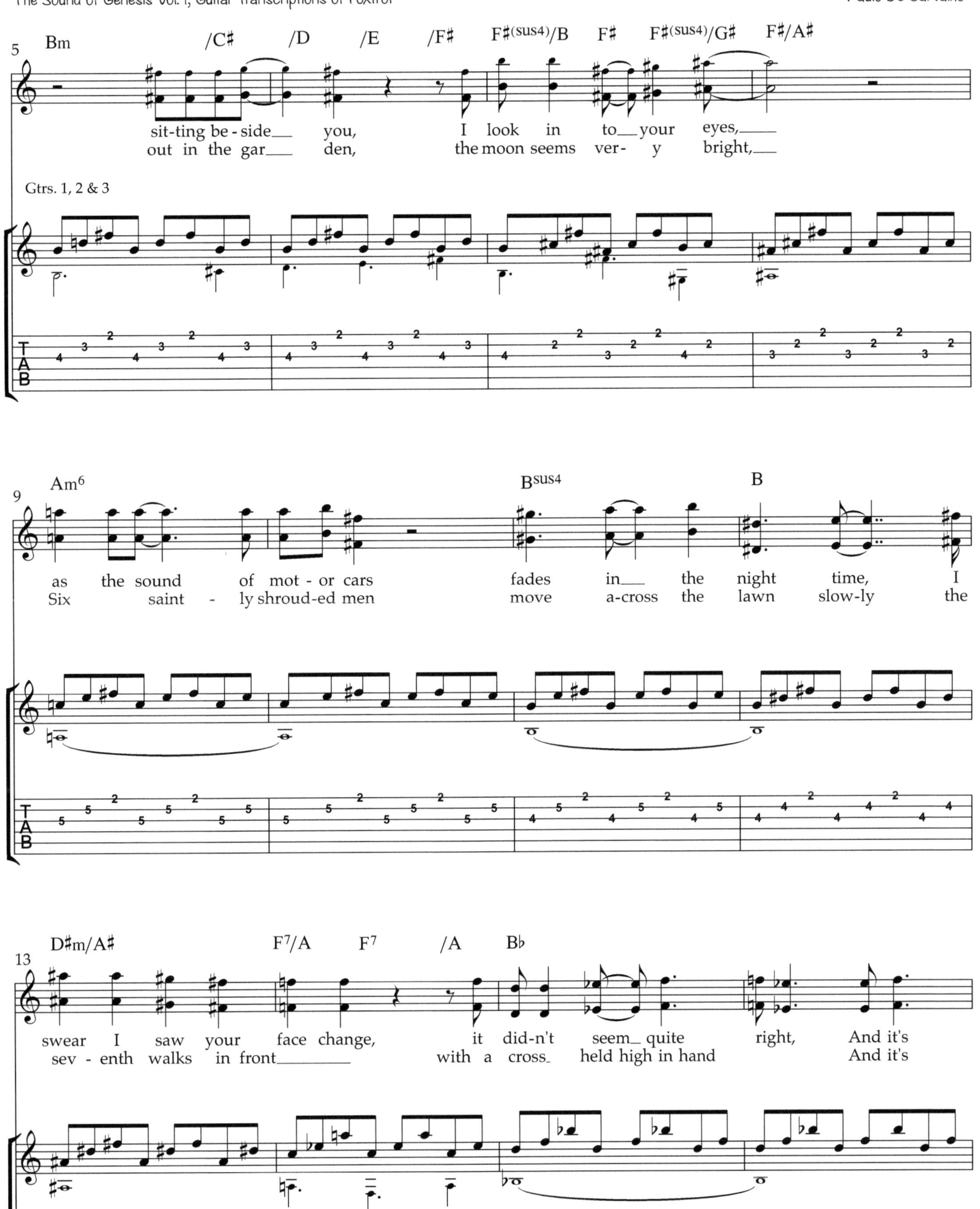
5
Bm /C♯ /D /E /F♯ F♯(sus4)/B F♯ F♯(sus4)/G♯ F♯/A♯
sit-ting be-side you, I look in to your eyes,
out in the gar den, the moon seems ver- y bright,
Gtrs. 1, 2 & 3
9
Am6 Bsus4 B
as the sound of mot-or cars fades in the night time, I
Six saint - ly shroud-ed men move a-cross the lawn slow-ly the
13
D♯m/A♯ F7/A F7 /A B♭
swear I saw your face change, it did-n't seem quite right, And it's
sev - enth walks in front with a cross held high in hand And it's

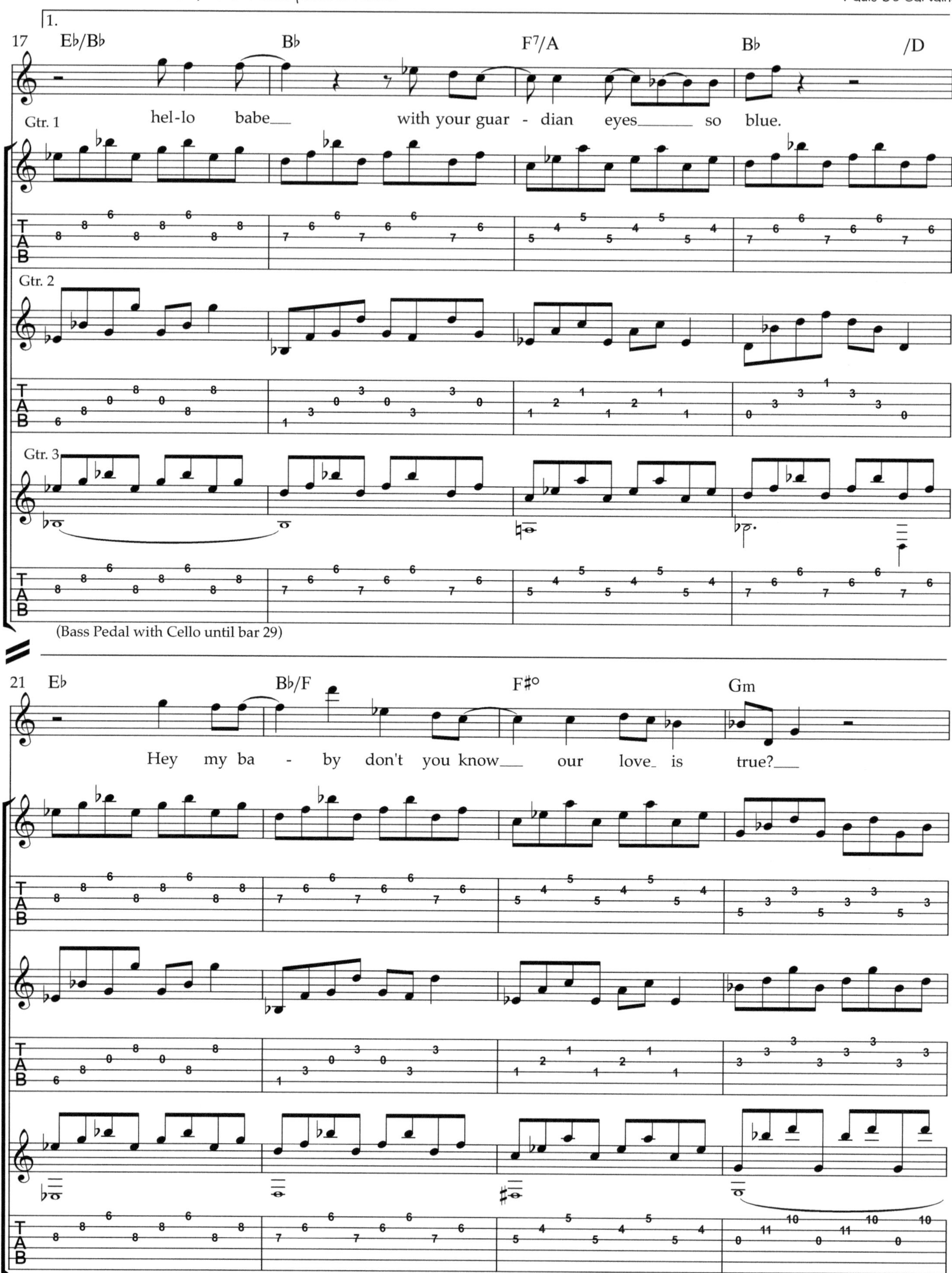
1.
17
Eb/Bb
Bb
F7/A
Bb
/D
hel-lo babe
with your guar - dian eyes so blue.
Gtr. 1
Gtr. 2
Gtr. 3
(Bass Pedal with Cello until bar 29)
21
Eb
Bb/F
F#o
Gm
Hey my ba - by don't you know our love is true?

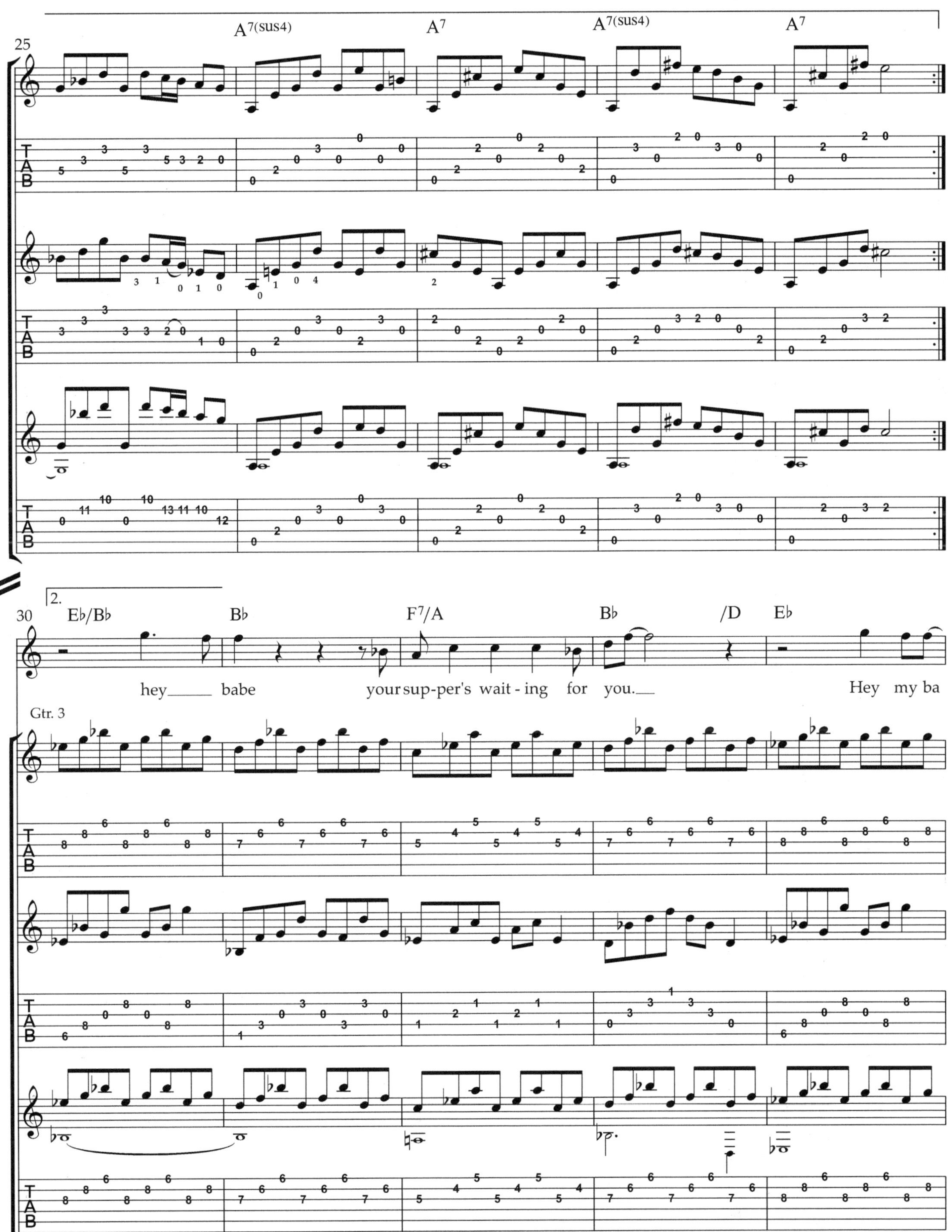
25
A7(sus4)
A7
A7(sus4)
A7
30
2.
E♭/B♭
B♭
F7/A
B♭
/D
E♭
hey___ babe your sup-per's wait - ing for you.__ Hey my ba
Gtr. 3

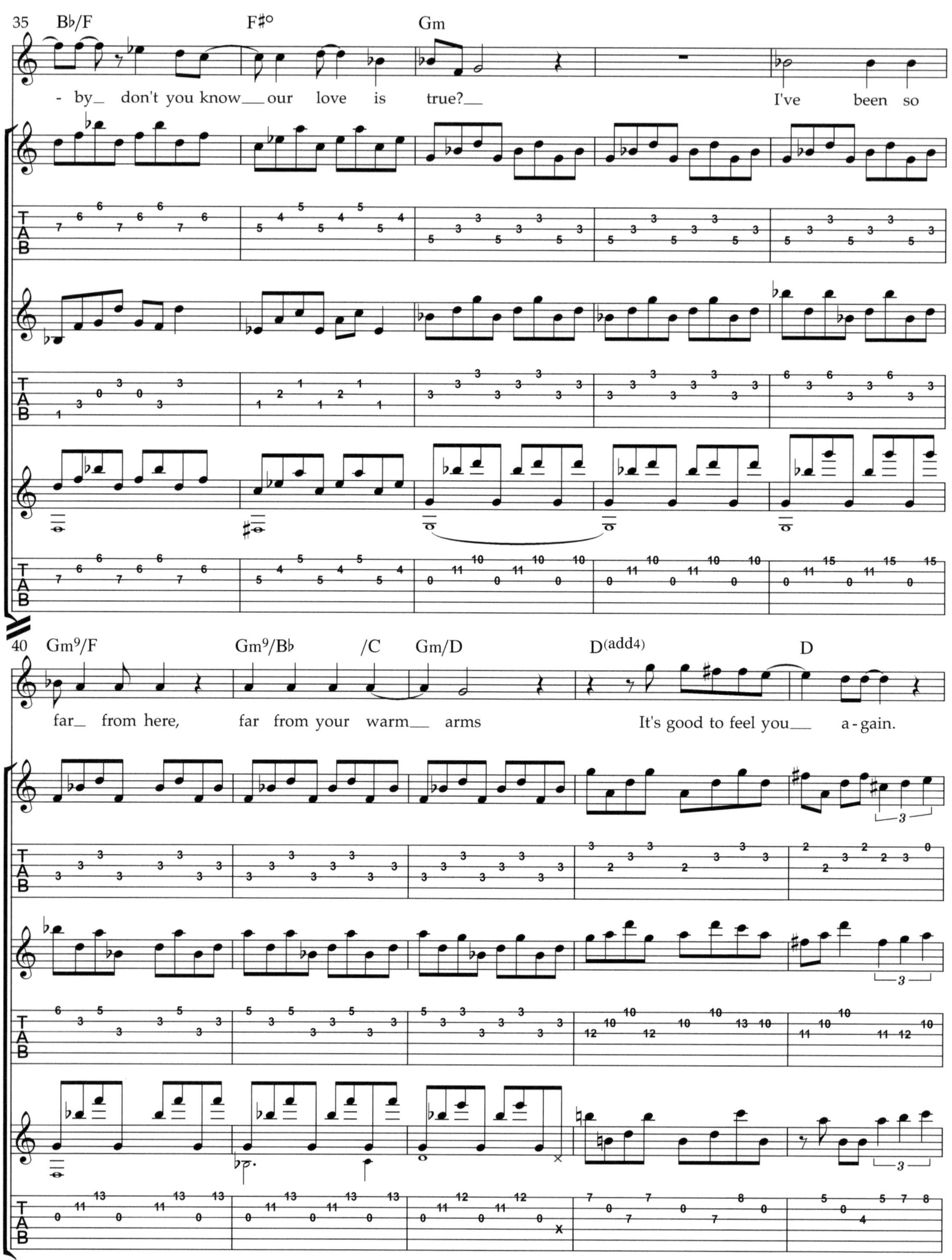
35
B♭/F
F♯o
Gm
- by_ don't you know__ our love is true?__
I've been so
40
Gm9/F
Gm9/B♭
/C
Gm/D
D(add4)
D
far_ from here, far from your warm__ arms
It's good to feel you__ a-gain.

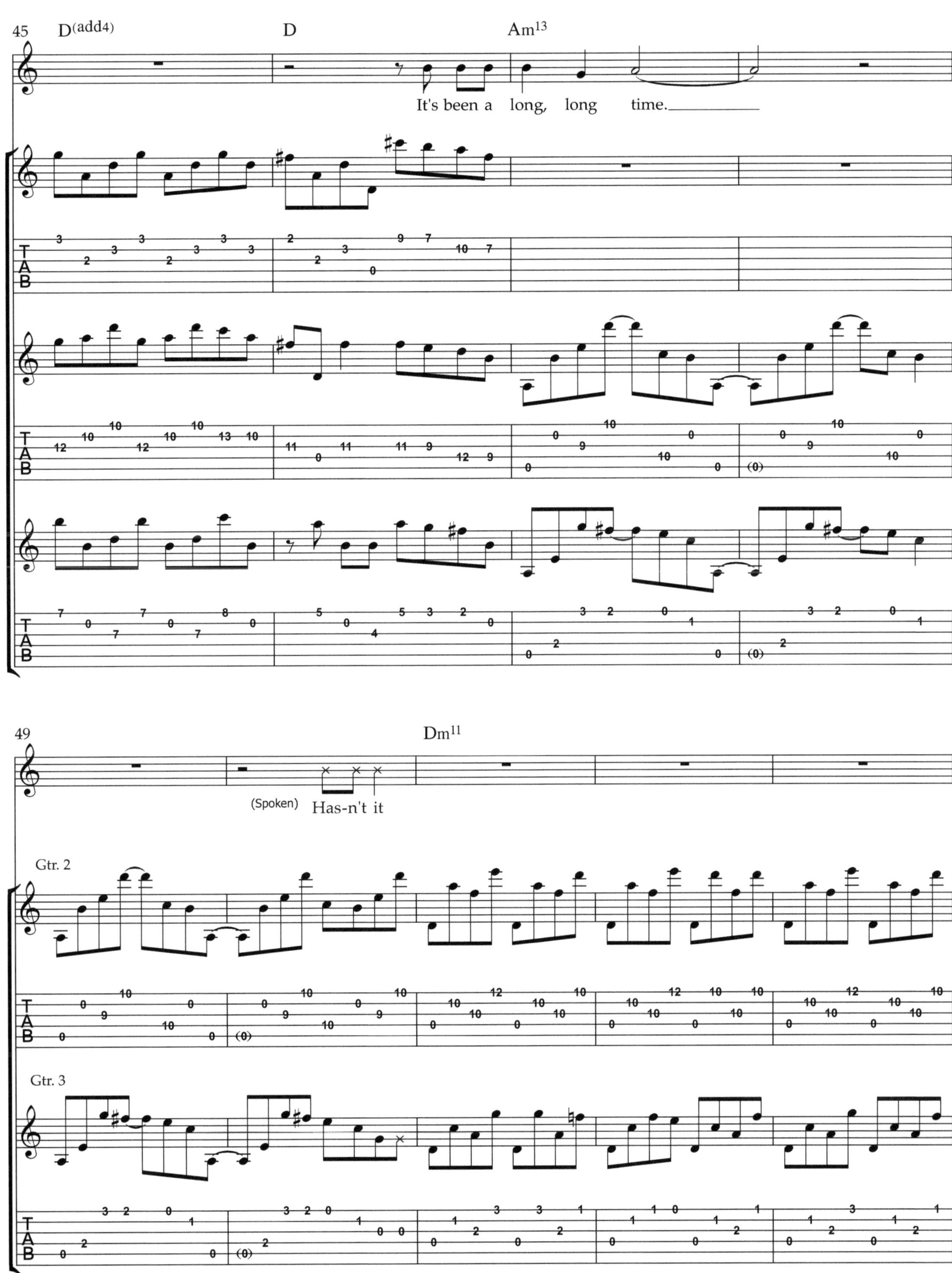
45
D(add4)
D
Am13
It's been a long, long time.
49
Dm11
(Spoken) Has-n't it
Gtr. 2
Gtr. 3

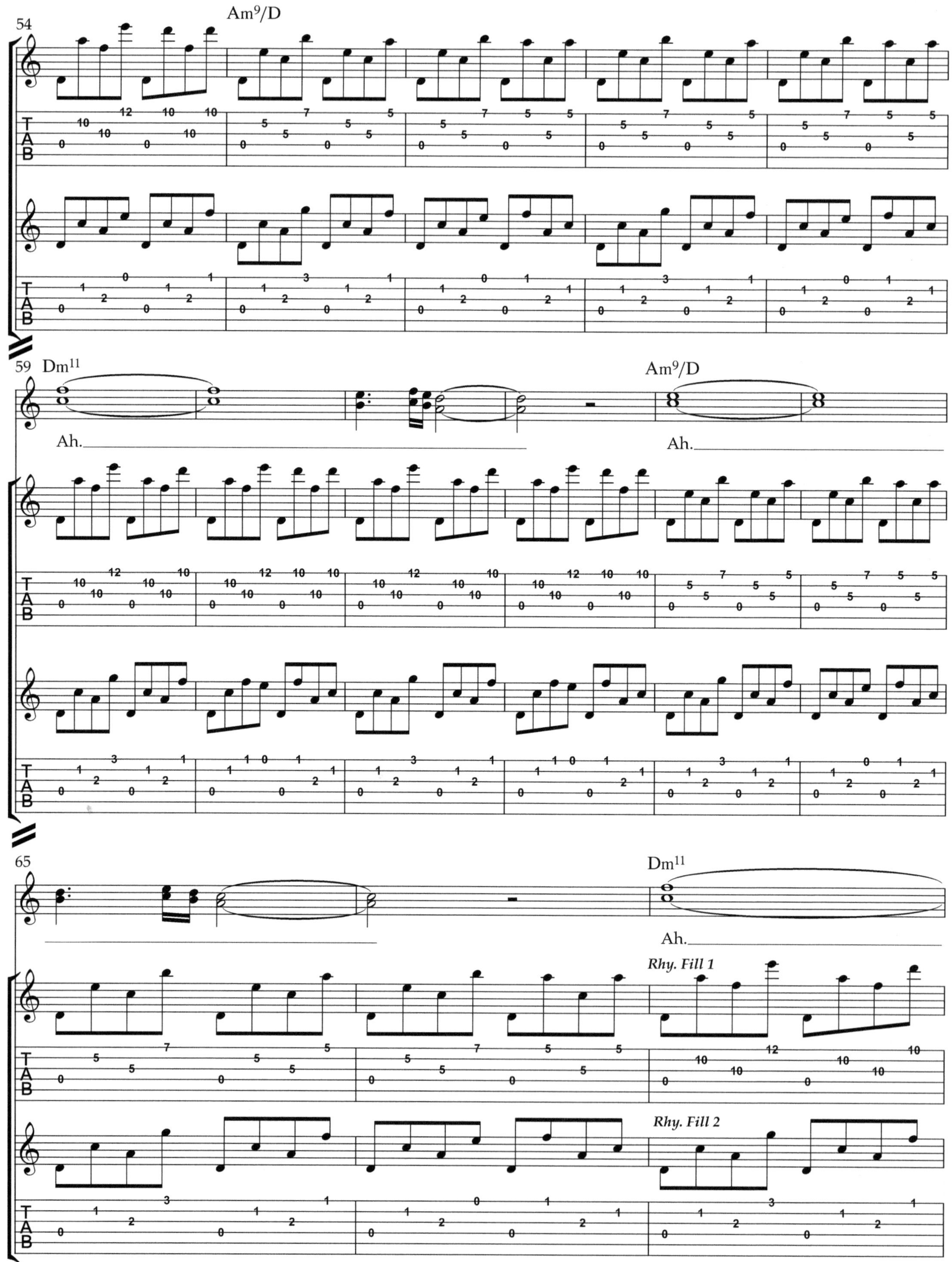
54
Am9/D
59
Dm11
Am9/D
Ah.
Ah.
65
Dm11
Ah.
Rhy. Fill 1
Rhy. Fill 2

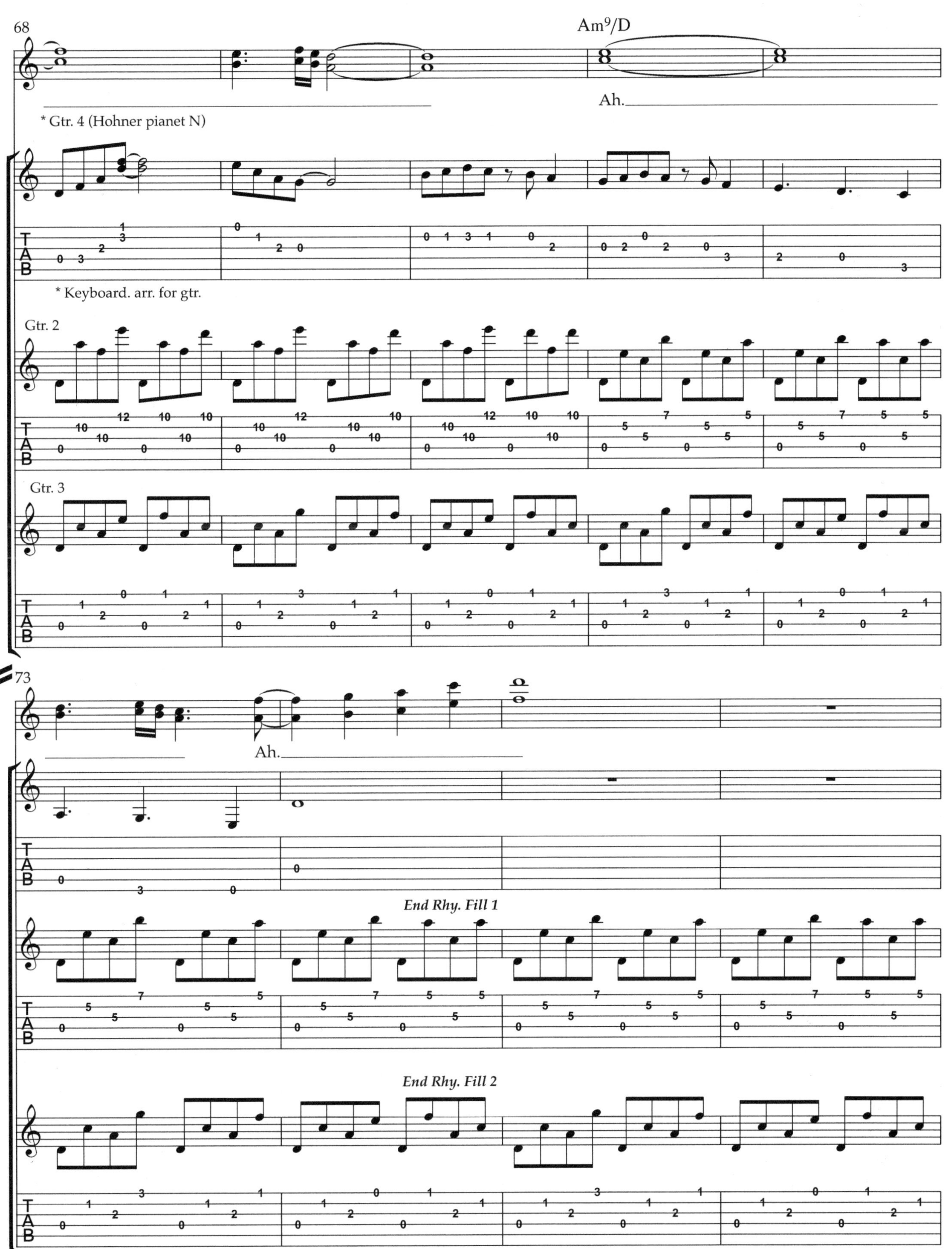
68
Am9/D
Ah.
* Gtr. 4 (Hohner pianet N)
* Keyboard. arr. for gtr.
Gtr. 2
Gtr. 3
73
Ah.
End Rhy. Fill 1
End Rhy. Fill 2

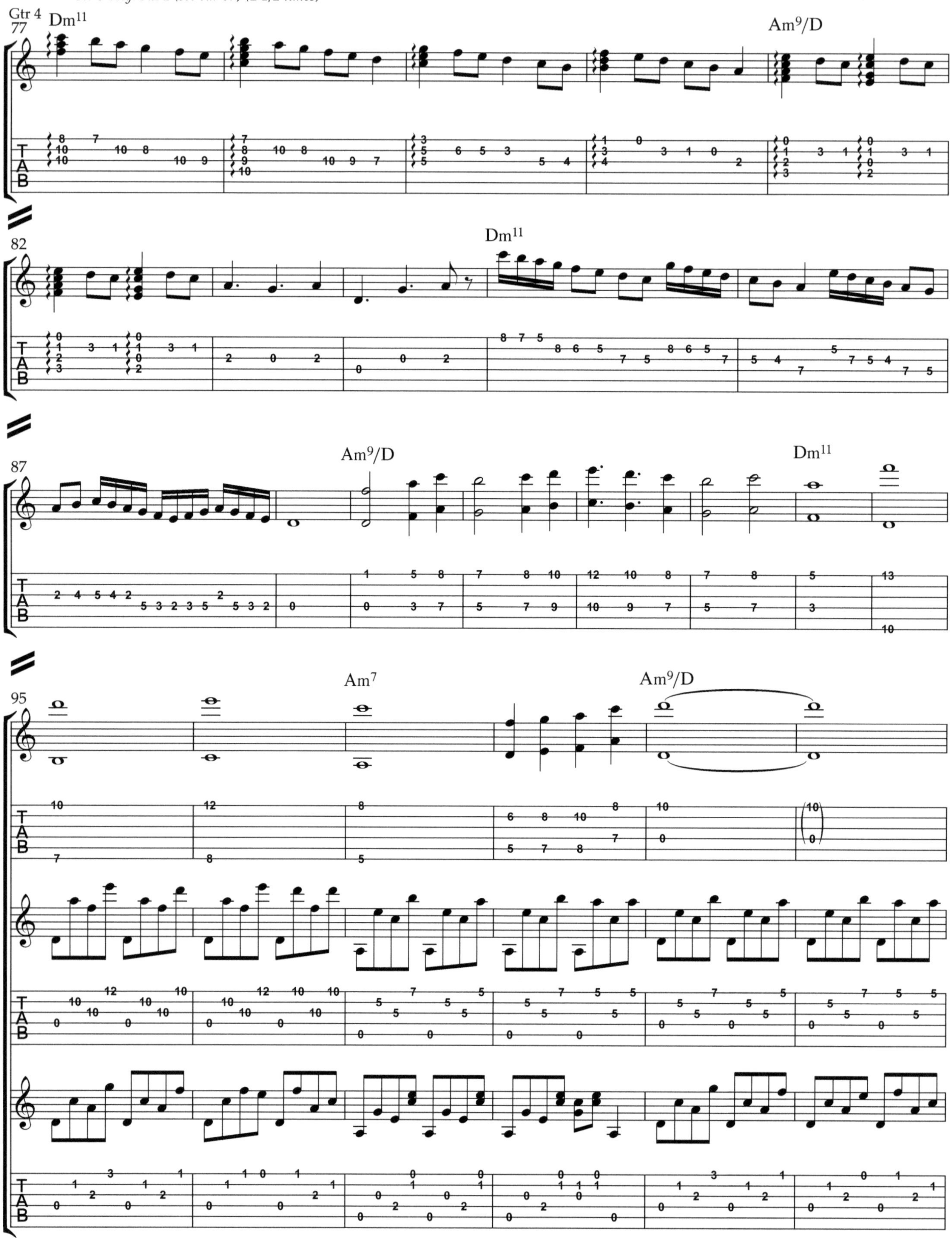
Gtr 2 Rhy. Fill 1(see bar 67) (2 1/2 times)
Gtr 3 Rhy. Fill 2 (see bar 67) (2 1/2 times)
Gtr 4
77
Dm11
Am9/D
82
Dm11
87
Am9/D
Dm11
95
Am7
Am9/D

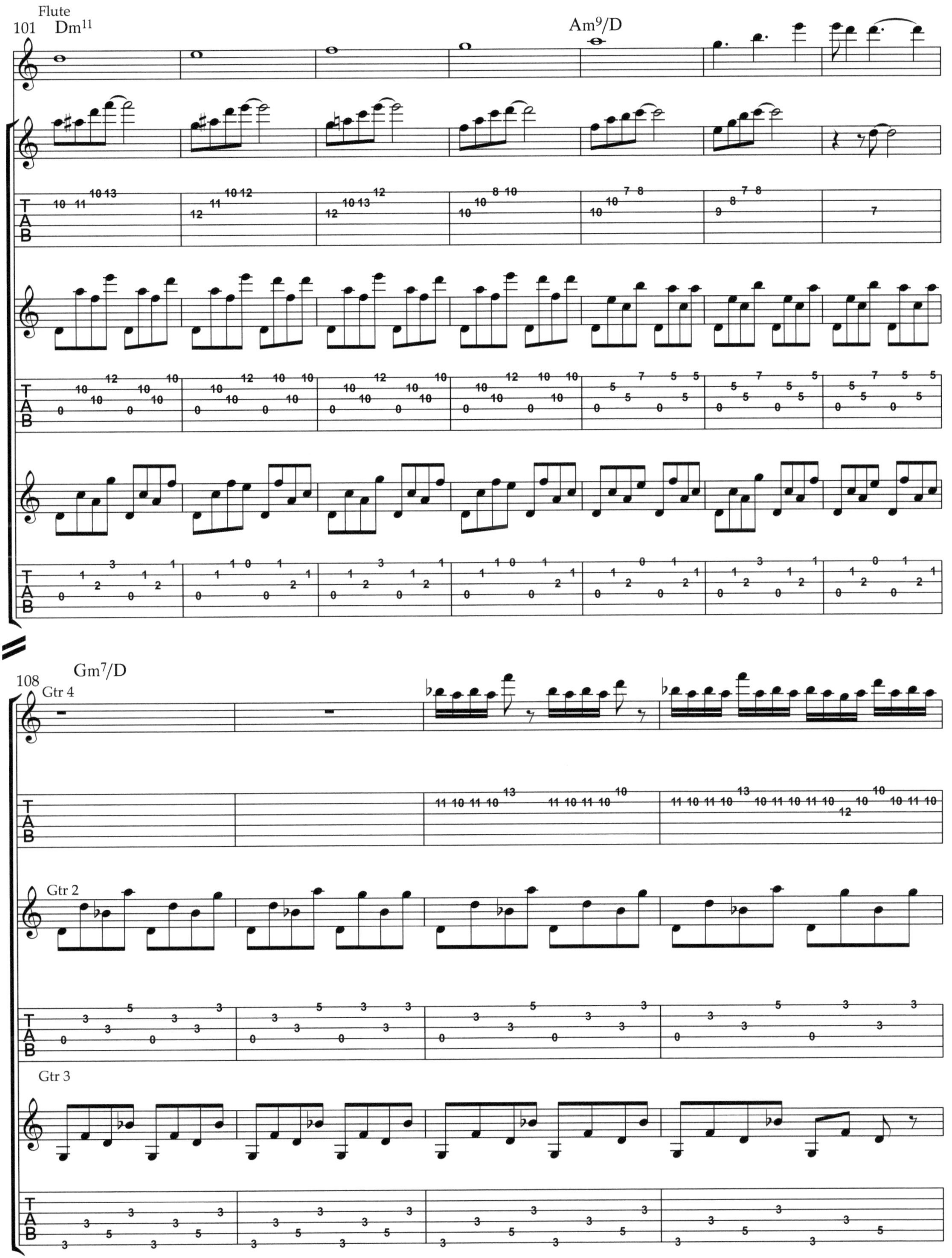
101
Flute
Dm11
Am9/D
108
Gm7/D
Gtr 4
Gtr 2
Gtr 3

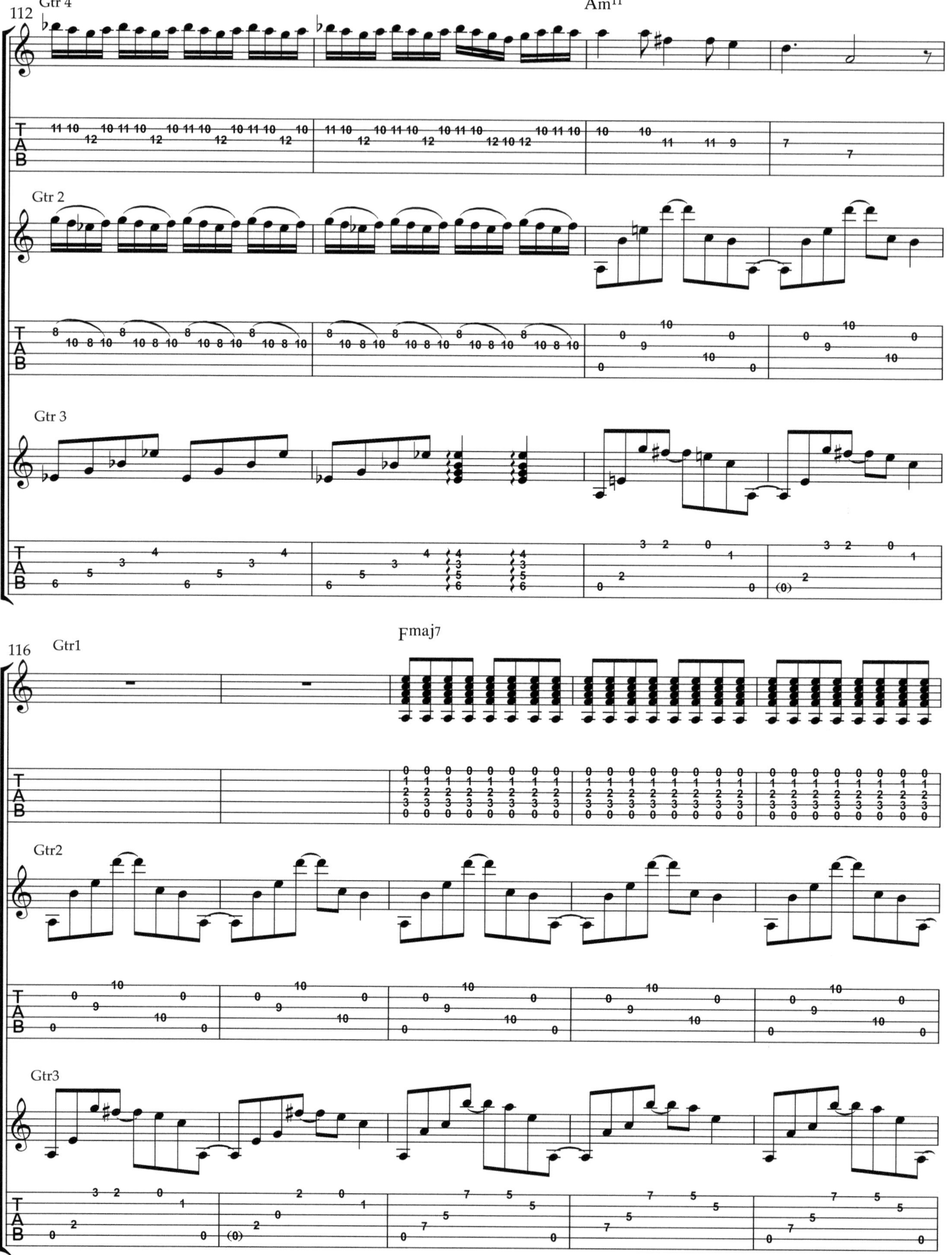
112
Gtr 4
Am11
Gtr 2
Gtr 3
116
Gtr1
Fmaj7
Gtr2
Gtr3

II. THE GUARANTEED ETERNAL SANCTUARY MAN

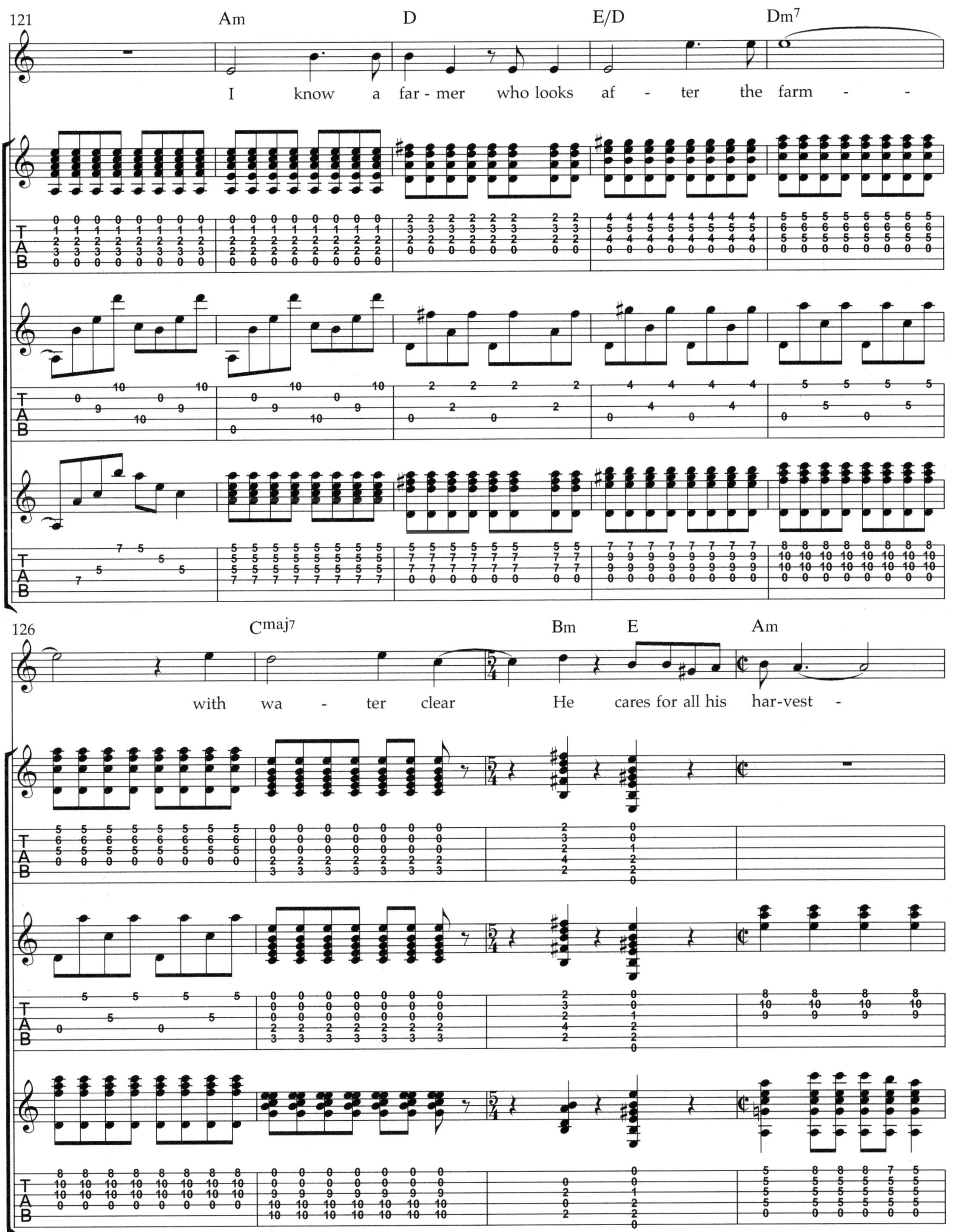

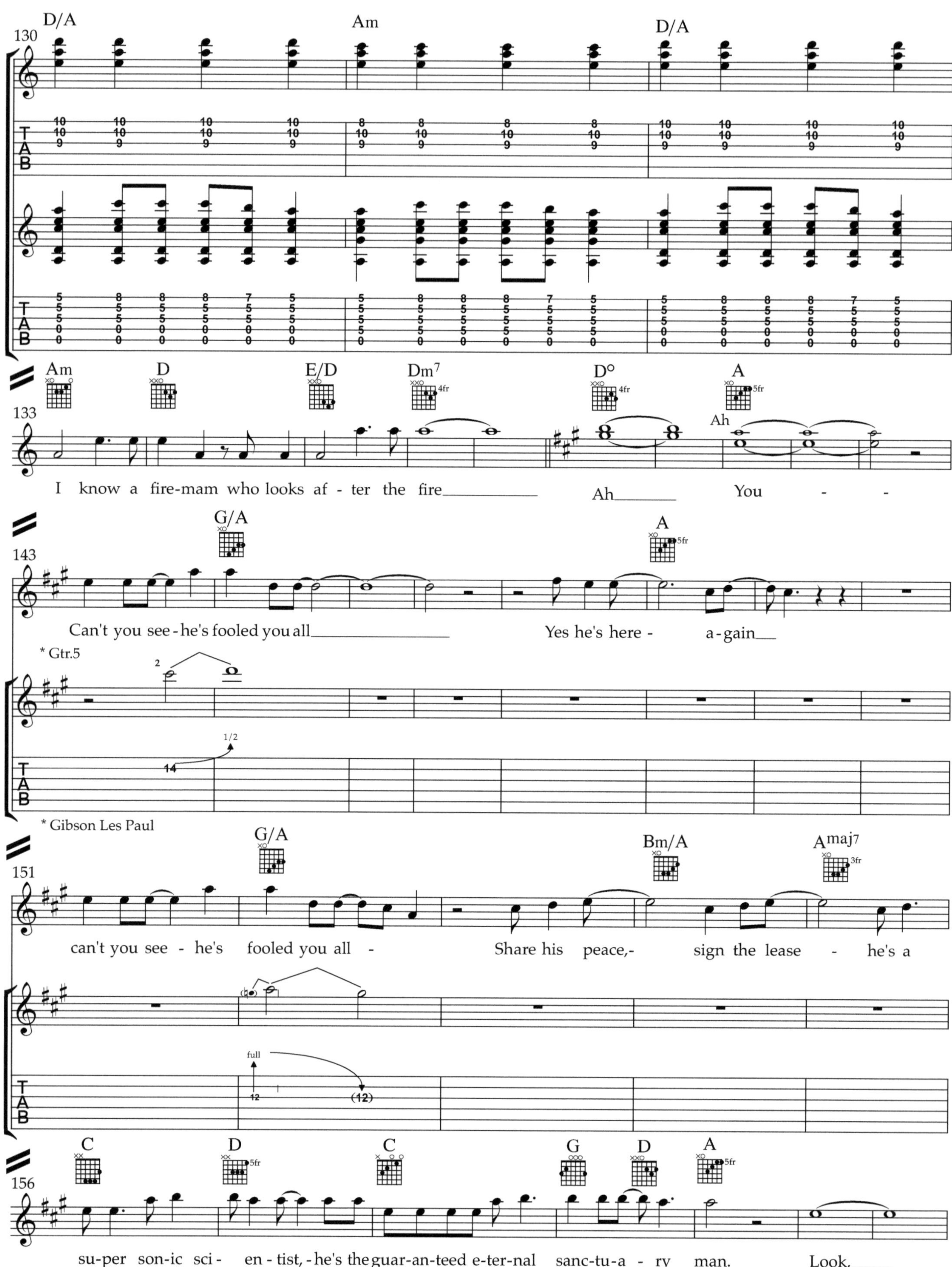
D/A
130
Am
D/A
Am
D
E/D
Dm7
4fr
D°
4fr
A
5fr
133
Ah
I know a fire-mam who looks af - ter the fire
Ah
You - -
G/A
A
5fr
143
Can't you see - he's fooled you all
Yes he's here - a - gain
* Gtr.5
1/2
* Gibson Les Paul
G/A
Bm/A
Amaj7
3fr
151
can't you see - he's fooled you all -
Share his peace,- sign the lease - he's a
full
C
D
5fr
C
G
D
A
5fr
156
su-per son-ic sci - en - tist, - he's the guar-an-teed e-ter-nal sanc-tu-a - ry man.
Look,

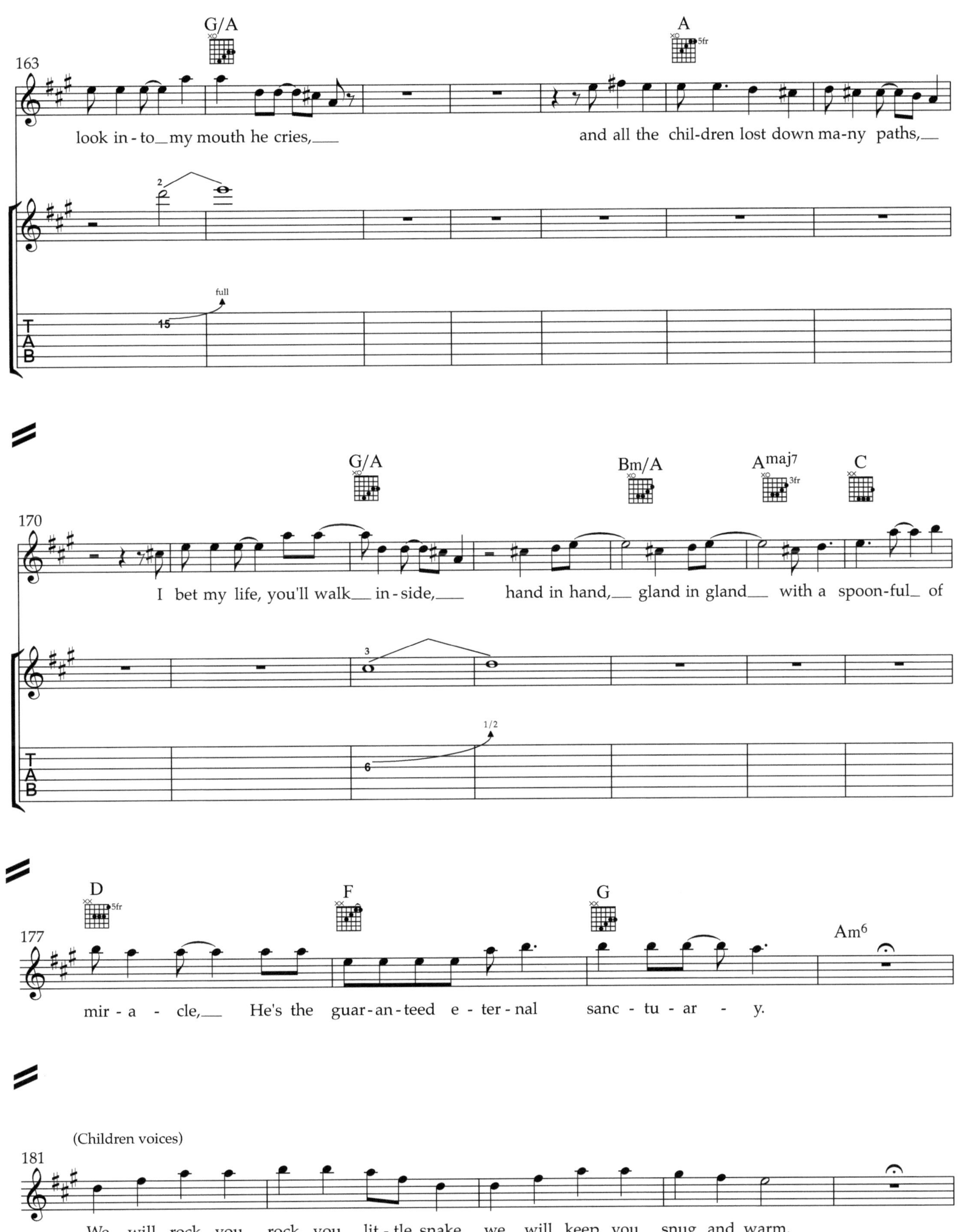
G/A
A
5fr
163
look in - to_ my mouth he cries,___
and all the chil-dren lost down ma-ny paths,___
2
full
15
T
A
B
G/A
Bm/A
Amaj7
3fr
C
170
I bet my life, you'll walk___ in - side,___
hand in hand,___ gland in gland___ with a spoon-ful_ of
3
1/2
6
D
5fr
F
G
Am6
177
mir - a - cle,___ He's the guar-an-teed e - ter - nal sanc - tu - ar - y.
(Children voices)
181
We will rock you, rock you lit - tle snake, we will keep you snug and warm.

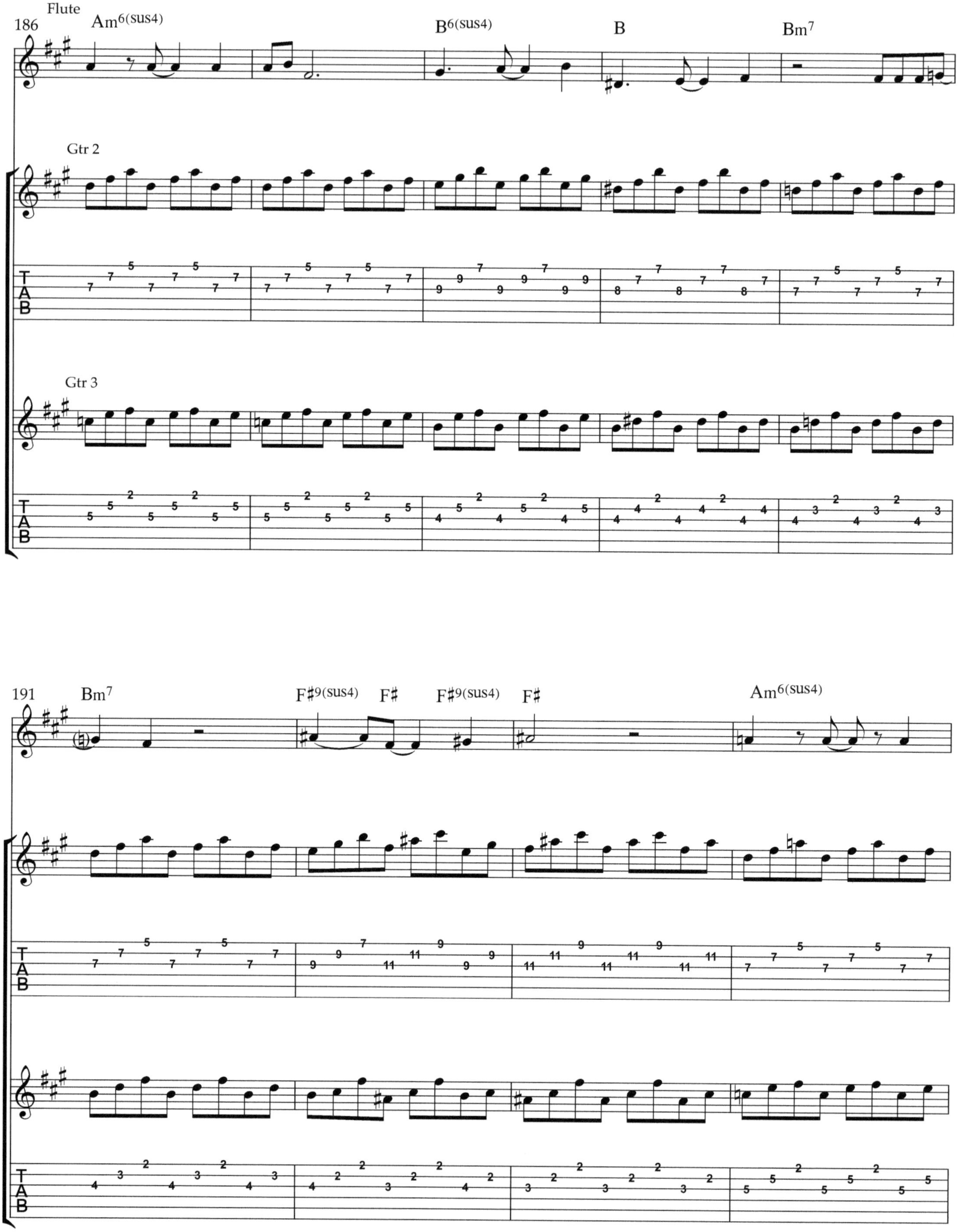

186 Flute

Am6(sus4) B6(sus4) B Bm7

Gtr 2

TAB

Gtr 3

TAB

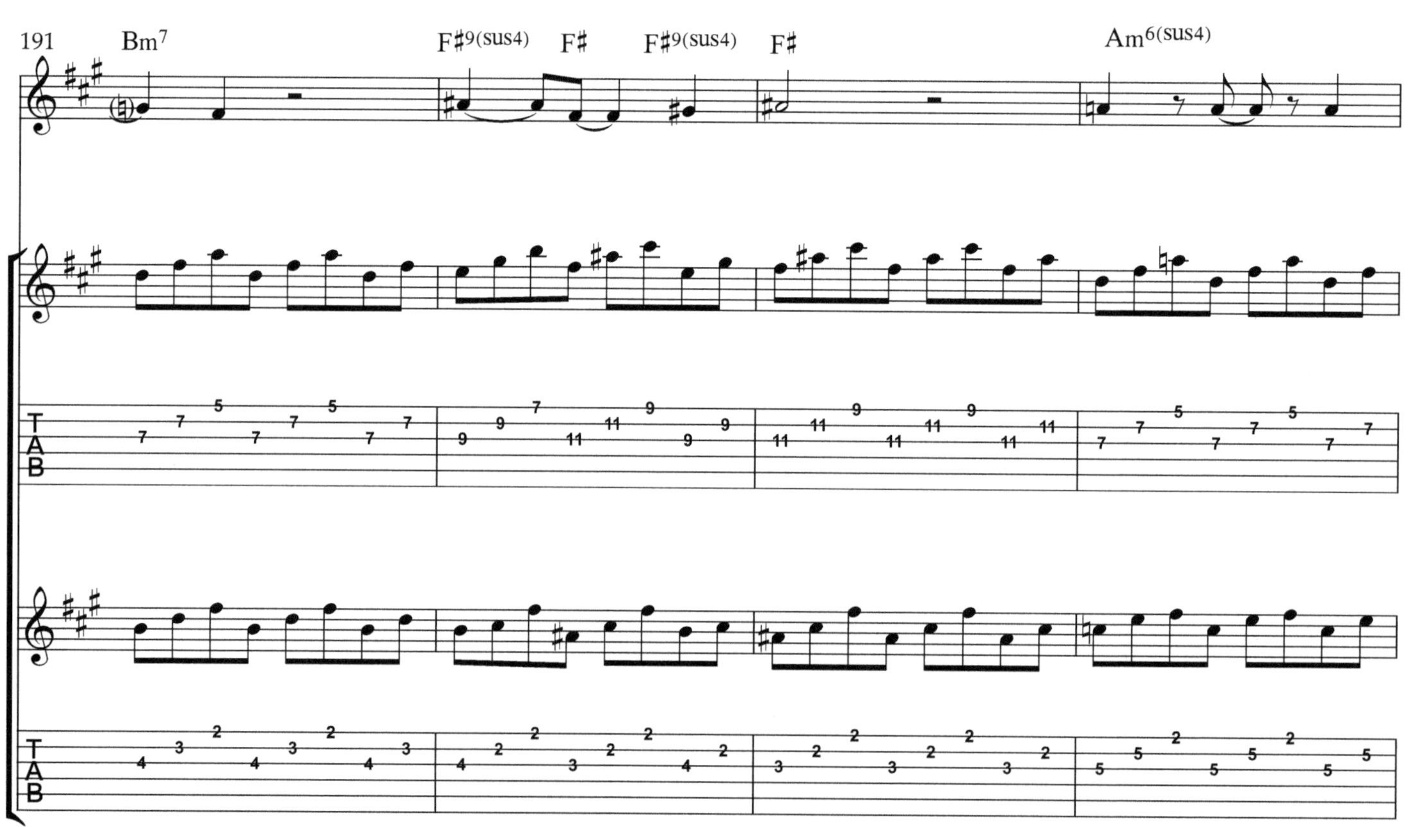

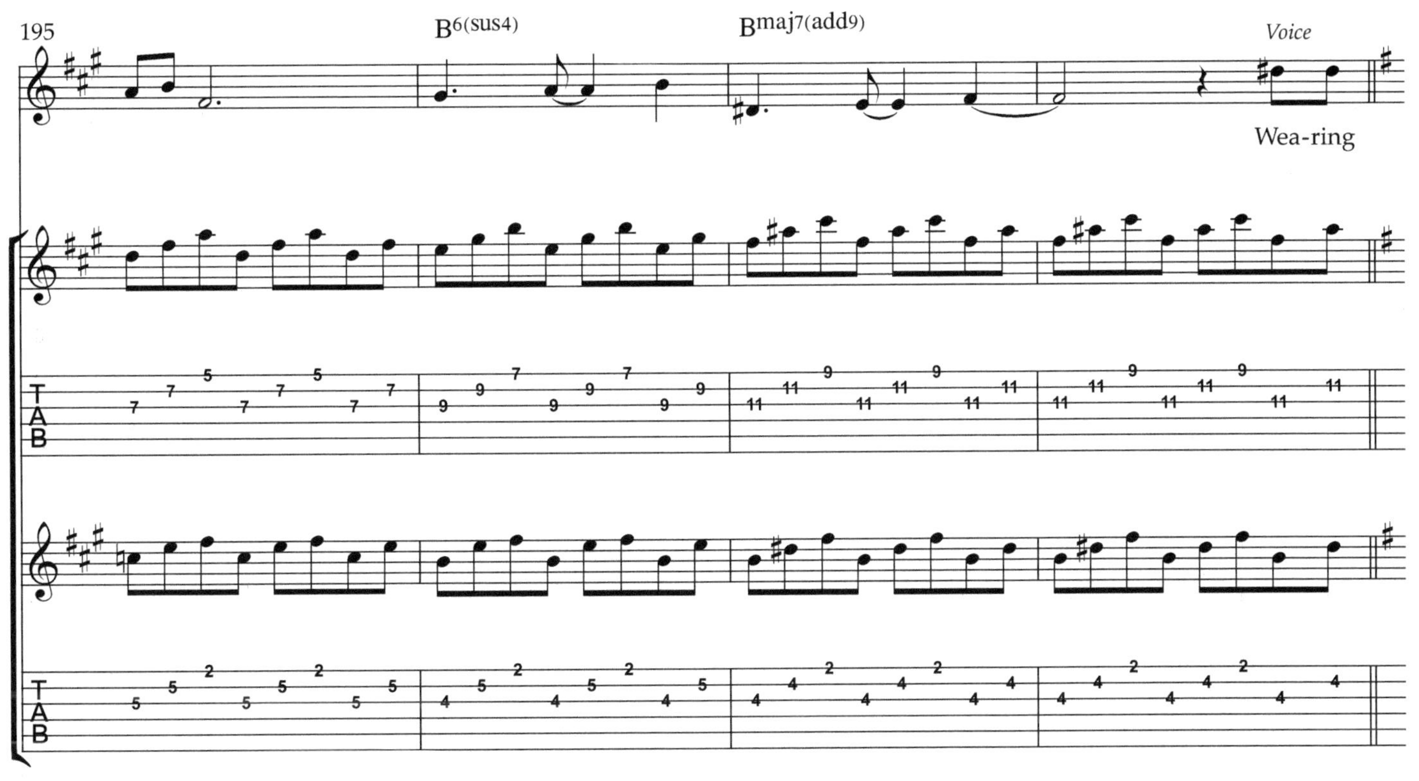

III. IKHNATON AND ITSACON AND THEIR BAND OF MARRY MEN

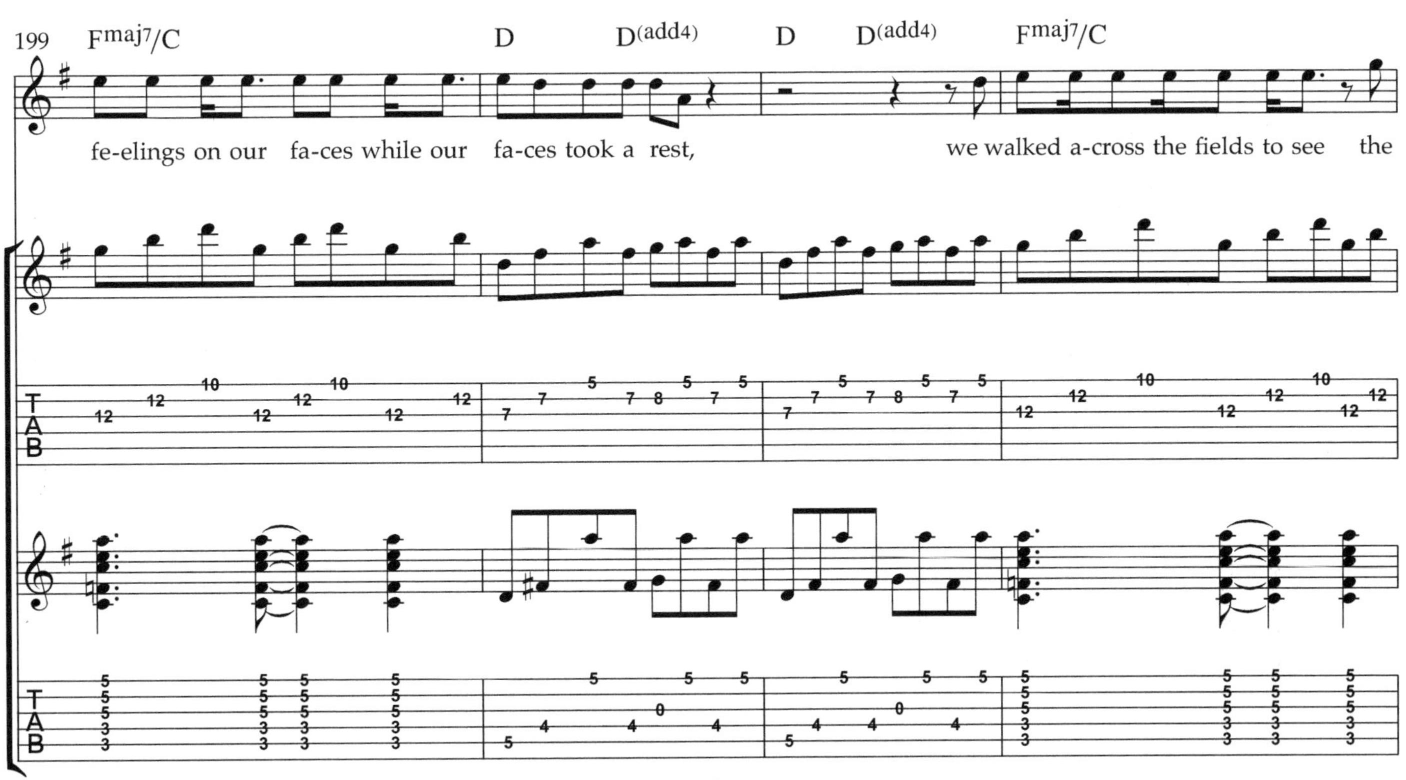

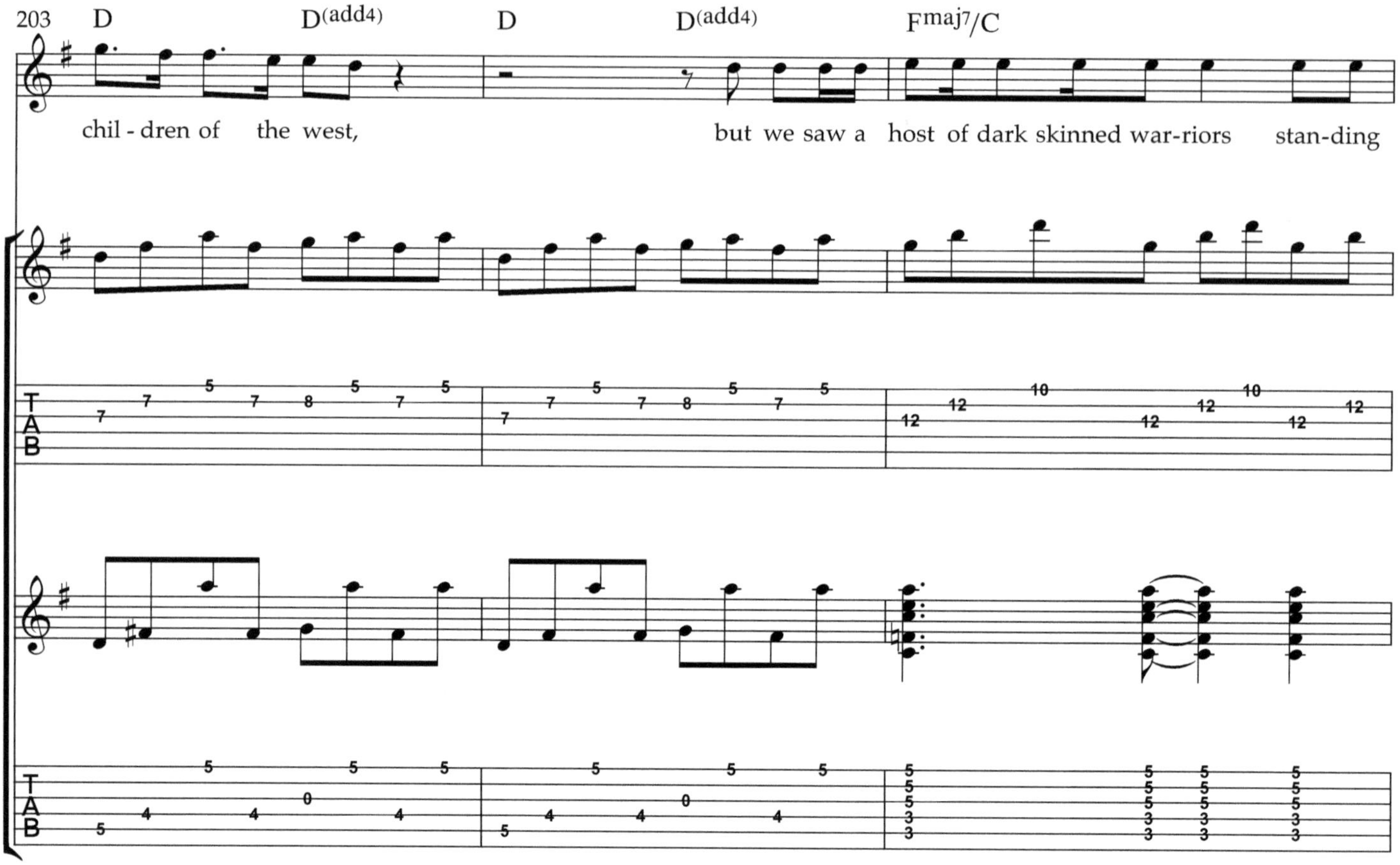

203 D D(add4) D D(add4) Fmaj7/C

chil - dren of the west, but we saw a host of dark skinned war-riors stan-ding

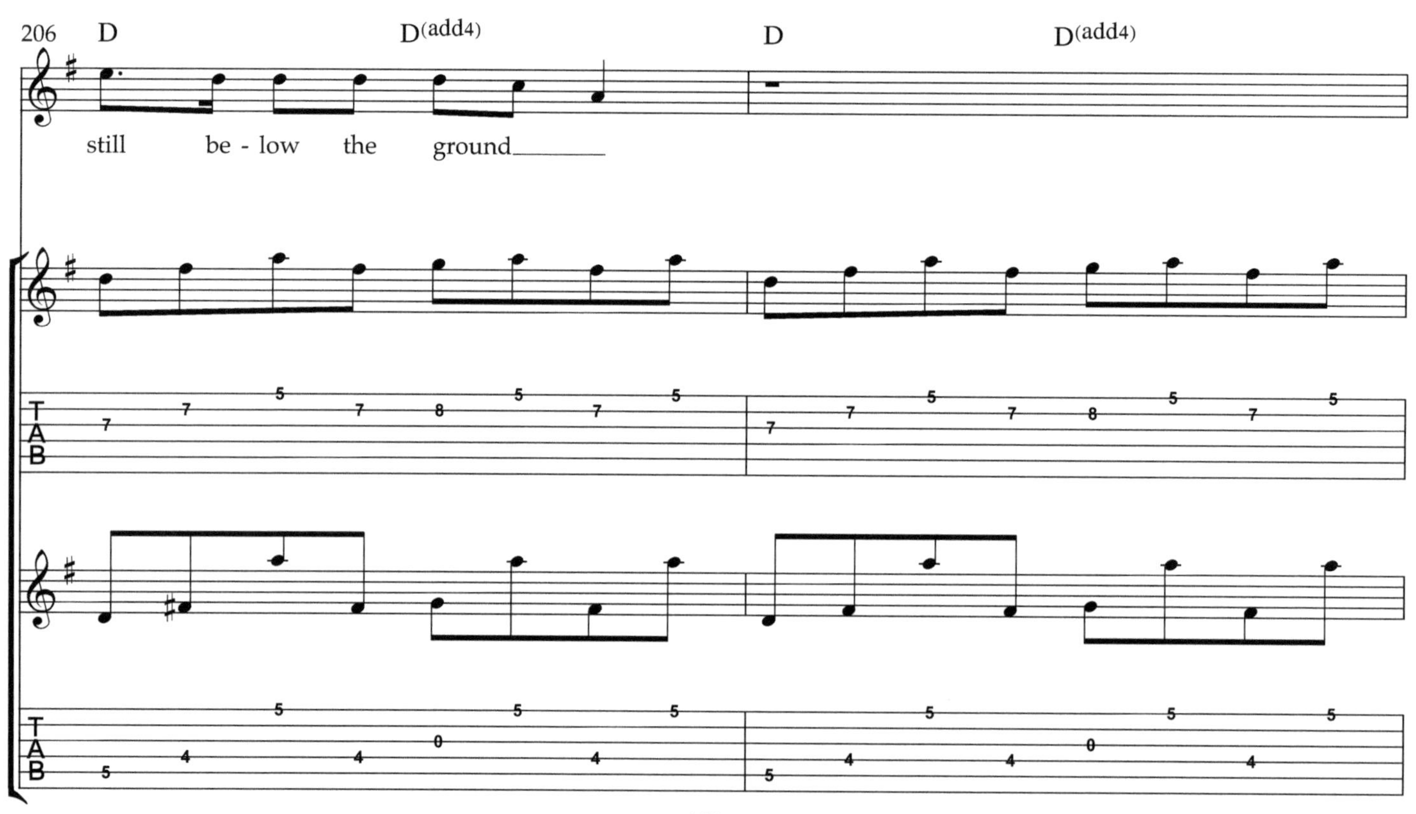

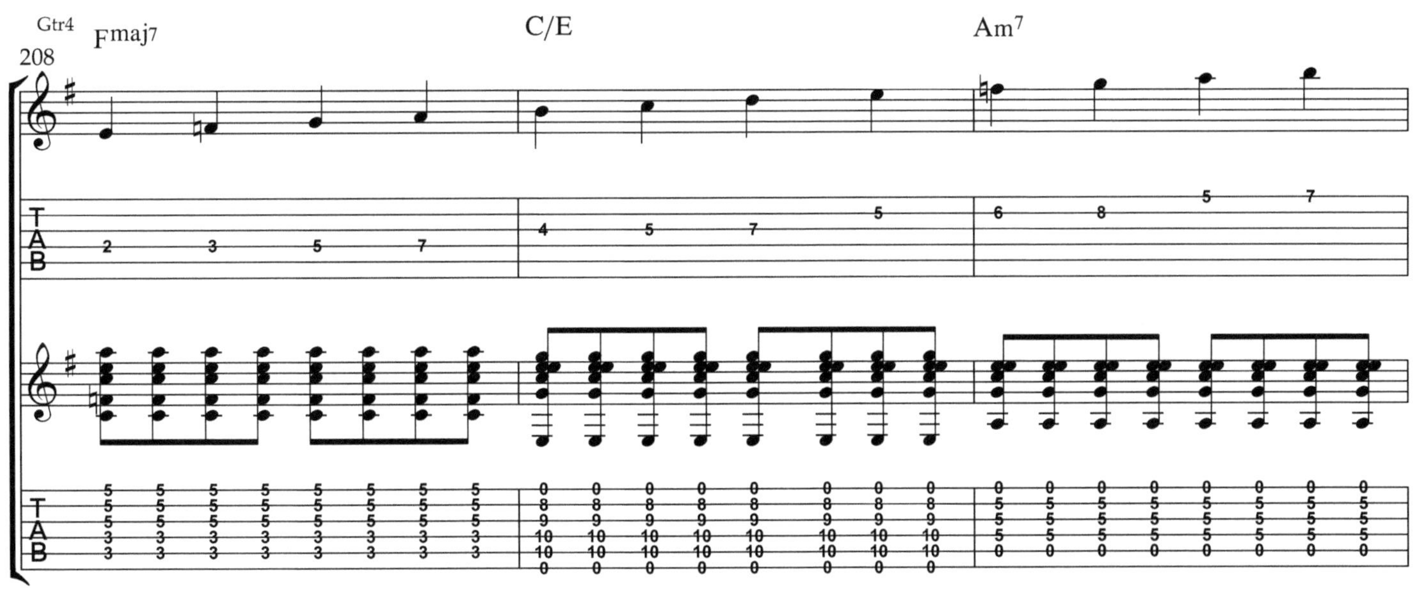

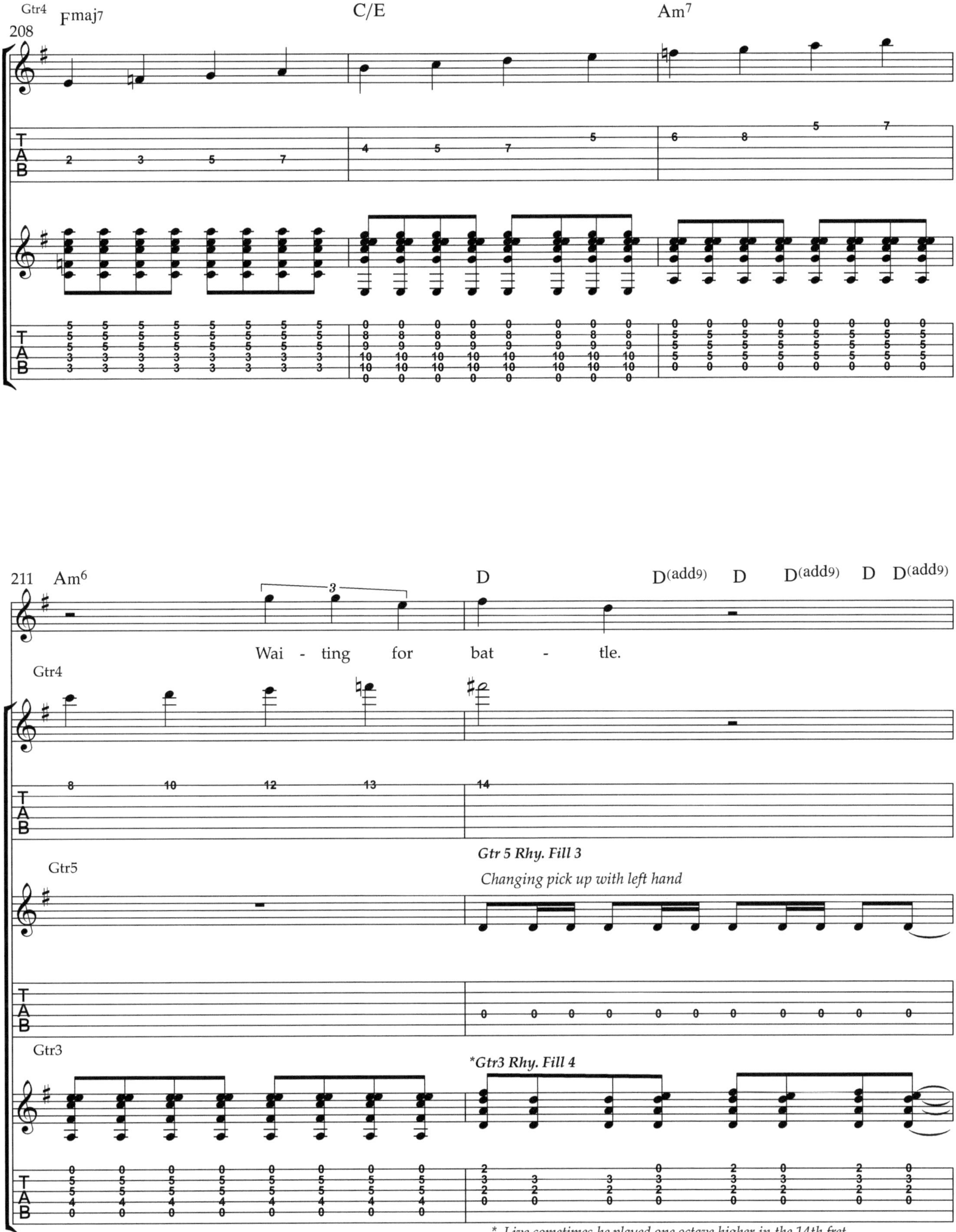

211 Am6 D D(add9) D D(add9) D D(add9)

Wai - ting for bat - tle.

Gtr4

Gtr 5 Rhy. Fill 3

Changing pick up with left hand

Gtr5

Gtr3

***Gtr3 Rhy. Fill 4**

* *Live sometimes he played one octave higher in the 14th fret*

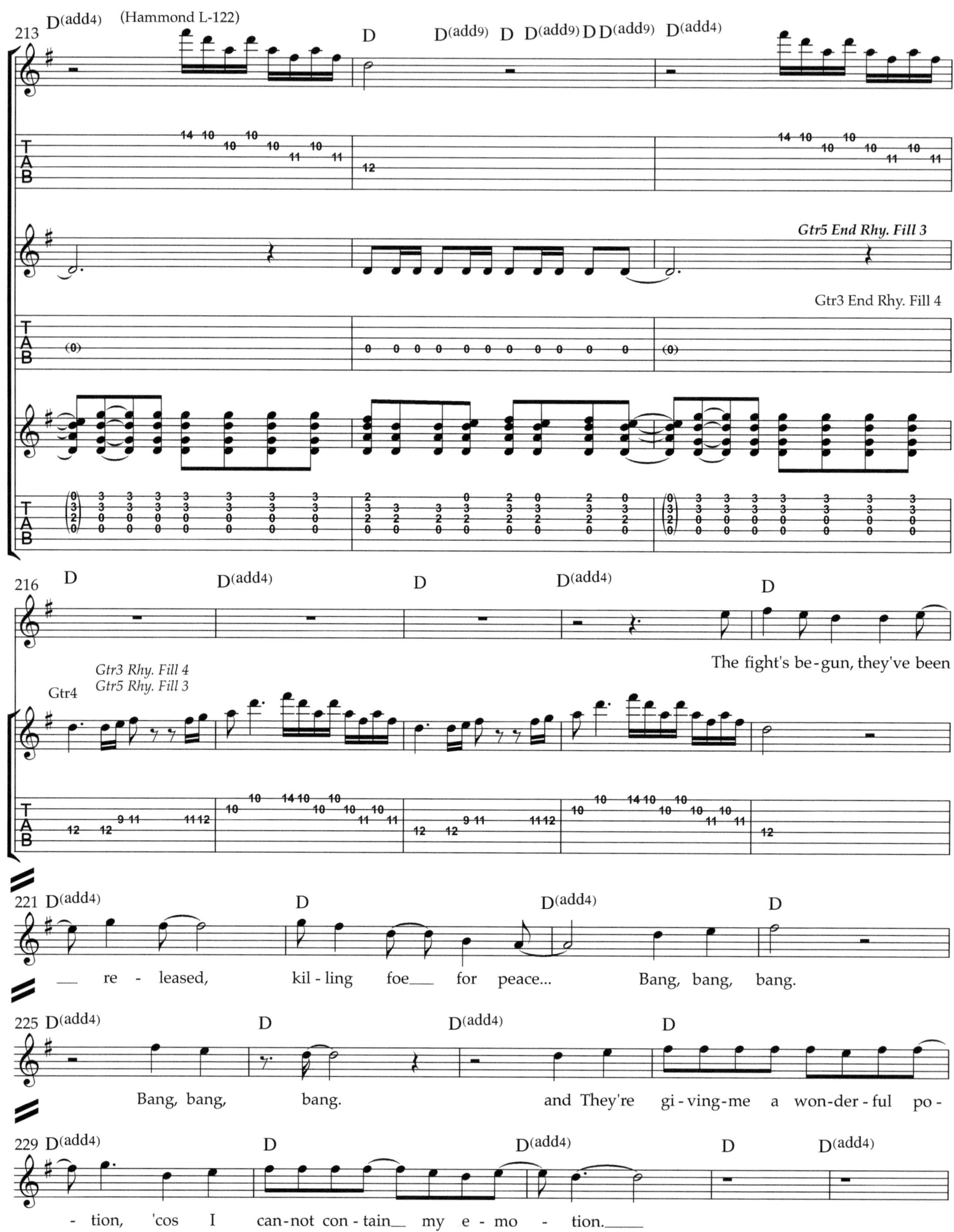
213
D(add4)
(Hammond L-122)
D
D(add9)
D
D(add9)
D
D(add9)
D(add4)
Gtr5 End Rhy. Fill 3
Gtr3 End Rhy. Fill 4
216
D
D(add4)
D
D(add4)
D
The fight's be-gun, they've been
Gtr3 Rhy. Fill 4
Gtr5 Rhy. Fill 3
Gtr4
221
D(add4)
D
D(add4)
D
re - leased, kil - ling foe for peace... Bang, bang, bang.
225
D(add4)
D
D(add4)
D
Bang, bang, bang. and They're gi - ving-me a won-der - ful po -
229
D(add4)
D
D(add4)
D
D(add4)
- tion, 'cos I can-not con - tain my e - mo - tion.

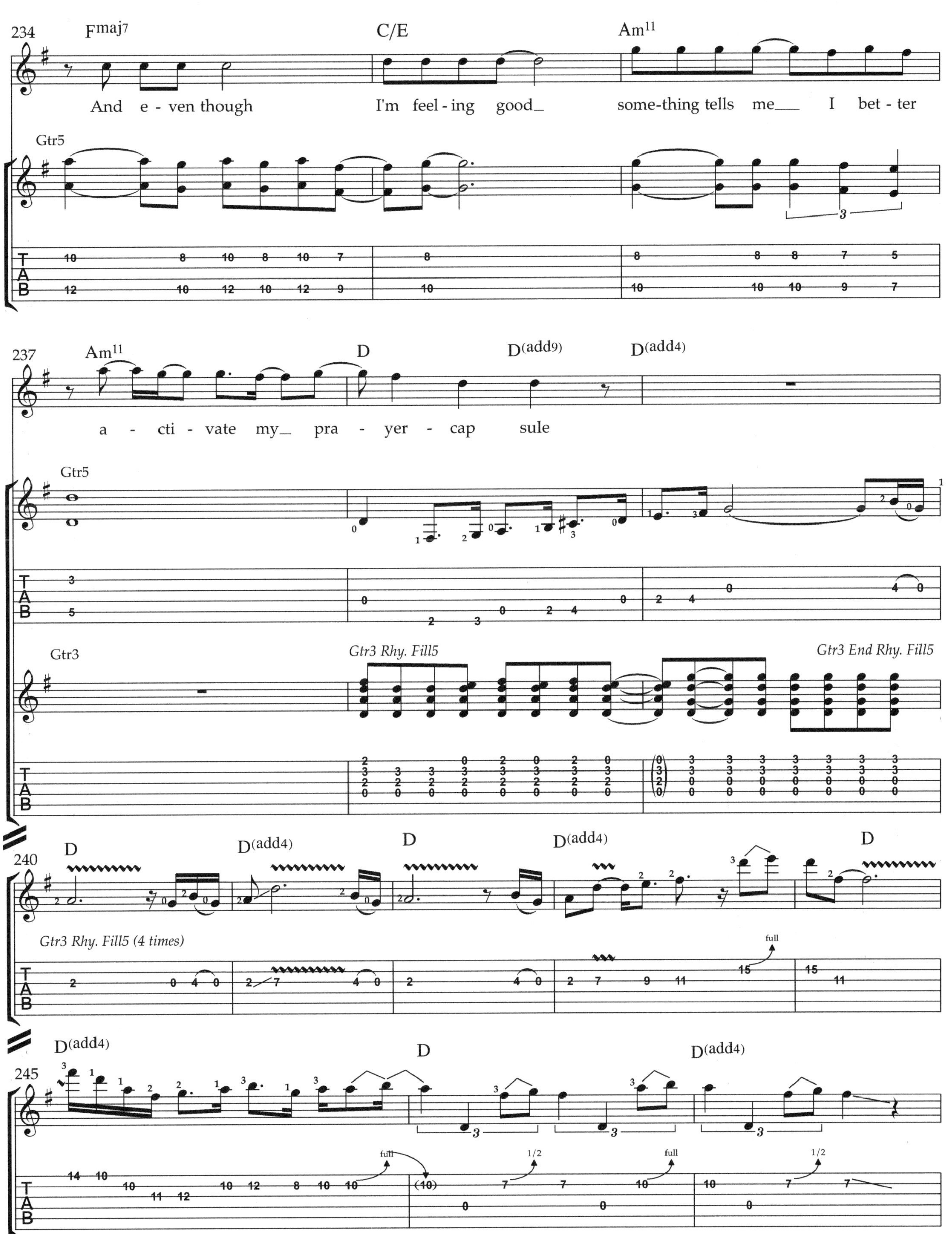
234
Fmaj7
C/E
Am11
And e - ven though I'm feel - ing good_ some-thing tells me__ I bet - ter
Gtr5
237
Am11
D
D(add9)
D(add4)
a - cti - vate my_ pra - yer - cap sule
Gtr5
Gtr3
Gtr3 Rhy. Fill5
Gtr3 End Rhy. Fill5
240
D
D(add4)
D
D(add4)
D
Gtr3 Rhy. Fill5 (4 times)
full
245
D(add4)
D
D(add4)
full
1/2
full
1/2

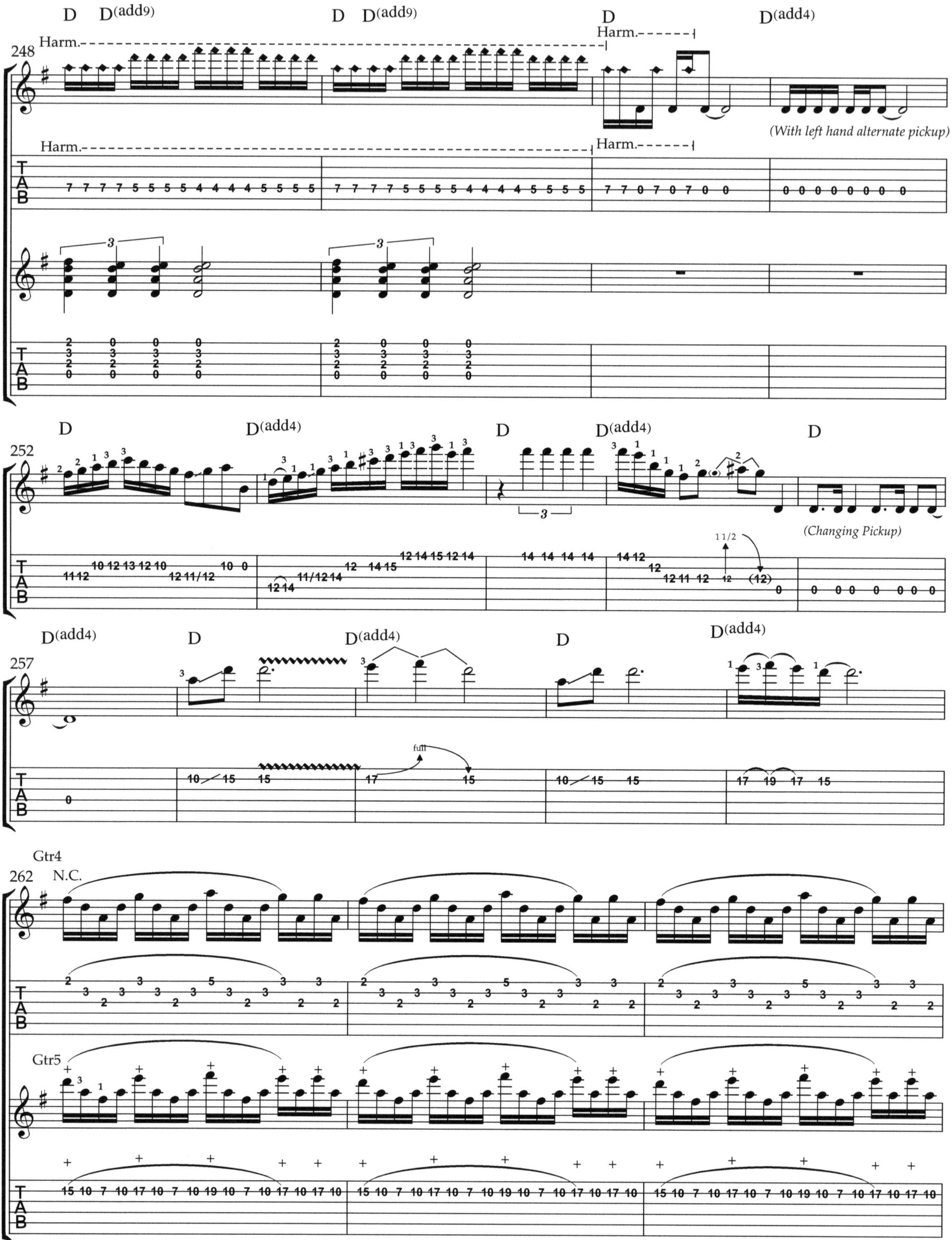
D
D(add9)
D(add4)
Harm.
(With left hand alternate pickup)
(Changing Pickup)
N.C.
Gtr4
Gtr5
full
1 1/2

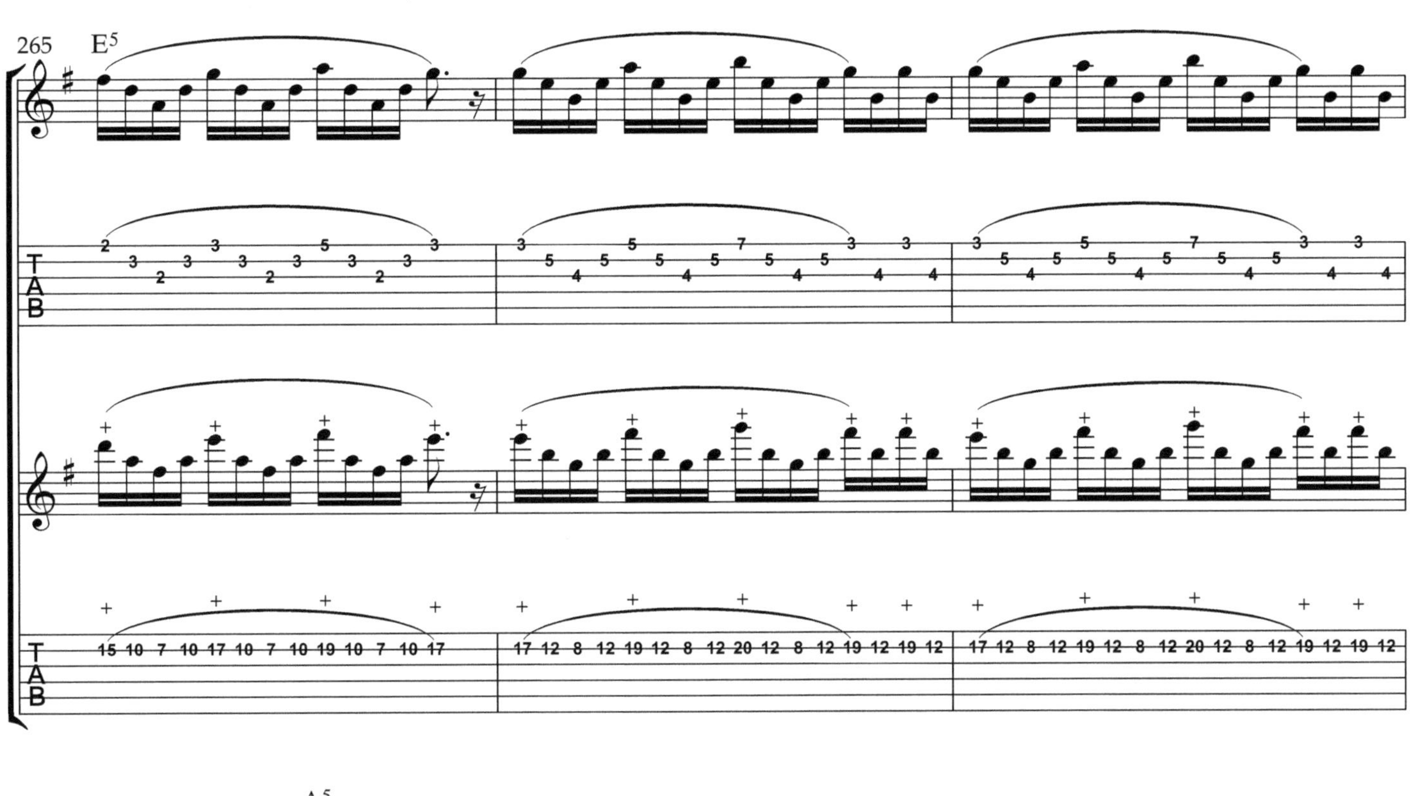

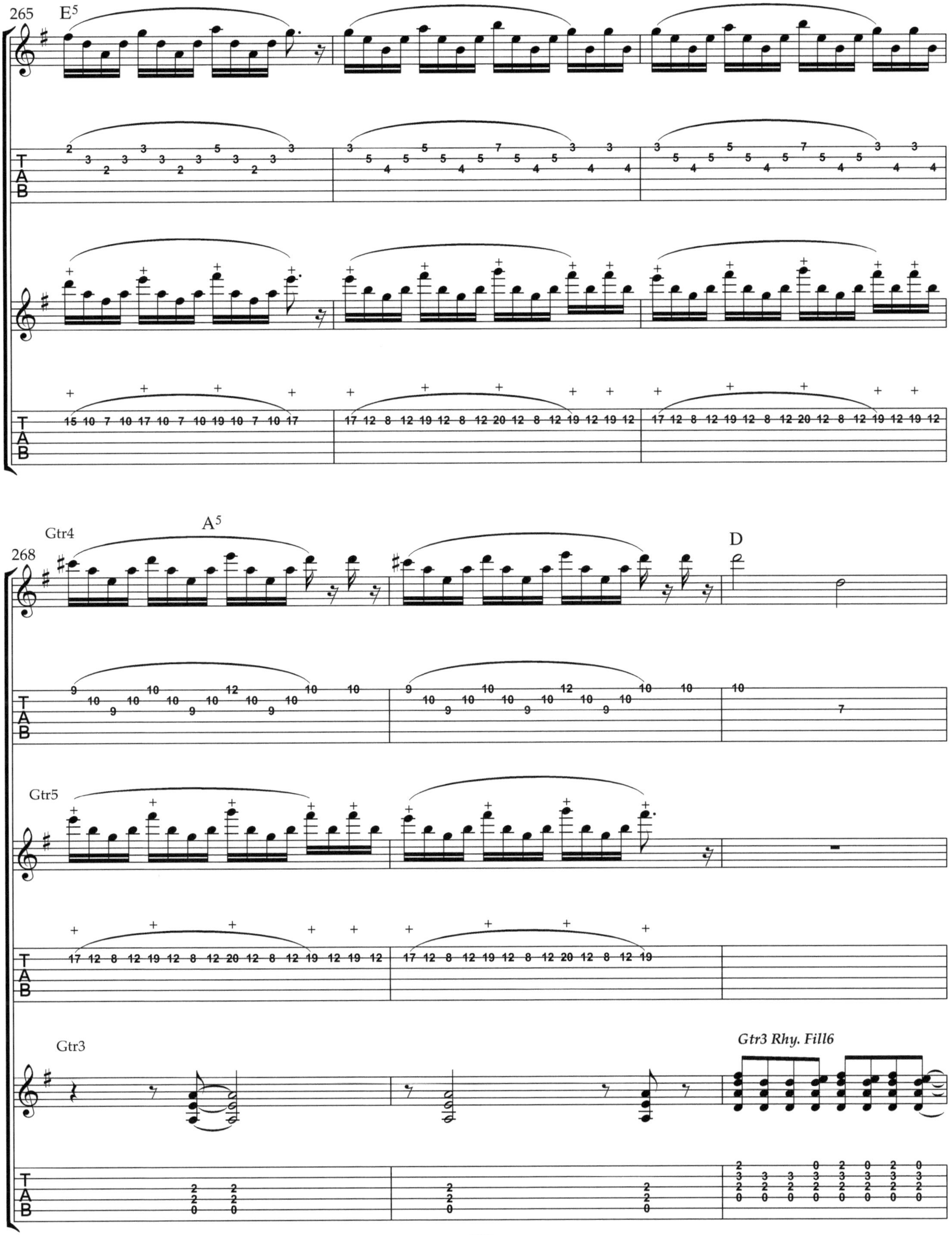

Gtr4

A5

268

D

Gtr5

Gtr3

Gtr3 Rhy. Fill6

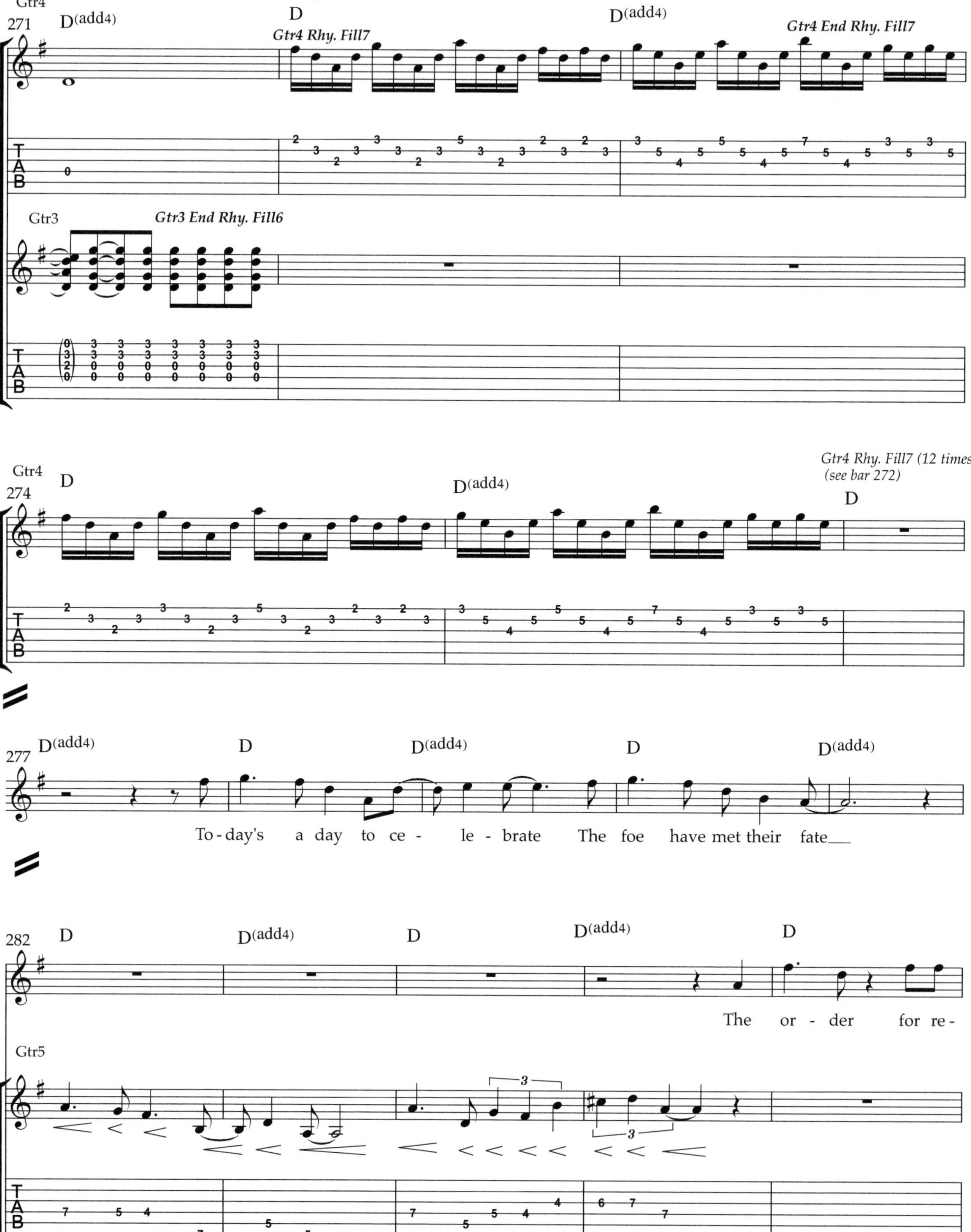
Gtr4
271
D(add4)
Gtr3 Rhy. Fill6 (13 times)
D
Gtr4 Rhy. Fill7
D(add4)
Gtr4 End Rhy. Fill7
Gtr3
Gtr3 End Rhy. Fill6
Gtr4
274
D
D(add4)
Gtr4 Rhy. Fill7 (12 times)
(see bar 272)
D
277
D(add4)
D
D(add4)
D
D(add4)
To-day's a day to ce - le - brate The foe have met their fate
282
D
D(add4)
D
D(add4)
D
The or - der for re -
Gtr5

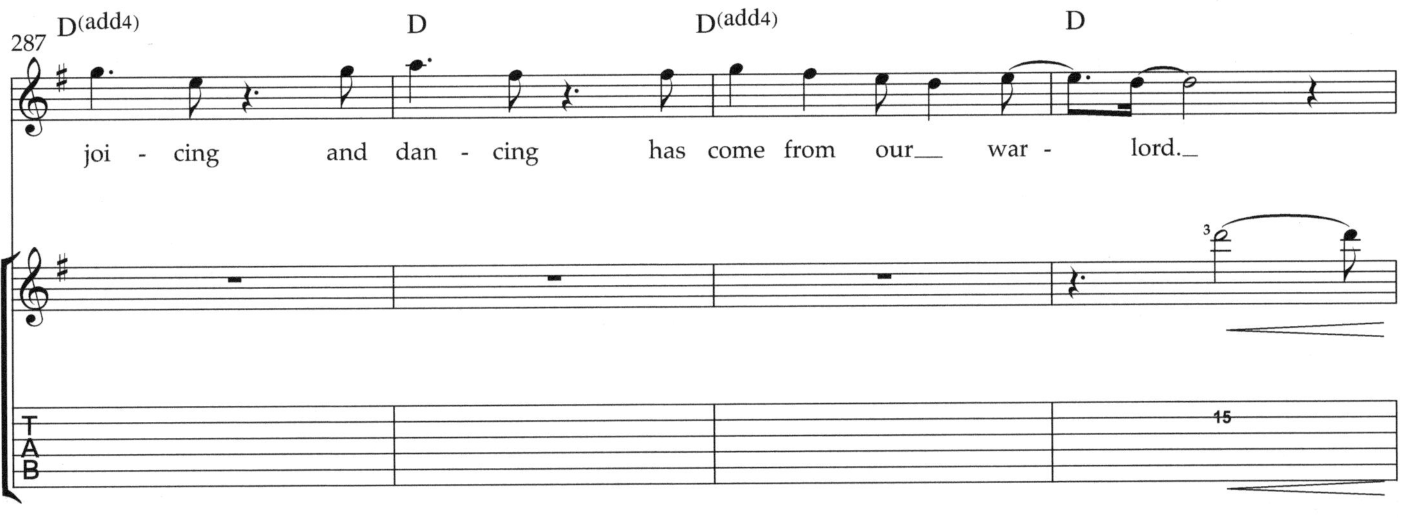
287
D(add4)
D
D(add4)
D
joi - cing and dan - cing has come from our__ war - lord._
15

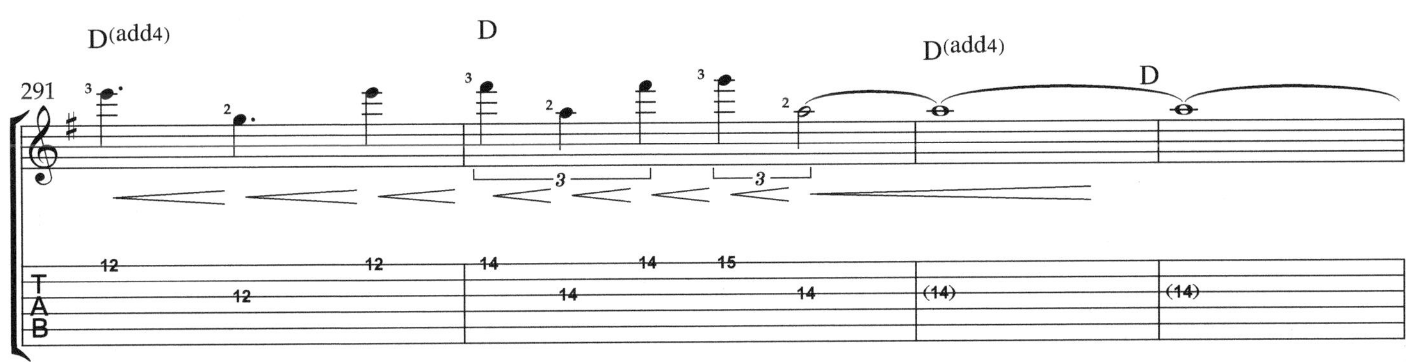
291
D(add4)
D
D(add4)
D
12 12 12 14 14 14 15 14 (14) (14)

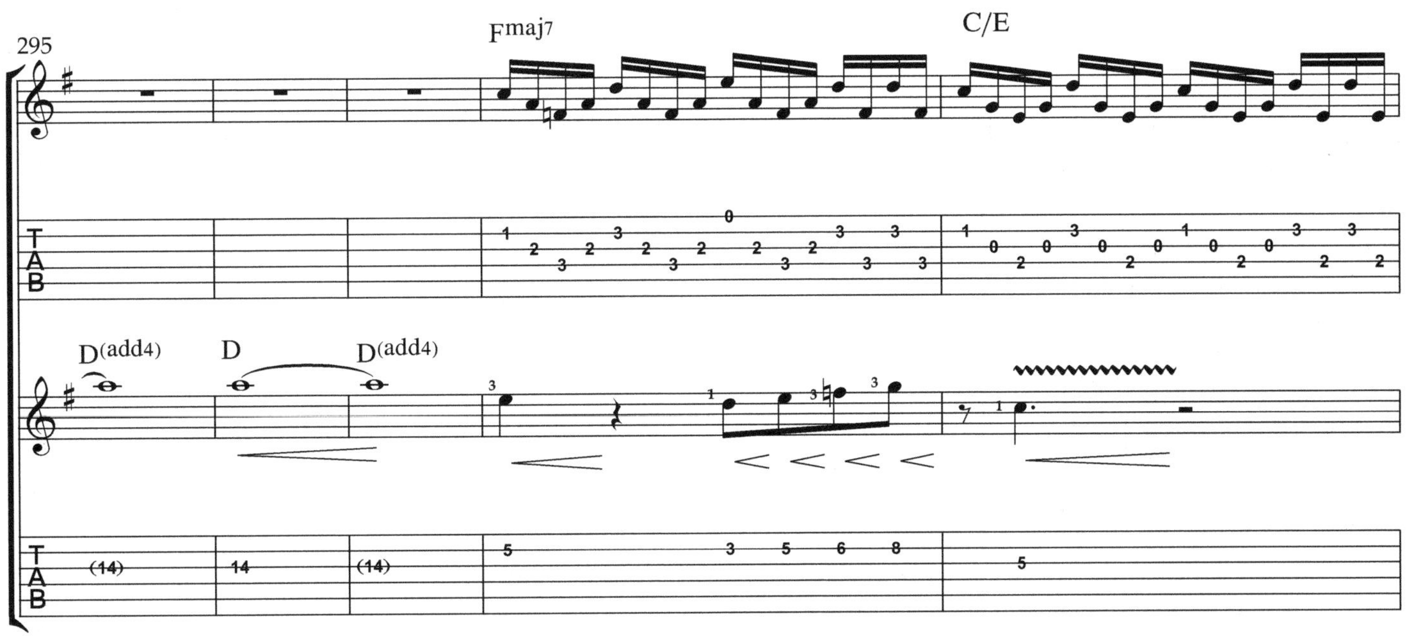
295
Fmaj7
C/E
D(add4)
D
D(add4)

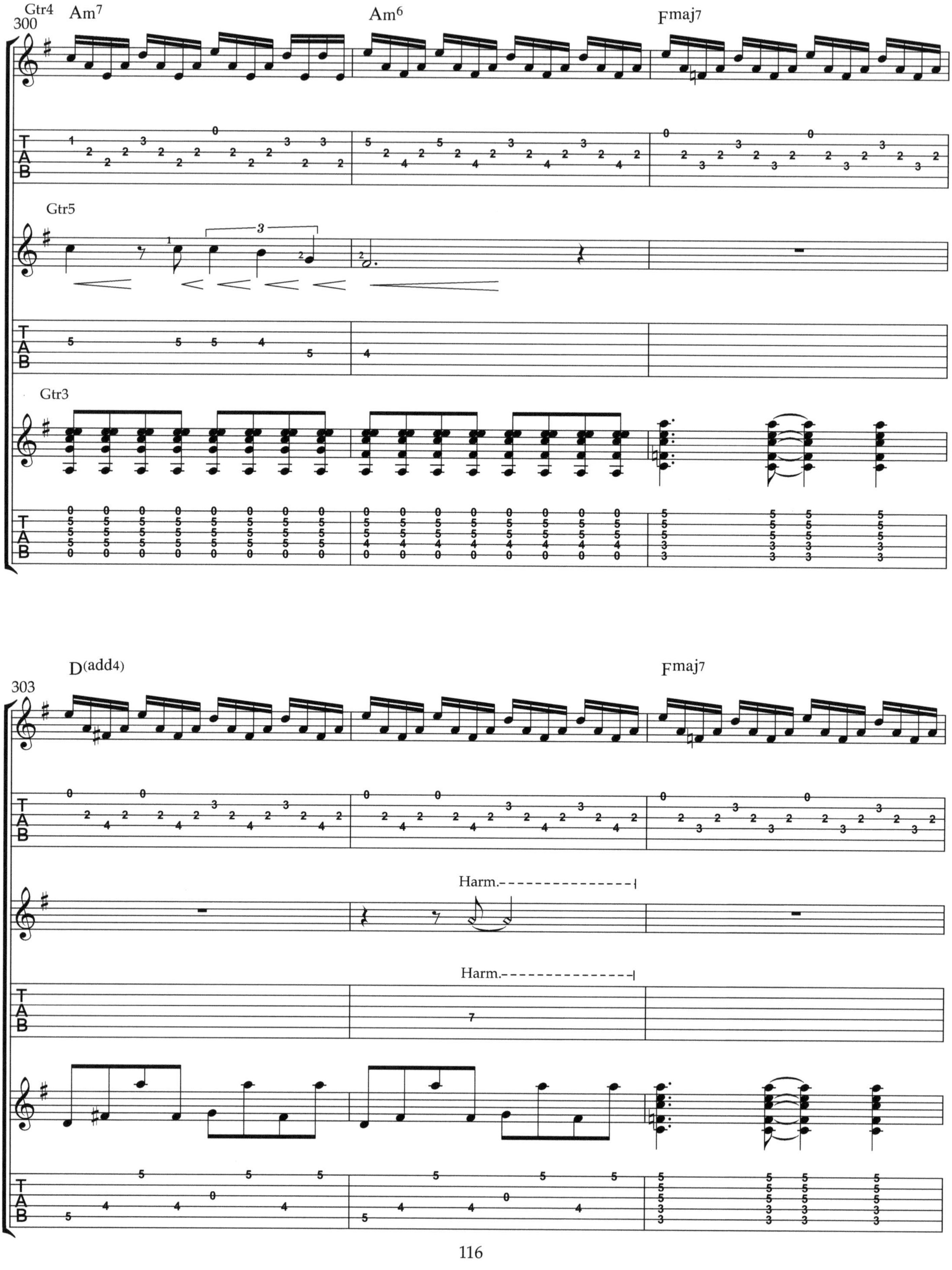

Gtr4
300
Am7 Am6 Fmaj7

Gtr5

Gtr3

303
D(add4) Fmaj7

Harm.

Harm.

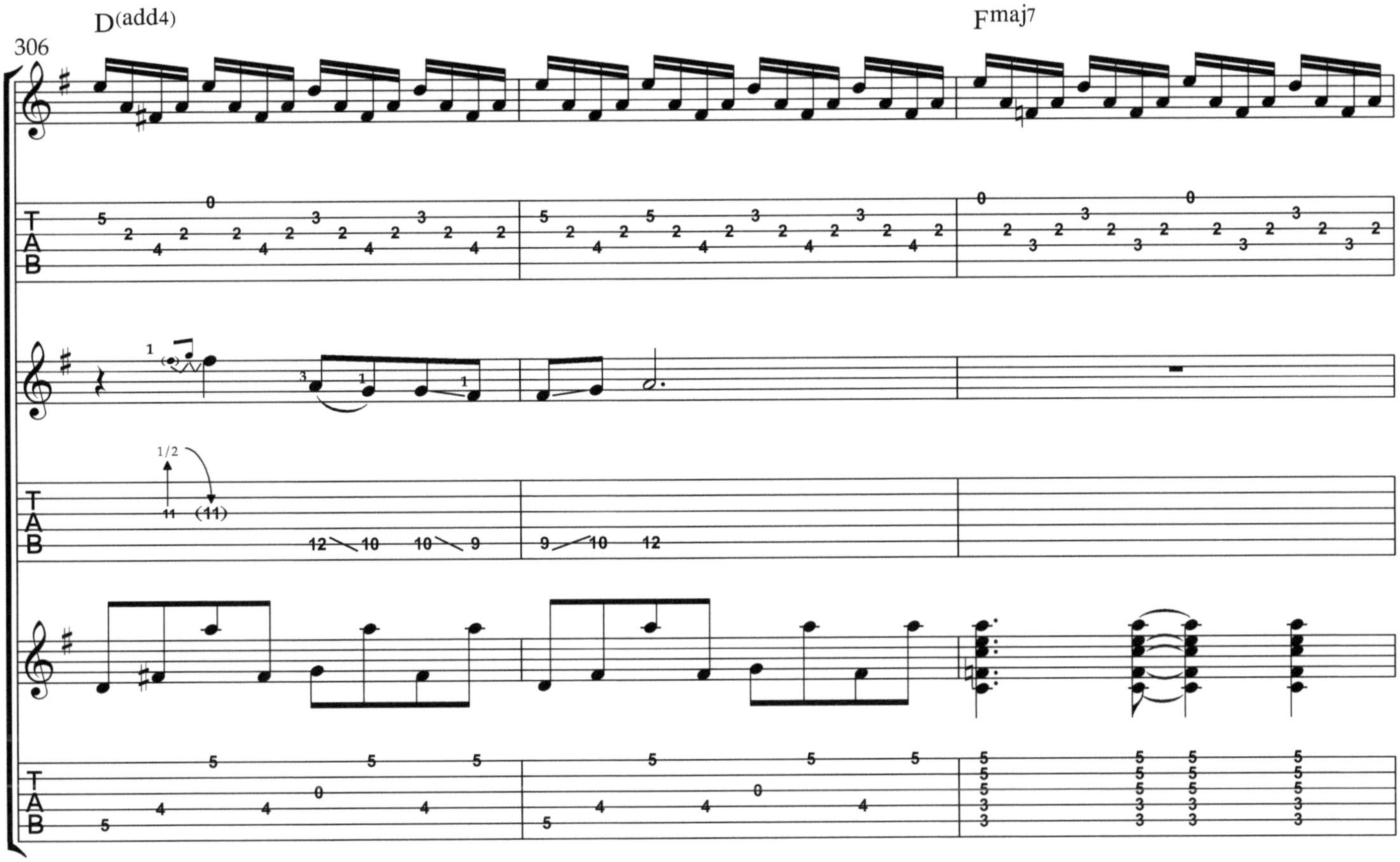

D(add4)
Fmaj7
306

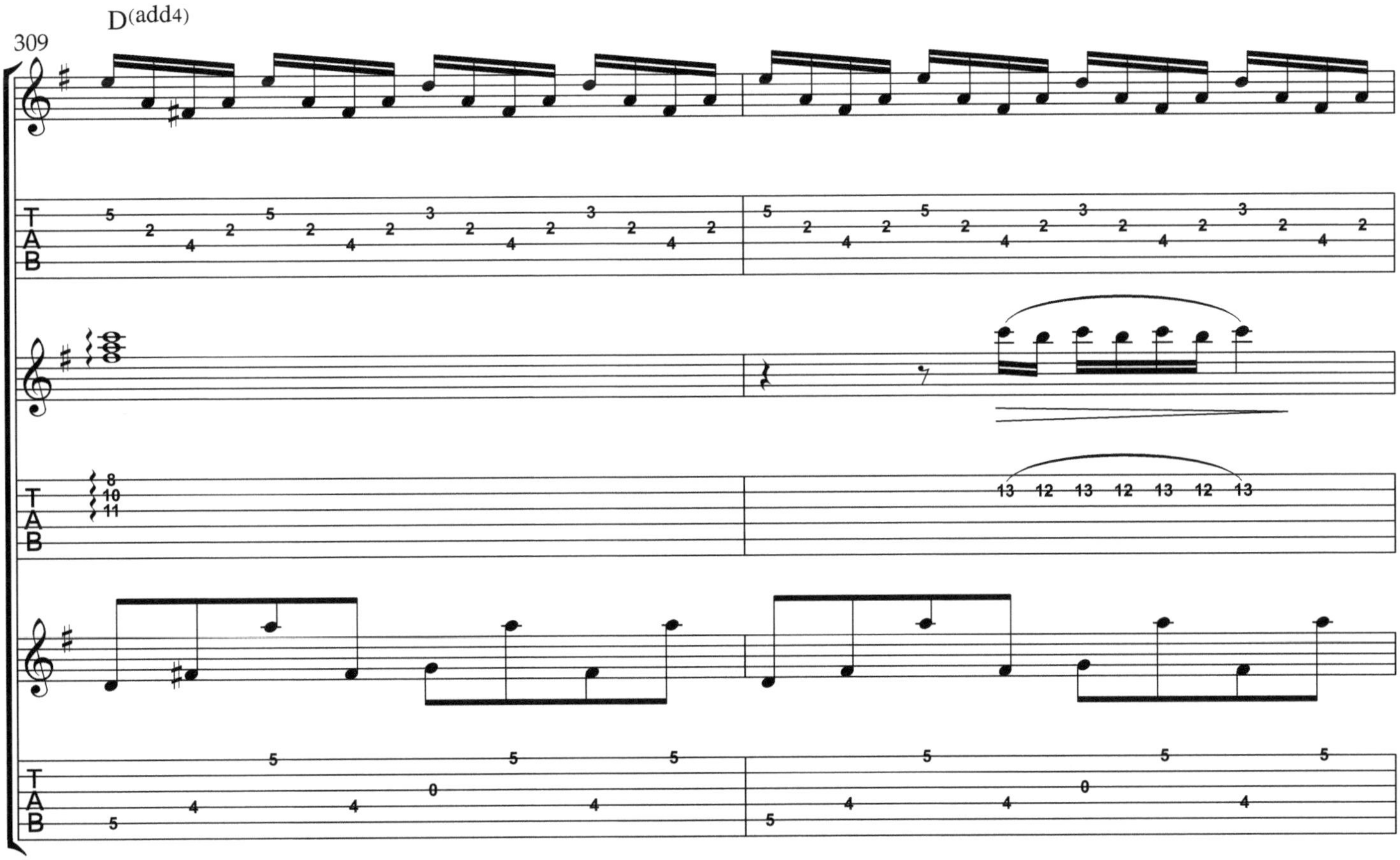

D(add4)
309

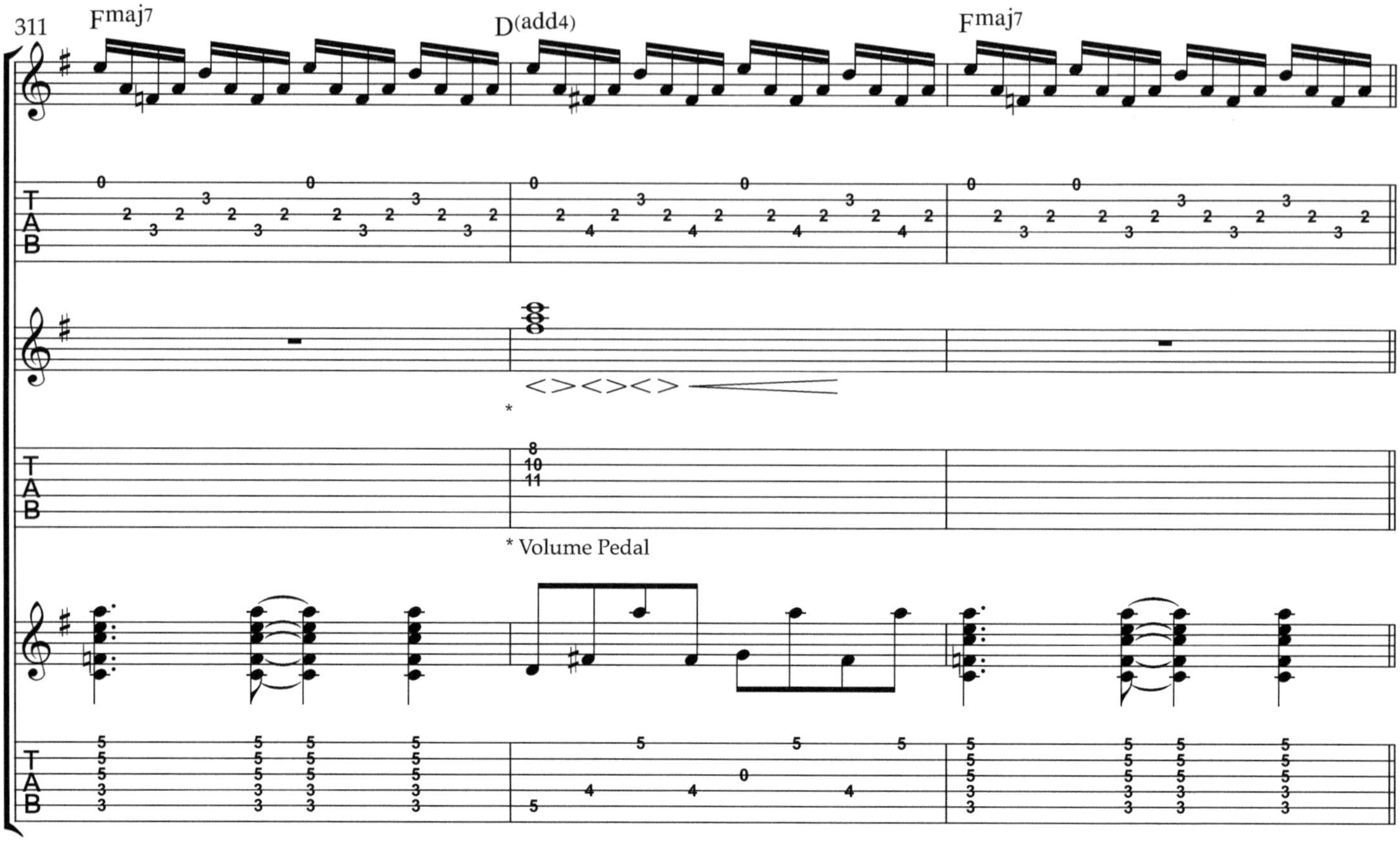

311 Fmaj7 D(add4) Fmaj7

TAB

* Volume Pedal

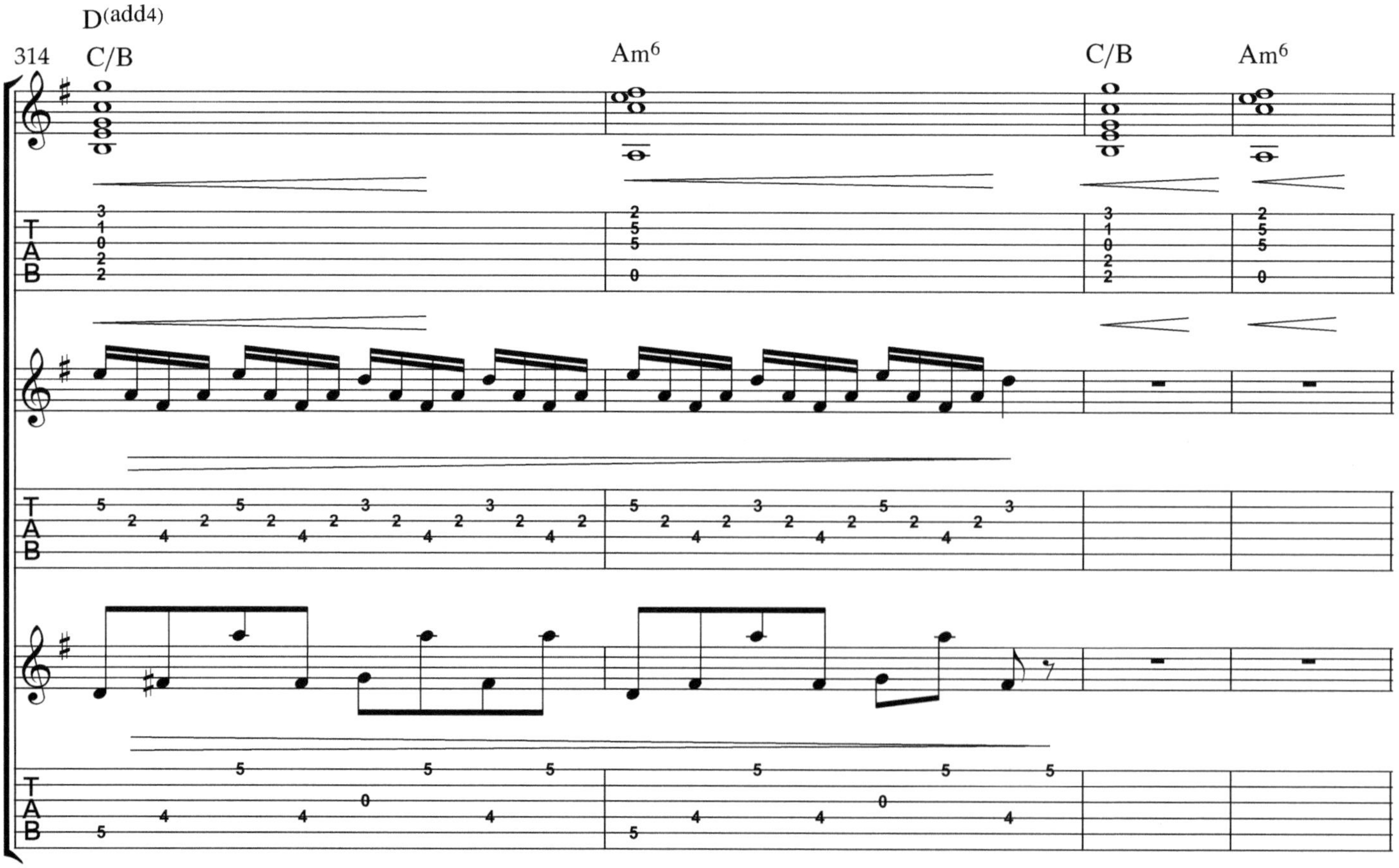

314 D(add4) C/B Am6 C/B Am6

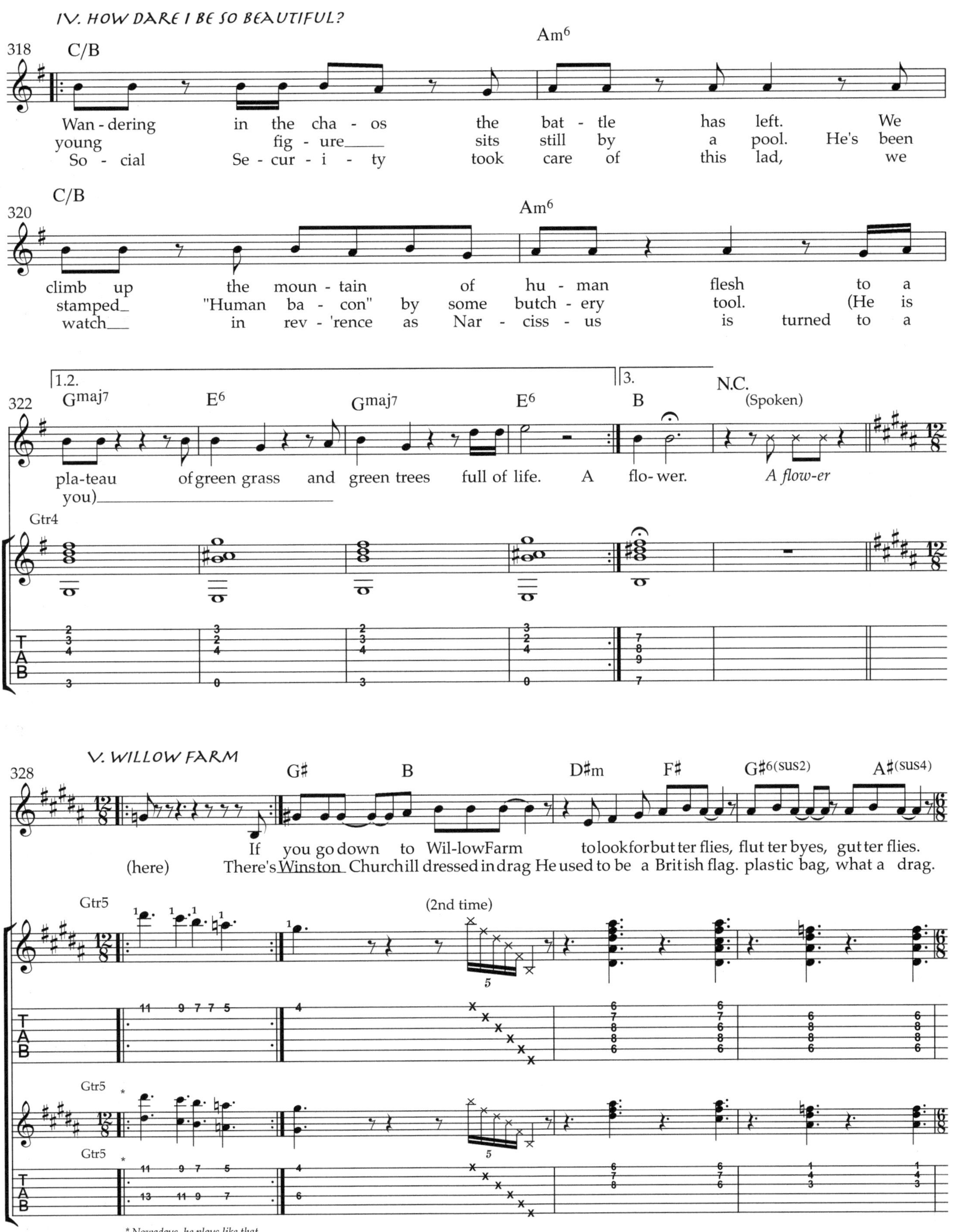

* Nowadays, he plays like that

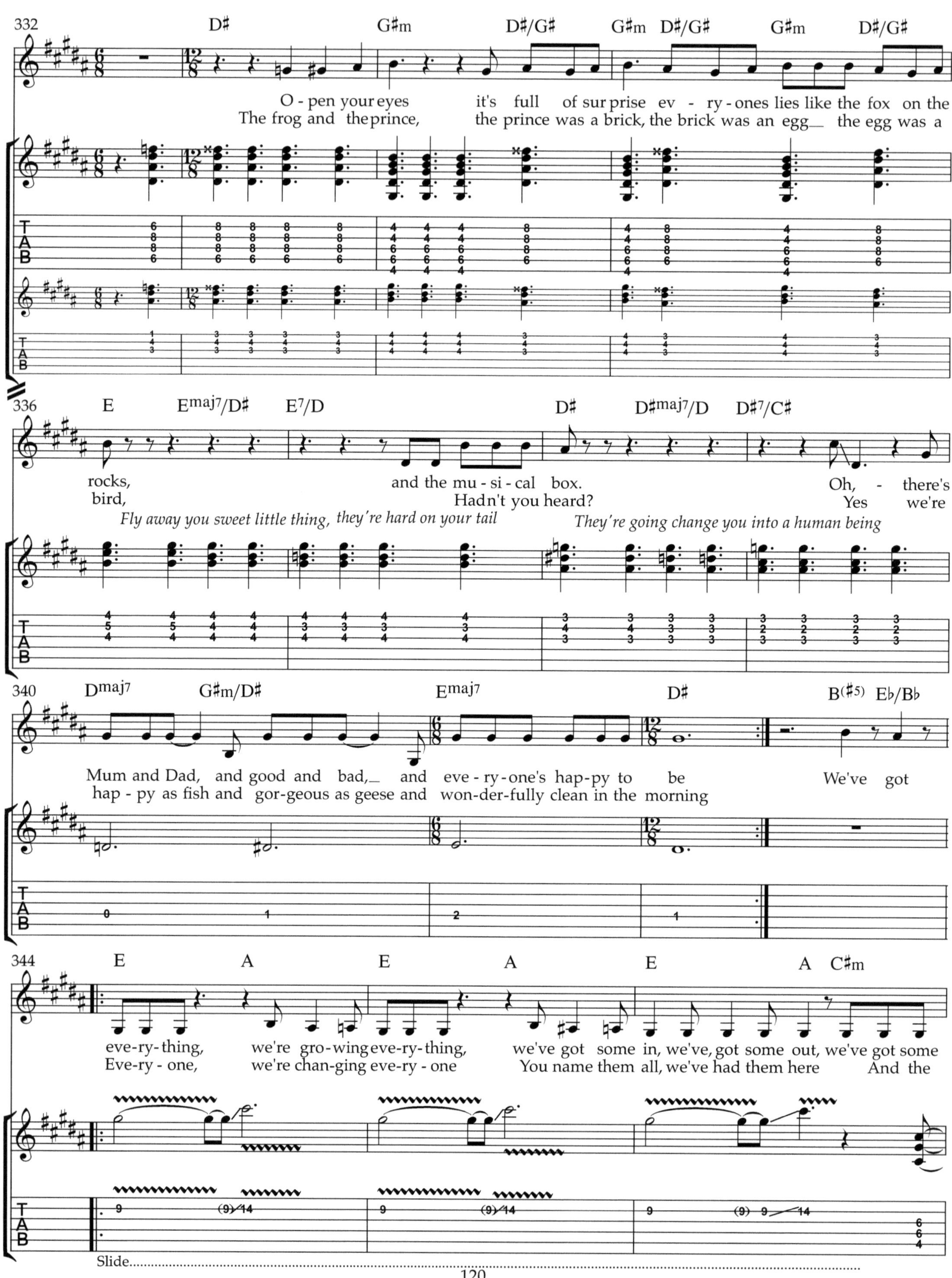
332
D♯
G♯m
D♯/G♯
G♯m D♯/G♯
G♯m
D♯/G♯
O - pen your eyes it's full of sur prise ev - ry - ones lies like the fox on the
The frog and the prince, the prince was a brick, the brick was an egg the egg was a
336
E
Emaj7/D♯
E7/D
D♯
D♯maj7/D
D♯7/C♯
rocks, and the mu - si - cal box. Oh, - there's
bird, Hadn't you heard? Yes we're
Fly away you sweet little thing, they're hard on your tail
They're going change you into a human being
340
Dmaj7
G♯m/D♯
Emaj7
D♯
B(♯5) E♭/B♭
Mum and Dad, and good and bad, and eve - ry - one's hap - py to be We've got
hap - py as fish and gor - geous as geese and won - der - fully clean in the morning
344
E
A
E
A
E
A C♯m
ev - ery - thing, we're gro - wing ev - ery - thing, we've got some in, we've, got some out, we've got some
Eve - ry - one, we're chan - ging eve - ry - one You name them all, we've had them here And the
T
A
B
Slide

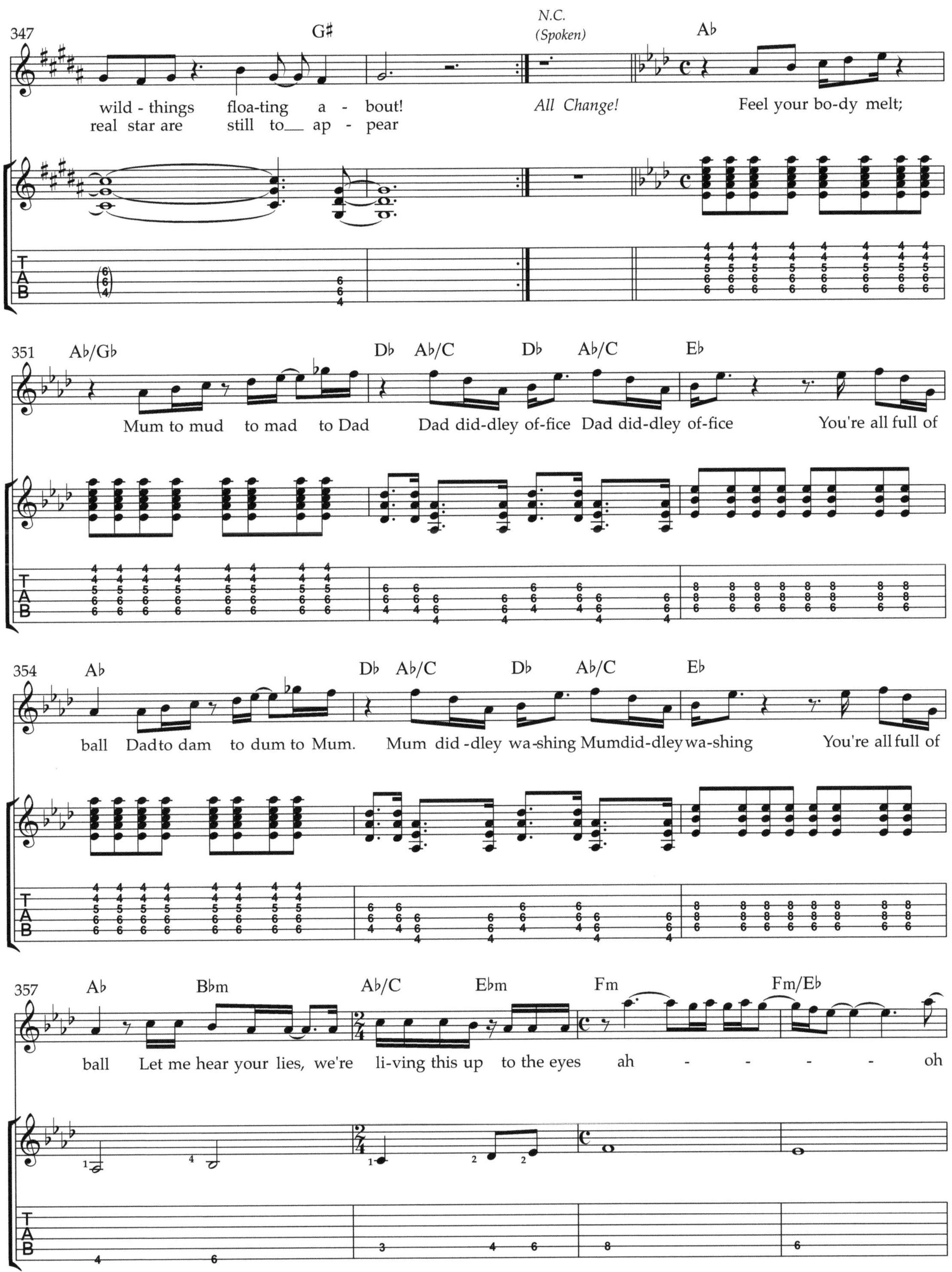
347
G♯
N.C.
(Spoken)
A♭
wild - things floa-ting a - bout!
real star are still to__ ap - pear
All Change!
Feel your bo-dy melt;
351
A♭/G♭
D♭
A♭/C
D♭
A♭/C
E♭
Mum to mud to mad to Dad
Dad did-dley of-fice Dad did-dley of-fice
You're all full of
354
A♭
D♭
A♭/C
D♭
A♭/C
E♭
ball Dad to dam to dum to Mum.
Mum did-dley wa-shing Mum did-dley wa-shing
You're all full of
357
A♭
B♭m
A♭/C
E♭m
Fm
Fm/E♭
ball Let me hear your lies, we're li-ving this up to the eyes ah - - - - - oh

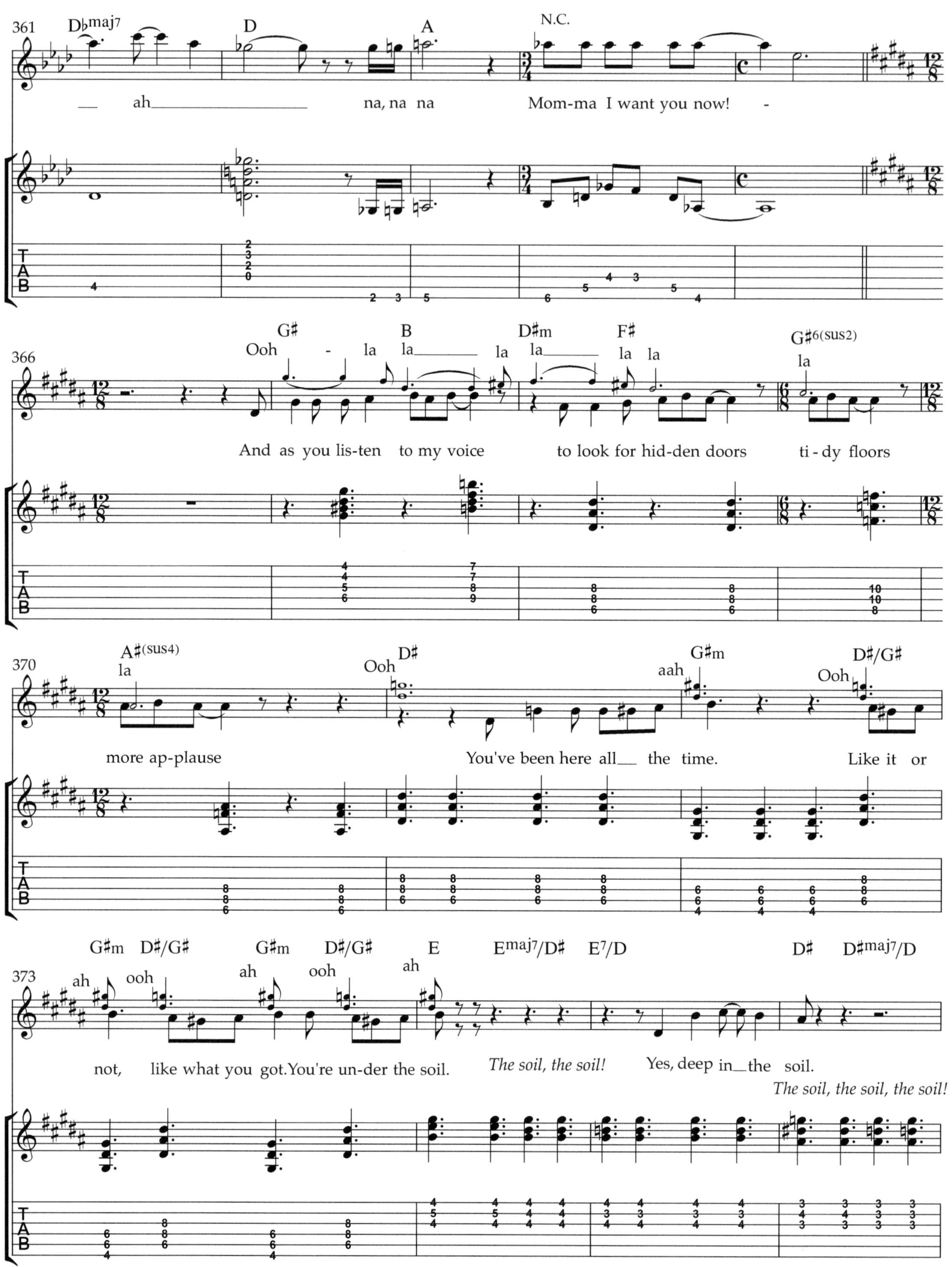
361
D♭maj7
D
A
N.C.
ah
na, na na
Mom-ma I want you now!
366
G♯
B
D♯m
F♯
G♯6(sus2)
Ooh - la la la la la la
la
And as you lis-ten to my voice
to look for hid-den doors
ti-dy floors
370
A♯(sus4)
D♯
G♯m
D♯/G♯
la
Ooh
aah
Ooh
more ap-plause
You've been here all the time.
Like it or
373
G♯m
D♯/G♯
G♯m
D♯/G♯
E
Emaj7/D♯
E7/D
D♯
D♯maj7/D
ah ooh ah ooh ah
not, like what you got. You're un-der the soil.
The soil, the soil!
Yes, deep in the soil.
The soil, the soil, the soil!

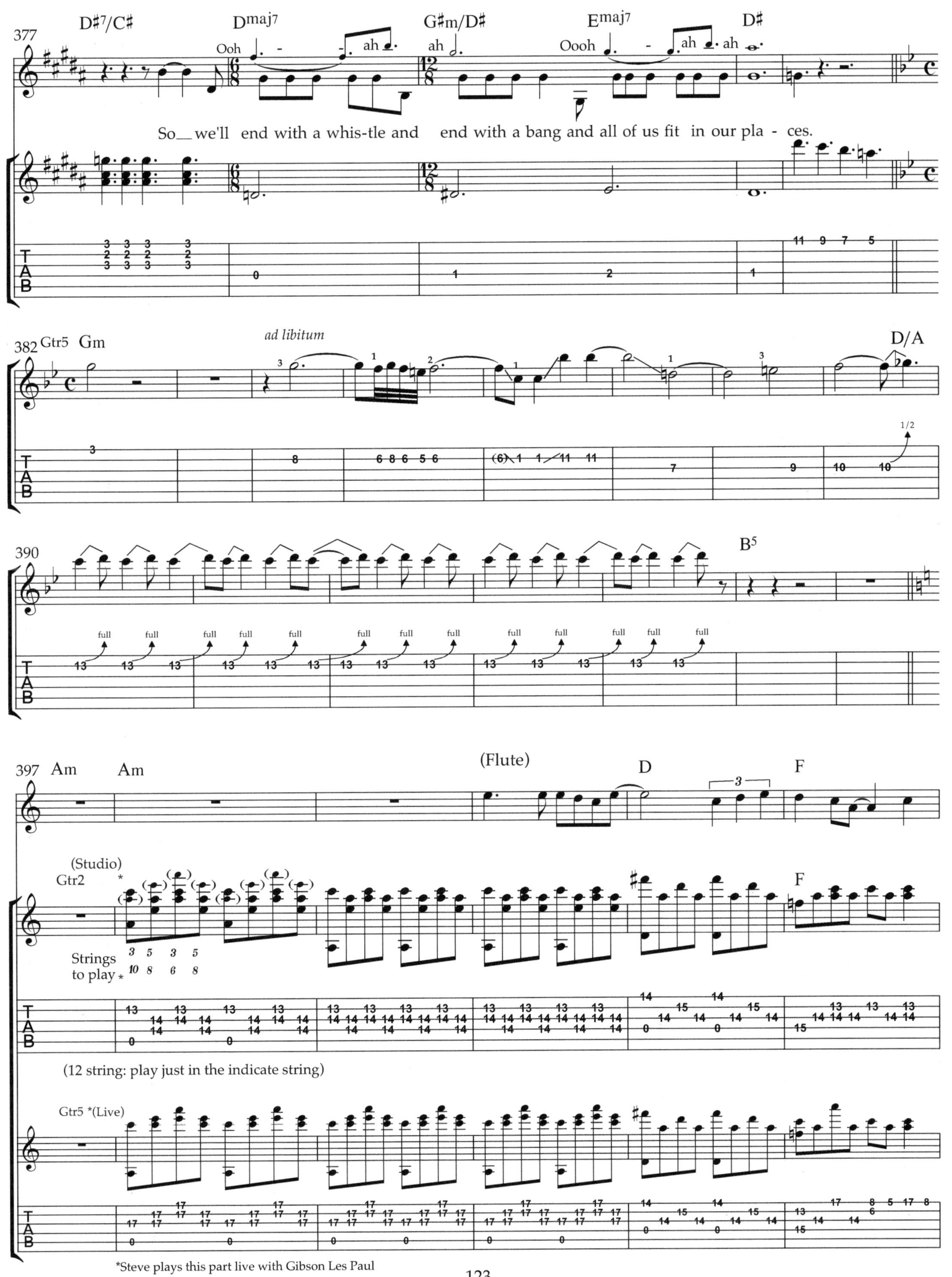

*Steve plays this part live with Gibson Les Paul

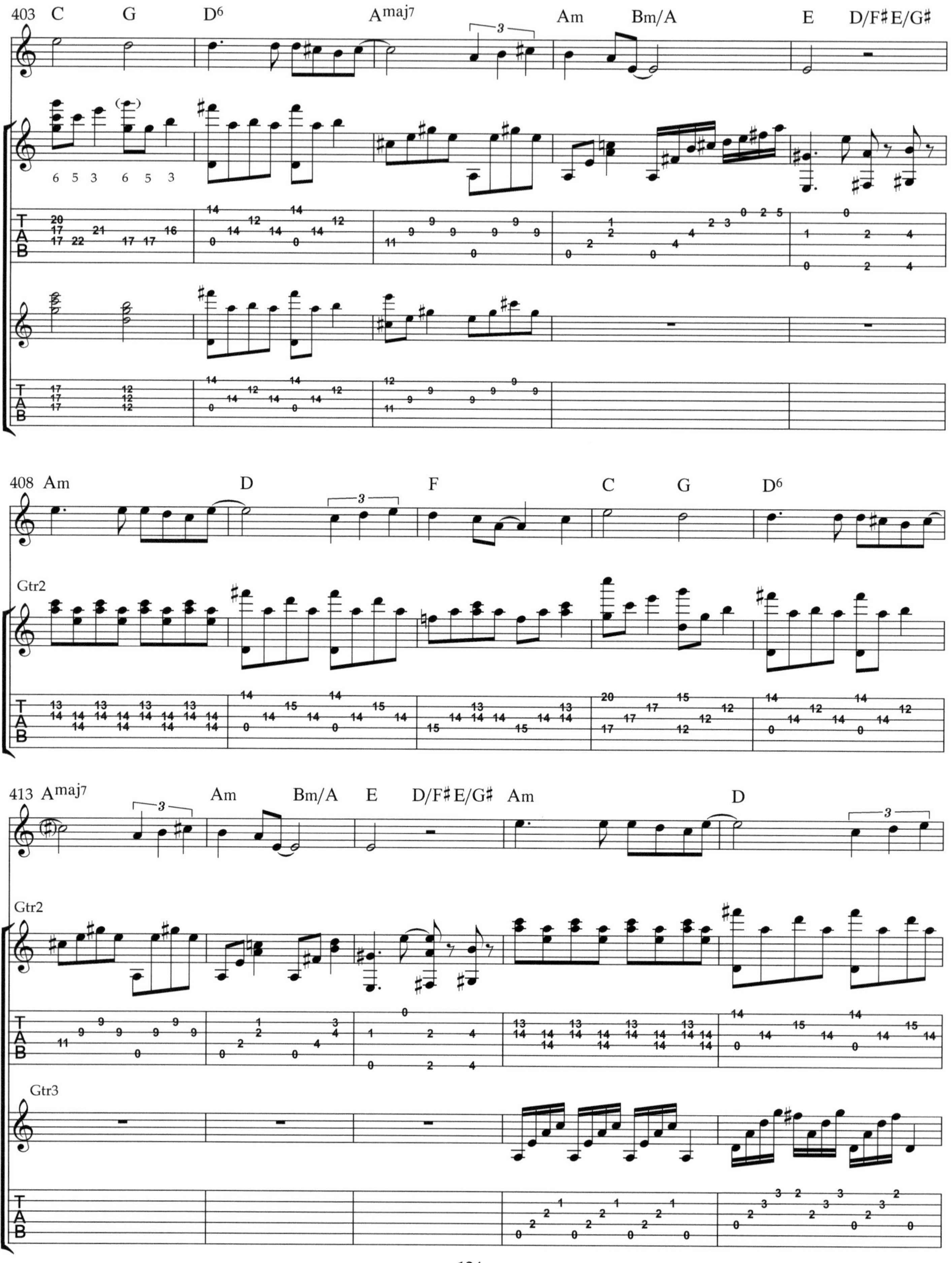
403
C
G
D6
Amaj7
Am
Bm/A
E
D/F♯
E/G♯
408
Am
D
F
C
G
D6
Gtr2
413
Amaj7
Am
Bm/A
E
D/F♯
E/G♯
Am
D
Gtr2
Gtr3

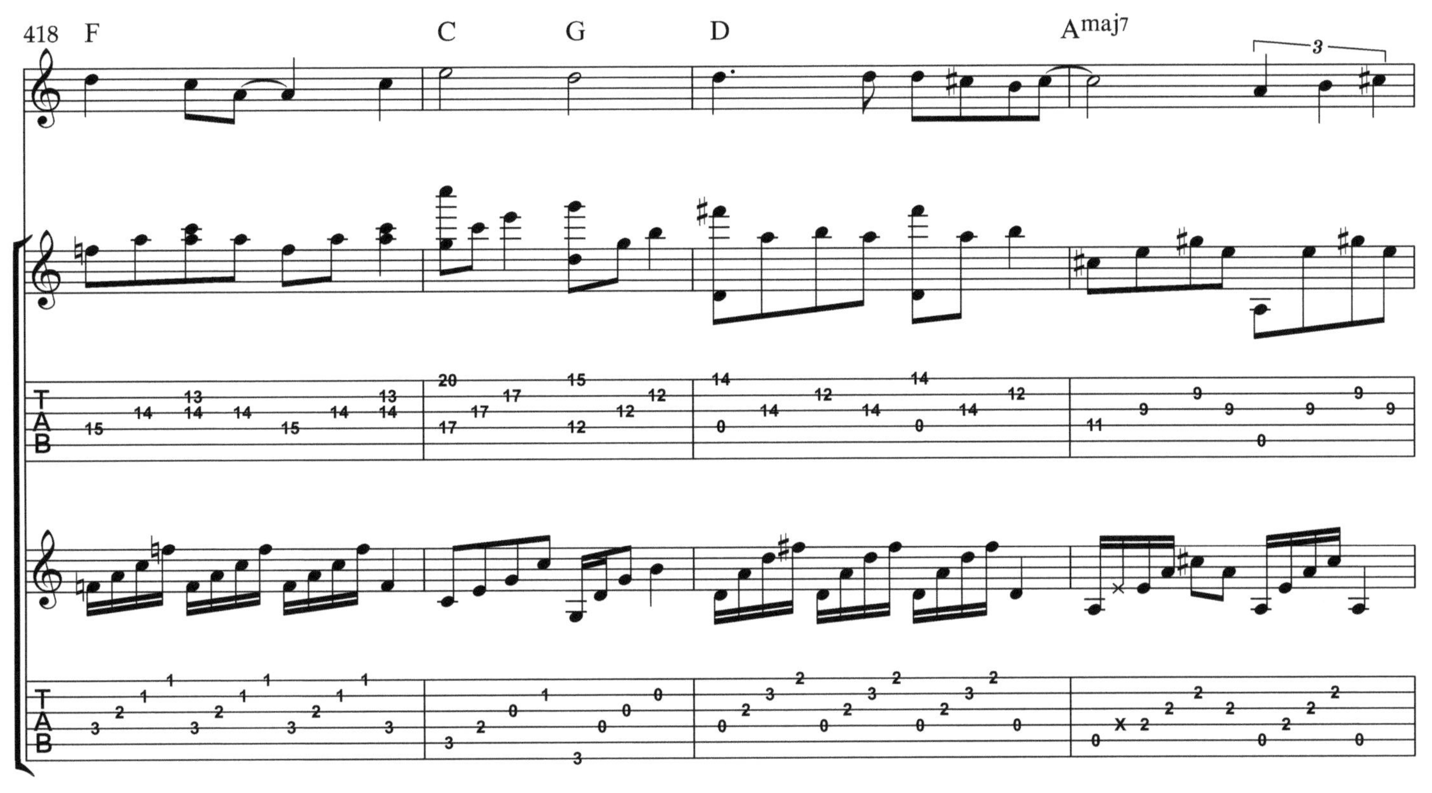
418
F
C
G
D
Amaj7

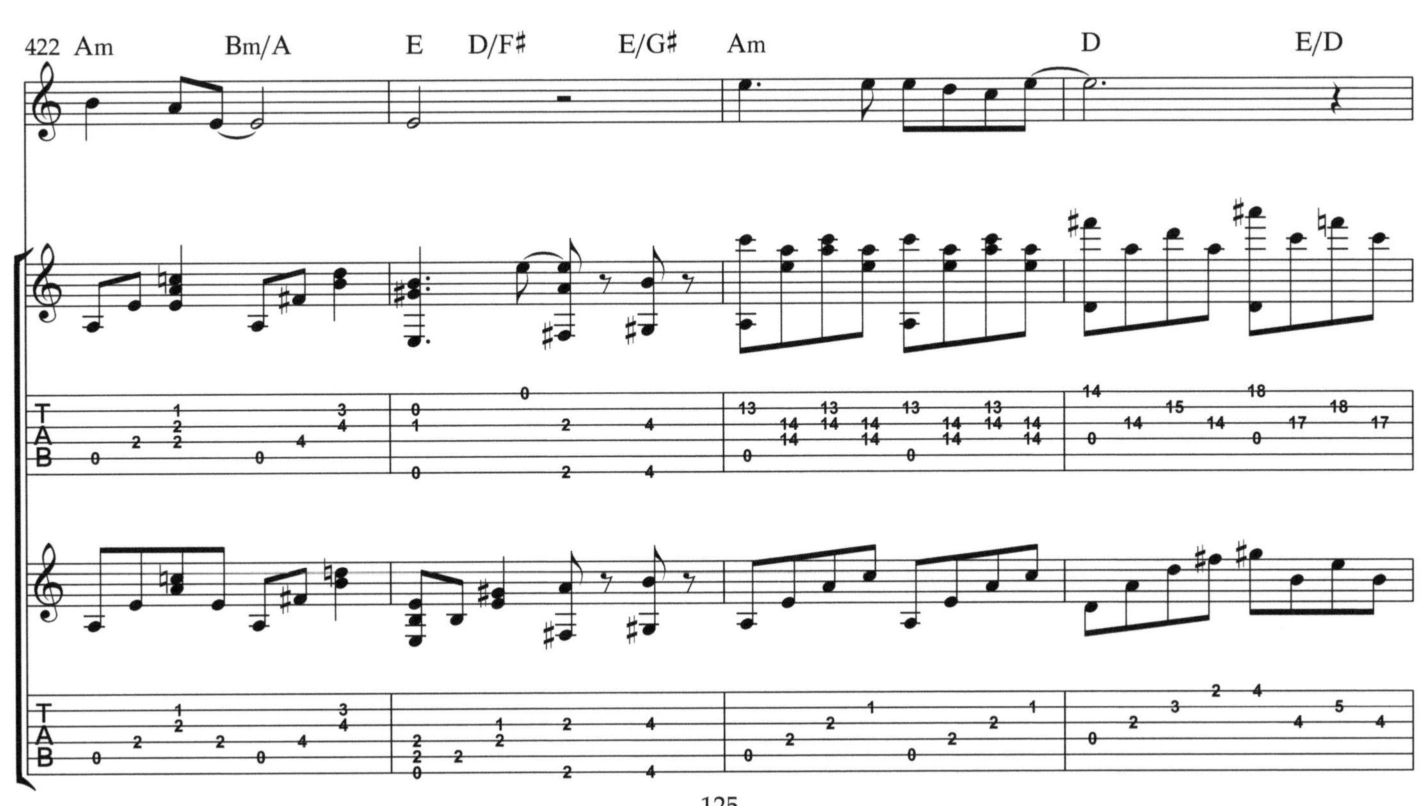
422
Am
Bm/A
E
D/F♯
E/G♯
Am
D
E/D

VI. APOCALYPSE IN 9/8 (CO-STARRING THE DELICIOUS TALENTS OF GABBLE RATCHET)

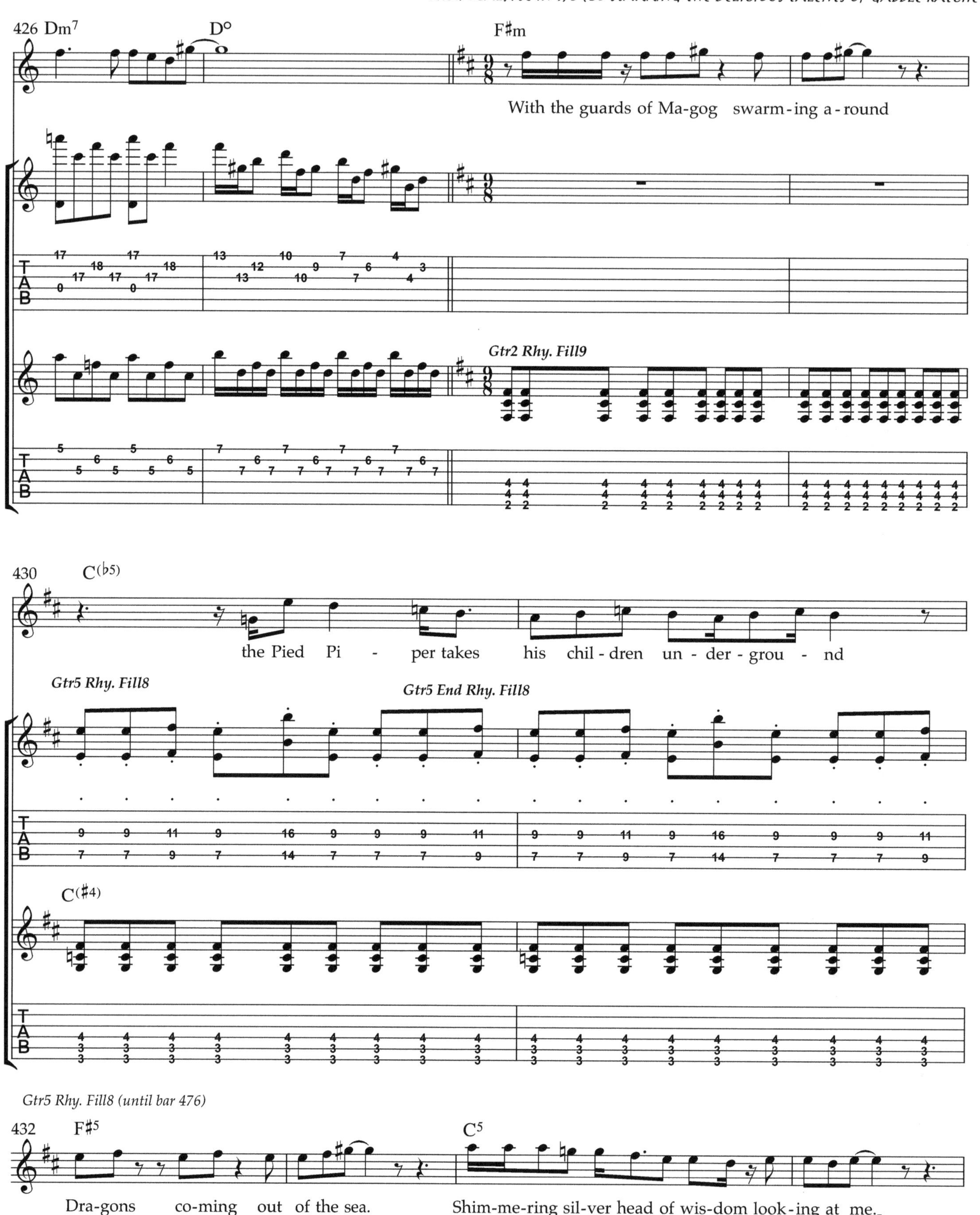

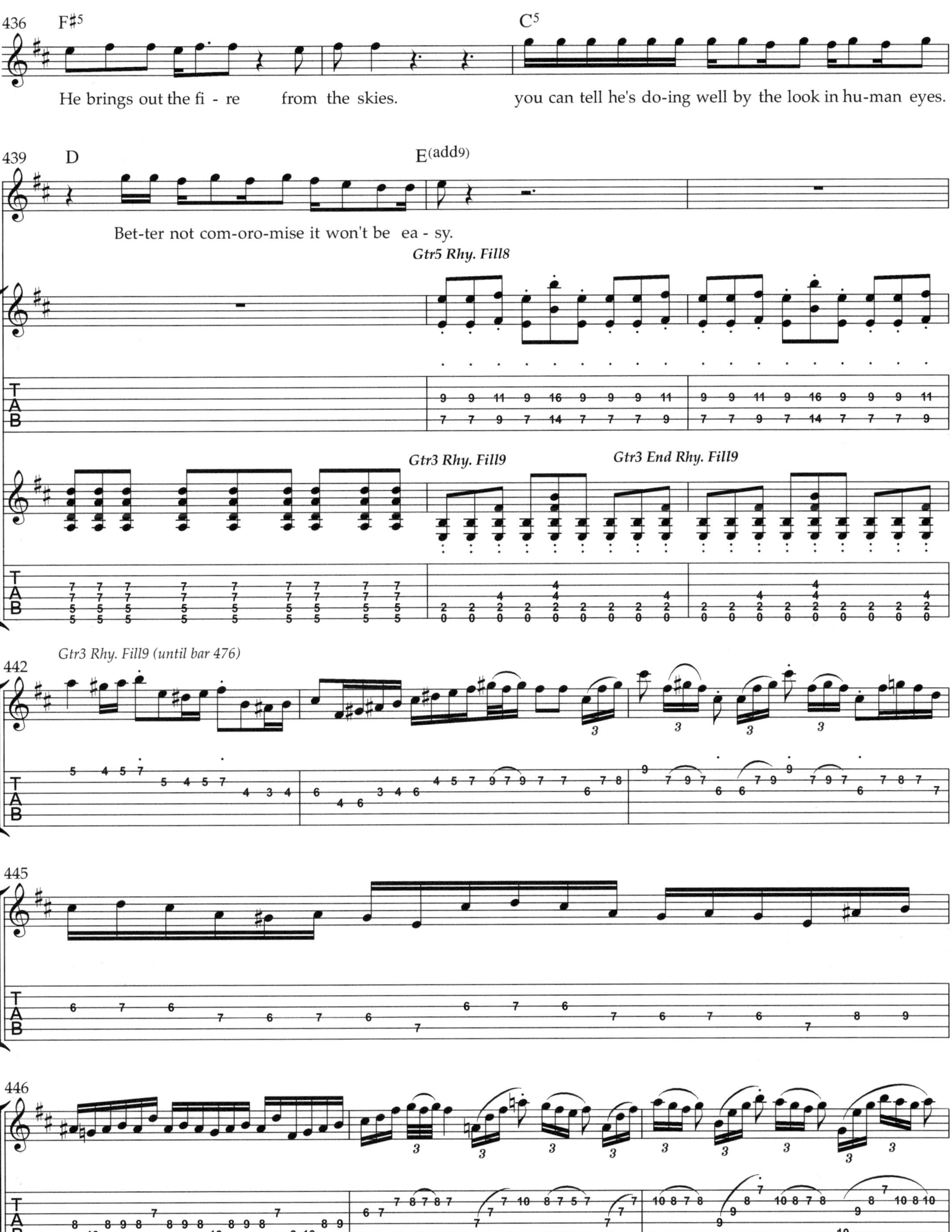
436
F♯5
C5
He brings out the fi - re from the skies.
you can tell he's do-ing well by the look in hu-man eyes.
439
D
E(add9)
Bet-ter not com-oro-mise it won't be ea - sy.
Gtr5 Rhy. Fill8
Gtr3 Rhy. Fill9
Gtr3 End Rhy. Fill9
442
Gtr3 Rhy. Fill9 (until bar 476)
445
446

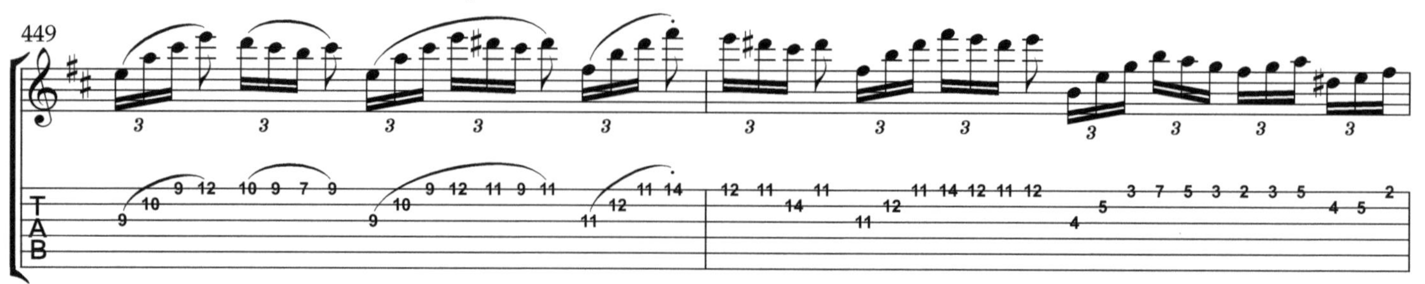
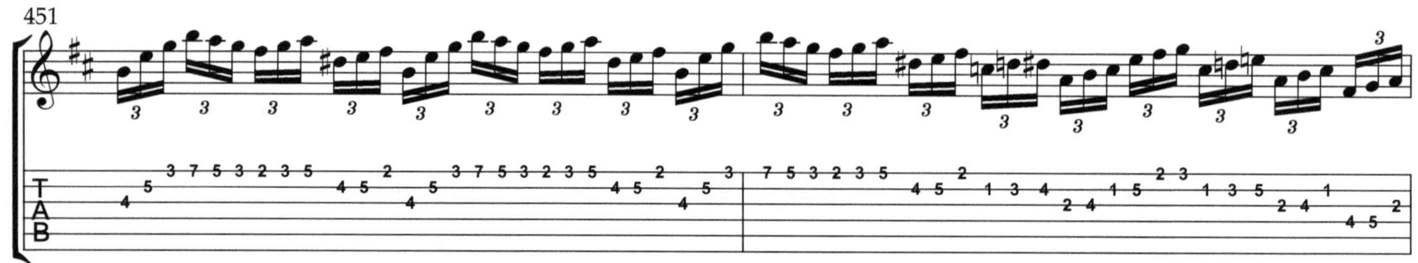
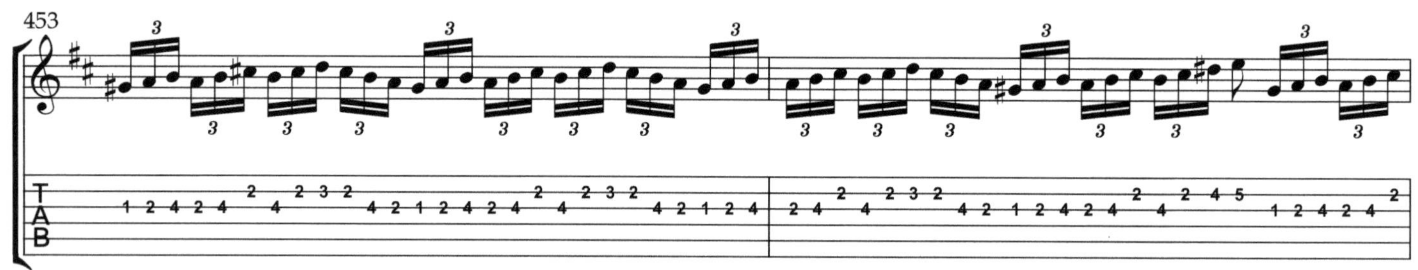
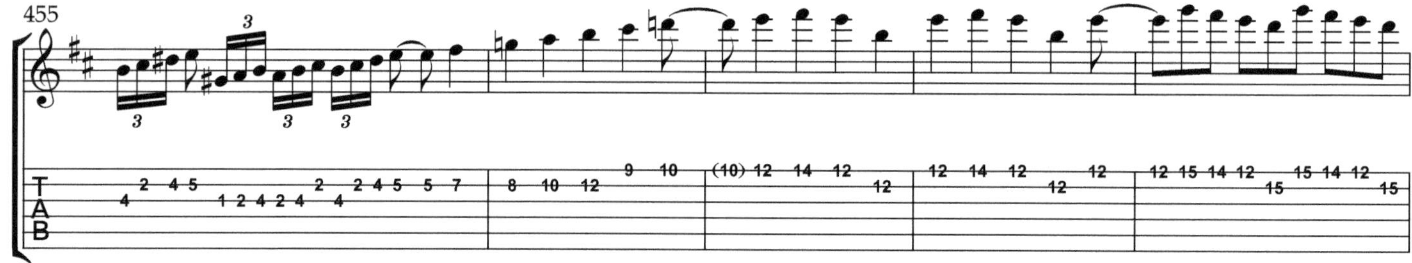
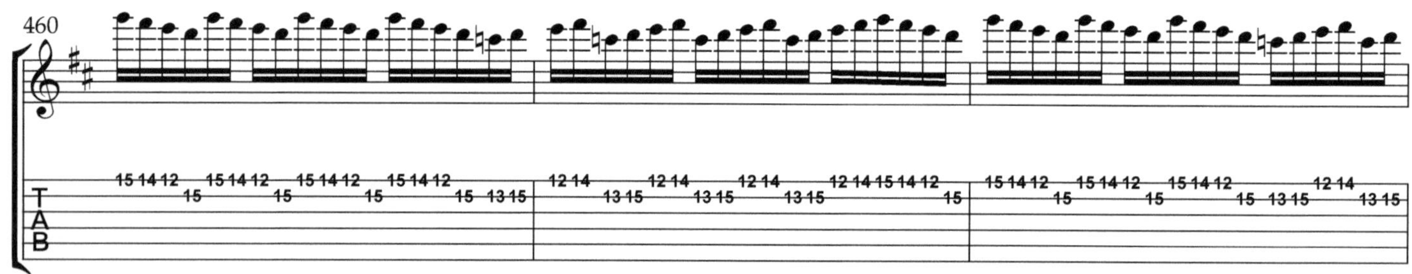
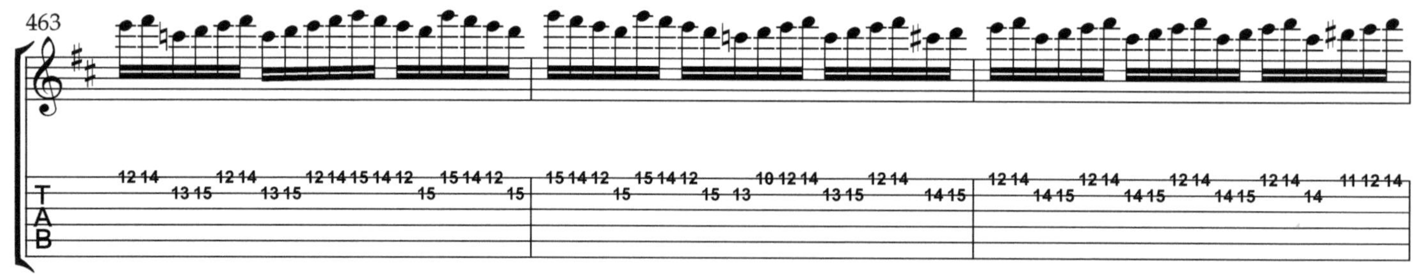

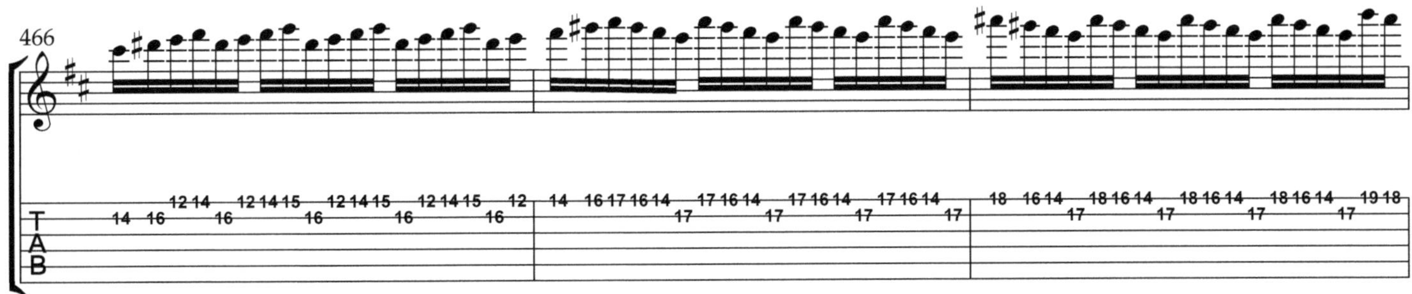

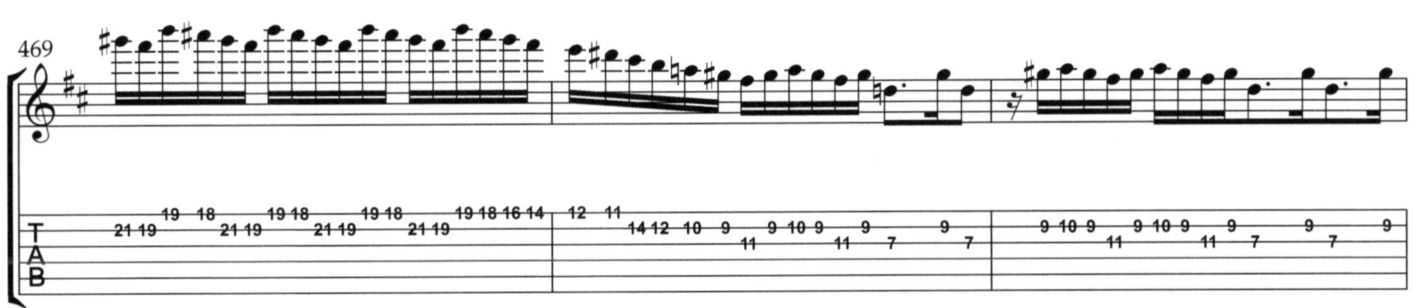

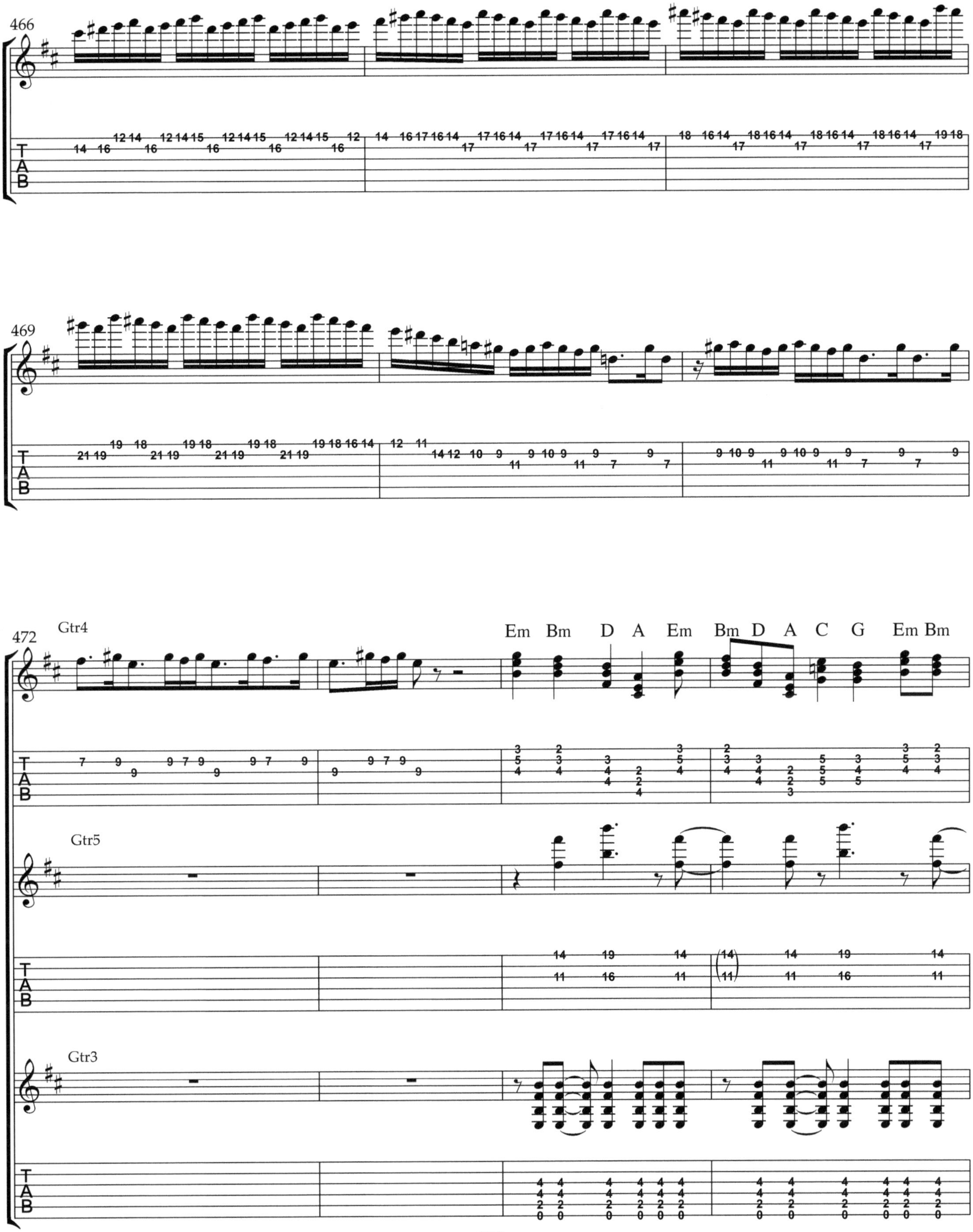

472 Gtr4

Em Bm D A Em Bm D A C G Em Bm

Gtr5

Gtr3

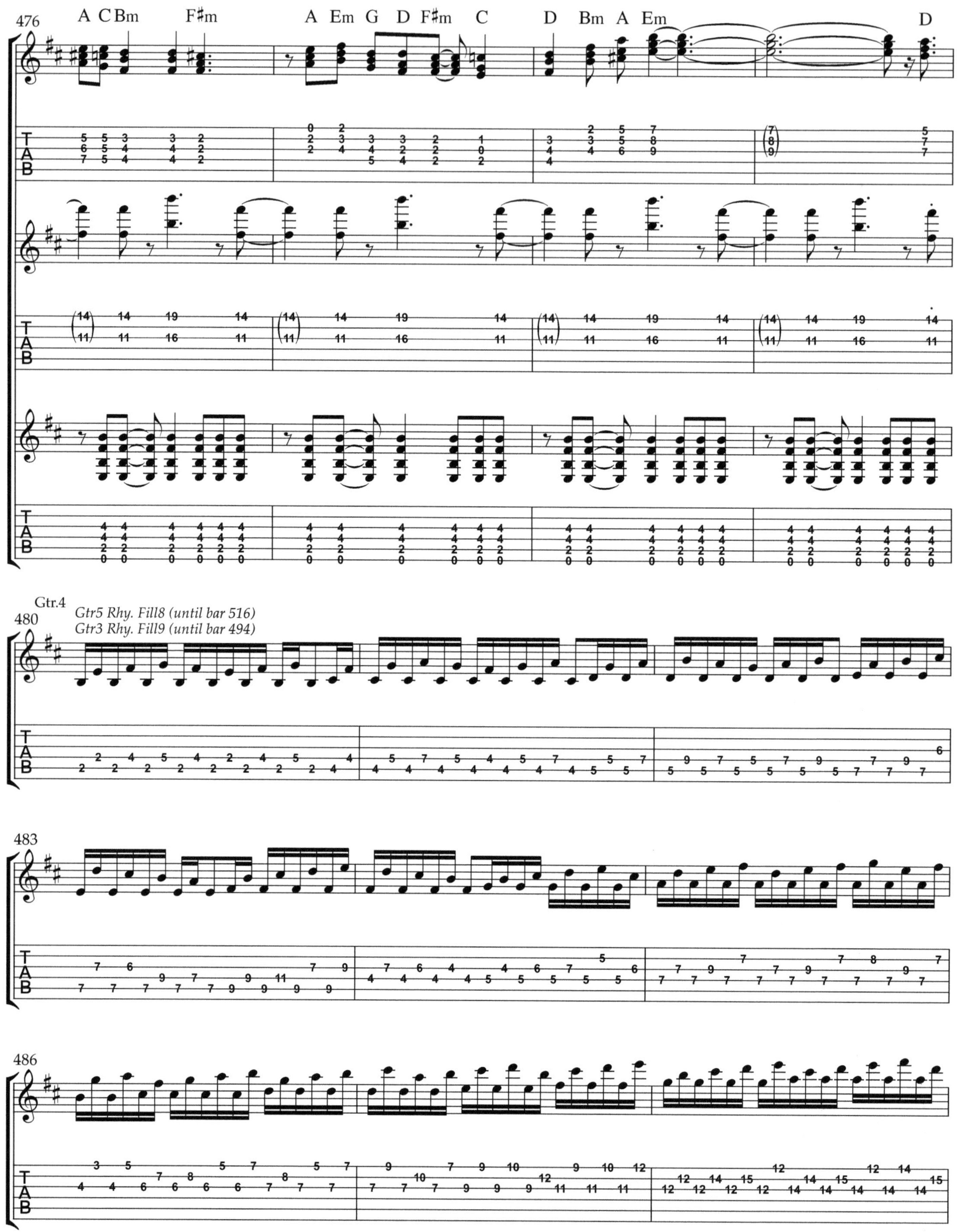
476
A C Bm
F♯m
A Em G D F♯m C
D Bm A Em
D
Gtr.4
480
Gtr5 Rhy. Fill8 (until bar 516)
Gtr3 Rhy. Fill9 (until bar 494)
483
486

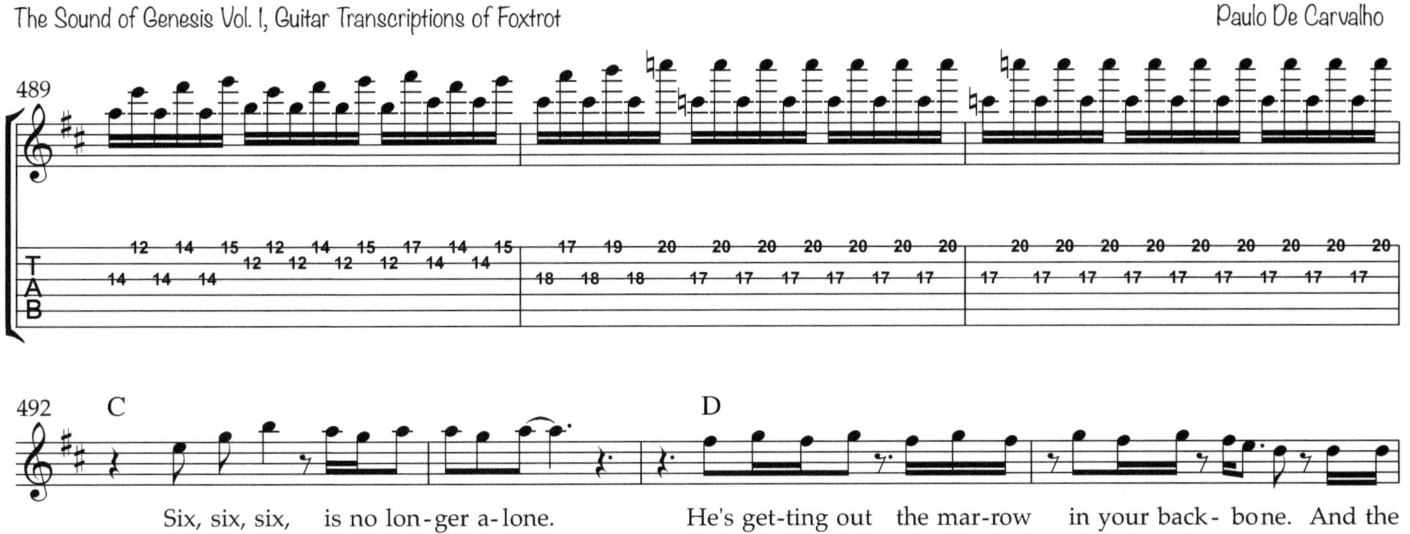

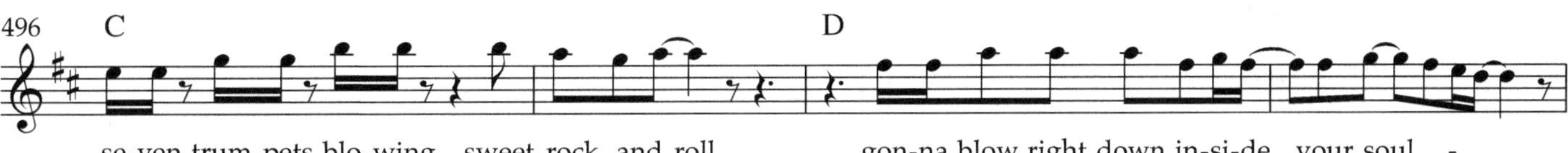

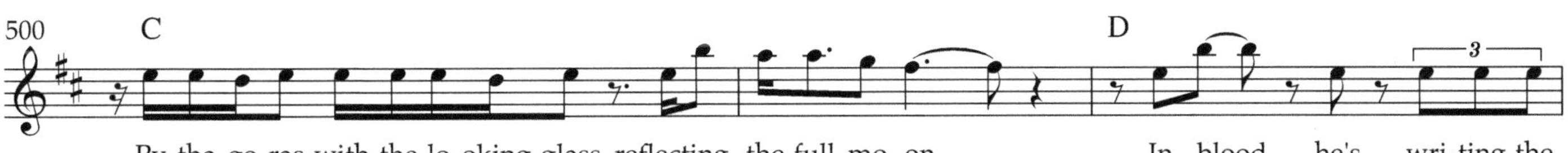

500 C D

Py-tha-go-ras with the lo-oking glass reflecting the full mo-on. In blood he's wri-ting the

503 E G♯m D Am E G♯m D Am

ly-rics of a brand new tu - ne

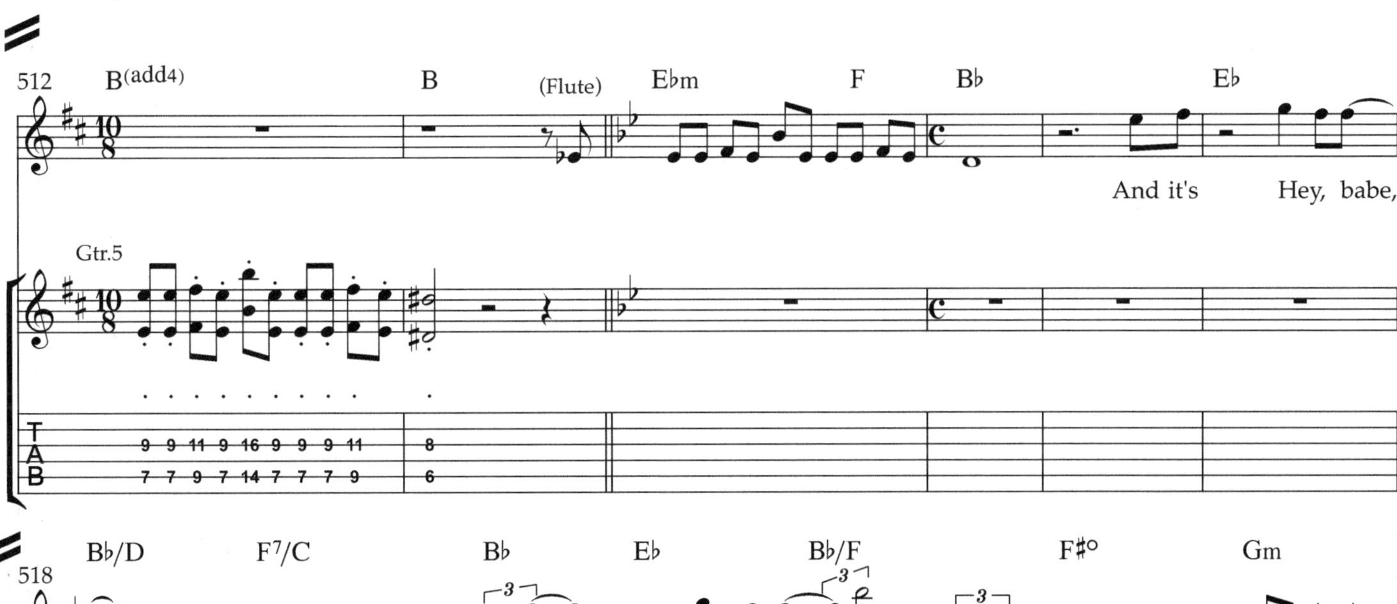

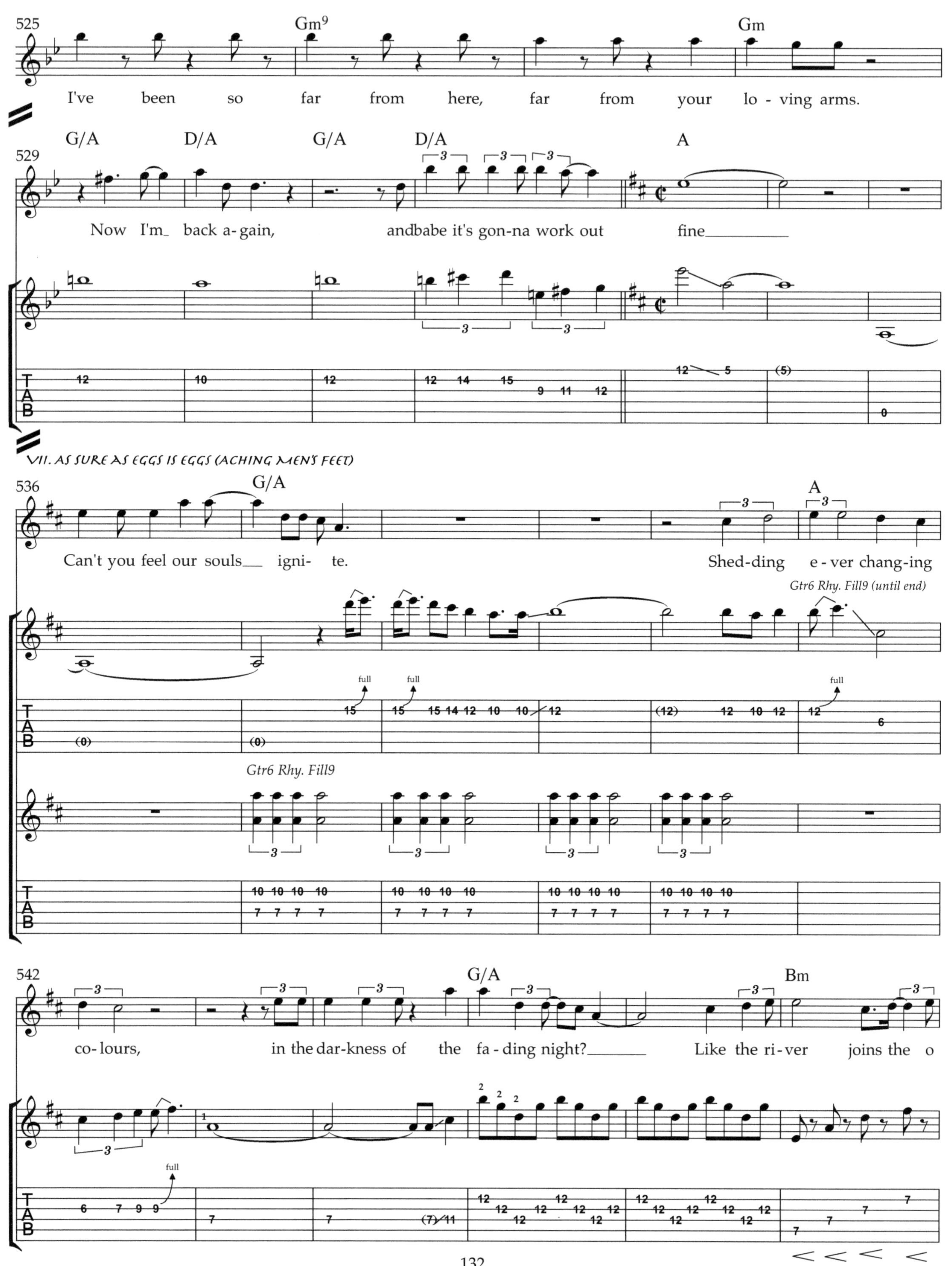
525
Gm9
Gm
I've been so far from here, far from your lo - ving arms.
529
G/A D/A G/A D/A A
Now I'm back a-gain, andbabe it's gon-na work out fine
VII. AS SURE AS EGGS IS EGGS (ACHING MEN'S FEET)
536
G/A A
Can't you feel our souls igni- te. Shed-ding e-ver chang-ing
Gtr6 Rhy. Fill9 (until end)
Gtr6 Rhy. Fill9
542
G/A Bm
co-lours, in the dar-kness of the fa-ding night? Like the ri-ver joins the o

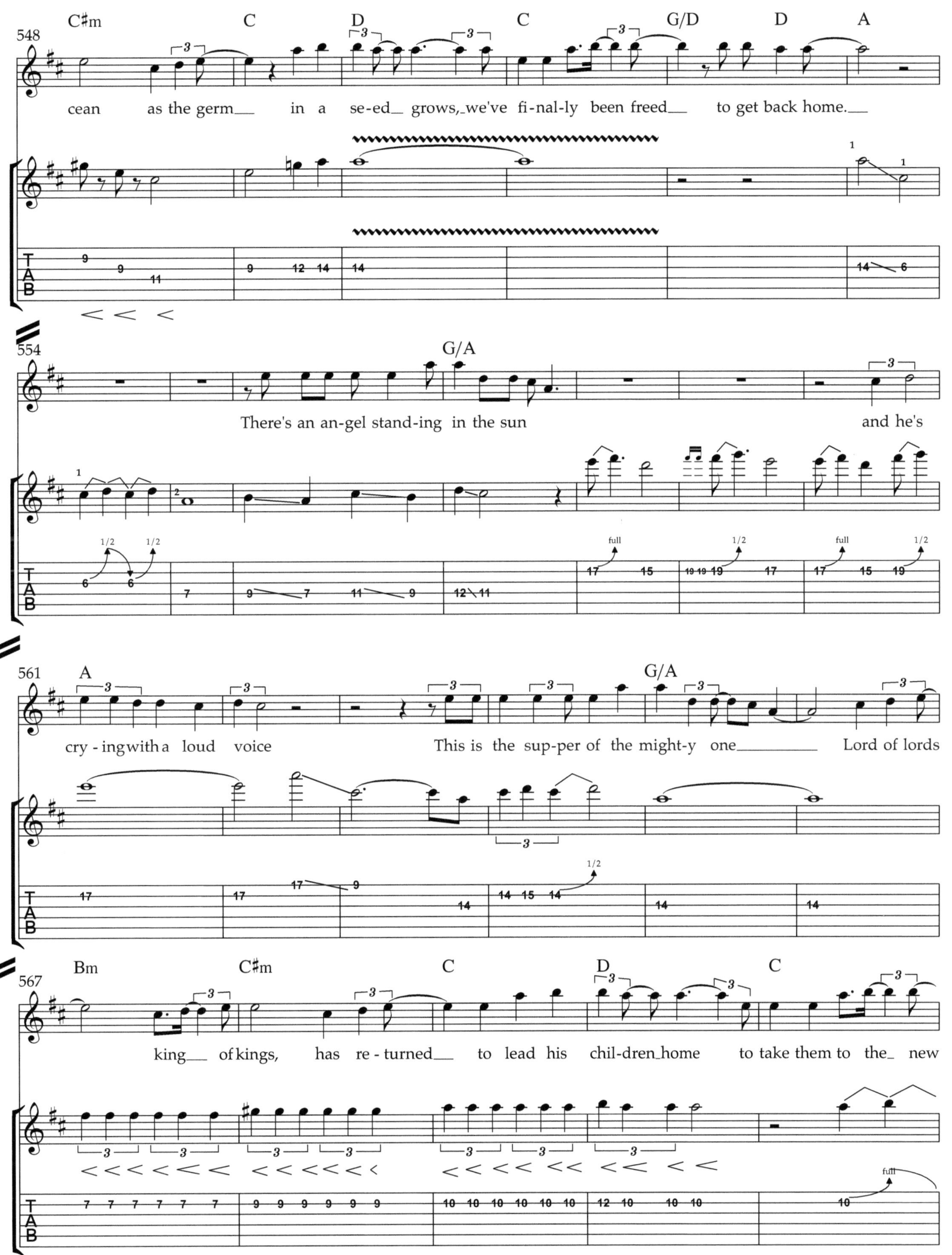
548
C♯m C D C G/D D A
cean as the germ__ in a se-ed__ grows,_we've fi-nal-ly been freed__ to get back home.__
554
G/A
There's an an-gel stand-ing in the sun and he's
561
A G/A
cry-ing with a loud voice This is the sup-per of the might-y one____ Lord of lords
567
Bm C♯m C D C
king__ of kings, has re-turned__ to lead his chil-dren_home to take them to the_ new

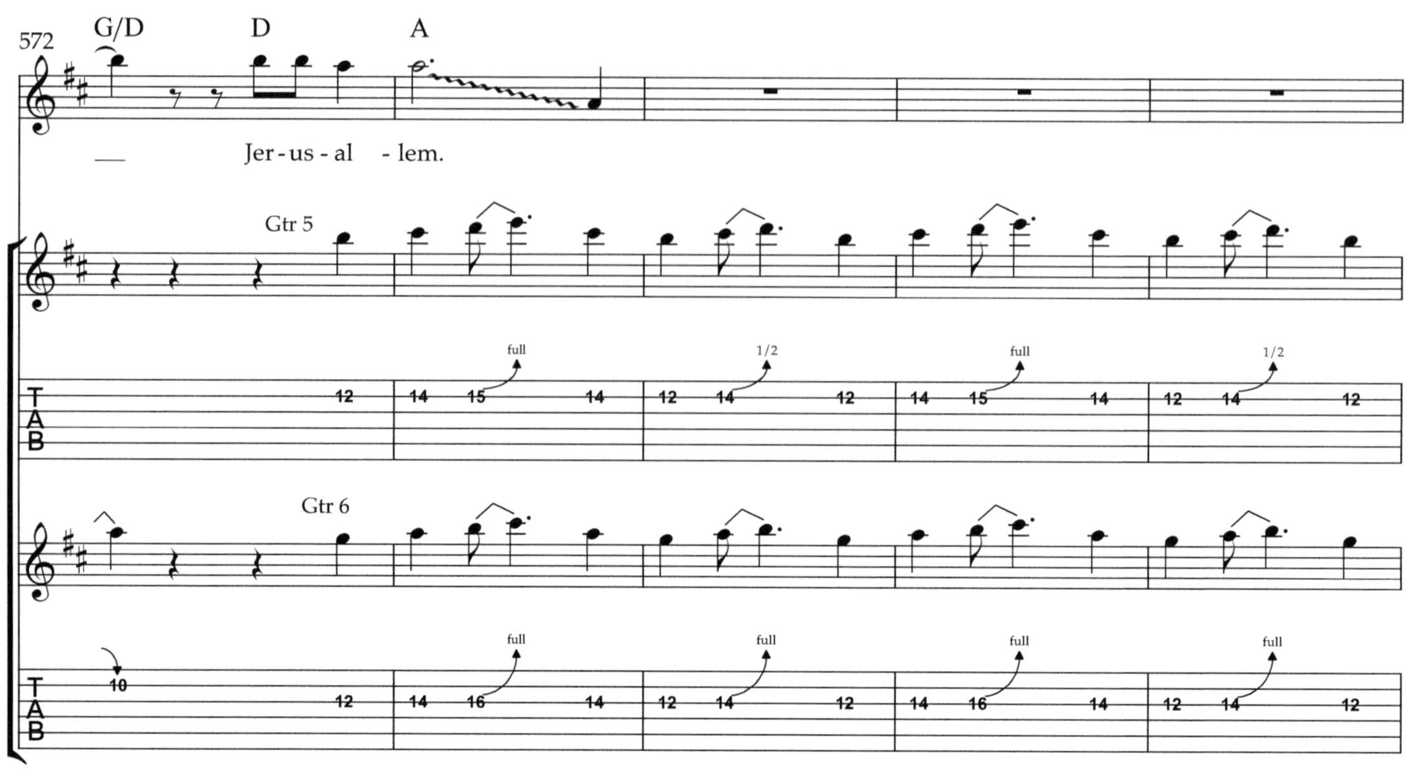

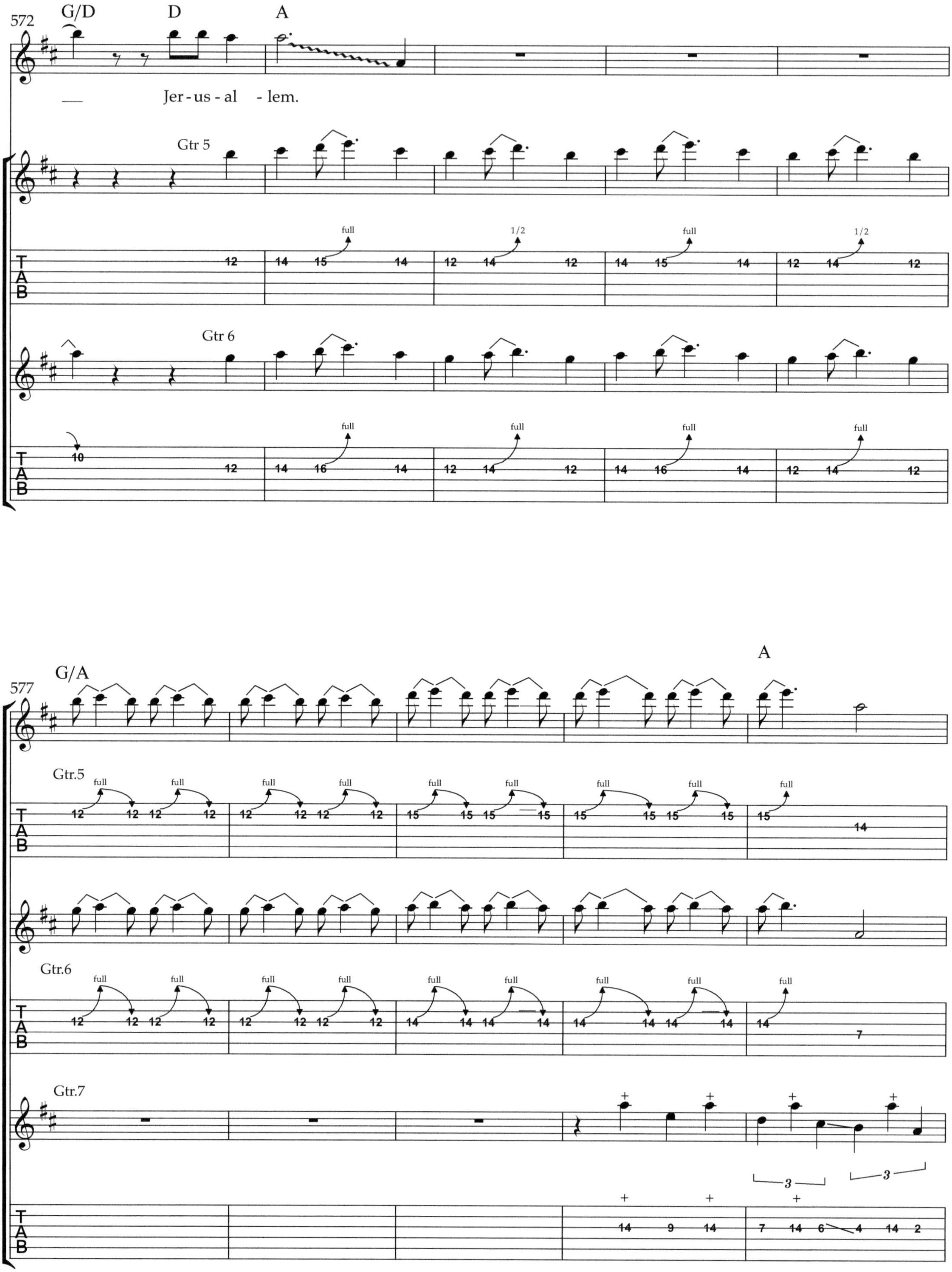

577
G/A
A

Gtr.5
full full full full full full full full full
12 12 12 12 12 12 12 12 15 15 15 15 15 15 15 15 15 14

Gtr.6
full full full full full full full full full
12 12 12 12 12 12 12 12 14 14 14 14 14 14 14 14 14 7

Gtr.7
+ + + +
3 3
14 9 14 7 14 6 4 14 2

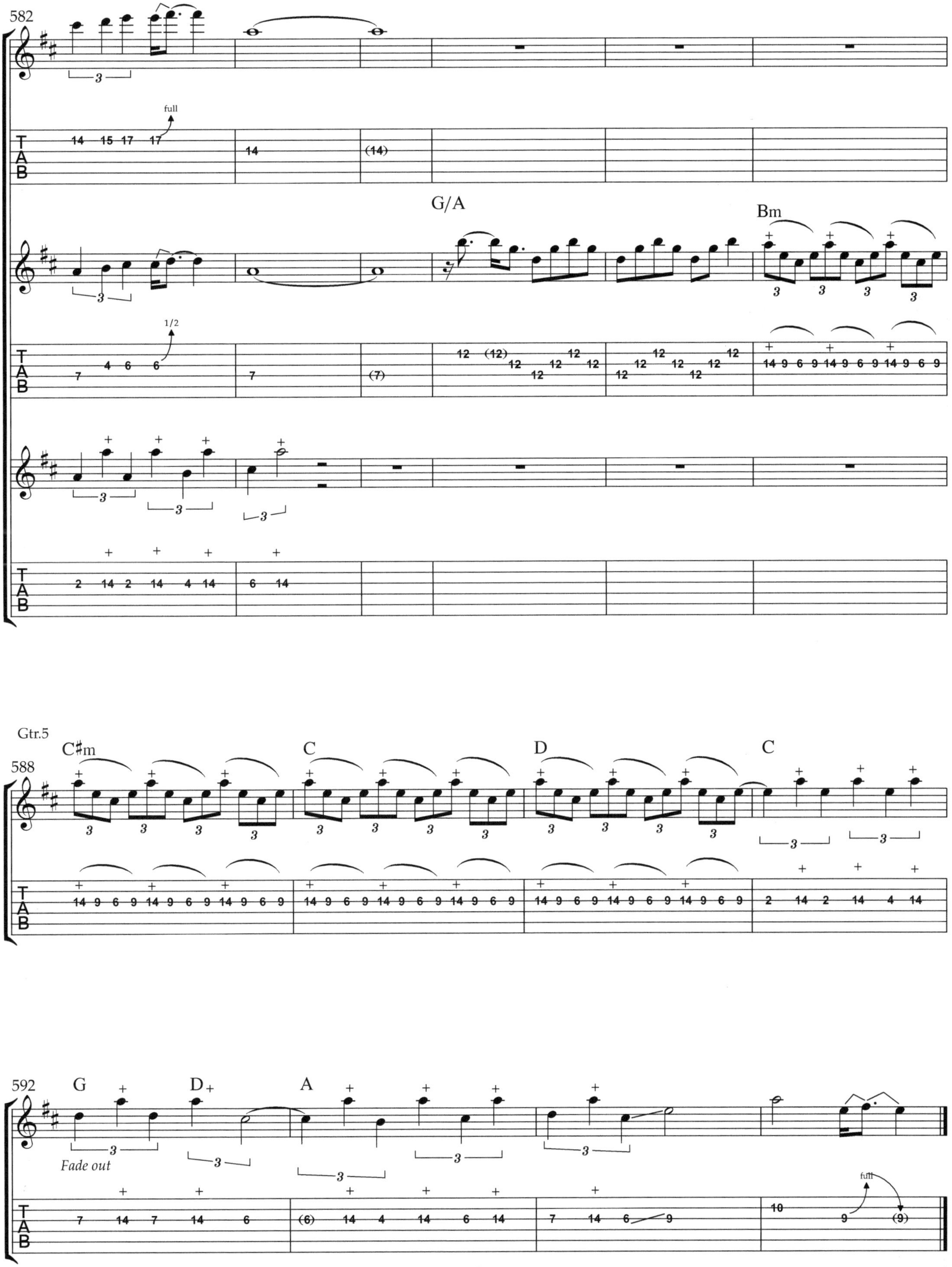

582

full

G/A

Bm

1/2

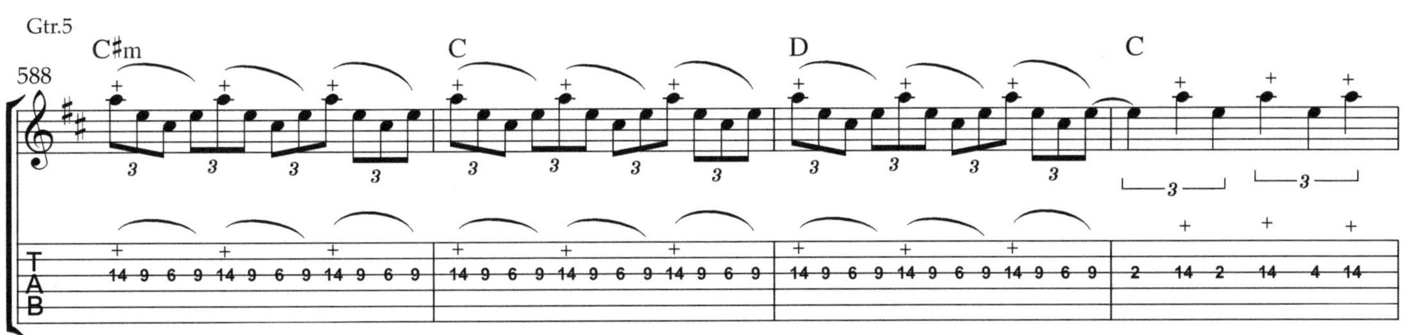

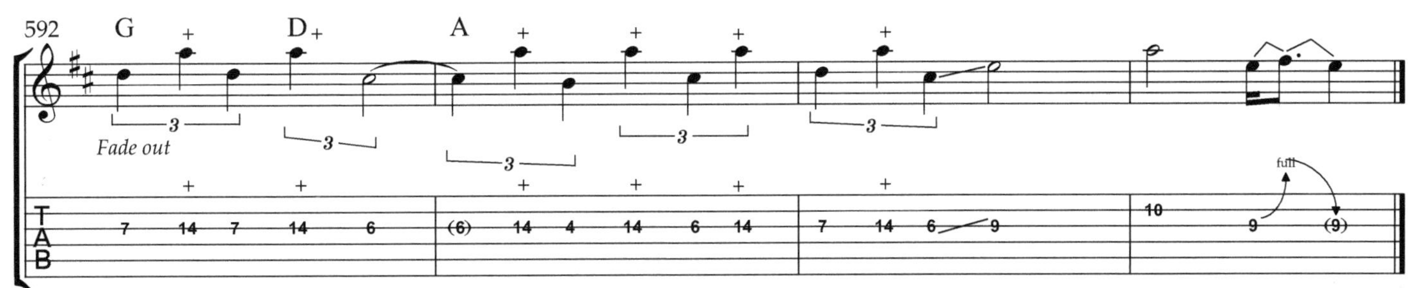

SUPER'S READY
BY GENESIS

1. LOVER'S LEAP

```
Am6                                          Bsus4          B
WALKING ACROSS THE SITTING-ROOM, I TURN THE TELEVISION OFF

Bm          /C#     /D      /E  /F#   F#sus4/B   F#  F#(sus4)/G#   F#/A#
   SITTING    BESIDE    YOU,       I LOOK    INTO    YOUR EYES

Am6                                 Bsus4          B
AS THE SOUND OF MOTOR CARS FADES IN THE NIGHTTIME

 D#m/A#                         F7/A  F7        /A    Bb
I       SWEAR I SAW YOUR FACE CHANGE,      IT DIDN'T SEEM QUITE RIGHT
...AND IT'S

Eb/Bb           Bb                     F7/A            Bb      /D
      HELLO BABE    WITH YOUR GUAR - DIAN EYES SO BLUE

Eb              Bb/F                   F#o             Gm
   HEY, MY BA  - BY, DON'T YOU KNOW    OUR LOVE IS TRUE?

| Gm       | A7(sus4)   | A7     | A7(sus4)   | A7       |


Am6                                    Bsus4                      B
COMING CLOSER WITH OUR EYES, A DISTANCE FALLS AROUND  OUR BODIES

Bm              /C#     /D     /E  /F#       F#sus4/B   F#   F#(sus4) /G#   F#/A#
   OUT IN THE  GARDEN,               THE MOON SEEMS VER-Y           BRIGHT

Am6                           Bsus4         B
SIX SAINTLY SHROUDED MEN MOVE ACROSS THE LAWN SLOWLY

    D#m/A#                        F7/A  F7    F7/A    Bb
THE SEVENTH WALKS IN FRONT                WITH A CROSS HELD HIGH IN HAND
...AND IT'S

Eb/Bb      Bb           F7/A                       Bb     /D   Eb
     HEY, BABE, YOUR SUPPER'S WAITING FOR YOU

Eb              Bb/F                  F#o             Gm
   HEY, MY BA  - BY, DON'T YOU KNOW    OUR LOVE IS TRUE?

Gm              Gm9/F               Gm9/Bb           /C        Gm/D
I'VE BEEN SO FAR FROM HERE, FAR FROM YOUR WARM   ARMS

D(add4)                          D          D(add4)
         IT'S GOOD TO FEEL YOU AGAIN

D6               Am13
  IT'S BEEN A LONG, LONG TIME, HASN'T IT?


||: Dm11 | 2 | 3 | 4 | Am9/D | 2 | 3 | 4 :|| (play 3 times)
| Am9/D | 2 ||: Dm11 | 2 | 3 | 4 | Am9/D | 2 | 3 | 4 :||
| Dm11 | 2 | 3 | 4 | Am7 | 2 | Am9/D | 2 |
| Dm11 | 2 | 3 | 4 | Am9/D | 2 | 3 |
| Gm7/D | 2 | 3 | 4 | 5 | 6 |
| Am11 | 2 | 3 | 4 | 5 | 6 | 7 | 8 ||
```

II. THE GUARANTEED ETERNAL SANCTUARY MAN

```
Am          D                        E/D          Dm7                 Cmaj7
I KNOW A FARMER WHO LOOKS  AFTER THE FARM             WITH  WATER CLEAR

Bm  E                 Am
HE  CARES FOR ALL HIS HARVEST

| D/A       | Am     | D/A     |

Am          D                        E/D          Dm7  |
I KNOW A FIREMAN WHO LOOKS AFTER THE FIRE

Ddim     A                                 G/A
AH,      YOU,          CAN'T YOU SEE HE'S FOOLED YOU ALL?

              A                                G/A
YES, HE'S HERE   AGAIN,          CAN'T YOU SEE HE'S FOOLED YOU ALL?

                   Bm/A                Amaj7      C          D
     SHARE HIS PEACE,          SIGN THE LEASE    HE'S A SUPERSONIC SCI-  ENTIST

        C                        G       D      A
HE'S THE GUARANTEED ETERNAL SANCTUA- RY MAN

 [                          G/A
LOOK,      LOOK INTO MY MOUTH, HE CRIES

                 A
AND ALL THE CHILDREN LOST DOWN MANY PATHS

                                G/A
 I BET MY LIFE, YOU'LL WALK INSIDE

                   Bm/A                Amaj7          C          D
 HAND IN HAND,     GLAND IN GLAND      WITH A SPOONFUL OF MIRACLE

        F                       G                Am6
HE'S THE GUARANTEED ETERNAL SANCTUARY

[Am6]
WE WILL ROCK YOU, ROCK YOU LITTLE SNAKE

WE WILL KEEP YOU SNUG AND WARM
```

FLUTE SOLO

```
| Am6(sus4)    |        | B6(sus4)  | B      | Bm7  |          |
| F#9(sus4) F#   F#9(sus4) | F#     | Am6(sus4)  |          | B6(sus4)  | Bmaj7(add9)
```

III. IKHNATON AND ITSACON AND THEIR BAND OF MERRY MEN

```
              Fmaj7/C                                 D             D(add4)
WEARING  FEELINGS ON OUR FACES WHILE OUR FACES TOOK A REST

D   D(add4)      Fma7/C                                D                      D(add4)
          WE WALKED ACROSS THE FIELDS, TO SEE THE CHILDREN OF THE WEST

D     D(add4)            Fma7/C
          BUT WE SAW A HOST OF DARK-SKINNED WARRIORS
             D          D(add4)         D     D(add4)
STANDING STILL BELOW THE          GROUND
```

GUITARS SOLO
Fmaj7 C/E Am7 D7/A D D(add9) D

WAITING FOR BATTLE
D(add4) D D(add4) D D(add4) D D(add4)

D D(add4)
THE FIGHT'S BEGUN, THEY'VE BEEN RELEASED

D D(add4) D D(add4) D
KILLING FOE FOR PEACE.... BANG, BANG, BANG BANG, BANG, BANG...

D(add4) D D(add4)
AND THEY'RE GIVING ME A WONDERFUL PO - TION

D D(add4) D D(add4)
'COS I CANNOT CONTAIN MY EMO - TION

Fmaj7 C/E
AND EVEN THOUGH I'M FEELING GOOD

Am7 Am6 D D(add9) D(add4)
SOMETHING TELLS ME, I'D BETTER ACTIVATE MY PRAYER CAPSULE

GUITARS SOLO
D |D(add4) |D |D(add4) | D|D (add4) |D |D(add4) |

D D(add9) |D D(add9) |D |D(add4) |D |D(add4) |D |D(add4) |D |D(add4) |

D |D(add4) |D |D(add4) |N.C. | N.C. | N.C. |

E5 | | | A5 | D | D(add4) | D | D(add4) |

D D(add4) D D (add4)
TODAY'S A DAY TO CE – LEBRATE

D D(add4) D D(add4) D D(add4)
THE FOE HAVE MET THEIR FATE

D D(add4) D. D(add4) D
THE ORDER FOR REJOICING AND DANCING HAS COME FROM OUR WAR-LORD

D(add4) |D |D(add4) | D |D(add4) | D |D(add4) |C6(add4) |Em7 C/E |
Am7 |Am11 |C6(add4) |D(add4) | |C6(add4) |
D(add4) | | C6(add4) | D(add4) | |C6(add4) |D(Add4) | C6 (add4) |
C/B | Am6 | C/B | Am6 |

IV. HOW DARE I BE SO BEAUTIFUL

C/B Am6
WANDERING IN THE CHAOS THE BATTLE HAS LEFT

C/B Am6
WE CLIMB UP THE MOUNTAIN OF HUMAN FLESH

Gmaj7 E6 Gmaj7 E6
TO A PLATEAU OF GREEN GRASS, AND GREEN TREES FULL OF LIFE

C/B Am6
A YOUNG FIGURE SITS STILL BY A POOL

C/B Am6
HE'S BEEN STAMPED "HUMAN BACON" BY SOME BUTCHERY TOOL

Gmaj7 E6 Gmaj7 E6
(HE IS YOU)

C/B Am6
SOCIAL SECURITY TOOK CARE OF HIS LAD

C/B Am6 B N.C.
WE WATCH IN REVERENCE, AS NARCISSUS IS TURNED TO A FLOWER. A FLOWER?

V. WILLOW FARM

G# B
IF YOU GO DOWN TO WILLOW FARM

D#m F# G#6(sus2) A#(sus4)
TO LOOK FOR BUTTERFLIES, FLUTERBYES, GUTTERFLIES

D# G#m D#/G# G#m D#/G# G#m
OPEN YOUR EYES, IT'S FULL OF SURPRISE, EVERYONE LIES

D#/G# E Emaj7/D# E7/D D# D#maj7/D
LIKE THE FOCKS ON THE ROCKS, AND THE MUSICAL BOX

D#7/C# Dmaj7 G#m/D#
OH, THERE'S MUM AND DAD, AND GOOD AND BAD

Emaj7 D#
AND EVERYONE'S HAPPY TO BE HERE

G# B
THERE'S WINSTON CHURCHILL DRESSED IN DRAG

D#m F# G#6(sus2) A#(sus4)
HE USED TO BE A BRITISH FLAG, PLASTIC BAG, WHAT A DRAG

D# G#m D#/G# G#m D#/G# G#m
THE FROG WAS A PRINCE, THE PRINCE WAS A BRICK, THE BRICK WAS AN EGG,

D#/G# E Emaj7/D# E7/D D# D#maj7/D
THE EGG WAS A BIRD, HADN'T YOU HEARD?

D#7/C# Dmaj7 G#m/D#
YES, WE'RE HAPPY AS FISH, AND GORGEOUS AS GEESE

Emaj7 D#
AND WONDERFULLY CLEAN IN THE MORNING

G/B G/A E A E
WE'VE GOT EVERYTHING, WE'RE GROWING EVERYTHING

140

A E A
WE'VE GOT SOME IN, WE'VE GOT SOME OUT

C#m G#
WE'VE GOT SOME WILD THINGS FLOATING ABOUT

E A E
EVERYONE, WE'RE CHANGING EVERYONE

A E A C#m
YOU NAME THEM ALL, WE'VE HAD THEM HERE

G# N.C.
AND THE REAL STARS ARE STILL TO APPEAR, ALL CHANGE!

Ab Ab/Gb
FEEL YOUR BODY MELT MUM TO MUD TO MAD TO DAD

Db Ab/C Db Ab/C Eb Ab
DAD DIDDLEY OFFICE, DAD DIDDLEY OFFICE. YOU'RE ALL FULL OF BALL

[Ab] Db Eb
DAD TO DAM TO DUM TO MUM, MUM DIDDLEY WASHING, MUM DIDDLEY WASHING

[Eb] Ab
YOU'RE ALL FULL OF BALL

Bbm Ab/C Ebm Fm Fm/Eb
LET ME HEAR YOUR LIES, WE'RE LIVING THIS UP TO THE EYES AH OH

Fm Fm/Eb Dbmaj7 D A
AH OH AH LA, LA LA

N.C.
MOMMA I WANT YOU NOW
G# B D#m F# G#6(sus2)
AND AS YOU LISTEN TO MY VOICE TO LOOK FOR HIDDEN DOORS, TIDY FLOORS

A#(sus4). D# G#m D#/G# G#m
MORE APPLAUSE. YOU'VE BEEN HERE ALL THE TIME, LIKE IT OR NOT

D#/G# G#m D#/G# E Emaj7/D# E7/D D# D#maj/D
LIKE WHAT YOU GOT, YOU'RE UNDER THE SOIL YES, DEEP IN THE SOIL

D#7/C# Dmaj7 G#m/D#
SO, WE'LL END WITH A WHISTLE AND END WITH A BANG

Emaj7 D# D#
AND ALL OF US FIT IN OUR PLACES

|Gm | 2 | 3 | 4 | 5 | 6 | 7 | D/A| 2 | 3 | 4 | 5 | 6 |B5 |B5 |
Am | 2 | 3 | 4 |D |F |
C G |D6 | Amaj7 |Am Bm/A |E D/F# E/G#| Am |D |F |C G |D6 |
Amaj7 | Am Bm/A| E D/F# E7/G# | Am | D | F | C G | D | A maj7 |
Am D/A| E D/F# E/G# | Am | D E/D |Dm7 | Do ||

VI. APOCALYPSE IN 9/8 (CO-STARRING THE DELICIOUS TALENTS OF GABBLE RATCHET)

F#m
WITH THE GUARDS OF MAGOG, SWARMING AROUND

C(b5)
THE PIED PIPER TAKES HIS CHILDREN UNDERGROUND

F#5
DRAGON'S COMING OUT OF THE SEA

C5
SHIMMERING SILVER HEAD OF WISDOM LOOKING AT ME

F#5
HE BRINGS DOWN THE FIRE FROM THE SKIES

C5
YOU CAN TELL HE'S DOING WELL, BY THE LOOK IN HUMAN EYES

D E(add9)
YOU'D BETTER NOT COMPROMISE, IT WON'T BE EASY

GUITARS SOLO
(34 measures) Em Bm D A Em Bm D A C G Em Bm A C G Bm F#m
A Em G D F#m C D Bm A G D (12 measures)

C
SIX SIX SIX IS NO LONGER ALONE

D
HE'S GETTING OUT THE MARROW IN YOUR BACKBONE

C
AND THE SEVEN TRUMPETS BLOWING SWEET ROCK AND ROLL

D
GONNA BLOW RIGHT DOWN INSIDE YOUR SOUL

C
PYTHAGORAS WITH THE LOOKING GLASS, REFLECTING THE FULL MOON

D E
IN BLOOD, HE'S WRITING THE LYRICS OF A BRAND-NEW TUNE

G#m D Am E G#m D Am B(add4) B Ebm F Bb.

Eb Bb/D F7/C Bb
AND IT'S HEY, BABE, WITH YOUR GUARDIAN EYES SO BLUE

Eb Bb/F F#o Gm
HEY, MY BABE, DON'T YOU KNOW OUR LOVE IS TRUE?

Gm9 Gm
I'VE BEEN SO FAR FROM HERE, FAR FROM YOUR LOVING ARMS

G/A D/A G/A D/A A [A] [A]
NOW I'M BACK AGAIN, AND BABY, IT'S GOING TO WORK OUT FINE

142

VII. AS SURE AS EGGS IS EGGS (ACHING MEN'S FEET)

A G/A
CAN'T YOU FEEL OUR SOULS IGNITE

A G/A
SHEDDING EVER CHANGING COLOURS, IN THE DARKNESS OF THE FADING NIGHT?

Bm C#m C D
LIKE THE RIVER JOINS THE OCEAN, AS THE GERM IN A SEED GROWS

C G/A D A
WE'VE FINALLY BEEN FREED TO GET BACK HOME

G/A A
THERE'S AN ANGEL STANDING IN THE SUN, AND HE'S CRYING WITH A LOUD VOICE

G/A Bm C#m
"THIS IS THE SUPPER OF THE MIGHTY ONE", LORD OF LORDS, KING OF KINGS

C D C G/D D A
HAS RETURNED TO LEAD HIS CHILDREN HOME TO TAKE THEM TO THE NEW JERUSALEM

GUITARS SOLO **(22 measures)**

PAULO DE CARVALHO

www.paulodecarvalhogtr.com

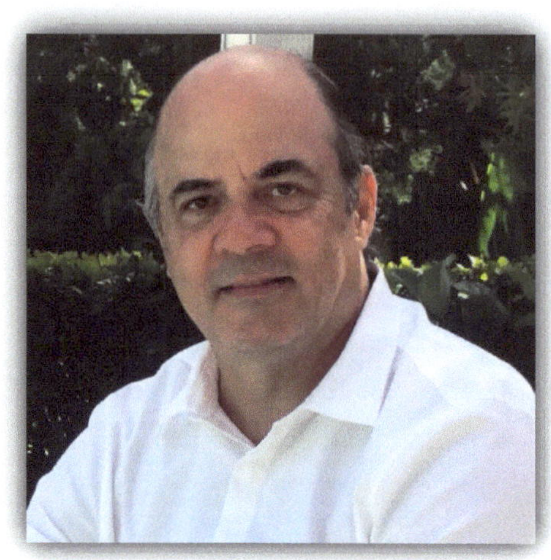

Paulo de Carvalho is a guitar player, composer, arranger, and audio engineer. He earned a bachelor's degree in music composition from the Federal University of Rio de Janeiro, Brazil. He regularly performs and records Brazilian Jazz/Bossa Nova.

4 Oaks Band, the group that Paulo put together with his wife and kids, performs Paulo's arrangements.

www.4oaksband.com

ALSO BY PAULO DE CARVALHO

The Sound of Steve Hackett:
A Selection of Guitar Transcriptions
from His Solo Career

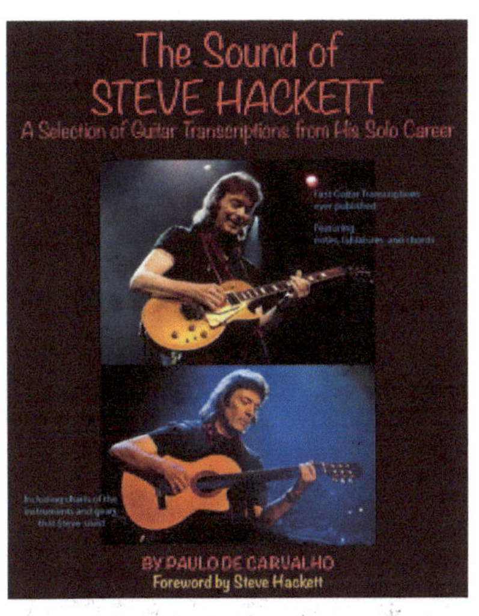

The Sound of Steve Hackett, Vol. 1:
The Complete Guitar Transcriptions of
Voyage of the Acolyte

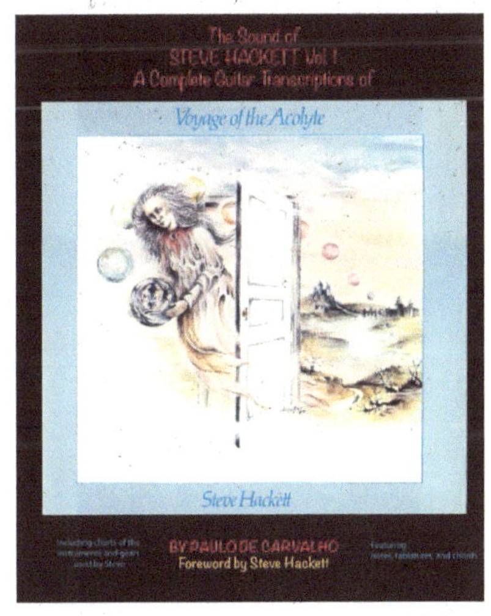

The Sound of Steve Hackett, Vol. 2:
The Complete Guitar Transcriptions of
Please Don't Touch

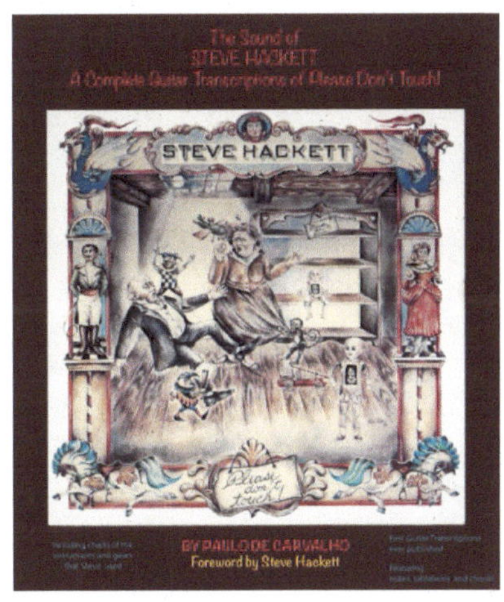

www.ingramcontent.com/pod-product-compliance
Lightning Source LLC
LaVergne TN
LVHW070124110826
845147LV00002B/183
* 9 7 8 0 5 7 8 9 4 0 1 1 3 *